Essays for Buddhist Trainees

Essays for Buddhist Trainees

Seikan Hasegawa

GREAT OCEAN PUBLISHERS
MARSHALL near ASHEVILLE, NORTH CAROLINA

Essays for Buddhist Trainees is the fourth in a series of books by Seikan Hasegawa to be published by Great Ocean Publishers. The first book in the series is *The Cave of Poison Grass, Essays on the Hannya Sutra*, the second is *Essays on Marriage* and the third is *Mind to Mind*. The books deal with various subjects, but their common theme and purpose is that of Zen training: The practical study of how to live best in each and every situation. The series is entitled COMPANIONS OF ZEN TRAINING.

Copyright © 2012 by Seikan Hasegawa

Cover: Statue of Sakyamuni Buddha on pilgrimage (made in Thailand, date unknown).

Photograph copyright © 2012 by Elizabeth Hasegawa.

All rights reserved. No part of this book may be used or reproduced in any manner whatsoever without written permission from the publisher.

First Printing

Printed in the United States of America

For further information contact:
> Great Ocean Publishers
> 1885 Long Branch Road
> Marshall, North Carolina, 28753

Library of Congress Control Number: 2011938066
ISBN 978-0-615-53668-2

Acknowledgement

*I'm always thankful for my wife Betsy
who corrected and improved my English.
My thanks to Ashley who worked for the chores
to be able to print and publish this book.
I also thank those who participated to form this book:
Dale, Drake, John, Paul C, Paul D and Tim.*

Contents

Shyuansha	11
Putting Down Our Thought and Emotion	81
Matzu's "Sunface Buddha, Moonface Buddha"	115
Jaujou's Weed Stem	184
The Meaning of the Eighth Primary Precept	207
Baijang's Wild Fox: Buddhist Causation	223
Essays on Jaujou's Twelve Hours Verses	250
Notes	344
Index	345

Essays for Buddhist Trainees

Shyuansha

Shyuansha Shybei (835-908) was born in Min, Fukien, according to *Chuandeng lu*, vol. 18:

> He liked fishing and from his infancy got to know fishermen.

Dogen says in his *Shobogenzo*: *Ikka no Meishu* [A bright crystal orb]:

> He must have not been waiting for the fish that come on board without being caught.

A legendary strategist, Taigung-wang, in the BC age in China was fishing daily on the Weishuei River until he was found by Emperor Wen. His line had no hook, so he took only the fish that jumped into his boat. Dogen here regards such fish that come without any bait as talented Buddhists. Nobody recommends, nobody invites, yet they come to study Buddha's Dharma. Such will study Buddha's Dharma only for the sake of Buddha's Dharma.

It is said "He must have not been waiting for." So Shyuansha wasn't even expecting to become a great Buddhist talent. Dogen meant he was greater than those who wish to become great Buddhist heroes someday. Dogen believed the Dharma within Shyuansha would someday be naturally awakened and lead his life. (Dogen when he wrote this fascicle knew of Shyuansha's successful life as a Buddhist patriarch. He also was writing from the Dharma side rather than from the perspective of human social reality.)

In social reality Shyuansha was born poor, child of a fisherman's house. He was fishing day after day without engaging in any intellectual study. He wasn't even the family's eldest son but was third son, regarded as useless and unwanted, given the name Shie Sanlang ("family Shie, third boy"). Dogen is interpreting such an innocent boy in the kindest way ever thinkable.

Being Shie Sanlang must have been Shyuansha's deep-rooted concern from infancy. In later days he brings up "Shie Sanlang" in his sermon:

> "Sakyamuni Buddha and I were contemporaries."
> A monk came forward and asked, "Could you tell me from whom did you learn?" Shyuansha said, "From Shie Sanlang on a fishing boat." (*Liandeng hueiyau*, vol. 23)

Both Sakyamuni Buddha and "I" (Shyuansha) are the activity of sunyata, and thus they are contemporaries. So when asked by the monk, why didn't Shyuansha reply that his teacher as well as Sakyamuni Buddha's teacher was sunyata? The reason is that sunyata is rupa, and rupa is sunyata; in other words, Shyuansha is Shie Sanlang, and Shie Sanlang is Shyuansha. Here sunyata and rupa are melting or freely exchanging position, as is Holy Sage freely exchanging with poor third son. Shyuansha thus purified his deep-rooted complex of being born third son of a poor fisherman. He did it by seeing through the fundamental mechanism of the world. Indeed Shyuansha is his priest's name, that is, sunyata, and Shie Sanlang is, as we know, his birth name, rupa.

In *Chuandeng lu* it is said:

> At age thirty he suddenly wished to leave family, and he abandoned his boat and received the shaving of his head by Furung Lingshyun (?-?).

Other records describe the circumstances of his determination to leave family:

> His father lost his balance on his boat and he drowned.
> Then a bright moon rose.

What does this moon symbolize? It couldn't have been the mysterious spirit of his father, as was said of the mother of Huangbo (Huangbo Shiyun, ?-856). When she drowned at a ferry port, it was said her spirit rose to heaven like a moon. The similarities of Shyuansha and Huangbo are that each lost a parent in the water and it strongly influenced them each to leave family.

Now, in the case of Shyuansha, the moon couldn't have been a symbol of his future social well-being. If so, he wouldn't have left family but would have continued faithfully in his father's business, as we often hear in such sayings as "What my dad was doing is a good thing." For a person to leave family there must be some strong dissatisfaction in the person's life. What was Shyuansha's dissatisfaction and for what did the moon symbolically rise?

Being a fisherman and third son set him in the lowest class. Catching smelly fishes and selling them daily in the market barely sustained his life and status such as it was. So did he complain about his situation? Or was his concern coming from the mentality of interpreting everything negatively? If a complaint about his situation, he needn't have had to leave family but could have tried within society to solve his problem. He left family. So his case was a deeper negative, that is, he couldn't see all sentient and insentient beings, including mountains and rivers, weeds and trees, are attaining Buddhahood. So he would try to solve his life problem through religious study instead of trying to improve his social status. In that sense his religious way was highly psychoanalytic too. There is a dialogue from his later days with one of his students:

> One day all monks went to an inlet and engaged in gathering firewood. A monk saw a tiger and said, "My Reverend, there's a tiger!" The Teacher [Shyuansha] said to him, "You are a tiger."
>
> When they returned to their temple the monk asked, "A little while ago we saw a tiger and you said I was a tiger. Could you clarify your meaning?" The Teacher said, "There are four kinds of obstacles in this saha world [world of endurance]. If you go through them you will be able to transcend the phenomenal world.
>
> (*Chanyuan mengchiou*, vol. 1)

The four obstacles are 1) *Klesa-avarana* (fundamental ignorance), 2) *karma* caused by all sorts of sins we committed in past lives, 3) having no time to study Buddha's Dharma because of our sins committed in past lives, and 4) having no opportunity to meet with a good teacher. Among these, the first is for us enough of a problem. In modern terminology, fundamental ignorance is largely coming from the oldest part of our brain, formed during the amoebic age through the animal age. Our old brain makes a clear distinction between self and others, protects self by any means, is suspicious of others, aggressive, pessimistic and negative in appraisal, and is doomed to have us make dualistic valuations. This old brain influences most of our new brain, and only the newest brain in our frontal lobe has the function to check and reflect on the workings of our old brain. Shyuansha is teaching his monk to function fully with his newest brain. This is the only way we can transcend the phenomenal world. For Shyuansha a zoological tiger wasn't enough to be feared. What he truly feared was the ignorant function of our old brain. Thus the moon bright and clear was a symbol of Buddha's bright and clear state free of his old brain. Buddha's bright and clear state was:

> Sentient and insentient beings have at once attained the Way, grasses, trees, land, all have attained Buddhahood.
>
> (The purport of the Nirvana Sutra
>
> [*Mahaparinirvana-sutra*], vol. 7)

The same meaning as Buddha's declaration is expressed in the Avatamsaka Sutra (*Mahavaipulya-buddhavatansaka-sutra*):

> How wonderful, there is not a single being that has no Tathagata's wisdom and virtue.

Now we can understand Shyuansha wanted to solve his life problem by means of the religious way. This was to confront his own old brain with the light that was Buddha's Dharma. Then he "suddenly wished to leave family" and went to Furung Lingshyun.

There he met with a senior Dharma brother who was Shyuefeng (Shyuefeng Yitsun, 822-908) and soon Shyuefeng would become his teacher.

In *Chuandeng lu* it is said:

> Shyuansha strictly kept modesty in dress and food, and he loved meditation to the degree that other monks felt strange. He became intimate with Shyuefeng as if they were student and teacher. Shyuefeng respectfully addressed him as 'Bei Dhuta ["Diligent" (Shy)bei].

Thus when Shyuefeng opened his temple, Shyuansha followed him. Mt. Shyuefeng was said to have many scenic rocky hills, its borders in four counties.

Later Shyuefeng shared with Shyuansha half his seat, and Shyuansha assisted him in lecturing and guiding the monks. Shyuansha and Shyuefeng were contrasting and were likened to Mahakasyapa and Sakyamuni Buddha. Shyuansha was born poor as we studied and was already as old as thirty when he left family, whereas Shyuefeng was born into a family dedicated to serving Buddha for generations, and left family at the early age of twelve accompanied by his father. Shyuefeng visited Toutzy three times, Dungshan nine times, and finally under Deshan with the help of his senior Dharma brother Yantou, he could come to the realization without any doubt. Shyuansha attempted to pilgrimage only once and even that he cancelled:

> One day he set out on a pilgrimage to visit masters countrywide. On the way he struck his toe on a stone. In bleeding pain he reflected, This body is not real being—from where does the pain come?"
> With this reflection he quit his pilgrimage and returned to Shyuefeng.
> (*Shobogenzo: Ikka no meishu* [Bright crystal orb])

Here it is described, "With this reflection he quit his pilgrimage and returned to Shyuefeng." It doesn't mean he gave up halfway toward what he wanted to achieve. It means he completed his pilgrimage goal. For those true Buddhists in the Tang dynasty, "pilgrimage" meant "to clarify the life problem and to establish one's peace." So what was the good of Shyuansha's striking his toe with the result that he could solve his life problem? His problem was his old brain, or tiger more fearful than any zoological tiger: being depressive, greedy, vain, unconfident, arrogant, wrathful, negative, prone to hate, suspicious, worrying, and more and more, counted as 108 or 84,000 unpleasant emotions and thoughts about everything internal and external.

Shyuansha's reflection was "This body is not real being—from where does the pain come?" It may seem abrupt to remember here the case of the Sixth Patriarch, Hueineng (Dajian Hueineng, 638-713), but he was one who suddenly left family and abruptly quit his pilgrimage, and he experienced a hard-laboring youth. He who became the Sixth Patriarch was selling his gathered firewood in town, and he chanced to hear a hotel guest reciting the Diamond Sutra. The passage that struck him was:

> Indeed there is no place to dwell, yet the mind should rise.

This passage is from a scene in which Buddha is telling Subhuti that Bodhisattvas should raise pure mind because the nature of the world, including our life, is ungraspable at the core, yet unlimited phenomena emerge (meaning "sunyata is rupa"). Pure mind means to raise our emotions and thoughts freely, without being possessed by concepts, prejudices or presumptions formed through past matters, sounds, smells, tastes, touches, and laws. Hueineng too must have been suffering from the *klesa* (impurity) that is emotions and thoughts. Hearing the passage from the Diamond Sutra, he came to a great realization instead of merely hearing a theory of "sunyata is rupa" as if to put another candy into his mouth. For him the passage was liberation from every bondage, purification of every filth, and conversion of every negative value to a positive value. The greatness of Hueineng is that at the very moment of hearing he determined to perfect his realization. Soon he visited the Fifth Patriarch, Hungren (Daman Hungren, 601-674), in order just to help others suffering as he had.

Now, there is no important difference between Shyuansha's realization, "This body is not real being—from where does the pain come?" and Hueineng's realization on hearing the passage from the Diamond Sutra, "Indeed there is no place to dwell, yet the mind should rise." Shyuansha's unpolluted and unpremeditated question was for him at once a confident assertion.

Shyuefeng must have noted that Shyuansha on the way of his pilgrimage came back with bright confidence and careful exemplary behavior instead of stuck in depressive endurance. Shyuansha became more active rather than passive in his understanding of Buddha's, "the mind should rise." Yes, we should raise our mind to practice whatever our pure mind tells us and be creative to help other beings.

> One day Shyuefeng asked him, "Who is 'Bei Dhuta?" Shyuansha responded, "I dare not mislead others."

> (*Chuandeng lu*, vol.18)

Shyuansha must have detected that Shyuefeng was understanding "'Bei Dhuta" is "Who," which can't be simply defined as sunyata, or rupa, or Buddha, or ignorant being. Isn't it delightful to hear Shyuansha's saying, "I dare not mislead others"? It means he is not more than what he is and not less than what he is. Everybody else too is like that. So, don't wait for someone else to define what you are. See by yourself. You are Buddha. Here Shyuansha is no longer seeking his own satisfaction. He doesn't care who he is. But he began to care deeply for those who are in the sediment of self-complex, self-devaluation, and self-binding.

There is a translation problem in Shyuansha's response "I dare not mislead others," because the original Chinese gives this sentence no subject. A complication is that not specifying the subject is right as far as the content of their interest goes. Shyuefeng did ask "Who is 'Bei Dhuta?" So we translated Shyuansha's response beginning with "I" assumingly and conveniently. For the same theme with Shyuefeng, the Sixth Patriarch asked Dahuei (Nanyue Huairang, 677-747) "What comes thus?"

"From where did you come?" Dahuei answered, "I came from National Teacher Hueian of Mt. Sung." The Patriarch said, "What comes thus?" Dahuei couldn't respond and thereafter he spent eight years attending the Patriarch.

> One day Dahuei came to the realization and he told the Patriarch, "I now understand. When I first came here you asked me 'What comes thus?'"
> The Patriarch said, "Now how do you understand?"
> Dahuei said, "Even if I tell you, nothing will come of it."
> (*Chuandeng lu*, vol. 5)

For patriarchs this "Who" and this "What" blend well and alternate freely. Sometimes the patriarchs distinguish these interrogatives and sometimes they don't. They think they are the Whole World in the Ten Directions. Changsha (Changsha Jingtsen, ?-?) defines what the monk's life should be, as follows:

> The Whole World in the Ten Directions is the whole body of the Buddhist monk. (*Chuandeng lu*, vol. 10)

Keizan (Keizan Jhokin 1268-1325), in the fourth generation of Dharma transmission from Dogen, could easily interpret Sakyamuni Buddha's Great Realization as we see in his *Denko roku*, vol. 2:

> Sakyamuni Buddha attained the Way at the sight of Venus and said: "I and my companions the great earth and sentient beings at the same time have attained the Way."
>
> Even though his three hundred sixty-some formal sermons throughout his forty-nine years were each unique, all his topics, metaphors, and discourses present only the truth of this episode. The "I" of this episode is not Sakyamuni Buddha, because from there he too came out. When we raise a big fishing net, every one of its knots is raised; when Sakyamuni Buddha attained the Way, the great earth and all sentient beings attained the Way. Not only the great earth and sentient beings but also all Buddhas in the Three Worlds attained the Way.
>
> Yet in Sakyamuni Buddha there was no awareness of attaining the Way. Do not see Sakyamuni Buddha outside of the great earth and sentient beings. Even though mountains, rivers, the great earth, and all the million phenomena are inexhaustible, they all enter the eye of Gautama Siddhartha. Not only do they enter his eye, his eye is replaced by the eyes of us all as well. Then, all phenomena also become the physical eyes of Gautama Siddhartha, and then [for his eyes] each person's whole body is as aloof as a precipitous cliff. Therefore the Bright Eye always was, is, and will be the whole body of each person.

Thus when Shyuansha replied "I dare not mislead others," he was already the person who could transcend his biological and biographical name Shie Sanlang without disdaining it. For him, seeing "Who is 'Bei Dhuta?" or "What comes thus?" was the surest way to transcend his biological and social problems.

A few days later Shyuefeng asked Shyuansha again:

> "'Bei Dhuta, why don't you make a pilgrimage to visit masters countrywide?"

Shyuefeng of course knew Shyuansha had with satisfaction quit his pilgrimage. So what Shyuefeng wanted to hear wasn't Shyuansha's personal affair and conventional reasoning, but his capable linguistic expression about the fundamental truth related with Buddhist training. Shyuefeng's mind was "You completed your training so thoroughly! Could you give me your own definition of what training is while you are excellent with language too?" Unlike Shyuefeng, not so many bodhisattvas like to hear the good expressions of others. Also, how we define what training is, is no different from how we live.

Shyuansha responded, "Bodhidharma never came to this eastern land and the Second Patriarch never went to the land under the western sky." (*Chuandeng lu*, vol. 18)

Shyuefeng is said to have been delighted to hear Shyuansha's response and this dialogue became a conspicuous event for them, such that the Dharma was thus transmitted. The same thing had happened in the dialogue between the Sixth Patriarch and Dahuei. That dialogue, given above, continues:

> Then the Patriarch said, "Is there the necessity of training and realization?"
> Dahuei said, "There may very well be, but training and realization shouldn't be polluted."
> The Patriarch said, "This non-pollution is the concern kept up by all Buddhas. You also do like this, I also. All patriarchs under the Western sky also do like this."
>
> (*Chuandeng lu*, vol. 5.)

Here Buddhist training isn't denied. The training is human participation in the activity of Buddha nature and there is no reason it should be denied. But it should be the right training. The training and the realization are considered in the relation between cause and effect. However, for true Buddhism this relation should be resolved as soon as it appears in our consciousness because cause and effect should be perfectly equal in content. When we aren't dazzled by the temporary form of phenomena, cause is effect and effect is cause, so when we are engaging in either cause or effect the other is included. In the above-quoted dialogue, disturbing this equation is referred to as being polluted. For instance, the training of an ignorant man to attain Buddhahood is a polluted way of training and accordingly pollutes the realization.

Shyuansha's definition of training reveals more about right training. His saying "Bodhidharma never came to this eastern land" isn't denying the historical fact of Bodhidharma's coming to China. First of all, when a Buddhist patriarch says "east," he doesn't mean east contrasting west. His "east" means the Whole World in the Ten Directions, and likewise his "west." Second of all, east—the Whole World—is his body. Bodhidharma is east, east is Bodhidharma. So it is a wrongful redundancy to say "Bodhidharma came to this eastern land." And third, such a patriarch who could live his life as the Whole World happened to be the teacher of Hueike (Second Patriarch, Hueike Shenguang, 487-593).

When Bodhidharma transmitted the Dharma to Hueike, there was no longer any Bodhidharma. The transmission, which is the precise relation of cause and effect, can occur only in the relation of A to A, B to B, or Hueike to Hueike. Buddhist transmission is possible when Bodhidharma enters Hueike without retaining his trace, or likewise when Hueike enters Bodhidharma. This is the relation between Buddhist teacher and Buddhist student, and while this is Buddhist cause and effect, it will define how our training should be. We must keep this equal relation of cause and effect between ourselves and our environment, and between rupa and sunyata. Thus for Shyuansha our training is to maintain this dynamic equality in every relation.

Yunmen's "Peony garden" is adopted in *Biyan lu* as Case 39:

> A monk asked Yunmen, "What is the pure Dharma-kaya?"
> Yunmen said, "The peony garden fenced and shelved."
> The monk: "How about if I am like that?"
> Yunmen: "A golden-haired lion."

The pure Dharma-kaya is universal in place and time and is the same as Buddha nature. It isn't polluted by human desires and value judgments, so for the human being it can be intellectual Reason. Because of this universal and pure nature, Yunmen spontaneously pointed out the peony garden fenced and shelved at near sight of the monk. The perilous pass of this case is in the second question and answer. The first question and answer is as if to define one of the important Buddhist terms, the pure Dharma-kaya. The second is about how to make such pure Dharma-kaya in actual daily life. Therefore this case is also after all concerned with training, how we should engage in Buddhist training to make our innate purity come true in everyday life through our phenomenal life.

This monk says boldly to his teacher, "How about if I am like that?" It is as if to say "I am daily practicing the mind of the Diamond Sutra. Indeed there is no place to dwell, yet the mind should rise. I am also living at such a height where the flood of the sewage of human concepts such as Training and Realization cannot lick my feet." To this Yunmen gave the comment "[You are] A golden-haired lion." Yunmen knew how hard it is to keep the peony garden in good condition, giving suitable fertilizer, timely disinfection, watering, drainage, trimming, renewal of shelves. It is hard to not make our klesa act evil but to make it express its innate purity. "A golden-haired lion" Yunmen said. It could be a low murmur breaking from his lips, and furthermore his mental eyes could be looking at wild peonies in the mountain depths that never bloomed for the sake of human appreciation.

Yuanwu (Yuanwu Kechin, 1063-1135) in his lecture for this case quoted Shyansha's response to the same question:

A monk asked Shyuansha, "What is the pure Dharma-kaya?"
Shyuansha said, "With the Diamond Eye, seeing oozing pus."

Then Yuanwu asks his monks whether Shyuansha's response is the same as Yunmen's. "Oozing pus" is the sight of the battlefield of our life-maintaining force against outside invaders, including infectious disease, and this sight is commonly regarded as impure and a sad state for us. However, Shyuansha was by then a well-seasoned trainee and must have been living with Buddha's declaration "Sentient and insentient beings have at once attained the Way." So Shyuansha didn't take the meaning of "pure" in "the pure Dharma-kaya" as a relative value, and meanwhile Yunmen went along with such a relative value when he was asked by the monk. For Shyuansha and his monk their dialogue's main subject wasn't about pure Dharma-kaya. It was about the eye to make every phenomenon pure Dharma-kaya. So Shyuansha said "With the Diamond Eye."

About "Diamond Eye" there is a sutra called *Mahakarunikacita-dharani*. Therein Avalokitesvara tells us that whoever keeps this *dharani* will raise Bodhisattva mind, help all sentient beings, and cure eighty-four thousand illnesses. The sutra also says "If we wish to obtain Buddha's wisdom we should hold the Treasured Orb." "The Treasured Orb" is

Buddha's wisdom and is Avalokitesvara's compassion. Thus Shyuansha said "With the Diamond Eye, seeing oozing pus." It seems for Shyuansha this world and its phenomena are the ocean of wisdom upon wisdom or compassion upon compassion. Now we can reply to Yuanwu: "Put aside whether Shyuansha's response is the same as Yunmen's. In which ocean are you bathing yourself, the ocean of wisdom or the ocean of compassion?"

Years ago,

> Purnamaitrayaniputra asked Buddha, "If all these worlds—the six worlds of our sense organs, the six worlds of the objects sensed by our six sense organs, and the six worlds formed when our six sense organs blend with the six worlds of the objects we sense—if they all are the primordially pure contents of the Tathagata, how is it that such mortal forms as mountains, rivers, and the great earth repeatedly rise, change, and ruin?"
>
> (*Surangama-sutra*, vol. 4)

It seems the idea of being mortal in each mortal phase and yet phase after phase endlessly continuing was for the ancient Indian a dreadful transmigration. To be such a reincarnating member was dreadful, and most people wished to finish such karma by behaving well and by contracting with the gods.

This idea was deeply rooted in Indian culture, probably five thousand years before Buddhism appeared on their earth. Buddhism also adopted to a certain degree this doctrine of transmigration. The main reason for adopting it was that Buddhism too needed to explain the phase of this life in the chains of causations. Buddhism rejected the idea of eternal authority and understood that 1) this world keeps changing, and 2) nothing has an everlasting self. Therefore every being exists in causations and mutual relations.

Even now Buddhism doesn't reject such ideas as karma and transmigration. The reason is that we want to know the cause and effect of this life and haven't yet found any better explanation than the traditional and obviously imperfect ideas or imagination of karma and transmigration. It is thankful that the newest study of genetics or such science begins to provide some explanations for the cause of our present physical problems. Yet we are very far from the stage where we can provide a better explanation than those ancient people about why we were born in a particular country, age, and race, with a particular feature, talent, and so forth.

Actually the ancient ideas of karma and transmigration aren't so far from our everyday life. The worlds to transmigrate are rich in variety; twenty-four in total including fourteen in the worlds of desires, seven in the worlds of form, and four more in the worlds of no form; and which world we must go to depends on our accumulation of karma, how we lived in previous lives. To understand how ancient people feared and disliked this transmigration, we must put ourselves in the position of being an incurable patient in a fine twenty-four-story general hospital. We will be sent to one department after another while we suffer from pain, itch, nausea, and dullness, until finally we are put in a cool dark room left for dead, and then (49 days after, it is said) we will be reborn just to find ourselves again on a floor of a twenty-four-story general hospital.

Buddhism understood 3) this world is peaceful Nirvana for Buddha, though 4) all events and affairs are, for ordinary beings, suffering. These, 1) through 4), distinguish Buddhism from other religions and thoughts. To be beneficial Buddhists, we must well understand this 3) the worlds of karma and transmigration are peaceful Nirvana for Buddha. Buddhist training means to understand this truth and to teach it to others.

About five hundred years after Purnamaitrayaniputra, the Mahayana lay Buddhist Vimalakirti answered his question to Buddha with this:

If your mind is pure, the mountains and rivers are pure.

(Vimalakirti-nirdesa-sutra)

This answer helped many people but also misled. Many Vimalakirti followers thought every human problem could be solved by holding the right mental state. They mistook his word "mind" to be merely our physical, mental, psychological, or cerebral mind. Being peaceful for one's cognition or feeling often doesn't ensure any world peace. Buddhist Nirvana isn't such a particular view. So about another thousand years later, the monk Changshuei (Changshuei Tzyshyuan, ?-1038) brought Purnamaitrayaniputra's same question to his teacher Langshie (Langshie Heuijyue, ?-?).

Langshie was contemporary with Shyuedou (Shyuedou Jungshian, 980-1052), who made a hundred gathas (to which Yuanwu later gave introductions, comments and lectures and it became *Biyan lu*). Shyuedou for his first case chose Bodhidharma's "Vacancy and No Holiness," and for his last, "Baliang's Sword That Can Cut a Blown Hair." Without attending a fireworks display we must be able to understand the importance of choosing which for the first and last case. In the first, Bodhidharma loudly invites us to the world where there are no dualistic valuations such as holy or humble, a powerful refusal of any practice of discrimination including discrimination of birth, sex, rank, and even by knowing or not knowing. In the last case:

> A monk asked Baliang: "What is the sword that can cut a blown hair?"
> Baliang: "Each coral twig holds a moon."

On a moonlit night, whether any human being is watching or not, each twig of the millions of corals contains a "dewdrop" and in each a "moon" is held. This is referring to the fact that every individual being in the past, present, and future in the ten directions has indispensable value. Recognizing this amazing fact is wisdom ("sword"), and after all, wisdom means compassion, and if so, after all, Baliang expressed the same thing as Sakyamuni's declaration: "All sentient and insentient beings, including mountains and rivers, weeds and trees, are attaining Buddhahood."

Hungjy (Hungjy Jengjyue, 1091-1157) also made a hundred gathas (later Wansung followed Yuanwu's manner for *Biyan lu* and it became *Tsungrung lu*). Hungjy chose "The World Honored One Takes His Seat" for his first case:

> The World Honored One took his seat. Manjusri struck the wooden instrument to indicate the close of the sermon and said: "Let me wish that you clearly understand the Dharma of the Dharma King. The Dharma of the Dharma King is like this." The World Honored One descended from his seat.

This case is telling us that in short all beings including Sakyamuni Buddha are preaching the undeniable truth with their form and function not only their mouth. If this interpretation is not far from the core of the case, can't we say it is after all the same as Sakyamuni's declaration "All sentient and insentient beings, including mountains and rivers, weeds and trees, are attaining Buddhahood." Now Hungjy for his hundredth case, which is his final concern for us, placed this Langshie and Changshuei dialogue:

> A monk [Changshuei] asked, "If all worlds are primordially pure, how do such mortal forms as mountains, rivers, and the great earth repeatedly rise, change, and ruin?"
> Langshie replied, "If all worlds are primordially pure, how do such mortal forms as mountains, rivers, and the great earth repeatedly rise, change, and ruin?"
> *(Tsungrung lu,* Case 100)

For true Mahayana Buddhists, this world is Buddha's body and the nature of this world and Buddha is compassion. Therefore, after every explanation throughout history, Langshie could only utter a lamentation. He was like a mother crying over her child who stole their money to live on, went away somewhere and now comes a phone call from a big city police officer. Or a mother crying over her child who can't enjoy this life and is detesting, complaining, and getting suffering instead of enjoyment.

In Langshie's lamentation, however, there is a growing power, the power of compassionate eyes to see oneself first of all. Buddhism in the past recommended that people reflect on themselves to gain their own peace. But this recommendation wasn't always heard with pleasure. It often became a pressure for people already suffering. Langshie here with his student reflects instead of recommending. With this light of sensitivity we will return to Shyuansha, with another episode:

> A monk asked, "Whatever involves language makes us fated to be trapped. Your Reverence, without being trapped could you talk with me?"
> Shyuansha responded, "Come after destroying every measuring device." (*Chuandeng lu,* vol.18)

We are often trapped in the direction of the overwhelming misunderstanding that this world is an impure burning house filled with sufferings and we helplessly misunderstand that we are ignorant, sinful, humble, worthless, and meaningless beings. And we are as often trapped in the opposite direction of helplessly misunderstanding that this world is a beautiful pleasant garden filled with enjoyments and we helplessly misunderstand that we are wise, virtuous, noble, valuable, and indispensable beings. Instead of all this, we must without any measuring devices see the world. For Buddhists, all units of measure are limitless.

Part of the greatness of Buddha is that he clearly told us how to reach the truth he advocated. Teaching right methods or devices to reach the truth is a very compassionate deed.

> A monk asked, "I have just begun to study here. Could you tell me from where should I begin?"
> The Teacher [Shyuansha] answered, "Do you hear the sound of the creek?"
> The monk, "Yes, I do."
> The Teacher: "That is your place to begin."
>
> (*Chuandeng lu*, vol. 18)

This dialogue is interesting because it mentions a view of the temple where Shyuansha dwelled. A good master will reply instantly to a student's question. Although his answer came instantly, the content of Shyuansha's life that produced the answer came after living for years faithfully to the answer. For the same question Jaujou (Jaujou Tsungshen, 778-897) replied simply:

> A monk asked, "I have just begun to study here. Could you tell me from where should I begin? "
> Jaujou replied, "That is really too bad!"
>
> (*Jaujou lu*, entry 371)

Jaujou is criticizing the monk's attitude toward the study of his own truth, his asking others as if the truth is in places other than his own place. Buddhist truth is in one's own life. In the same *Jaujou lu*, entry 291, the same question is again recorded:

> A monk asked, "I have just begun to study here. Could you tell me from where should I begin? "
> Jaujou said, "Did you have breakfast?"
> The monk: "Yes, I did."
> Jaujou: "Then carefully wash your bowls."

This second dialogue will be adopted by *Tsungrung lu* as Case 39, but there the monk's question is recorded differently.

The monk asks:

"Could you tell me what is myself?"

In the flow of time, unsure is which question was the monk's question. Again it is interesting that the questions "From where should I begin?" and "What is myself?" are easily convertible.

To resume with Shyuansha's answer, it wasn't simply picking up (with very little sense of responsibility for the monk's training) the notion ("sound of the creek") that happened to come to mind. Shyuansha was contemporary with Jaujou, but it seems he was more cautious in guiding the monks than Jaujou, who became famous with his easy and light eloquence. About two hundred years after them, Su Dungpo, (1036-1101) indeed by seeing and hearing a vale and rill, came to a great awakening. It is also well known that Avalokitesvara reached the truth by the occasion of hearing a sound. This awakening through our sense organs and sense objects shouldn't be despised, because some people misunderstand that the teaching to meditate by "abandoning all relations and ceasing a million affairs" means to make our sense organs dysfunction. Neither that nor being led by them is the ideal state, which is the subject of study in *Biyan lu*, Case 78:

> Sixteen bodhisattvas, including Bhadrapala, took a bath at the usual time, but on this occasion they all suddenly came to an awareness of the nature of water.
> Now Shyuedou asks you, all reverend monks:
> "How do you understand what they said? They said 'The wonderful sense is in clarity, and we have accomplished to dwell in the rank of Buddha's children.'"
> Shyuedou adds his comment: "Their accomplishment is not enough. We must attain the freedom to help others."

In order to understand their astonishing greatness, we had better add to "took a bath" the words "of suffering." This "wonderful sense is in clarity" is the very thing that Second Patriarch Hueike was helped to understand by Bodhidharma in the deep snow at Shaulin Temple.

> Shenguang [Hueike Shenguang, 487-593] said: "Can we understand the Dharma evidence of all Buddhas by

hearing?"

> The Teacher [Bodhidharma] said, "Dharma evidence is not the thing to obtain from a person." Shenguang said, "My mind is not yet settled. Teacher, I beg you, please settle it."
> The Teacher said, "Bring your mind and I will settle it for you."
> Shenguang: "I cannot hold my mind no matter how much I try to do so."
> The Teacher said, "Now I have settled it for you."
> (*Chuandeng lu*, vol. 3)

Shyuansha experienced this "wonderful sense is in clarity" when he struck his toe on a stone and then quit his pilgrimage of study. So his teaching to a novice isn't a slight matter. He is telling the novice, "Respect your six sense organs and their six objects as Buddhas. By any means do not devaluate them. It is the beginning of study."

Now, is the following sermon for the beginner or for the veteran trainee?

> Shyuansha on the way to deliver his sermon heard the sounds of swallows. In his sermon he said: "The swallows talk profoundly about True Form and well preach the Essence of the Dharma." Then he descended from his lecture seat.
> A monk asked him, "I cannot understand what you said, please would you further explain?"
> Shyuansha: "You are dismissed. Nobody believes what you say." (*Sanbyaku soku*, vol. 3, case 41)

Swallows are usually busy chirping and feeding when nursing their young. They must have made a nest under the roof of the open corridor between the master's quarters and the lecture hall. Did Shyuansha see their strenuous life as True Form and as the Essence of the Dharma? It could be, but how can an animal become competent to teach Buddha without studying Buddha's teaching? There are many things to study from this sermon. Here it is uncertain what Shyuansha concretely meant with the words "Essence of the Dharma"; but with association of the *Dharmapundarika* term "True Form," it couldn't be so far an assumption to remind ourselves of the following passage to understand what Shyuansha concretely meant:

Always thinking thus: How should I make sentient beings enter the Unsurpassed Way and quickly attain Buddha's body?
(*Dharmapundarika-sutra* [Lotus Flower Sutra], chap. *Tathagata-ayus-pramana* [Life duration of the Tathagata])

"The Essence of the Dharma" is to understand that Buddha, every being, is always devoting to make others Buddha, that is, Buddha is making Buddha out of Buddha. This is the world of oneness, and this world of oneness is "the Essence of the Dharma."

A similar passage can be found in the chapter *Upaya*, in the same sutra:

Sariputra, you must know I once upon a time vowed to make all sentient beings equal with me and no different. Now I have accomplished my vow and taught all sentient beings and enabled them to enter Buddha's Way.

Here in this passage the details of "Essence of the Dharma" are spelled out. Buddha shed himself and made all other sentient beings no different from himself. Then in his world there was no distinction between sage and ordinary people. Buddha's body was not a being among millions. His body was "the Great Body," as is said in the Seventh Precept, Neither admiring oneself nor depreciating others:

Kyoju kaimon: The body of Buddha and the patriarchs is realized in the entire sky and everywhere on the great earth. At times they present the Great Body and in the sky no distinction exists between inside and outside. At other times they present the Dharma-kaya and not an ounce of soil exists anywhere on earth.

So the swallows were preaching "the Essence of the Dharma," which means they were not distinguishing themselves from others, and especially not dividing the one who preaches from the one who listens. The relation between the one who preaches and one who listens is like the relation between a flower and spring; spring enters flower and flower enters spring. Thus no one distinguishes between a flower and spring. About this area Shyuansha and his teacher Shyuefeng had an important dialogue:

> Great Teacher Jenjiau at Mt. Shyuefeng said in his sermon: "All Buddhas in the Three Worlds are residing in the flame of fire and turning the Great Dharma Wheel."
> (*Yuanwu lu*, vol. 19)

> Great Teacher Tzungyi in Shyuansha Temple said: "When the flame preaches for all Buddhas in the Three Worlds, all Buddhas in the Three Worlds listen, standing attentive."
> (*Shobogenzo: Gyo butsuyigi* [Practicing Buddha's Behavior])

Seeing all Buddhas in the flame of fire was Shyuefeng's inventive virtue. Even now people see fire as only the process of combining oxygen and hydrogen while separating carbon and water from burning materials. Shyuefeng first of all clarified the place where Buddhas dwell. The flame of fire is a metaphor for the burning worlds, according to the Lotus Flower Sutra. But it is also a representation of any being or function. Shyuefeng therefore second of all clarified that the existence of Buddha, which is any phenomenal being or function, is the very act of helping (turning the Great Dharma Wheel, or Buddha's Deed).

On the other hand, what did Shyuansha do here? He didn't add anything to his teacher's words, but just mumbled that the one who preaches and one who listens are equal in value: Through the flame of fire, Buddha preaches the Dharma, and through the flame of fire Buddhas listen to it. Shyuansha was the first in history to tell that the one who preaches and one who listens are equal. Thus this fire can become a symbol of wisdom too. Wisdom equalizes all beings.

Shyuansha neither denied nor applauded his teacher's words. He simply mumbled an equality. He didn't even comment on his teacher's discovery that Buddhas, phenomenal beings, and turning the Dharma wheel are the same thing. We should be alert to his reserve. His inventive virtue in this dialogue was to show us that the greatness of most things is that they don't tell us anything but keep silent, all for our benefit.

For instance, turning in at a mailbox, seeing a dreary-looking driveway showing age with no virtue of aging, at the left a raw cliff made for human convenience with no nourishment or moisture for its healing. At the right, a valley covered in briars, vines, and naturalized plants. Ascend the driveway of coarse railway blast and see thorny locust trees with tent caterpillar webs, the leaves showing a decayed color in early June, then pines eager only to grow tall while losing their lower branches on both hillsides.

The truth is these beings, materials, and phenomena on the highways and off-roads don't tell us as much as this. It is thankful they keep silent. Shyuansha was the first with his expression to appreciate their silence.

After exposing ourselves to the flame of fire, it is easy for us to understand that the swallows, the beings as swallows, are already engaging in preaching, which is helping sentient beings, and their preaching is at once their listening. In other words, these self-perfecting beings or functions are "True Form" and "the Essence of the Dharma."

In detailed study, "True Form" is a concept coordinate with our phenomenal form, which is a temporary existence according to causation in time and mutual relations in space. So Shyuansha is saying the swallows' nest-building is True Form. He means the phenomenal form of their nest-building is transcending such relative phenomena as being or non-being, and moving or non-moving, but is presenting true, absolute form. In short he recommends that we see Buddha nature in the given phenomenon because the given phenomenon is shedding itself and showing its True Form, which is Buddha nature.

In the chapter *Upaya* (Devices) of the same sutra, it is mentioned that Buddha understands the world in ten aspects, which are Like This Form, Like This Nature, Like This Body, Like This Power, Like This Function, Like This Cause, Like This Indirect Cause, Like This Fruit of Training, Like This Karmic Reward for Training, and Like This All Above-listed Ultimately Equal. Each isn't easy to understand without the devotion of a Tiantai monk, but it is good enough if we gain the flexibility to convert them each freely according to our situation. For instance, when we talk about Form we must understand we are talking about Nature too, Body too, Power too, etc.

Similarly, when we hear Shyuansha's saying "The swallows talk profoundly about True Form and well preach the Essence of the Dharma," we must understand it as "The swallows talk, preach, study, practice, believe, teach, prove, (and all other important verbs)." Daily Buddhist life is to practice the life of no division between oneself and one's environment and not fall into dualistic valuation. In such a life, making the habit to find synonymy in all antonyms, contrary concepts, and contrary terms is a useful mental device.

In popular Buddhism it is said Buddha preaches the Dharma to sentient beings. In true Buddhism, Buddha is the Dharma and is also sentient beings. Buddha is True Form and sentient beings are phenomena. Buddha is the one to preach and sentient beings are the listeners. Preacher and listeners are of equal value. To be as a Buddha means to preach as a Buddha. Preaching is Buddha's function. Being is functioning as a being and is practicing Buddha's function. Being as a being is perfecting being. When being (a phenomenon) is perfecting its being, it sheds its form and becomes True Form. When True Form preaches, True Form is perfecting its form, Buddha is practicing Buddha's function. When True Form perfects its form, True Form sheds its form and becomes a phenomenal form, that is, in this case "the swallows."

Now how should we understand this dialogue that follows Shyuansha's sermon?

> A monk asked him, "I cannot understand what you said, please would you further explain?"
> Shyuansha: "You are dismissed. Nobody believes what you say."

Traditionally there are three interpretations. The first takes the monk's question literally and interprets that he really didn't understand what Shyuansha said. But the dynamic of True Form is a phenomenal form and it is always preaching the Dharma as universal fact. The monk's life is a very such being, and this fact has nothing to do with whether or not he understands. It is more like saying "I wish to touch the universe." The fact is, "I am the very universe." So Shyuansha in telling the monk he is dismissed, nobody believes what he says, is strongly urging the monk to reflect for himself.

The second interpretation is the monk well understands what Shyuansha says. But the deepest understanding is to become the object to be understood, and when we do, we won't have any consciousness of our understanding. It is Fayan's "Not knowing is the most intimate [knowing]."

Actually Fayan (Fayan Wenyi, 885-908) is the grandson of Shyuansha in the Dharma transmission. For this advanced knowing, Shyuansha said "You are dismissed. Nobody believes what you say." This is his approval of the monk.

The third interpretation is by Dogen. His focus is on the words "Nobody believes." He takes it to mean the absence of any person. The world addressed by the saying that the phenomenal swallows talk about True Form and preach the Essence of the Dharma is the world of Buddha or the Dharma, who, or which, is endlessly recycling in a self-perfecting process. Such a pure dynamic of the world is going on regardless of our understanding. Our ultimate goal is to participate in this world of Buddha. We are able to participate only when we shed human survival instincts, including dualistic conflicting views, and become Buddha or the Dharma. So Shyuansha for this reason said "You are dismissed. Nobody believes what you say."

Dogen's interpretation is glorifying Buddha's world and is almost metaphysical. We should always be careful not to indulge in any metaphysics of theology and also not to fall irretrievably into any chemical or zoological reality. It is right that the world of True form, or the world of Buddha or the Dharma, is beyond human discrimination. Even so, we can't ignore the fact that only through our consciousness can we sense the world of Buddha, and only through our consciousness can we understand that such a world has nothing to do with whether we understand it or not.

The second interpretation is theoretically possible but is unlikely to have actually happened historically. Would a monk who attained the high understanding that the ultimate understanding should be no understanding step forward voluntarily to show his advance in question form?

The first interpretation is the most natural to the recorded episode. With this interpretation Shyuansha appears as a really kind master.

While studying the case in its recorded form, we should always respect the literature. The recorder of this short episode gave us three hints, which set the right atmosphere for the right understanding of the content. The three hints are "on the way," "descended," "dismissed." The words are common as to the point that they clearly suggest the change of the engagement of the subject. "On the way" is from "Shyuansha on the way to deliver his sermon," and quietly Shyuansha was engaging in something related with a sermon in his residence before going to the Dharma Hall. This "on the way" gave him the topic of his sermon almost accidentally. "Descended" is from "he descended from his lecture seat," and it means his engagement has shifted to the practice of what he has just said in his sermon. Therefore the act of his descending must be True Form, and the Essence of the Dharma.

"Dismissed" is directly related with how to understand the monk's question and Shyuansha's answer, and it is from "You are dismissed." The meaning is to tell the monk to resume his daily chores either in gardening or office work or in fixing utensils.

When we consider these three hints and translate Shyuansha's answer into a modern outspoken mode, his words become, "I understand you don't understand what I said in my sermon. You must be frustrated. But even I your master can only glimpse in a passing moment. As soon as I see it, it disappears. When I engage in tangible work with my whole body and mind, it fully functions, but I can't see it. So you are now dismissed from the theological study. Resume your chores if you don't understand that every part of you is True Form and the Essence of the Dharma. Nobody doubts about this, including me. Live your earnest life of alternating physical practice and scripture study. Someday you will understand to your satisfaction."

Shyuansha's teacher Shyuefeng said:

> Every part of the great earth is the gate to attain Freedom.
> I lead people there, but they do not consent to enter.
>
> (*Liandeng hueiyau*, vol. 21)

Obviously a lamentation. Even though always having around fifteen hundred students, Shyuefeng had to lament. Like Shyuansha's swallows, Shyuefeng is saying every phenomenon is a device to attain Freedom. For Buddhists, Freedom (*vimukti* or *vimoksa*) means to be free of the restraint of one's own klesa and transmigration in the Three Worlds. So we gaze at a device or at a swallow, like a bird watcher. No Buddhist wisdom comes until we realize that the bird is ourselves. In short, every phenomenon is the device only when we make equality between it and ourselves. The swallows were preaching the Essence of the Dharma only when Shyuansha was them. Another expression is that our life in these suffering worlds is the very device to make us aware that we each are Buddha and that the worlds are the pure world of Nirvana.

When we see our own life in each phenomenon, we are using our own life as a device. At such a time it is nonsense to mention coming and going through the gate, or to mention ourselves coming and going through, because our own life is the very gate. For now we had better believe, even if we don't understand, that when any phenomenon is ourselves, our life is Buddha's device to free us from suffering no matter how much we are suffering. This is the dynamic of Buddha's cycle of suffering, gate, device, freedom.

In Buddha's world there's no division between self and other being, True Form and phenomena, the one who preaches and the one who hears, gate inside and out, device and real. To practice the Ninth Precept, Not Angering, means to live in such a dynamic of Buddha's cycle. Therefore it is stated in *Kyoju kaimon*:

> Not regressing and not advancing, not true and not false, everywhere the ocean of bright clouds, the solemnly ornamented ocean of clouds.

So, for those who are innocent about True Buddhism, Shyuefeng lamented, but he was expecting some heroic Buddhist would appear and say, "I knew it would be shabby, the world that would open only when we knocked. That's not how it is, for all worlds, inside, outside, and in between, are equally open for attaining Freedom, or, all worlds are various forms of attained Freedom." The following creative case also resembles a lamentation or sympathy on the surface, but Shyuefeng's expectation is to free people from worldly suffering:

> One day Shyuansha said to the assembly, "All respectable teachers everywhere claim they are trying to be beneficial and helpful for all sentient beings. Now I ask you how you will help such as those who suffer from the three disabilities identified as blind, deaf, and mute?
>
> "Even if you strike the wood instrument and raise your whisk, such persons cannot see you. Even if you speak, they

cannot hear nor can they speak. If you be of no help, Buddhism will have no miraculous virtue."
(*Chuandeng lu*, vol. 18)

Chuandeng lu continues the record:

> Then a monk stepped forward and asked,
> "Your Reverence, will you allow one who suffers from those three disabilities to debate the Dharma?"
> Shyuansha replied, " I allow you unlimited debate."
> The monk spoke a farewell and left.
> The Teacher said, "Wrong, wrong."

Chuandeng lu here inserts an added comment in smaller font:

> Fayan said "I understood the case of 'one who suffers from those three disabilities' at a time when Priest Luohan was introducing us to the monk's words."

Chuandeng lu resumes the record in regular font:

> Luohan said, "I who am Gueichen have eyes and ears. Your Reverence, how will you help me?"

Shyuansha's topic in those days gained popularity and was adopted as Case 88 in *Biyan lu*. It goes in the following manner, directly connecting with Yunmen's example and how Yunmen made use of it:

> A monk, in order to clarify further, asked Yunmen.
> Yunmen said, "Make your bows."
> The monk did, then stood there. Yunmen pushed him with his staff and the monk withdrew.
> Yunmen said, "You aren't blind" and he told the monk to come close. The monk did.
> Yunmen said, "You aren't deaf" then he asked, "Do you understand?"
> The monk said, "No, I don't."
> Then Yunmen said, "You aren't dumb,"
> and just then the monk attained insight.

Thanks to Shyuedou with his gatha, we try to understand the right direction and right concern of the case:

> The world of blind, deaf, and dumb
> is beyond our thought and judgment.
> The whole of heaven and earth

> is laughable and also sorrowful.
> Lilou could not discern the true color,
> nor Shykuang the sound out of scale and melody.
> Meditate alone by the window,
> at the right time the flowers open and the leaves fall.
> [Shyuedou adds] Do you get the point?
> It is an iron mallet without a handle hole.

Yunmen told the monk "You aren't blind," "You aren't deaf," "You aren't dumb." With actual demonstration he encouraged the monk who was excusing himself from awakening to the world of true blind, true deaf, and true dumb. The monk was weak-spirited, declining from awakening, almost violating the First Precept, Not Killing. It is said in *Kyoju kaimon*:

> Life cannot be killed; Buddha's seed keeps increasing.
> The life of Buddha's wisdom is to be continued; life is not to be killed.

"Life" is Buddha nature and is the life of Buddha. Yunmen believes no matter how our sense organs and intellectual powers are weak, they aren't too weak for us to be aware that our life is Buddha and that we needn't live a suffering life as ignorant beings. The world of true blind, deaf, and dumb is described by the first two lines of Shyuedou's gatha:

> The world of blind, deaf, and dumb
> is beyond our thought and judgment.

He means "The world of true blind, deaf, and dumb is beyond our dualistic view such as to see or not, to hear or not, and to speak or not.

Lilou (a person of 4th century BC) could see a piece of animal hair as far away as a hundred steps, and Shykuang was said to have excellent ears to hear the fighting of ants beyond a mountain. But Shyuedou says they weren't enough able to see true color and hear true sound.

> Meditate alone by the window,
> at the right time the flowers open and the leaves fall.

Shyuedou says meditation is the way to understand "the world of true blind, deaf, and dumb," and more, meditation enables us to know "the right time" for the flowers to open and the leaves to fall. These seventh and eighth lines are his answer to Shyuansha's original case. Shyuansha said "If you can be of no help, Buddhism will have no miraculous virtue." Buddhist miraculous virtue doesn't mean to be Annie Sullivan or Helen Keller. Buddhist miraculous virtue means to understand the most important causation. Buddha appeared in this world to enable sentient beings to enter the Unsurpassed Way and enable them to quickly attain Buddha's body. At the right time we will be "the flowers open" and will be "the leaves fall," just as we will be Buddha to help sentient beings and also will be sentient beings to be helped by Buddha.

When we are Buddha we shouldn't forget we are sentient beings and when we are sentient beings we should not forget we are Buddha. It is ideal not to see while we are seeing, not to hear while we are hearing, and not to speak while we are speaking. But to attain this sort of freedom, what sort of careful study and practice must we go through? Shyuedou therefore added:

> Do you get the point?
> It is an iron mallet without a handle hole.

These lines are related with the annexed episode:

> Then a monk stepped forward and asked,
> "Your Reverence, will you allow one who suffers from those three disabilities to debate the Dharma?"
> Shyuansha replied, "I allow you unlimited debate."
> The monk spoke a farewell and left.
> The Teacher said, "Wrong, wrong."

Shyuansha said that one who suffers from those three disabilities is allowed unlimited debate ("I allow you unlimited debate"). This means that a person with those disabilities has an unlimited and indefinable ability to preach the Dharma. The asking monk was understanding the unlimited and wonderful Dharma as if to see the depths of astronomical space. But unfortunately he thought such wonderful Dharma is endlessly developing in nature and that when we are disabled we can be a part of such profound nature. He was taking literally the proverb Silence is golden. For such a monk, Shyuedou's nature was phenomenal nature: Meditate alone by the window,

> at the right time the flowers open and the leaves fall.

This springtime is Buddhist spring, To raise Bodhi mind; and this autumn is Buddhist autumn, To attain the realization. Here summer (to practice what we intellectually understand) and winter (to attain Nirvana by living with intuition) are abbreviated. We must keep building the Buddhist World and the Buddhist Season instead of being victims of phenomenal causation. The monk made an immature but decisive conclusion, said farewell and started to leave. To the back of this departing blind, deaf, and mute monk, Shyuansha could only mutter "Wrong, wrong."

Luohan (Luohan Gueichen, 867-928) was a trusted disciple of Shyuansha and later becomes one of his Dharma heirs. To help junior monks deepen their understanding, he asked Shyuansha:

"I who am Gueichen have eyes and ears. Your Reverence, how will you help me?"

In the record, to this, Shyuansha spoke nothing further, meaning he approved of what Luohan expressed by his question. After all, Buddhism should "not have any miraculous virtue" whether we are physically blind or not, mentally blind or not, or whether we are sage or not, or ignorant beings or not, because all worlds in the ten directions in the past, present, and future are Buddha upon Buddha and nothing else. (Buddhists transcend both seeing and also blindness.) So, it is recorded:

Fayan said, "I understood the case of 'one who suffers from those three disabilities' at a time when Priest Luohan was introducing us to the monk's words."

In this way of understanding, doesn't Shyuedou's iron mallet become soft, bright, even warm?

[Shyuedou adds] Do you get the point?
It is an iron mallet without a handle hole.

One of Shyuansha's most important teachings is how to put into daily life the understanding of the Three Worlds are One Mind. To express this he made use of his longtime disciple Luohan. Luohan too began his study under Shyuefeng and became a disciple of Shyuansha continuously. When he became independent he dwelled first in Ditsang Temple and later in Luohan Temple. His posthumous name is Great

Teacher Jenying. (Luohan is called "Teacher" in the following episode, but at that time he was Shyuansha's disciple.)

> To the Great Teacher Jenying in Ditsang Temple Shyuansha asked, "How do you understand 'The Three Worlds are One Mind'?"
> The Teacher [Luohan] pointed to a chair and said: "Your Reverence, what do you call this?"
> Shyuansha said: "A chair."
> The Teacher: "Your Reverence does not understand 'The Three Worlds are One Mind'."
> Shyuansha: "I call it wood and bamboo. What do you call it?"
> The Teacher: "I too call it wood and bamboo."
> Shyuansha: "Even if we look for a person who understands Buddha's Dharma, we cannot find."
> (*Sanbyaku soku*, vol. 2, Case 12)

"The Three Worlds are One Mind" is the basic Buddhist view about what the world is and how we should accordingly live in it. Yet this basic Buddhist view is unfortunately not well understood and is regarded as a primitive, difficult, and impractical theology. Indeed Buddhism has lagged behind modern science in the study of the constituents of the elements, the mechanism of phenomenal functions, and the change of mutual relations. But Buddhism is even now effective to know the fundamental character of the world and ourselves, and how to make our life most meaningful.

Shyuansha and Luohan weren't local furniture makers. To appreciate their dialogue, we must study the following gatha known as "The Three Worlds are One Mind":

> The Three Worlds are One Mind.
> Outside this Mind there are no other beings.
> Mind, Buddha, and sentient beings
> are not three different things.
> (*Shobogenzo: Sangai yuishin* [The Three Worlds are One Mind])

We have been cherishing this gatha as a teaching of Sakyamuni Buddha, though there isn't the exact same gatha in any sutra. The first line can be found in the Avatamsaka Sutra, the second line in the Lankavatara Sutra. The last two lines are again from the Avatamsaka Sutra, where they are preceded by the sentences "Mind is like a painter who paints various materials, and there is nothing in the whole world that is not painted. Buddha is so, and so are sentient beings."

Here, Mind is likened to a painter, as are Buddha and sentient beings. In other words, Mind is a synonym for Buddha, and Buddha is a synonym for sentient beings. So this Mind doesn't mean the sensing and thinking faculty of our brain. It means the more universal and invisible nature of the universe that can be recognized by our intelligence when we transcend dualistic valuation.

The latter half of the gatha states "Mind, Buddha, and sentient beings are not three different things." So we can re-write the first half in the following ways:

> The Three Worlds are Buddha.
> Outside this Buddha there are no other beings.

Or:

> The Three Worlds are sentient beings.
> Outside these sentient beings there are no other beings.

Even this much seemingly automatic work of re-writing must be very hard to be achieved by guinea pigs and by most human beings. The gatha is declaring rather quietly and as a matter of fact that Mind, Buddha, and sentient beings are not different things but are the same one thing. Mind is the fundamental cause of every phenomenon, including the distressed human being, which is an effect. The gatha says cause and effect are the same one thing. The distressed human being wishes to be helped by a capable, wise, and compassionate Buddha. The gatha says the one who helps and the one who is helped are the same one being, and more, the one who helps is the cause of distressed human beings, who are the effect. This is the meaning of the passage in the Diamond Sutra that struck Sixth Patriarch Hueineng:

> Indeed there is no place to dwell, yet the mind should rise.

"Indeed there is no place to dwell" is Buddha, and "yet the mind should rise" is sentient beings.

It is said in the Brahma's Net Sutra, fasc. 2:

> When sentient beings receive Buddha's precepts

> they instantly enter the rank of all Buddhas
> and their rank equals that of the Greatly Realized One
> and they are truly Buddha's children.

When sentient beings receive the precepts they transcend dualistic valuations and there is no division between them and Buddha. So it is easy to understand sentient beings become equal with Buddha. But in an annotation to Dogen's *Kyoju kaimon*, on the First Precept, Not Killing, there is this special caution:

> Because it was said "their rank equals that of the Greatly Realized One," this "equals that of the Greatly Realized One" should be understood as "their rank equals that of sentient beings."

When we transcend dualistic valuations we are immediately Buddha, and when we are bound by dualistic valuations we are immediately sentient beings. Sentient beings are not comprising one third of the world. We already studied that the Three Worlds are sentient beings. Outside sentient beings there are no other beings. When we see the worlds as sentient beings there is no Buddha, no Mind, and of course no wall or pebble, not even a tree. All things inside and outside the world are only sentient beings. When all worlds are sentient beings, even sentient beings transcend sentient beings, and there won't be a single distressed sentient being to be helped.

It is important to see the worlds purely or whole-heartedly. When we see the worlds as Mind, they should be Mind and nothing else; when we see the worlds as Buddha, they should be Buddha and nothing else; and when we see the worlds as sentient beings, they should be sentient beings and nothing else. If we are strictly loyal to this "nothing else," we cannot say even "Mind is Buddha and is also sentient beings," because it should be truly "nothing else." In other words, the worlds are Mind and *period* (.) The worlds are Buddha and. The worlds are sentient beings and. Or we cannot say even as much as "The worlds are Mind." It is because "The worlds" and "Mind" don't coexist to be equaled. None of the worlds, Mind, Buddha, and sentient beings, know one another in truth. They know one another only in our intellectual world, which isn't the real existing world. Fayan was one of the conspicuous

Dharma heirs of Luohan and was regarded in a later age as the founder of the Fayan school.

> Fayan was studying under Changching [Changching Hueileng, 854-922] in Fujou, yet he could not settle his mind and set forth on a mendicancy with his friends to the outskirts of the Hushiang district. On the way he met a great rain and a swollen gorge and he happened to visit the priest Ditsang [Luohan] at Ditsang Temple at the west end of a town.
> Ditsang asked, "Your Reverence, where are you going?"
> Fayan replied, "I am only going along the meandering mountain skirts."
> Ditsang: "What is the meaning of your mendicancy?"
> Fayan: "I do not know."
> Ditsang: "Not knowing is the most intimate [knowing]."
> Fayan suddenly came to the realization.
> (*Chuandeng lu*, vol. 24)

By this reflection Fayan could realize that the life of Buddhism is in daily innate practice and not in a wide study of theology or in meticulous *vinaya* behavior. His recorded sayings (*Jinling Chingjing-yuan Wenyi Chanshy wulu*) continue to describe more of his realization opportunities:

> Then these three monks [Fayan and his companions Shaushiou and Fashin] were discussing Dharma Teacher Sengjau's *Jaulun* and they came to the passage "Heaven-and-earth and I are of the same root. All things and I are of one body."
> Ditsang asked, "Reverend Trainee, are mountains-and-rivers and you the same one thing or different things?"
> Fayan responded, "Different."
> Ditsang raised two fingers.
> Fayan said, "The same thing."
> Ditsang again raised two fingers and left.

It is interesting that in Case 40 in *Biyan lu*, Nanchyuan's "as if in a dream" treats the exact same theme. There Nanchyuan (Nanchyuan Puyuan, 748-834) had to be cautious because he was dealing with a government officer who had power to influence his temple. So it is described:

> Nanchyuan pointed to the flowers in the garden and guided the officer over to them and said, "People nowadays see these flowers as if in a dream."

In Buddhism too there are dreams and they are given a positive meaning. For Buddhists, phenomenal worlds are the dreams (rupa) of Buddha (sunyata). In another expression Buddhist dreams are the actualization of Buddha nature. Therefore our intellectual reasoning, judgment, and colligation are regarded as dreams of dreams, or illusions, (and those Freudian objects are dreams of dreams of dreams, or an imperfect combustion of our brain). Therefore Shyuedou said in his gatha:

> Mountains and rivers should not be viewed in a mirror.

The world (or life) should be seen (lived) directly instead of trifled with in one's mental mirror, which is our intelligence.

Now, Ditsang (Luohan) strongly urged Fayan to see the world (or life) directly by raising a second time his two fingers and leaving, thus telling Fayan that intellectual investigation is fated to endlessly bring dualistic arguments without any solution and it pushes us farther away from the true life, which we can't catch by our thought. Leave from intellectual trifling and put oneself in the center of Life.

Fayan's Record continues the episode:

> The snow stopped and they bid farewell.
>
> Ditsang saw them off at the gate, and there he addressed Fayan, "Your Reverence, you always state the Three Worlds are One Mind and the million phenomena are only *vijinaptimatrata* [Universal Mind]." So saying, he pointed to a fragment of stone in the garden and asked, "Tell me, where is this fragment of stone, inside your mind or outside?"
>
> Fayan said, "It is inside."
>
> Ditsang: "By what queer causation should a pilgrimage monk carry a fragment of stone his head?"
>
> Fayan was frustrated and could not respond. He finally unwrapped his travel pack and took the seat of resident monk in order to clarify. For nearly one month he kept presenting his views and reasoning to Ditsang. But Ditsang kept telling him "Buddha's Dharma is not like that."
>
> Then Fayan said, "I have exhausted all my words and reasoning."
>
> Ditsang said, "If I must say to you about Buddha's Dharma, I'll say everything is manifesting."
>
> Under these words Fayan came to the great realization.

Fayan saw the totality of the world. When we divide worlds, oneself from others, rupa from sunyata, time from materials, here from there, now from then, life from death, and such, we aren't seeing the totality of the worlds, which is we ourselves.

We now go back to the study of The Three Worlds.

Other names are World of Desires, World of Materials, and World of No Materials. The World of Desires is equivalent to sentient beings, The World of Materials is equivalent to Buddha, and The World of No materials is equivalent to Mind.

There is one more set of names for The Three Worlds, and they are Dharma-kaya, Sambhoga-kaya, and Nirmana-kaya. Dharma-kaya is equivalent to Mind, Sambhoga-kaya to Buddha, and Nirmana-kaya to sentient beings.

These are The Three Bodies of Buddha (*tri-kaya*, "three bodies"). Dharma-kaya is universal reason, beyond any restriction of time and form. The Body of Buddha, which is Dharma-kaya, is connected with our intuition. Sambhoga-kaya is Buddha having perfected his training through countless kalpas of training and yet enjoying to keep studying and increasing his virtue. Examples are the Buddhas Amitatathagata, Bhaisajyaguru, and Vairocana. This kind of Buddha helps our understanding of endless stretches of time and space. Nirmana-kaya is like our Sakyamuni Buddha, who shows up according to the talent and environment of sentient beings. In this category we can include showing up as cat, dog, flower, thunder, any phenomenal function. This Buddha deepens the meaning of phenomena.

It looks as though each of the three is different, but in this case too it is wrong to understand that the worlds consist of Three Buddha's bodies, for each is the same as the others. Dharma-kaya is Sambhoga-kaya, and Sambhoga-kaya is Nirmana-kaya. Therefore when we say Dharma-kaya, the two other kayas will be hidden in Dharma-kaya. Likewise when we say Sambhoga-kaya, Dharma-kaya and Nirmana-kaya will be hidden in Sambhoga-kaya.

At any rate these Three Worlds are Buddha. So wherever we go, whatever happens for us, we will fall into Buddha's body. This is a point to establish our peace.

Dogen says about the gatha "The Three Worlds are One Mind":

> The gatha was expressed by using all his life power, and using all his power was the total expression of the total power, and this expression was done naturally even if done artificially.
> Therefore "The Three Worlds are One Mind" expressed by the Tathagata is the total manifestation of all Tathagatas.
> *(Shobogenzo: Sangai yuishin* [The Three Worlds are One Mind])

Dogen saw all of Sakyamuni Buddha's power in this gatha. He isn't saying Sakyamuni Buddha poured all his life power into this gatha but saying this gatha is equal with all the life of Sakyamuni Buddha.

More, Dogen says "using all his power was the total expression of the total power." First Dogen is making the gatha equal with all the life of Sakyamuni Buddha. Now he is making "all the life of Sakyamuni Buddha"—historically a lifetime of about eighty-two years—equal with "the total expression of the total power." Then what is "the total expression of the total power"? "The total power" means the power that exists throughout the three times, past, present, and future. In other words all life of Sakyamuni Buddha is Nirmana-kaya, and it is Sambhoga-kaya, and it is Dharma-kaya. In short "the total power" means another expression of the gatha, which above we have already rewritten:

> The Three Worlds are Buddha.
> Outside this Buddha there are no other beings.

Dogen understood the gatha was the expression given by Sakyamuni Buddha, who was The Three Worlds, or Buddha. He therefore concluded that "this expression was done naturally even if done artificially." Dogen saw in this gatha a perfect blend of human effort and worlds function.

In the Lotus Flower Sutra, it is Chapter 16, Life Duration of the Tathagata (*Tathagata-ayus-pramana*) that has been regarded as the eye of the sutra. This chapter expresses that Sakyamuni Buddha, who attained Buddha's Way in the vicinity of Buddhagaya, was in fact the primary Buddha who attained Buddha's Way eons ago.

In the same chapter it is said:

> There is no better view than [The Three Worlds] see The Three Worlds as The Three Worlds.

It is a headache that translations don't agree with one another about this important passage. About this particular passage too, since old times a different translation with a completely opposite interpretation has been circulated. For instance, the English translation *Scripture of the Lotus Blossom of the Fine Dharma* by Leon Hurvitz (publ. Columbia University Press, 1976) is written as follows (p. 239), I underline the related line:

> The Thus Come One in full accord with reality knows and sees the marks of the triple sphere. There is no birth-and-death, whether withdrawal from or emergence into the worlds, nor is there any being in the world nor anyone who passes into extinction. [The triple sphere] is neither Reality nor vanity, neither likeness nor difference. <u>Not in the manner of the triple sphere does he view the triple sphere.</u> Such matters as these the Thus Come One sees clearly, without confusion or error.

The translator evidently understood the meaning of the passage as "The Thus Come One because he is a sage does not view the triple sphere in the same manner as ignorant residents in the triple sphere view it."

Genshin (942-1017), founder of the Japanese Pure Land sect, rejected this kind of interpretation because he believed ignorant sentient beings have equal Buddha nature with Buddha even though they aren't yet awakened to it. Dogen too took this ground. My translation is along this line. Otherwise Buddha must propagate the difference between himself and all others in the very paragraph here, in which he is denying every dualistic view. Just as we have studied that The Three Worlds are Buddha upon Buddha and nothing else, we must read this sutra passage from Buddha's eye and not from theologians' eyes, which are fated to see things with conflicts.

In the above words of Buddha according to my translation, a very important attitude about how we should see ourselves is suggested: "There is no better view than [The Three Worlds] see The Three Worlds as The Three Worlds." It means the best view for A is A sees A as A. Here we are reminded of Buddha's respect for all beings, including himself: "In all heaven and on earth I alone am respectable," and "Make yourself like an island in the ocean, and depend on yourself. Make the Dharma your torch, rely on the Dharma, rely on nothing else." (Here it becomes evident "yourself" and "the Dharma" are synonymous.) It is right to establish oneself as the core of the world because The World in the Ten Directions, as well as in the past, present and future, is Buddha upon Buddha.

Then what is the meaning of "[The Three Worlds] see The Three Worlds as The Three Worlds"? It is that sentient beings should see the burning worlds as burning worlds, and not see them as 'One Mind' or any such thing. (The point is, when we are sentient beings we should confront The Three Worlds as the place for sentient beings, and not blur our recognition by bringing other notions such as One Mind, or Buddha.) Directly face the burning worlds, and don't dream of going elsewhere, such as to a 'Pure Land.'

By directly facing the burning worlds, we who are functions of Buddha are going to meet the burning worlds, which are functions of Buddha. When Buddha's functions meet Buddha's functions, both the burning worlds and we ourselves are shed. In other words, we and our object blend to build primordial Buddha's worlds. The sight of this blending is like sight of the two raised fingers of one hand. The very time two functions of Buddha are blending with each other is the very time The Three Worlds are transcending The Three Worlds. This is the Buddhist's transcending of The Three Worlds, which are we ourselves. When we see The Three Worlds in front of our very eyes as what they are, we are transcending ourselves and our objects without destroying, distorting, or ignoring either ourselves or our objects, our environment.

When we keep transcending ourselves and our objects in this Buddhist way, we are inevitably repeating the endless cycle of raising Bodhi mind, actually training, attaining the realization, and attaining nirvana. It is also true to say that unless we are not participating in this endless cycle we are unable to transcend ourselves and our objects. The reason is that we won't see Buddha's functions but will see only forms, nature, and the powers of ourselves and our objects.

It is odd that we are functions of Buddha and our sufferings too are functions of Buddha. Yet in order to understand that the one who causes the suffering and the one who struggles with the suffering are the same one Buddha, we must go through the endless cycle of raising Bodhi mind, actually training, attaining the realization, and attaining nirvana. For Buddhists, what life means is to keep this cycle endlessly turning. When we are suffering we are sentient beings, and when we transcend the suffering we are Buddha.

Actually when we are engaging in any stage of the endless cycle we are already transcending the suffering or The Three Worlds, and this is important—that we are actually transcending the sufferings or The Three Worlds even when we are in the midst of the suffering. Here we must remind ourselves of the virtue of Sakyamuni Buddha, who taught us the way to transcend The Three Worlds by engaging in the endless cycle. Without his teaching our body must face fire, our liver must face cancer, our toe must strike a stone, and our brain must face irritation. Thanks to his teaching of the endless cycle, we now know that the function of Buddha is meeting Buddha's function. After all, it isn't the work of Buddhist monks to engage with militaristic and undemocratic governments. What monks should do is teach us how to make one function meet another function without our defiling them with our illusions in the name of our thought and emotion.

When we see The Three Worlds as The Three Worlds, The Three Worlds transcend The Three Worlds and become Buddha's body, which can appear as Dharma-kaya, Sambhoga-kaya, or Nirmana-kaya. They are three bodies of One Buddha and are not outside of us.

Jaujou said in his sermon:

> A metal Buddha will not survive a smelting furnace, a wooden Buddha will not survive fire, and a mud Buddha will not survive water. True Buddha is in the depths of the Hall. Bodhi, Nirvana, Tathata, and Buddhata all are decorative robes, and are called klesa.
>
> (*Jaujou lu,* entry 209; this part adopted into *Biyan lu*
> as Case 96)

Those Buddha images don't survive the harsher environments. So too should be any form and concept, such as superstitions, thoughts, and emotions. The true Buddha is reliable throughout time and space for everyone. So we must intuitively sense the existence of the true Buddha. Then where is it? Jaujou said: "The true Buddha is in the depths of the Hall."

Jaujou continues his sermon:

> There is no klesa if you do not ask. Where are you going to place a mental state such as True Ultimate Existence? 'Only if one's mind is not born do all phenomena have no problem.' Meditate in seeking Reason for twenty or thirty years and cut off the head of this old monk if you are not yet going to arrive at the understanding.

Practicing meditation means to live with all our might with our body and mind. When we are forced to live with total devotion, we have no surplus to be bothered by dualistic thoughts. At such meditation time we are with true Buddha. So the residence of true Buddha isn't in space but in the activity of functions. This meditation enables the best of each function to meet function. Thus when a metal Buddha melts in a furnace, when a wooden Buddha burns in fire, and when a mud Buddha dissolves in water, "true Buddha" is acting steadily "in the depths" of our daily function. To listen to the teaching of "[The Three Worlds] see The Three Worlds as The Three Worlds" means to act as a metal Buddha and melt, to act as a wooden Buddha and burn, and to act as a mud Buddha and dissolve.

In the Lotus Flower Sutra, Chapter 3, *Aupamya* (Metaphor), the secret of transcending The Three Worlds is suggested as quietly as a standing shadow:

> I tell you, Sariputra, I too am like this,
> being the most venerable among saints,
> father of the world.
> All the living beings, all my children,
> are profoundly addicted to worldly pleasure
> and have no wise thoughts.
> The Three Spheres, completely unsecure,
> are just like a house afire,
> full of many woes most frightful,
> constantly marked by birth, old age,
> sickness, death, and care—
> fires such as these, raging without cease.
> The Thus Come One, having already left
> the burning house of the Three Spheres,
> is quiet and unperturbed,
> dwelling securely in forest and field.

> Now these Three Spheres are all my possession,
> the living beings within them all my children.
> (*Scripture of the Lotus Blossom of the Fine
> Dharma*, p. 72, Leon Hurvitz, ref. above)

The lines in our current topic are:

> The Thus Come One, having already left
> the burning house of the Three Spheres,
> dwelling securely in forest and field.

It is said "The Thus Come One, having already left," and we would like to know when was (is) the exact time of this "having already left." It is when he or The Three Worlds "see The Three Worlds as The Three Worlds," and it is the time when he melts in the furnace, burns in the fire, or dissolves in the water. Here the time now (to melt) is already (gone), and there is no time gap between. Likewise, where is there such an ideal place referred to as "in forest and field"? It isn't any geographical suburb. The "quiet and unperturbed" mentality is called "in forest and field." So the place here (burning worlds) is there (nirvana), and for true Buddhists here is the burning worlds and there too is the burning worlds, as well as here is nirvana and there too, nirvana. Truly to be a true Buddhist we should be heroic and wise like Shyuansha. But before returning to Shyuansha's Three Worlds, "A chair," we will study a little more the last lines of the quoted gatha:

> Now these Three Spheres are all my possession,
> the living beings within them all my children.

Originally the sutra was written in a feudalistic culture, and the words "my possession" must be likened to land for the king, and "my children" to the people. But for us who have studied that Buddha is The Three Worlds, The Three Worlds are of course the possession of The Three Worlds. This is as if to say in English "I have my hands." It means "The Three Worlds are with The Three Worlds," or "The Three Worlds consist of The Three Worlds." It means all parts and functions within The Three Worlds are all parts and functions of Buddha's body and here they are called "my children."

However, we must be careful when we read "the living beings within them all my children." The Three Worlds are Buddha, and the content of The Three Worlds is Buddha. If so, then "the living beings within them" are The Three Worlds, and therefore "all my children" must mean "all The Three Worlds," or Buddha. In short, Buddha is calling himself here a child (children). When the sutra describes The Three Worlds in the mode to be taken care of, The Three Worlds are children upon children. And in the mode of caretaker, The Three Worlds are father upon father. And when the sutra describes The Three Worlds in the mode of The Three Worlds, then The Three Worlds are The Three Worlds upon The Three Worlds. And in the mode of Buddha, they are Buddha upon Buddha. By any means, in the mode of "children" there will be no existence of "father," and vice versa. It is like just saying "The Three Worlds," for when we say "The Three Worlds," all worlds are only The Three Worlds and nothing else. When we say "Mind," every phenomenon is only Mind and nothing else. Bringing any of these pairs together in the same place and time is dualistic thought.

Now finally we can return to the dialogue between Shyuansha and his disciple Ditsang. On the surface they are having a pleasant talk on a veranda with an evening ocean breeze. It is in a subtropical zone rich in both woods and bamboo. But they were presenting themselves as examples of Buddhist monks who have completely digested such big sutras as the Avatamsaka Sutra and the Lotus Flower Sutra instead of being crushed under their weight.

> To Great Teacher Jenying in Ditsang Temple, Shyuansha asked, "How do you understand 'The Three Worlds are One Mind'?"

Shyuansha wasn't asking Luohan (Jenying) for theological knowledge. As far as we studied The Three Worlds are One Mind, it seems we can understand The Three Worlds in any way (because The Three Worlds are Buddha upon Buddha wherever and whatever happens), and yet we shouldn't adhere to any of our understandings (because of Buddha nature, which keeps transcending itself), and yet we also have to understand The Three Worlds by ourselves in each situation with our own freedom and responsibility (because we each are a particular life, which is the medium for universal truth, or life).

> The Teacher [Luohan] pointed to a chair and said: "Your Reverence, what do you call this?"

Shyuansha said: "A chair."
Your reverencee does not understand 'The Three Worlds are One Mind.'"

Luohan sensed his teacher Shyuansha wasn't asking for an explanation or definition of The Three Worlds and he rather asked back, "What do you call this?"—pointing to a chair. Shyuansha said it was a chair. There Luohan saw through that his teacher Shyuansha wasn't understanding The Three Worlds are One Mind. For them understanding the concept The Three Worlds are One Mind wasn't a matter deserving special mention. Their grave concern was whether they were living as The Three Worlds are One Mind. If living as The Three worlds are One Mind, they wouldn't know what is The Three Worlds are One Mind. They were neither spectators nor critics of life. So disciple Luohan was admiring his teacher: "Your Reverence does not understand 'The Three Worlds are One Mind.'"

Shyuansha wanted to make sure his disciple Luohan was in any changes thoroughly and therefore flexibly mastering the life to live as one who is living (instead of observing or dreaming), living the life of The Three Worlds are One Mind through daily life. So he asked:

"I call it wood and bamboo. What do you call it?"
Luohan: "I too call it wood and bamboo."
Shyuansha: "Even if we look for one who understands Buddha's Dharma, we cannot find."

Here Shyuansha's admiration is important. "Even if we look for one who understands Buddha's Dharma, we cannot find." Yes, all true beings including Luohan are not understanding themselves, and this great activity of not understanding themselves is the life of Buddha's Dharma. The more we act in no understanding, the more we can participate in the activity of The Three Worlds, or One Mind, as expressed:

Always thinking thus: How should I make sentient beings enter the Unsurpassed Way and quickly attain Buddha's body?
(Lotus Flower Sutra, chap. *Tathagata-ayus-pramana* [Life Duration of the Tathagata])

What we study through the dialogue between Shyuansha and Luohan is after all a practical understanding of the Tenth

Primary Precept: Not Devaluating the Three Treasures. The first half of the annotation clarifies for us:

> Annotation: In Buddha there is each. First, Dharma-kaya Buddha: Dharma-kaya's wonderful substance is the original Buddha. In talking, when we mean 'universal Dharma world,' we should not say such a particular thing as Western Buddha or Eastern Buddha. In this context there is only one Buddha. In this one Buddha there are the Eastern Tathagata [Bhaisaiyazuru-vaiduryaprabha] and Western Tathagata [Amitabha, or Amitayus]. Now, what is universal when we say 'universal'? 'Universal' has no place to be placed and is described as "not blue, not yellow, not red, not white, not black," and also "neither coming nor going."

You might take too easily Dharma-kaya thus explained. When we deal with the worldly world, Dharma-kaya is blue, yellow, red, white, and black. In Buddha's Dharma, Dharma-kaya is said to be "not blue, not yellow, not red, not white, not black." Sometimes it is expressed as "rupa is sunyata, sunyata is rupa." At other times it is expressed as "all dharmas," "True Form," "One Mind," "Dharma nature," and "truth such as it is." About these, no questions should remain in the context of "all dharmas," which we see, are "True Form." It is regretful if we do not fully understand this truth because of our unfamiliarity with it. The point is we should abandon our ego and customary daily views.

It is said "If you earnestly wish to see Buddha, do not be sparing with your life." What is to be abandoned and what not spared while the waterside or foot of the tree where you abandon your life and the fields and village too are all Dharma-kaya? What we must abandon is only the body and mind of our ego and self. We must dedicate ourselves to the body of the Dharma, Dharma-kaya. Dedicating means, not holding onto, not loving, oneself. At such a time who will not come to the realization "by seeing peach blossoms," who will not realize the Way by "hearing the sound of the bamboo"? Such is the very time we are Not Devaluating the Three Treasures. Coming and going is within Dharma-kaya. Blue, yellow, red, white, and black are the Dharma substance of Dharma-kaya. This is called Not Devaluating the Three Treasures.

After studying "wood and bamboo," understanding the following episode should be easier:

> Shyuansha offered cakes to General Wei.
> Wei asked, "How come not knowing how to make these, though we make use of them daily?
> Shyuansha raised a cake and said, "Have it."
> Wei ate it and again asked the same question.
> Shyuansha: "We daily make use of them but do not know how to make them." (*Chanyuan mengchiou*, vol. 3)

This episode teaches the importance of concentration, of devoting the whole of ourselves to one thing at a time. Concentration doesn't divide our ability and in consequence doesn't divide us and our environment. No division gives us the best mutual relation between we who wish to know and the object that by us should be known. This best mutual relation is called wisdom (*prajna*). In short, concentration (*dhyana*) is wisdom. This wisdom is to know without an object to know and is also the world of the precepts (*sila*). Intellectual knowing, on the contrary, disturbs our dhyana and in due course leads us to violate the precepts. It is said in the Brahma's Net Sutra:

> To keep the precepts means to restrain.

To restrain oneself from going elsewhere, by the declaration:

> Sentient and insentient beings have at once attained the Way; the grasses, trees, and land have all attained Buddhahood. (The purport of the Nirvana Sutra, vol. 7)

Confucius too restrained himself from wandering about:

> "Sy, do you regard me as an erudite man?"
> "Yes, you are, are you not?"
> "I am not. I carry One throughout." (*Lunyu*, chap. 13)

This "One" is our dhyana power. Shyuansha was asking General Wei to nurse it. By devoting ourselves to eating, for instance, such as General Wei was asked to do, the worlds of these sutras will be presented as actual existence, whereas trying to know them by means of our intelligence will dissipate them like moonlight on rough water.

Shyuansha visited an elder priest, Shautang, in Putian county, and was welcomed with all sorts of entertainments.

> Next day Shyuansha asked him: "Where have those noises of yesterday gone?"
> The elder priest Shautang raised a corner of his kasaya.
> Shyuansha said: "Between them there is no relation."
>
> (*Tsungrung lu*, Case 81)

This episode is of interest for preserving some custom of the late Tang, unanticipated by the recorder. Shyuansha was then master of a conspicuous monastery always containing eight to nine hundred monks. Born third son of a poor fisherman, he was now a celebrity, teacher of the local independent and powerful Governor Bin.

He was welcomed by an elder priest, Shautang, who also must have been a well-to-do priest. He and his entire manor welcomed Shyuansha, and the occasion could be combined with the autumn harvest festival. The locals must have cheered with an acrobatic circus, theatrical company, exhibit of local products, and many small temporary shops, with noisy music and firecrackers.

When Shyuansha asked the elder priest Shautang "Where have those noises of yesterday gone?" he must have been remembering the quiet moon rising over the harbor. We occasionally experience such a difference that we express as yesterday was noisy and today is quiet, and vice versa. In the age of jet airplanes, yesterday I could be on a quiet hill of persimmon orchards in a suburb above a stretching city, today airsick in a busy airport, and tomorrow on a hillside against a dark blue sky. A person in a responsible position like the elder priest Shautang, who had to organize the festival and direct and watch it, should be much relieved when things go as planned. Or was he dispirited after achieving the stressful task?

It is amazing he didn't show any disturbance or take any stance either to defend himself or gather himself up for a good answer. He just raised a corner of his kasaya to indicate "those noises of yesterday" didn't go anywhere, they are here now. By raising his kasaya corner, he is gazing at the nature underlying such contrasting forms as noise and quiet. He won't be influenced by the endless change of forms.

His answer contains three contrasting terms: noise and

quiet, yesterday and today, and here and there, and he answered at once for all three. For his skilled way of answering, Hungjy (Hungjy Jengjyue, 1091-1157) made this gatha line of admiration:
> A well-mannered old turtle settled in among the lotus roots.

Before Shautang finished the motion of raising his kasaya corner, Shyuansha said: "Between them there is no relation." We must thank him for speaking so. Otherwise, about Shautang's teaching we almost wanted to complain, "We didn't ask are noise and quiet two different things or one same thing. We don't care whether today and yesterday are the same one time or two different times. We don't care how much distance is between here and there. Our care is happy days now gone, when our parents cheered our childhood with presents. Where did those days go? Now we are in a corner of a cold dark room without light and heat, to save electricity. We don't care about Buddhist ontology, cosmology, and epistemology. Only we wish to be relieved of our present sorrows and pains."

So Shyuansha said "Between them there is no relation." The theology tells indeed that noise and quiet, yesterday and today, and here and there, are each not one and also not two. Shyuansha's interest is how to use such a theology in daily actual life.

For everyone's sense, noises and quietude are obviously different from each other in form, so too yesterday and today, here and there. So the only way to be free of the sufferings coming from their difference is to solve by seeing their hidden sameness. (Likewise, to be free of the sufferings that come from their sameness, we must find their difference.) However, through our intelligence we have no way to see their true sameness, because the function of our intelligence is to see the difference.

Our intelligence sees differences even in the midst of our insisting that the objects we see are equal. When noises are equal with quietude, why should we say noises are equal with quietude? If they are equal, then noises = noises, and quietude = quietude, and just to say noises or quietude should be enough. When we say noises, quietude is included; when we say quietude, noises are included. Thus in the true equal world, noises and quietude never coexist. In effect, when equal, "They have no relation with each other." This is the teaching "Not knowing is the most intimate [knowing]."

In order not to bring contrasting terms to this one place and time, what furious assiduity must be continuously carried on? Once Shyuansha was admirably called 'Bei Dhuta by his teacher Shyuefeng, and even to the day when he could relish a festival feast he was keeping up his assiduous life as well as his youth, after all. It was his dhyana power, which can be interpreted as vitality for life, his virtue of keeping sila, which can be the same as a thankful attitude and his happiness of living in an environment where prajna was commonly cared for.

When there are noises, the whole world is noises, with no quiet anywhere, and vice versa. Noises aren't some part of phenomena but are the totality of the world. It is like Yuanwu's "Life is the total function, death is the total function." When we see life, the whole world is life upon life and there is no death. When we see death, the whole world is death upon death and there is no life. When the whole world is life, for instance, even this one life too will disappear because nothing remains to be compared. This is the vacancy in fullness. Thus Shyuansha's greatness in this episode was to bring all available contrasting terms including life and death, while the elder priest Shautang only suggested three sets of contrasts. More, Shyuansha gave all contrasting terms the opportunity to transcend, made them enter the ocean of Buddha nature.

When we see this episode in this light, Hungjy was wrong because he saw Shyuansha and Shautang as equal in greatness, recognizing their easy and prompt response to each other. He thus made another gatha line of admiration, this time for Shyuansha:

> A colorful fish swims free among the water grasses.

Among Shyuansha's implied contrasting terms, the most important are "knowing" and "not knowing." For these very terms his comment "Between them there is no relation" was a most effective crushing blow. Extend his words and they can be read as "Between the truth of the world and our understanding of it there is no relation." Hungjy overlooked this important awareness of Shyuansha's contained in his response to the elder priest Shautang.

Then what was Shyuansha's intention in making this statement? Indeed when transcending any contrasting terms by concentrating on the function before our very eyes, we experience our not knowing state. Shyuansha's "no relation" is by no means a pessimistic sigh over the inefficiency of our knowing facility. Rather, when we concentrate we are in the midst of participating in the function, which is always carried in mutual synergy between us and our object. In this most vital combustion of life, the need of knowing is fully satisfied.

So his "no relation" must have a more positive meaning. It must be the goal or glory in Buddhist study instead of being negative and pessimistic. It is a graduation from the thirst for knowing, or, freedom from the obsession to know. Shyuansha was, so to speak, personally witnessing Buddhism's farewell departure from Greek philosophy, which has long been the core of science. Both Greek philosophy and science started from the wish to know oneself and others. But before science, Buddhism attained the peace of "not knowing" in which every being is functioning best in equality.

This "not knowing" is the ultimate knowing and has always been the goal of Buddhist study. The study begins from faith, Buddhist faith, which is the belief that our intelligence can solve our problems, as Nagarjuna beautifully defined:

> Faith enables us to enter the great ocean of Buddha's Dharma, and wisdom can free us from sufferings.
> (*Maha-prajnaparamita-sastra*, vol. 1)

Having this faith is to raise Bodhi mind, and what Nagarjuna is saying is that to raise Bodhi mind means to contemplate mortality. He especially means to face the death of one's loved ones and all else, including the imminent death of one's own life. When we contemplate mortality in our near vicinity we won't insist on our ego or self, and naturally we won't care for worldly fame and profit. This mentality is already the content of wisdom. The more we are imminent with our mortality, the more we will wish to study Buddha's view instead of our own view, and wish to practice Buddha's deeds instead of our own behavior.

When we raise Bodhi mind, we inevitably believe we are capable of understanding and practicing Buddha's teaching because Buddha says we are Buddha and we are living in Buddha's body (The Three Worlds are Buddha's possession), and Buddha said:

> Sentient and insentient beings have simultaneously attained the Way; grasses, trees, land, all have attained Buddhahood. (The purport of the *Nirvana Sutra*, vol. 7)

And:

> The great faith is Buddha nature, and Buddha nature is the Tathagata. (Ibid., vol. 33)

And the Avatamsaka Sutra (60-volume version) ensures the virtue of faith:

> When for the first time raising Bodhi mind, if a Bodhisattva is simple-hearted, firm, and immobile in seeking Bodhi, the virtue of his momentary notion will be so boundless in depth and width that it cannot be perfectly calculated even if the Tathagata for kalpas attempts to do so by exercising his discriminatory faculty.
> (Vol. 8: *Bhadrapala Bodhisattva*)

This "When for the first time raising Bodhi mind" means:

> It is possible to raise Bodhi mind as the result of having from the depths of the heart pure faith in Buddha, Dharma, and Sangha, and hence having grave respect for The Three Treasures. (Ibid.)

The same sutra states the importance of faith:

> Faith is the foundation of the Way, mother of virtues. It makes all good dharmas grow, extinguishes all doubt, and opens the Unsurpassed Way. This pure faith enables us to detach from filth, strengthens our determination, annihilates our arrogance, and nurses our piety.
>
> Faith is the first Dharma treasure, which purifies our hand to receive the teachings and practice the deeds.

By the way, from this first line Dogen got his name. In Japanese pronunciation, "foundation" is gen, and "Way" is Do.

Dogen too emphasizes the importance of faith:

> Those who wish to study Buddha's Way should first of all believe in Buddha's Way. Those who believe in Buddha's Way should believe their self is primordially on the Way and not confused, not deluded, not upset in view; their view faultless and neither going to increase nor decrease. Raising this sort of faith and clarifying this sort of Way is the foundation of studying the Way.
> (*Gakudo yojin shu* [Cautionary Advice for Studying the Way])

Once more, by the way, this Buddhist faith is for trusting human intelligence after all and it is fundamentally different from the faith of other religions.

Jesus couldn't see any salvation on this earth (in the phenomenal worlds or in The Three Worlds):

> For we know that the law is spiritual: but I am carnal, sold under sin.
> (Romans 7.14)

> For the good which I would I do not: but the evil which I would not, that I practice.
> (Ibid., 7.19)

> ...for all have sinned, and fall short of the glory of God; being justified freely by his grace through the redemption that is in Christ Jesus.
> (Ibid., 3.23, 24)

> ...in this adulterous and sinful generation
> (Mark 8.38)

So he pursued eternal life in heaven,

> And Jesus answered and said, O faithless and perverse generation, how long shall I be with you, and bear with you? Bring hither thy son.
> (Luke 9.41)

Thus the content of Christian faith is the atonement of Jesus and is God's blessing.

> For ye died, and your life is hid with Christ in God.
> (Colossians 3.3)

> ye have put off the old man with his doings.
> (Ibid., 3.9)

> I have been crucified with Christ; and it is no longer I that live, but Christ living in me: and that life which I now live in the flesh I live in faith, the faith which is in the Son of God, who loved me, and gave himself up for me.
> (Galatians 2.20)

What Shyuansha has arrived at, in the ultimate knowing, is "not knowing," and it is the exact same attitude he should have at the start of his study. This "not knowing" and "no relation" tell us that "not knowing" can enable us to participate in

Buddha's activity or Truth of the universe, whereas knowing doesn't enable us so. This "not knowing" and "no relation" give supportive evidence to Sakyamuni's declaration: "All sentient and insentient beings, including mountains and rivers, weeds and trees, are attaining Buddhahood."

In the manner of keeping for final enjoyment the most favorite food among servings of food, we are waiting to study Shyuansha's most important teachings, which are condensed in the following episode:

> A monk asked, "I have heard Your Reverence has the saying 'The Whole World in the Ten Directions is a bright crystal orb.' How should I your student understand it?"
>
> The Teacher said, "The Whole Worlds in the Ten Directions is a bright crystal orb. What is the use of understanding?"
>
> Next day the Teacher asked him, "How do you understand 'The Whole World in the Ten Directions is a bright crystal orb'?"
>
> The monk replied, "The Whole World in the Ten Directions is a bright crystal orb. What is the use of understanding?"
>
> The Teacher: "It is obvious you are vigorously living in a demons' cave under a dark mountain."
>
> (Chuandeng lu, vol. 18)

This monk must have been a visiting monk rather than a resident monk, for he started his question with the introduction "I have heard." Not only Shyuansha but all good patriarchs were kind in teaching even temporary visitors.

Now did this monk ask with or without understanding Shyuansha? Which is the case makes a big difference in interpreting this episode from beginning to end. If this monk is an ignorant, then Shyuansha's answer "What is the use of understanding?" will in return to the monk become a question of the validity of his understanding. It suggests some kind of negative valuation towards human intelligence before the vast nature of the worlds.

According to negative interpretation, the truth of The Whole World in the Ten Directions can't be experienced by our senses, perceptions, and judgments. It is like a colorless crystal orb, it can't be grasped by any means. Still the monk tried to understand such truth of the world and asked "How should I understand it?" So Shyuansha answered "What is the use of understanding?" meaning "You are good just for asking such a question. By us the truth of the Whole World cannot be understood. What we can do as our best is ask 'How?' such as you do."

For us human beings, the truth is presented in the form of this "How?" and we are living with this "How?" and in such a life, come to think of it, it is possible to live, thanks to a bright crystal orb. So we mustn't seek any solution and profit from "How?" It is the way the world is. Just keep the practice of not seeking any profit and realization (Just Sitting Meditation). With this understanding Shyuansha encouraged the monk to continue his No-profit-seeking training, "It is obvious you are vigorously living in a demons' cave under a dark mountain."

Well, we don't go along with this negative interpretation. When there are plural interpretations, which should we take? Of course we can't ignore the grammar and usage of the time in which the records were written. However, in studying any sutras and patriarchs' words, it is recommendable to "first grasp what they meant to say, then study the words and phrases actually spoken." It is no mistake if we choose such interpretations that give the deeper Buddhist meaning and more compassion to our actual life. The following interpretation is to regard the monk as well-matured, and this interpretation follows Dogen's *Ikka no Meishu* (A bright crystal orb).

"The Whole World in the Ten Directions is a bright crystal orb" Shyuansha creatively said. The theological meaning of his saying is the same as saying "rupa is sunyata" (*Prajnaparamita-hrdaya-sutra*), but Shyuansha's value is that he said it in his own words and with his own nuance. Buddhism has no complication. "Buddha's Dharma is consistent!" Linji declared. This truth can be expressed one way or another to define it in one's own words.

Keizan (Keizan Jyokin, 1268-1325) was in the fourth-generation descent from Dogen, and he made Dogen's teaching more approachable for his age. Many years he was studying the koan "The ordinary mind is the Way" under the instruction of his teacher Gikai (Tettsu Gikai, 1219-1309). One day while engaging in daily temple activities, he shed himself and came to realize his ordinary mind was indeed the Way, manifestation of the Treasure Repository Housing the Eye to See the Right Dharma.

He went to his teacher to say "Now for the first time I understand the ordinary mind is the Way." The teacher asked him, "How do you understand it?" "The pitch-black grindstone vigorously flies about in the night," Keizan answered. "Not complete, say more," said the teacher. So Keizan added, "I have rice at mealtime and tea when it arrives." In this, his concrete behavior, sunyata was hidden in rupa. Ordinary mind backed by the Way is the Buddhist ordinary mind.

Some people interpret that Shyuansha scolded his monk for satisfying himself in a state of basic equality, sunyata: The monk had replied, "The Whole World in the Ten Directions is a bright crystal orb. What is the use of understanding?"—the equivalent of Keizan's saying to his teacher Gikai "The pitch-black grindstone vigorously flies about in the night." Shyuansha had said to his monk "It is obvious you are vigorously living in a demons' cave under a dark mountain." Shyuansha's words are equivalent to Gikai's "Not complete." Next we will see Shyuansha's more positive meaning:

First we will study in more detail "The Whole World in the Ten Directions." Second we will study "a bright crystal orb." Third we will study the "How" and "What" in the episode. And finally, fourth, we will study "a demons' cave under a dark mountain."

Hearing the words "The Whole World in the Ten Directions," we imagine the vast universe. This is fine, but we must understand there is also The Whole World in the Ten Directions even in a poppy seed, in a strand of hair. The Whole World in the Ten Directions can be big, also small. Even in a thing big as a nebula, there it is; even in a thing small as a mosquito's eye, there too. It transcends both large and small, and likewise transcends things of any shape. Not only in physical beings, it is in our conducts, our going, dwelling, sitting, reclining, also in our mental states—illusion, awakening, ordinary, holy. Our life is The Whole World in the Ten Directions, as is our death. It is in beings both active and inactive. It can be a certain thing but also will not be limited by any certain thing. In that sense it isn't a certain thing but can be a certain thing. In other words, it doesn't repeat to come and go, or to be born and to die, but can repeat to come and go, or to be born and to die. Here too we must remember Shyuansha's striking his toe:

> On the way he struck his toe on a stone. In bleeding pain he reflected, "This body is not real being—from where does the pain come?"
> (*Shobogenzo: Ikka no Meishu* [A bright crystal orb])

The pain obviously came from The Whole World in the Ten Directions because everything is The Whole World in the Ten Directions. When his toe healed, where went the pain? It went to The Whole World in the Ten Directions because everything is The Whole World in the Ten Directions. Wherever the pain comes to and wherever it goes is the same Whole World in the Ten Directions. This same place can be experienced when we become only the pain. When we strike our toe, our whole body is the pain. When our toe heals, our whole body is free of the pain.

Where the pain originates is in The Whole World in the Ten Directions, and where the pain departs to is also to there. All times, past, present, and future, are the same Whole World in the Ten Directions. Before we came to this life on earth, our life was in The Whole World in the Ten Directions. While we are now here, our life is in The Whole World in the Ten Directions. After this life also, our life will be in The Whole World in the Ten Directions. Our life is always in The Whole World in the Ten Directions. So naturally Shyuansha responded to Shyuefeng:

> "Bodhidharma never came to this eastern land and the Second Patriarch never went to the land under the western sky."

Both eastern land and land under the western sky are the same Whole World in the Ten Directions. There is no coming and going of Bodhidharma and the Second Patriarch. Even coming and going are The Whole World in the Ten Directions, not only Bodhidharma and the Second Patriarch are so. Thus The Whole World in the Ten Directions is The Whole World in the Ten Directions. In other words, it is the absolute world and not a relative world. So when The Whole World in the Ten Directions is entirely itself and nothing else, we have no way to "mislead others."

Shyuefeng asked "Who is 'Bei Dhuta?" The past life of Shyuansha—'Bei Dhuta—was The Whole World in the Ten Directions; his present life too, the Whole World in the Ten Directions, and his future life too; his every gesture and thought too. So Shyuefeng expressed this marvelous indefinable fact as "Who is 'Bei Dhuta," a statement meaning whatever everything is, is 'Bei Dhuta. Thus Shyuefeng's words were an affirmation. Likewise, when he asked Shyuansha "'Bei Dhuta, why don't you make a pilgrimage to visit masters countrywide?" his question contained "You are great for completing your pilgrimage, for mastering The Whole World in the Ten Directions! Yesterday was The Whole World in the Ten Directions, your life. Today too and every time is The Whole World in the Ten Directions, your life."

When we begin to understand that our every act and thought, our every behavior and form, and our every state and function are the same Whole World in the Ten Directions, we begin to appreciate Shyuansha's unique expression "The Whole World in the Ten Directions is a bright crystal orb." Every one of our six sense organs, objects of our six sense organs, and world formed by our six sense organs and their six objects are each and all The Whole World in the Ten Directions. Everywhere is The Whole World in the Ten Directions, there's no place to escape from it. The Whole World in The Ten Directions is always existing through past, present, and future. We must train ourselves to see it in every being and phenomenon. (While talking about it we are talking as well about the bright crystal orb backing it.)

Our life with this body is The Whole World in The Ten Directions, and the life before we got our body (rhetorically we say "original face before our parents were born") is also The Whole World in the Ten Directions. The nameless and formless something (Whole World in the Ten Directions = True Form = sunyata) becomes each piece of being (Whole World in the Ten Directions = phenomena = rupa), and each piece of being becomes the nameless and formless something. This transition is endlessly carried on without time loss, without sunyata destroying rupa or rupa destroying sunyata

The nameless and formless something can become each piece of being without being destroyed, can become the nameless and formless something without destroying each piece of being. Therefore we can't say universal truth is only one of them—rupa or sunyata—that is, we can't say a nameless and formless something, as opposed to each piece of being. The truth is they are one, neither the one only nor the other only. This is Buddhist transition.

As we have at many opportunities already studied, whoever truly understands this transition will see only the nameless and formless something when the nameless and formless something comes, and will see only each piece of being when each piece of being comes. They are the same thing, thus having no relation with each other. Because our intelligence hasn't yet the flexibility to go straight ahead on a crooked path, our expressing the totality of this truth is extremely difficult. *Biyan lu*, Case 46, Jingching's Sound of Raindrops, treats this subject poetically. Jingching (Jingching Dafu, 864-937) was nearly thirty years younger than Shyuansha but was surely his Dharma brother:

> Jingching asked a monk, "What is the sound outside?"
> The monk said, "It is the sound of raindrops."
> Jingching: "Ignorant people are upside down, losing themselves and chasing after things."
> The monk: "How about Your Reverence?"
> Jingching: "I am almost not lost."
> The monk: "What do you mean by 'I am almost not lost'?"
> Jingching: "Transcending the body may be easy, expression free of substance is truly hard."

In this episode, "losing themselves" is "their original face" or "the nameless and formless something"; and "chasing after things" must be "each piece of being." Sunyata loses itself and is chasing after rupa. (When we focus on rupa, rupa loses itself and chases after sunyata.) Both rupa and sunyata are the same Whole World in the Ten Directions, and each is also different. Shyuedou, a poet even more than a teacher, created a poetic solution for this dilemma:

> Understanding and not understanding:
> Deluge upon deluge on the south and north mountains.

Being a patriarch, Shyuansha pointed out that our every thought, emotion, and act, including our suffering, depression, anxiety, and disappointment, are The Whole World in the Ten Directions. It might have been said by Shie Sanlang, "A family pleasantly chatting while watching fish in a pond, and another family blaming one another for their family misfortune — I was believing they are utterly different in nature, not only in outward appearance!"

Now we will study "a bright crystal orb." Shyuansha gave this name to the thing that has no name. Our work is to recognize what he was naming.

> The Teacher [Dungshan Liangjie, 807-869] asked Yunjyu [Daying, 835?-902], "What is your name?"
> Yunjyu said, "My name is Daying."
> The Teacher said, "Tell me a more advanced view."
> Yunjyu said, "In the advanced view I will not be called Daying." (*Dungshan lu*, entry 41)

Yunjyu's primary name Daying (Da Ying) means The Way Treasured, and his teacher Dungshan asked him to see free being before caught by concept. This "advanced view" means view transcending dualistic thought. Yunjyu understood that this nameless something is acting in reality as Daying. Daying is a name. We are able to understand the depth of the world only through named phenomenal beings, rupa, and we shouldn't expect another way to know any meaningful truth.

The bright crystal orb is the bright crystal orb throughout past, present, and future, (and throughout all worlds). For the bright crystal orb there is no division between past, present, and future. Only our intelligence puts a difference between our life and our death. All time is the bright crystal orb.

Not only time, every being is the bright crystal orb. So river is not river but a bright crystal orb, a weed not a weed either. Not only materials, for our notion and emotion, and each not-notion and not-emotion (if there are such), each is a bright crystal orb. By seeing a tangible being, we must recognize it isn't a being but a bright crystal orb (or Buddha nature, Dharma-kaya, unsurpassed Bodhi). As we studied, "Who is 'Bei Dhuta" wasn't a question; it is telling us that everything is 'Bei Dhuta (Buddha nature). Buddha nature sheds itself and becomes a pinecone, a pineapple, anything.

We must make each shed itself to become Buddha nature. When we see everything as Buddha nature, we can for the first time keep the Fourth Precept, Not Speaking Untruths. (Shyuansha: "I dare not mislead others.") Until then we are doomed to keep fighting by insisting on a particular view.

>4) Not Speaking Untruths. *Kyoju kaimon*: The wheel of the Dharma innately turns not too much, not too little. The sweet dew evenly distributes its moisture and all beings receive truth and substance.

When we see that every being in time and space is Buddha nature or Dharma-kaya, then great wisdom and compassion begin to turn as the Dharma wheel. There will be no false sight where ordinary people (student, ignorant person, poor nation, etc.) are attempting to get the Dharma from Buddha (teacher, wise person, rich nation, etc.) and Buddha taking the role of giving the Dharma to ordinary people. The beneficial Dharma isn't too much for Buddha and isn't too little for ordinary people. If people come to the awareness that everything is Buddha nature (the sweet dew evenly distributes its moisture), they will wish to be more active in constructing Buddha's world.

Seeing Buddha nature or the bright crystal orb in phenomena is essential work for the Buddhist. Changching Hueileng (854-922) studied from the master who was awakened by seeing peach blossoms (Lingyun Shichin, ?-?), and for twelve years he studied under Shyuefeng and Shyuansha. During those years, it was said he wore out seven meditation cushions, yet he couldn't come to a clear awakening to Buddha nature.

One day when rolling up a reed screen, he suddenly had a great awakening, and he made a gatha:

>What a great difference!
>Great difference!
>While rolling up a reed screen I saw the world.
>Straightaway I will whisk the mouth of anyone
>asking me what kind of religious truth I understand!
>
>*(Chanyuan mengchiou,* vol. 1)

Chuandeng lu, vol. 18, focuses more on Buddha nature:

On one occasion Changching asked, "Please teach me the path transmitted from ancient times by all sages."

Shyuefeng kept silent. Changching bowed and withdrew. Shyuefeng smiled in satisfaction.

On another day Shyuefeng told him, "I always tell my venerable monks there is a venomous turtle-nosed snake here on South Mountain and they had better see it well."

Changching responded, "Today in the Hall there is one who has completely lost his body and life."

Shyuefeng gave his approval.

Changching entered the Teacher's residence. "What now?" said Shyuefeng.

Changching replied, "Today is a fine day for everyone to work outside." Thereafter he had no ambiguity about any profound meaning and he described his realization in a gatha:

> The aloof body is exposed
> in the million phenomena
> One can be intimate with it only
> when acknowledging it by oneself.
> Until today I was gluttonously groping
> along the way.
> Now it is like seeing ice amid fire.

According to this episode, being killed by a venomous snake is important to see Buddha nature. Such a dead life is seeing not merely a new day but this day newly: "Today is a fine day for everyone to work outside." "The aloof body is exposed in the million phenomena"—this is the bright crystal orb. Shyuansha directly facing reality could see every phenomenon without destroying, deforming, or remodeling it, could see it as the most precious wisdom or compassion.

"I have heard Your Reverence has the saying 'The Whole World in the Ten Directions is a bright crystal orb.' How should I your student understand it?" It sounds as if Shyuansha's monk lost in a dense fog is asking for a beacon. But a compassionate teacher like Dogen sees great wisdom in the ignorant question. His greatness is to see with Buddha's eyes instead of with the eyes of ordinary people. It is painful to watch a person who suspects every event and happening by seeing from the position of being depressed, suppressed, disillusioned, and tortured. Dogen recommends that we quietly see from Buddha's side:

Just free and forget your own body and mind. Cast them into Buddha's house and let Buddha act. Follow the acts of Buddha. Then with no application of force, no consumption of your mind, you will graduate from life-death and become Buddha. (*Shobogenzo: Shoji* [Life-Death])

So Dogen sees the essence of Buddhist training in the monk's "How," which comes in his "I have heard Your Reverence has the saying 'The Whole World in the Ten Directions is a bright crystal orb.' How should I your student understand it?" Now we are entering the third study, about "How" and "What."

Not sure from exactly when, but in the Tang dynasty, in a newly risen Buddhist community they began to use such interrogatives as what, when, who, where, and how as new abstract nouns to express unknown, undefined, boundless ideas instead of relying on old generalized words. These new abstract nouns they used in established question sentences, and it was confusing for those outside their community to understand the language. After all, languages are signs and marks to communicate ideas among those with the same culture. So, because these texts were written by the Chinese of those days, we have difficulty to precisely and concisely translate them to English. Yet we do whatever we can to understand what they cherished.

To illustrate their usage of interrogatives, this between Yaushan (Yaushan Weiyan, 745-828) and a monk is typical:

When the Teacher [Yaushan] was sitting, a monk asked: "What should we think when we are singularly sitting?"
The Teacher: "Think the unthinkable."
The monk: "How to think the unthinkable?"
The Teacher: "Beyond thought."
(*Chuandeng lu,* vol. 14)

They are using interrogatives as abstract nouns, so it should be read as follows:

When the Teacher [Yaushan] was sitting, a monk said: "What is we think, and when is we who are singularly sitting."
The Teacher: "Thought is the unthinkable."
The monk: How (or However, or Whatever) is to think the unthinkable."

> The Teacher: "Beyond thought. (Beyond thought is our thinking-and-unthinking." (*Chuandeng lu*, vol. 14)

The following, the final part of this essay, is concerned with the translation of this new usage of interrogatives, and there could be some confusion in the process of putting them into English.

The truth is that a mountain is not a mountain, it is a bright crystal orb; a river is not a river, it is a bright crystal orb; a suffering is not a suffering, it is a bright crystal orb. However, on the other hand, a mountain is not a bright crystal orb, it is a mountain; a river is not a bright crystal orb, it is a river; a suffering is not a bright crystal orb, it is a suffering. So the essence of Buddhist training is to live our life such that we don't betray either the truth of being a bright crystal orb, or such that we don't conflict with the truth of being a mountain. Somehow we should find the way to satisfy both. This monk understood "How" is the way to understand the relation between The Whole World in the Ten Directions and a bright crystal orb. Thus the monk's words can be rewritten: "The relation between The Whole World in the Ten Directions and a bright crystal orb is like the relation between wave and water, or between heat and light. We must understand this relation however we can and use it in practical daily life somehow, mustn't we?"

To make sure, we are reminded of the Fifth Precept:

> Not Buying or Selling Intoxicants. *Kyoju kaimon*: Do not violate that which has not yet been brought. Not violating is Great Brightness.

"Buying or selling intoxicants" or "violating" means to see the truth only as "a mountain" or only as "a bright crystal orb." Though it is a very ancient example, Confucius was also concerned:

> The way a wise person behaves in the world is not to be surely definite to do or not to do. A wise person follows where righteousness goes. (*Lunyu*, chap. 4: *Liren*)

It is easy to live our life if there are no rigid undigested intoxicants, such as the concepts bright crystal orb, Buddha nature, mountain or river. As much as we have undigested intoxicants, we must suffer.

To the monk's comment "The Whole World in the Ten Directions is a bright crystal orb," Shyuansha responded "What is the use of understanding?" which is a slightly different expression of what the monk said, but the meaning is the same. The monk said in effect: "We must understand this relation 'however,' and must use it in practical daily life 'somehow,' mustn't we?" The monk's 'however understanding' or 'somehow using' became Shyuansha's 'What is the use of understanding,' which means 'Whatever we understand is a bright crystal orb (and therein is no use of understanding).' 'However' and 'whatever' are reflecting the indefinable and unlimited nature of the truth. Then why is it that "whatever we understand is a bright crystal orb"? The answer is that "The Whole World in the Ten Directions is a bright crystal orb." If so, The Whole World in the Ten directions is the Whole World in the Ten Directions or a bright crystal orb is a bright crystal orb. Then, instead of repeatedly saying The Whole World in the Ten directions is The Whole World in the Ten Directions, or a bright crystal orb is a bright crystal orb, we should say simply The Whole World in the Ten directions or a bright crystal orb. It means The Whole World in the Ten Directions is a bright crystal orb, and whatever we understand and however we understand it, it is a bright crystal orb. So in any World in the Ten Directions past, present, and future, and inside and outside, whether it is hell or heaven, whether we are a sage or not, whether we are happy or not, we can't find any spot that isn't "a bright crystal orb," and it is the ultimate way of understanding, here expressed as "What is the use of understanding?" In other words, this "What" isn't an interrogative suggesting a nihilism toward our itelligence. It is the positive and affirmative use of interrogation.

Alternative understandings such as 'The Whole World in the Ten Directions is a bright crystal orb' and vice versa are imperfect in practical life. The tautological non-alternation such as 'the Whole World in the Ten Directions is the Whole Worlds in the Ten Directions' or 'a bright crystal orb is a bright crystal orb' is practical. Therefore Dogen says:

> Bodhidharma when he was transmitting was Bodhidharma, and the Second Patriarch when he received the marrow was Bodhidharma.
>
> (*Shobogenzo: Katto* [Ivy and Wisteria])

Finally we will study about "a demons' cave under a dark mountain." But beforehand we must make sure why Shyuansha asked the monk the next day with the same words the monk asked on the previous day. This is evidently Shyuansha's kindness in wanting to make sure the monk was correctly understanding.

"The Whole World in the Ten Directions" is decisively "a bright crystal orb," and, yes, vice versa. Therefore to express such a dynamic of the world, the Buddhist says only "The Whole World in the Ten Directions" or only "a bright crystal orb." This situation is here expressed as "How" in Shyuansha's question "How do you understand 'The Whole World in the Ten Directions is a bright crystal orb'?" We must practice the truth that when we express one side the other should be hidden. We should be sensitive to detect the hidden side and not at the same time express both sides of the one truth.

Shyuefeng's "Who" of "Who is 'Bei Dhuta?" and the monk's "How" of "How should I your student understand it?" as well as Shyuansha's "How" of "How do you understand 'The Whole Worlds in the Ten Directions is a bright crystal orb'?" are used for the same meaning in the same creative way, which is to use the interrogative to name undefined and unsettled things in order to activate them.

> The monk replied, "The Whole World in the Ten directions is a bright crystal orb. What is the use of understanding?"

A negative understanding interprets this monk as falling short in power and parroting Shyuansha's words. Seeing the monk as a talented monk, Dogen expressed the non-division in understanding between him and Shyuansha. Shyuansha said "The Whole World in the Ten Directions is a bright crystal orb. What is the use of understanding?" It means there is no division, no seam, between The Whole World in the Ten Directions and a bright crystal orb. If we say "The Whole World in the Ten Directions is a bright crystal orb" or its vice versa, there will be a seam between. As far as the linguistic expression goes we must say only "The Whole World in the Ten Directions" or "a bright crystal orb," and there we must understand that when we say one side, the other is hidden and well satisfied. Such a way of understanding is the true understanding and it was expressed by Shyuansha as "What is the use of understanding?" and as "How do you understand 'The Whole World in the Ten Directions is a bright crystal orb'?" Shyuansha was seeing no seam and expected this talented monk wouldn't make one between his teacher and himself.

This no division or no seam is actually an important achievement we must wish to attain. We take a bath, and the bath takes us is one example of no division. Actually how many no divisions in relations do we cherish? Between us and a pet animal, husband and wife, parents and children, government and citizen, clothing and our body, body and mind, us and a tree, house, environment, neighbors, air, food? (All natural phenomena are without division: flower and warmth, wind and temperature, etc.) Unfortunately between us and most things and happenings we are making a great division. Yet we believe we have enough understood Shyuansha's saying "The Whole World in the Ten Directions is a bright crystal orb." When can we extinguish the division, when can we dissolve the seam?

Case 18, National Teacher Nanyang's Seamless Pagoda in *Biyan lu* is handling this subject:

> Emperor Sutzung asked National Teacher Nanyang Hueijung, "A hundred years hence, what may I do for you?"
> The National Teacher replied, "For this old monk, make a seamless pagoda."
> The Emperor asked, "Please, would you describe its design?"
> The National Teacher meanwhile kept silent, then asked, "Do you understand?"
> The Emperor said, "No, I do not."
> The National Teacher said, "I have a disciple called Danyuan, to whom I transmitted the Dharma Seal. He is well versed in this matter. Please invite him and ask him."
> After the National Teacher went elsewhere to teach, the Emperor invited Danyuan and asked him the meaning of this matter.
> Danyuan said in his gatha:
>
>> It is located south of Shiang and north of Tan,
>> (Shyuedou's comment: The sound of one hand scarcely resonates.)

where gold abounds, filling the land.
(Shyuedou's comment: A crude mountain staff.)
Take a ferry at the shadowless hour of high noon
(Shyuedou's comment: Clear river, calm sea.)
to the lapis palace, where you shan't find a single teacher.
(Shyuedou's comment: The meaning has been clarified.)

Emperor Sutzung asked what he could do for his teacher Nanyang (Nanyang Hueijung, ?-775). He didn't ask for his own benefit. Yet National Teacher Nanyang answered what the emperor should do for his own benefit. This dialogue itself illustrates already an ideal relation with no seam between. Later Nanyang told the emperor to ask his disciple Danyuan (Danyuan Yingjen, ?-?). This dialogue also suggests another good relation, between teacher and disciple.

What Nanyang wished for the emperor was excellent relationships with his all surroundings, a limitless number of pagodas. Nanyang "meanwhile kept silent" to instruct the emperor how to achieve such relationships; the meaning of his silence was to go beyond dualistic valuation. Danyuan also expressed the place(s) where the emperor could establish such relationships: "It is located south of Shiang and north of Tan, where gold abounds, filling the land." This "gold" is Shyuansha's bright crystal orb. Saying "south of Shiang and north of Tan" is more like saying "south of The Whole World in the Ten Directions and north of a bright crystal orb." When Buddhists say "south," the whole world is south, when "north," "north." South and north do not contrast. So when it is "south of Shiang," the whole world is south, when "north of Tan," the whole world is north. Therefore Shyuansha's "The Whole World in the Ten Directions is a bright crystal orb" and Danyuan's "It is located south of Shiang and north of Tan" are saying the same Buddhist truth, which is No division in one phrase.

Now Shyuansha said, "It is obvious you are vigorously living in a demons' cave under a dark mountain." This isn't a negative comment but is an admiration of no division between The Whole World and a bright crystal orb, between teacher and monk, between all sentient and insentient beings and

Buddhahood. The world of no division is expressed as "a demons' cave under a dark mountain." All worlds are filled with Buddha upon Buddha. It is admirable if there are those who can live such a life of Buddha upon Buddha from morning to night with whatever or whomever they meet.

With what evidence did Shyuansha judge the monk was living such a seamless life of Buddha upon Buddha? It is from the monk's words "What is the use of understanding?" When his words are positively activated, "The Whole World in the Ten Directions" is good enough and "a bright crystal orb" won't be expressed, or "a bright crystal orb" is good enough and "The Whole World in the Ten Directions" won't be expressed. In a northern climate when we say December we needn't say "It is cold." Such is the vigorous life in a demons' cave under a dark mountain.

When we say a bright crystal orb, the whole world is a bright crystal orb from beginingless beginning to endless end. Even an anonymous patient is a bright crystal orb, a renowned surgeon too is a bright crystal orb. Each of life's struggles is a bright crystal orb, being born, becoming ill, growing old, facing death. There are no comparative merits. Each is the Eye to See the Right Dharma, each is Buddha's body (True Body), the Illumination of Light. Each is the Total Body, which has no contrasting obstacle and freely keeps functioning. Each phenomenon in hell too is a bright crystal orb, and it means there is no hell. Even if we escape from a bright crystal orb, where we arrive is a bright crystal orb. This world is a bright crystal orb, that world too, because The Whole World in the Ten Directions is a bright crystal orb.

There is no division between us and peach blossoms, us and warm water, us and the sound of a pebble hitting bamboo. The persons are each a bright crystal orb, their object too. Each being is preaching through its actual body. Sentient and insentient beings are both preaching through their actual body because each is a bright crystal orb. There was, is, and will be trouble if we discriminate sentient beings from insentient beings. We shouldn't carelessly treat any being. For well-trained persons every being is preaching the Dharma and we shouldn't stare. We should politely keep a state of ignoring, positively, thankfully.

After all, the very first case of *Biyan lu* is also making a solemn declaration about the seamless worlds, a demons' cave under a dark mountain:

> Emperor Wu of Liang asked Great Teacher Bodhidharma, "What is the first principle of the holy teachings?"
> Bodhidharma: "It is vacancy and no holiness."
> Emperor Wu: "Who stands before me?"
> Bodhidharma: "I do not know."
> The Emperor could not grasp his meaning.

Emperor Wu could see only the difference between the holy teachings and the worldly teachings, between sage and ordinary person, good deeds and evil deeds. For Bodhidharma every being, every world, is a bright crystal orb, with no difference. So he directly answers "It is vacancy and no holiness."

Emperor Wu could see only the difference in front of himself: himself a layman and Bodhidharma a sage. He humbly asked "Who stands before me?" Bodhidharma didn't know Shyuansha's later naming "a bright crystal orb." He honestly replied "I do not know." Of course he knew the content of his own saying. The content was bright crystal orb upon bright orb and nothing else. Therefore it can be "vacancy." The Whole World is "a demons' cave," and at such a nice time there isn't even "a demons' cave": it can be expressed as "vacancy." "Under a dark mountain" could be suggesting the state where there is no negative insistence on any illusionary belongings, such as particular form, nature, substance, force, function, cause, indirect cause, and so forth—illusionary belongings, which are sometimes called "shadows." In Danyuan's gatha there is the line

> Take a ferry at the shadowless hour of high noon.

The latter half of *Biyan lu*, Case 1, exposes what Bodhidharma brought:

> The Emperor could not grasp his meaning.
> Having exhausted all means, Bodhidharma forded the river and went to the land of Wei.
> The Emperor then spoke to Jygung about this.
> Jygung: "Do you actually not know who he is?"
> The Emperor: "I do not know."
> Jygung: "He is the Bodhisattva Avalokitesvara, bearer of

Buddha's Heart Seal."

"Buddha's Heart Seal" was and is "a bright crystal orb," which is Avalokitesvara's Compassion.

    Greatly taken with regret, the Emperor longed to send for Bodhidharma.
    Jygung said, "No use in that. Even if all the people of your country go, he will not turn back."

After all, even if we see that everyone else has "a bright crystal orb," it's useless unless we come to the awareness that we ourselves are first of all "a bright crystal orb." Yungjia (Yungjia Shyuanjyue, ?-713, a disciple of the Sixth Patriarch) said in his *Jengda ge:*

Without leaving this very place we are always tranquil.
By searching we understand you cannot be found.

Here "you" is "a bright crystal orb." "By searching we understand you cannot be found" because "you" should be sought within ourselves, and also once we establish ourselves we will see everything else too is "a bright crystal orb." At such a nice time, in such a demons' cave, indeed we cannot see "you."

Related or not to this,

    A monk asked: "What is the most precious thing in the world?"
    The Teacher [Tsaushan Benji, 840-941] replied: "Most precious is the skull of a dead cat."
    The monk asked: "Why is the skull of a dead cat the most precious?"
    The Teacher: "Because no one has put on it any price."
    (Tsaushan lu)

Dogen says a bright crystal orb is for everyone whether enlightened or not, training or not. (His point is to say such as it is we should indeed train ourselves to become aware of and activate "a bright crystal orb.")

    It is not mere training during sitting meditation. It is more like the wonderful sound that keeps ringing before and after the stroke. (*Bendo wa,* [Essay on studying the Way])

So, universal being in time and space is a bright crystal orb, and it is The Whole World in the Ten Directions. How much we practice this truth determines whether we can live vigorously in a demons' cave under a dark mountain. If we can see both inside and outside our life as a bright crystal orb, and even before and after our life as a bright crystal orb, then we can take a demons' cave positively. Even if we must fall into hell, we now should know the cause to go there too is a bright crystal orb, and the effect we made to go there too is a bright crystal orb. For Buddhists, Cause and Effect are equal. Our emotions and thoughts keep appearing and disappearing every moment like flashing lights. There are lots of depressive notions such as separation from loved matters, frustration at being unable to obtain what we want, and meeting hated events. We must suffer each rather faithfully, and believing that these notions are ours, our life. Actually they aren't ours, aren't our life. Each is a bright crystal orb. Whatever happens for us is all the great activity of A Bright Crystal Orb.

  A monk: "How do you guide when a person of no understanding comes?"
  Luohan:"Who does not understand?"
(Chuandeng lu, vol. 21)

November 29, 2007

Putting Down Our Thought and Emotion

Putting down or transcending our thought and emotion is the central issue for Buddhism. Come to think of it, all human acts are based on thought and emotion, so controlling our thought and emotion is of vital importance for the survival of human culture. It is reasonable that the Japanese were forced to write Article 9 into their new Constitution after having two atomic bombs dropped on their country within a week.

Article 9 reads as follows:

1. Aspiring sincerely to an international peace based on justice and order, the Japanese people forever renounce war as a sovereign right of the nation and the threat or use of force as a means of settling international disputes.

2. In order to accomplish the aim of the preceding paragraph, land, sea, and air forces, as well as other war potentials, will never be maintained. The right of belligerency of the state will not be recognized.

These are great ideal articles. But shouldn't we be wary if not knowing how to control our thoughts and emotions? As for Article 9–2, it became an echo perfectly in vain as early as five years after this Constitution was made, by the creation of the Police Reserve Force, which was the beginning of the rearmament of Japan. Before the end of the 20th century, Japan achieved the third strongest army in the world. While this 9–2 is not kept up, we are most possibly right to say that 9–1 was kept up thanks to the world situation which doesn't owe much to Japan's effort or endurance. Here I'm not arguing for or against Article 9, but only pointing vaguely to the importance of our controlling our thought and emotion for the sake of world peace. And we must remind ourselves that the act endangering the survival of human culture isn't only warfare. The problem is that putting down or transcending our thought and emotion is actually very difficult to practice even though it is the central issue for Buddhism and of vital importance for us all. My Zen master lived eighty years with the motto Perfect

Combustion, and he summed up his life as Patience. Hearing this was a surprise for those of us who knew him intimately, because he was the one who scolded, insulted, and shouted at his disciples as much as he wanted, and he decided on whatever all by himself as he liked. We were the ones who were asked to have patience and he was the last one, we thought. He was successful at climbing to the top of the worldly hierarchy of the priest system, and as a single man he had no family worry. Yet he confessed that patience was the most fitting description of his life. Here I'm not going to estimate whether he was a great Buddhist priest but am just expressing the difficulty of putting down or transcending our thought and emotion.

Putting down or transcending our thought and emotion is so important and so hard to practice that it is regarded as one of the Six Paramitas to attain Nirvana and is called ksanti-paramita (endurance). These six are the perfect and ultimate virtuous deeds of Mahayana Bodhisattvas and they are dana, sila, ksanti, virya, dhyana, and prajna, all of which should be backed up by wisdom, and with compassion derived from wisdom. If putting down or transcending our thought and emotion isn't deeply linked to wisdom and compassion, it should be called mere patience, which can be an Asura's struggle ironically based on fighting spirit. My Zen master's haphazard patience throughout his life of power struggle belongs to this worldly patience, and of course the Japanese Constitution Article 9 is also dust floating on the worldly ocean.

The Mahayana Bodhisattva's endurance (ksanti) consists of three parts (according to Vasubandhu's *Mahayana-samgraha-bhasya*): 1) to endure the sufferings caused by the faults of others and rather try to benefit others, 2) to endure all sorts of sufferings that occur in maintaining life, and 3) to endure to keep studying the Dharma in detail in any situation and never give up doing so. These three parts aren't actually separate things. They are more like three aspects of one thing: to keep studying the Dharma. In this essay, ksanti is generalized as "Putting down or transcending our thought and emotion," and now it becomes clear that recommending to ourselves and to others to do so isn't different from recommending that we keep studying the Dharma.

Though we count putting down or transcending our thought and emotion as one of the Six Paramitas, now I will clarify that it cannot be merely confined as one of the six important Buddhist virtues. From the beginning it is the central Buddhist issue, for all Buddhist biographies tell us that Sakyamuni Buddha abandoned his six years of stoicism and after six more years training by the Middle Way he came to the great realization at the sight of Venus in the morning sky:

> Sakyamuni Buddha recognized the Way at the sight of Venus and said: "I and my companions the great earth and sentient beings have at the same time attained the Way."
>
> (Keizan Jhokin, *Denko roku*)

Here "I" is not Sakyamuni, for he is a member of "my companions the great earth and sentient beings." So in a later age, "I" became sunyata, and "my companions the great earth and sentient beings" became rupa. First Sakyamuni recognized that the total world is the endless recycling of sunyata and rupa. Second, he recognized that all things inside and outside the world, regardless of division of time, are equal in attaining the Way. The point of the words of this passage is to make sure that in "recognized" there is no sense of Sakyamuni. Sakyamuni isn't a hero, he is an equal member of sunyata's companions. It means he hasn't thought and emotion. In short, only when he put down or transcended his thought and emotion could he come to this great realization. Thus putting down or transcending our thought and emotion is the Buddhist's central issue.

Indeed, presented in the first Case of *Tsungrung lu* is Sakyamuni who has transcended thought and emotion:

> One day the World-Honored One ascended to the lecture seat. Then Manjusri struck the wood instrument and announced: "Understand the Dharma of the Dharma King. The Dharma of the Dharma King is like this." The World-Honored One descended from the lecture seat.

Bodhidharma in Case 1 of *Biyan lu* said only "It is vacancy and no holiness" and "I do not know," the same as Sakyamuni's transcending thought and emotion. These two examples can force us to see the tremendous positive meaning in transcending our thought and emotion instead of our keeping on grudgingly enduring patience. As written in

Baijang lu, Sakyamuni said:

Mt. Himalaya is like the Great Nirvana.

This Mt. Himalaya is not a literal mountain as a natural resource for people who keep using other beings for their desires, nor for alpinists cherishing memory of the infant joy in learning to climb. This is the sight of Mt. Himalaya seen by those who have put down or transcended their thought and emotion. Such a thing likened to Great Nirvana is rightly likened. At such a time, "is like" is the same as to say "is equal to." Sakyamuni is saying we are in Nirvana when we put down or transcend our thought and emotion.

About putting down thought and emotion, the young Hueineng, later the Sixth Patriarch in China, must have been well practiced. His father was relegated to the remote South and died there when Hueineng was only three, so mother and child had to endure a very poor life. When in a market selling firewood, the young Hueineng chanced to hear a guest at an inn chanting a sutra. It is said the sutra was the Diamond Sutra (*Vajracchedika-prajnaparamita-sutra*) and that the passage he heard was from Chapter 10, "To Ornament the Pure Land":

> All bodhisattvas should raise pure mind, which is to raise the mind without dwelling in form, should raise the mind without dwelling in sound, scent, taste, and touch. Indeed there is no place to dwell, yet the mind should rise.

The Diamond Sutra is dedicated to unfolding Buddhist Wisdom, which is to understand deeply and to utilize freely the relationship between sunyata and rupa. This passage describes bodhisattvas who can raise "Pure mind" when not attaching to any form, which is their thought and emotion. The young Hueineng hearing this passage must have been delighted as if he could feel he was beginning a second life. Later reflecting upon himself, he said "This must have been my karmic good fortune."

Here we mustn't be sloppy to run our thought to his delight. His delight couldn't have been from being illuminated by a new thought; rather, it was to find his understanding in the sutra, or we can venture to say it was his joy in giving more meaning to the sutra than the original presented, for he saw there is no place to dwell, yet the mind should be raised.

When Hueineng later became a teacher, a monk named Fada came to ask. For seven years he had been studying the Lotus Flower Sutra (*Saddharmapundarika-sutra*), but he said he had lost his mind and the heart of the sutra. Teacher Hueineng had never read it, so he asked Fada to recite it. He then kindly and logically explained its essence to the monk and concluded his teaching after all by saying:

> When our mind advances in practice, we can make use of the Lotus Flower Sutra. When our mind is stagnated, the Lotus Flower Sutra will make use of us.
> When our mind is right, we can make use of the Lotus Flower Sutra. When our mind is wrong, the Lotus Flower Sutra will make use of us.
> When we open Buddha's wisdom, we can make use of the Lotus Flower Sutra. When we open our worldly wisdom, the Lotus Flower Sutra will make use of us.
> (*Lioutzu Tanjing*, entry 16, ed. Fahai)

By hearing the Diamond Sutra, Hueineng understood that our thought and emotion aren't exceptions to rupa, and they rise from sunyata and yet aren't dwelling in any form of thought and emotion. In other words, our thought and emotion have a certain duration of form or life, but their nature is to transcend it. For Hueineng, thought and emotion weren't objects to be put down. Instead they were respectable and even lovable beings coming from sunyata, not bound by any form. The meaning of "Pure mind" is to not hinder this nature of thought and emotion. "Pure mind" means not giving our thought and emotion special love or hate. When we maintain "Pure mind," the endless recycling of sunyata and rupa will be manifested through our life scale too. Having attained confidence in his own understanding, the young Hueineng lost no time to enable himself to visit the Fifth Patriarch, Daman Hungren (601-674). The Fifth Patriarch saw that Hueineng was one who already understood "Pure mind."

> The priest Hungren asked Hueineng, "Which country person are you who comes to this mountain and is paying worship to me? What do you want here?"
> Hueineng replied, "Your disciple is a person of Lingnan, a commoner of Shinjou. I came far to pay worship to Your Reverence for no other reason than to ask you the way to become Buddha."

At last the Great Teacher accusingly said, "You are a person of Lingnan who has no Buddha nature. How can you become Buddha?"

Hueineng replied, "For the birth of a person there is South or North. For Buddha nature there is no South or North. I a barbarian am not the same as Your Reverence as to form, but our Buddha nature is not different."

(Ibid., entry 1)

Barbarians as barbarians might understand Hueineng's first encounter with the Fifth Patriarch to be like that of a youth with some talent and much hungry spirit who visits a boxing gym with the dream of becoming a champion. Hueineng was said to be then twenty-four, and, as we have studied, he understood that thought and emotion are not objects to be put down but are respectable pure mind transcending, now expressed as Buddha nature. According to Dogen (*Shobogenzo*, vol. *Bussho* [Buddha nature]), Hungren's first question to Hueineng is a positive statement in question form. He is stating "You are a person of which country." "Which country" is an abstraction to mean the truth of the sutra's passage "Indeed there is no place to dwell, yet the mind should rise." "What do you want here?" holds the meaning "You want what" and this "what" is the totality of Buddha nature. Great Buddhist patriarchs were always expressing the abstract universal truth while speaking about concrete particular phenomena.

Hueineng replied, "Your disciple is a person of Lingnan." This individual noun to express the South of China is here used as the Buddhist term for The Whole World in the Ten Directions. The initial dialogue should therefore be read as follows:

Hungren: "You come from purity, your body is Buddha nature, ever pure body."

Hueineng: "Yes, ever pure body."

Great persons are great from the start of their study. In Buddhism, Cause A always brings Effect A, and Cause and Effect are equal. The greatness of the Sixth Patriarch we have already studied is that he saw purity in the endless cycle of sunyata and rupa, so he recognized that thought and emotion too are respectable pure beings.

Hueineng replied, "Your disciple is a person of Lingnan,

a commoner of Shinjou. I came far to pay worship to Your Reverence for no other reason than to ask you the way to become Buddha."

Hueineng in his reply asked "the way to become Buddha." This is an example of Buddha nature asking to become Buddha. In true Buddhism there is no such truth that an ignorant or ordinary person can become Buddha. Only with Buddha nature can we become Buddha.

Hungren said "You are a person of Lingnan who has no Buddha nature. How can you become Buddha?" This is full approval of Hueineng. In his saying "a person of Lingnan who has no Buddha nature," Hungren is saying "a person of Lingnan who is no Buddha nature." It means all rupa or beings are No Buddha nature and sunyata is Buddha nature. Buddha nature and beings do not exist at one place and at one time. When beings appear, Buddha nature is hidden. When Buddha nature appears, all beings disappear. When we say not a thing has Buddha nature, we are confirming that all beings have Buddha nature.

Thus Hungren's saying that a person of Lingnan has no Buddha nature becomes the exact same meaning as Buddha's saying that all sentient beings have Buddha nature without exception. Hungren added "How can you become Buddha?" A strong cross-question, meaning "Is there any way to become Buddha other than in your way, which is Buddha nature becomes Buddha?"

> Hueineng replied, "For the birth of a person there is South or North. For Buddha nature there is no South or North. I a barbarian am not the same as Your Reverence as to form, but our Buddha nature is not different."

These words of Hueineng later to become the Sixth Patriarch aren't merely pointing out the diversity in rupa, or of forms. Hueineng is like Sakyamuni Buddha declaring that every being has Buddha nature. A person of the South has Buddha nature. So too has a person of the North. The Reverend Hungren has Buddha nature. So too has a barbarian. This understanding is possible when we see that it is the nature of all our thoughts and emotions thus to transcend. Our thoughts and emotions aren't objects to be put down, or to be dealt with, with patience. It is said the Sixth Patriarch entered a secluded life after receiving transmission of the Dharma from Hungren. After spending fifteen years with hunters, he showed up in the yard of Fashing Temple in Kwangtung, where a Dharma teacher, Yintzung, was lecturing on the Nirvana Sutra:

> The wind was blowing a banner. A monk said, "The wind is moving." Another said, "The banner is moving." The argument went on and on. Hueineng approached and said, "Not the wind, not the banner. The mind of the reverend monks is moving." The monks were surprised.
> *(Lioutzu Tanjing,* ed. Tzungbau)

The Sixth Patriarch isn't here an idealist insisting on superiority of mind over matter. He is seeing the movement of the banner, the wind, and our mind (thought and emotion) and at once is looking at no movement of the banner, the wind, and our mind. He is wishing us to see all at one time the movement of our thought and emotion while we are looking at their no movement, and at another time see no movement of our thought and emotion while we are looking at their movement. With this understanding we can appreciate these two gathas:

A monk recited a gatha by Zen Teacher Woshu:

> Woshu has the talent
> to sever a hundred thoughts.
> No mind rises in any situation.
> Bodhi thus grows daily

The Teacher [Hueineng] commented: "This gatha shows an unclarified mind. If people follow this gatha they will increase their bondage." He then made his own:

> Hueineng lost the talent,
> a hundred thoughts cannot be severed.
> Mind rises as often as any situation turns.
> How can Bodhi be grown?
> *(Ibid.,* ed. Tzungbau)

One of Hueineng's disciples, Yungjia Shyuanjyue, (?-713), clearly says in his *Jengda ge* (Verse about Realization of the Way):

> Being able to practice dhyana in desires
> depends on our power of knowing.
> The lotus in the fire will never ruin.

In these lines "desires" (klesa) is our thought and emotion. Dhyana originally meant to think quietly, or the calm mentality that comes from settling our concern in one subject, and therefore concentration and wisdom well balanced. Peace accompanied by wisdom can be obtained only when we see the purity of all beings. So the meaning of practicing dhyana can be defined as transcending all negative aspects of our thought and emotion by seeing the pure nature of our thought and emotion. This seeing is possible only through our intuition, while our intelligence keeps seeing dualistic value. Not exercising our intelligence leads us only to dullness and fatigue. After all, "our power of knowing" means "to endure to keep studying the Dharma in detail in any situation and never give up doing so," introduced as the third endurance (ksanti) at the start of this essay.

Yungjia advises us in the same verse:

> If you do not wish to create cause to enter the endless hell,
> do not devaluate the Tathagata's continuous turning of the
> Right Dharma Wheel.

The "Tathagata's continuous turning of the Right Dharma Wheel" means Buddha's Teaching. The evident virtue of the Sixth Patriarch and his descendants compared with his predecessors is that they directly saw Buddha in their life, not only in distant history or in the vast stretch of theological space. They saw in the function of their life Buddha's teaching. So for Yungjia, not devaluating Buddha's Teaching means not shutting our eyes from the fact that all beings are transcending what they are and are beyond our dualistic valuation. Here, transcending our thought and emotion and transcending our dualistic valuation are exactly the same thing. According to the Nirvana Sutra, when Sakyamuni Buddha as his former self was not yet transcending dualistic valuation on Mt. Himalaya, he could hear only the first half of the Yaksa's gatha:

> All beings are not eternal.
> This is the Dharma of birth and death.

When he transcended his dualistic valuation, he could for

the first time hear the latter half of the Yaksa's gatha:

> Completely extinguish birth and death.
> Quiet annihilation is the pleasure.

It was said by Nanyang (Nanyang Hueijung, ?-775), one of the forty-three next-generation Dharma inheritors of the Sixth Patriarch: "Fence, tiles and pebbles, all are the ancient Buddha." He was the teacher of two emperors, so his name came to be imposing, but actually he had been living a quiet life forty years on Mt. Baiyai until forced to go up to the capital after the death of his teacher, the Sixth Patriarch.

We can thank Nanyang all the more for his words if we apply them to our concrete life as "Yes, those people regarded as useless odds and ends are the very Buddha. Pebbles and pieces of tile are the very Buddha." Don't his words lead to Saicho (767-822), who opened Mt. Hiei in Japan? Saicho said: "Any person, any being, illuminating a corner is a national treasure."

At any rate, how can we possibly see Buddha in tiles and pebbles without transcending our thought and emotion? When we transcend our thought and emotion, we are able to see the function, nature, causation, influence, and such, of each, not only its form, for we can see how and where it is, not only what it is.

Nanyang is said to have been very young when he became a disciple of the Sixth Patriarch. This could be one reason why his way of teaching was very kind and faithful to Buddhist theology. Here is his teaching to a monk:

> A monk asked, "What does it mean to accomplish Buddhahood?"
> The Teacher: "All bondage will be shed from you when you abandon at once both Buddha and ignorant beings."
> Question: "How should I be to be like that?"
> The Teacher: "Think neither good nor bad and you will see Buddha nature."
> Question: "What does it mean to practice my own Dharma-kaya?"
> The Teacher: "It means to go beyond Vairocana [Universal Light]."
> Question: "How can I attain pure Dharma-kaya?"
> "By seeking Buddha with no attachment to Buddha."

"What is Buddha?"
"Our mind is Buddha."
"But isn't there klesa in our mind?"
"Klesa has the nature to transcend itself."
"So shouldn't we sever it deliberately?"
"Those trainees who sever klesa are called Hinayana [Dualistic View], and those trainees who do not make klesa rise are called Great Nirvana [Mahayana]."
"What do you say about observing purity by the practice of sitting meditation?"
"Our nature is neither impure nor pure. Why should we intentionally raise our mind to see the form of purity?"
Further question: "The Zen Teacher sees the void in all Ten Directions. Is that Dharma-kaya?"
"Any understanding by our thought in our mind is a deluded view."
"But if our mind is already Buddha, must we further practice intentional training in a million details?"
"All sages are solemnly ornamenting themselves with wisdom and compassion. Why should we live in opposition to them and from their life invite contradictory causation? There will be no end even if for kalpas I keep answering you in this manner. The more words, the farther the Way goes away. So it is said 'If there is something obtainable in preaching, such preaching is the snort of a wild boar. But such preaching that has nothing obtainable is a lion's roar.'"

(*Chuandeng lu*, vol. 5)

Here Nanyang's essential teaching to the monk is to see through the nature of our thought and emotion and not let them do evil ("Those trainees who sever klesa are said to be called Hinayana, and those trainees who do not make klesa rise are called Great Nirvana."). The difference between making klesa rise and not making klesa rise is the difference between seeking Buddha with attachment to Buddha and seeking Buddha "with no attachment to Buddha."

Nanyang's "with no attachment to Buddha" means of course to go beyond dualistic valuation, but before that it means to engage in our conduct thoroughly for the purpose of performing that very conduct regardless of its necessity and value, and regardless of our preference and ability. This was the ultimate happiness that Buddha originally found for himself and all others. Therefore, for Nanyang and all fortunate Buddhists thereafter, being faithful to Buddhist theology means to live the life in which we can keep confirming that what Buddha taught us is right for us each. What did Buddha originally teach us? First of all he said:

> In seeking happiness, no one in the world has exceeded me.
> (*Ekottaragama*, vol. 31-5)

What was his happiness, and how did he attain it?

> There is no better human happiness than realizing Nirvana by controlling oneself well, practicing the pure deeds, and understanding the Four Truths [= our life is suffering, our suffering comes from our various states contradictory to our desires, we must extinguish our desires, and thus comes peace].
>
> Thus our mind will not be upset by death and life, will not be disturbed by worldly praise and censure, and will not be distressed or angry. Thus we can stand in unsurpassed peace. There is no better human happiness.
> (*Mahamangala-sutta* in Sutta-nipata in Sutta-pitaka)

Here "controlling oneself well" means to be compassionate for the history of our thought and emotion. For our thought and emotion, we should take extenuating circumstances into consideration so both our thought and emotion can have ample opportunity to exercise their nature, which is to shed themselves. Klesa has tremendous power to rise, and just as well, tremendous power to shed itself. After all, klesa is Buddha nature, which is always taking any one of its basic four forms: raising Bodhi mind, actually practicing, coming to the realization, and attaining Nirvana.

The meaning of "practicing the pure deeds" is to keep the state in which our klesa sheds itself. Such a state can be kept only while we are actively practicing "seeking Buddha with no attachment to Buddha." This is the activity of transcending our thought and emotion. It isn't the passive and blank state of doing nothing, making no use of our intelligence, or having no emotions. Actually this activity of transcending our thought and emotion is our very true life or true self, which is claimed by Buddhism.

If we can live such a life as is said "seeking Buddha with no attachment to Buddha," what are we like? A good comparison is hard to find on this earth. Living such a life means to regain the center of the world and establish our subjecthood.

When we suffer we are forced to put down our thought and emotion, or transcend our thought and emotion. If thrown from the window of an airplane, we will suffer. It is because of being put extremely apart from our usual standard, which we firmly believe to be our center. Or in the minor event of being invited to a party and no one there cares about us, we will suffer, because we sense being put in a corner. We suffer if forced to detach from our usual living space, style, habit, and association; we suffer if we must live in a strange place. It is because we sense being put far apart from the world that was our habitual center. Any drastic change caused by any of the Four and Eight Sufferings is nothing other than the agony of being placed in a corner far from our usual geographic, cultural, social, physical, and psychological center.

When we are put far from our center we lose our mastery to cope with all sorts of affairs and concerns. We lose our identity, or subjecthood. Naturally we try to regain it, and if we come to realize there is no way, we are forced to put down or transcend our thought and emotion. Thus we can define that "seeking Buddha with no attachment to Buddha" means to regain our center of the world and establish our subjecthood.

As for this matter of regaining our center of the world and establishing our subjecthood, Copernicus and Galileo needed to be concerned about the totality of the world and needed to say more considerately: "When we think and feel, we are not the center of the world, we are orbiting the sun. When we go beyond our thought and emotion, we are the center of the world and the sun is orbiting us."

On each occasion of reading Shyuefeng's episode "Mt. Aushan attained the Way!" we are delighted as if sensing it our personal happening. The episode is lengthy; the needed part here is only the last paragraph, but I will quote it all, out of respect for the causation.

> Shyuefeng, Yantou, and Chinshan pilgrimaged to visit various teachers. Later when they came to Lijou, Chinshan remained in a temple and Shyuefeng and Yantou went on.
>
> At Mt. Aushan they were confined by snow. Yantou kept sleeping day after day, whereas Shyuefeng kept practicing sitting meditation. One day Shyuefeng addressed

Yantou: "Brother, get up!" Yantou said, "What is it?" Shyuefeng: "My life is not blessed. I, when on pilgrimage with Wensuei [Chinshan], was pulled by him into many chores. Now I've come along with you and all you do is sleep." Yantou reprimanded, "You too have kept sleeping! Day after day you sit on a meditation seat like a tutelary god in a rural village. Someday you'll charm boys and girls of good family!"

Shyuefeng clapped his hand to his chest and said, "I dare not deceive myself, truly here at heart I am not at peace." Yantou: "I have been thinking you are the one who will establish a hermitage on the summit of an aloof peak and spread the great teaching, but you talk like that." Shyuefeng: "Truly I am not yet at peace." Yantou: "Well then, spell out each of your views. I will certify those that are right and check off those that are wrong."

Shyuefeng: "I first visited Yanguan. Hearing his preaching on 'being is non-being,' I attained the entrance." Yantou: "A matter of thirty years ago, lamentable to keep carrying." Shyuefeng: "I saw Dungshan's gatha on fording the river, when he said it is detestable to seek after others, others are miles apart from oneself." Yantou: "With such an understanding you cannot help even yourself." Shyuefeng: "Later I visited Deshan and asked 'Has your student the talent to understand the essence of the heritage?' He struck me with his staff, 'What are you saying!' and I was like a bucket with a broken bottom."

Yantou raised his voice, "Do you not know whatever comes in through the gate is not the real treasure? If you'd like to spread the great teaching, make each thing overflow from your own bosom and yourself be all heaven and earth." Shyuefeng then and there understood and he came to the great realization. He paid worship to Yantou, then stood up and cried, "Brother, today for the first time Mt. Aushan attained the Way! Mt. Aushan attained the Way!"

(Tzutang ji. 7)

In the last paragraph Shyuefeng came to the great realization under Yantou's teaching "Do you not know whatever comes in through the gate is not the real treasure?" It means Yantou clearly denied our thought and emotion. Hearing others' thought and emotion, we are actually placing ourselves in a remote corner of the world. It is so even if we believe we are in the very midst of the world cultural center.

Yantou completed his teaching: "Make each thing overflow from your own bosom and yourself be all heaven and earth." It means "Put down or transcend thought and emotion and you will be the center of the world," or "Entirely devote yourself to any trifling being or affair and you will be practicing to seek Buddha with no attachment to Buddha."

"Let it go and it will fill your hands" Dogen said in his *Bendo wa*. Theologically what Yantou told Shyuefeng was the exact same dynamic analysis as the fragment of the Diamond Sutra that made Hueineng into a priest who sells fuel to burn up our klesa and prepare our compassion.

Shyuedou admires Huangbo (Huangbo Shiyun, ?-856) in the gatha he composed for *Biyan lu*, Case 11:

> Serene and aloof air contains no pride.
> Solemn in the Imperial sea, discerning dragon from snake.
> Prince Dajung once provoked him
> and thrice was intimately exposed to his fangs and claws.

The first two lines are recognizing Huangbo who established himself and was in the center of the world. Yuanwu's lecture brings record of the following episode:

> In the community of Yanguan [Yanguan Chian, ?-842], where Huangbo was head monk, Dajung was asked to become a secretary.
> One day Dajung was with Huangbo when Huangbo was paying homage to Buddha.
> Dajung asked: "We should seek Buddha without adhering to Buddha, seek Dharma without adhering to Dharma, and seek Sangha without adhering to Sangha. How are you seeking by your paying homage?"
> Huangbo: "We should seek Buddha without adhering to Buddha, seek Dharma without adhering to Dharma, and seek Sangha without adhering to Sangha. Then, I always thus pay homage."
> Dajung: "What is the use of your paying homage?"
> Huangbo gave him a slap.
> Dajung: "How rude of you!"
> Huangbo: "With what kind of understanding of this place are you fondling such a relative idea as rude versus gracious?" and again he slapped him.
> Later ascending the throne, Dajung honored Huangbo with the title "Rude Monk."

This episode is evidently concerned with the same world of regaining the center of the world by seeking Buddha with no attachment to Buddha, which is the content of transcending our thought and emotion. We know Huangbo from infancy needed to keep changing his dwelling place. Wherever he newly moved, he gave the mountain there the name of his native mountain, Huangbo. Separating from his native land, persons, and culture was to make him lose his sense of center. By transcending his thought and emotion, he needed to go beyond the form of beings and things. The center he regained was the spaceless center established in an actual corner in the world of form. Fortunately for us Huangbo understood that a great many people have lost their center, and he determined to donate his life to helping them regain their center. From this episode his circumstance permeates to us.

Dajung was also a one who had lost sense of center and by a political enemy his life was even endangered. But it seems he lacked sensitivity, as is often characteristic of those qualified people engaging in government works. He acts as if this is another person's matter, looking only at Huangbo's big seven foot-tall body, looking only at the form of him prostrating to Buddha, Dharma, and Sangha.

We usually pay homage to our parents, to other people, to the governor of the land, and to the Three Treasures. Such conducts have been practiced worldwide until recently, and they are an outcome of our thought and emotion.

Huangbo's paying homage was the act of transcending thought and emotion. He was paying homage in the place where there are no Three Treasures, making Buddha where there is no Buddha, Dharma where there is no Dharma, and Sangha where there is no Sangha. By twice giving Dajung a slap, Huangbo wanted give the secret of creation, to found Buddha's Country. The important point we shouldn't ride past like a sleepy bus driver skipping one or two stops is that Huangbo was building this Buddha's Country while actually prostrating physically many times a day, every day. Dajung could easily understand Huangbo's paying homage was within his thought and emotion. He could also easily understand Huangbo's paying homage was beyond his thought and emotion. However, Dajung was straying from understanding the wonderful blend of not beyond and beyond, or attachment and no attachment.

The truth is that those who can go beyond thought and emotion must also be able to live with thought and emotion. This is the difficulty of Buddhist training and the reason we don't see many Buddhist priests and we feel a bitterness.

Now, let's go back to how Huangbo mastered this hinge, this pivotal point, under his teacher Baijang (Baijang Huaihai, 749-814).

The totality of life is the wonderful blend of contradictory natures, which are the world of rupa as well as sunyata, and we can appreciate such natures when we exercise at one time our thought and emotion and when at another time we transcend them. To live a pure, free, happy life, Buddhists for long generations have been transmitting the right time to use this hinge for when we should use rupa (thought and emotion) or use sunyata (transcending thought and emotion). In Buddhism this is the foremost hinge, here below illustrated picturesquely in Yuanwu's lecture on *Biyan lu*, Case 11:

> When Huangbo came to Baijang for the first time, Baijang asked,
> "Lofty Dignified, from where did you come?"
> Huangbo said, "Lofty Dignified came from the Mountain Range."
> Baijang: "For what did you come?"
> Huangbo: "For nothing particular to do."
> Baijang recognized Huangbo as a great talent.

In Baijang's greeting and Huangbo's response, there is the awareness that they shouldn't only fall into the world of form (thought and emotion) while talking form. Hence "Lofty Dignified" was chosen to express Huangbo as Nirmana-kaya as well as Dharma-kaya. Huangbo's response "from the Mountain Range" is so too, a geographic identity as well as the abstraction "Dharma."

To Baijang's question "For what did you come?" Huangbo answered "For nothing particular to do." "Nothing particular to do" is the world of transcending thought and emotion, and this behavior demands of us the most energy among all our daily behaviors. It doesn't mean having no interest in or passion for human advancement. It means not to pollute naturally pure being by crowning human dualistic value on innate Buddha nature.

> Next day Huangbo bid Baijang farewell.
> Baijang asked, "Where are you going?"
> "To Jiansi to pay homage to Great Teacher Matzu."
> Baijang said, "He has already passed away."
> Here Yuanwu inserts this question to his students:
>> All of you, tell me, Baijang asked thus. Did he ask knowingly or not knowingly?

As a matter of human affairs, Baijang is asking knowingly (exercising thought and emotion), but in the sense of "Dharma seeks Dharma" he is asking unknowingly (transcending thought and emotion). But Yuanwu won't be satisfied by this kind of theological answer. Should we say "A fertilized egg well knows," or simply "I will plant one more seedling before lunch"?

> Huangbo said, "I was specifically going to pay homage to him, but my karma to bring happiness must be weak. Therefore I will be unable to have even a glimpse of him. I wish to know what were his daily words and phrases. Please tell me."

This paragraph appears to have no density of importance. But that isn't so. As I have already said, to live a pure, free, and happy life, Buddhists have for long generations been transmitting the right timing for using the hinge. People who are not eager but are selfish and sloppy in studying all of the Buddhist transmission will have all sorts of misunderstandings about Buddhism. Trying to be accurate in understanding is already the act of transcending one's own thought and emotion.

> Baijang at last narrated to Huangbo the episode known as "Studying from Matzu for the Second Time":

Baijang's "at last" indicates his delight in finding that he and Huangbo were born on the same branch. This "for the Second Time" is so because Baijang had already been taught for the first time by an experience with Matzu, which was adapted as "Baijang and Wild Ducks" in *Biyan lu*, Case 53":

> Great Teacher Matzu and Baijang as they were walking saw wild ducks take wing.
> The Great Teacher asked, "What are they?"
> Baijang said, "They are wild ducks."
> The Great Teacher: "Where have they gone?"

Baijang: "To somewhere they have flown away."
The Great Teacher after all twisted Baijang's nose.
Baijang yelped.
The Great Teacher said, "What? They didn't fly away."

Here Matzu helped Baijang understand the being that doesn't fly away. The thing that flies away most is time. Secondly, it is the change of matter/materials. In the world of time and material, which means in the world of our thought and emotion, only when we transcend our thought and emotion can we truly understand the thing that doesn't change. Though we can understand the thing that doesn't change when we transcend our thought and emotion, we can't understand it after all, for we haven't thought and emotion to understand it at such a time. So we must understand it in the manner of not understanding it, that is, to understand intuitively, or to acquire a belief as a development of the best part of our intelligence.

At last Baijang came to the realization about the being that doesn't fly away, universal, beyond chronological time, and it is the world of no thought and emotion. Now for him the ancestor of ducks wasn't *Archaeopteryx*, and primitive humans had nothing to do with *Homo erectus*, *Homo neanderthalensis*, or even *Homo sapiens*. For him the sound of the flute was sounding on and on before and after the breath through the flute. In short, he saw the positive meaning of transcending thought and emotion. But even this painful experience at the water's edge wasn't deep and wide enough for him. For him the world of thought and emotion (rupa) and the world of transcending thought and emotion (sunyata) were still as if two different worlds, which kept alternating within him, and often the world of thought and emotion seemed to him to be of less value than the world of transcending thought and emotion.

This area can be rather fussy and complicated to clarify for some people. So for them, disregarding sunyata and living only in chronological rupa may seem a straight, honest, dauntless life. As a result they divide their thought and emotion into two categories, good and bad, and try to put down their thought and emotion by some effort and outer help, or try to rescue their thought and emotion by improving their objects and circumstances, or try to substitute other thought and emotion, or they depend on the most effective solution, which is to be benefited by loss of memory or by decline of their temporary harmonious form. The solution for Buddhists is not to avert our eyes from the nature of being. So Baijang had to visit Matzu again, as he here to Huangbo relates:

> The Patriarch [Matzu] when he saw me approach raised his whisk.
> I asked, "Is it detaching itself while fulfilling its function?"
> After an interval the Patriarch hung the whisk on a corner of the meditation seat and continued to keep silent.
> He then replied, "In the future, by speaking, how will you help people?"
> I took and raised the whisk.
> The Patriarch stated: "It is detaching itself while fulfilling its function."
> I returned the whisk to the corner of the meditation seat.
> The Patriarch gave a thunderous shout.
> I was instantly deafened and for three days I could not hear."
> Huangbo unconsciously stuck out his tongue in amazement. (*Biyan lu*, Case 11, Yuanwu's lecture)

The whisk for a priest is like the baton for a conductor, a convenient extension of the body. Workers of all kinds have tools they are accustomed to using and keeping always within reach. In this episode, whisk is a tool symbolizing language, or our thought and emotion. Take note of Matzu's words to Baijang: "In the future, by speaking, how will you help people?"

As Baijang approached, Matzu without a word raised his whisk to present the subject of their dialogue. Baijang asked "Is it detaching itself while fulfilling its function?"

Here we must come to the realization that our thought and emotion are, as are all other beings, detaching themselves while fulfilling their function. The ducks as they fly away are detaching themselves and aren't ducks, they are Nirmana-kaya. Whisk wasn't whisk when Matzu raised it.

Why then did Baijang use question form instead of statement? Was it politeness to his teacher? No. The whisk was a whisk when Matzu raised it and was functioning perfectly well as a whisk. To sum up, the whisk wasn't a whisk, as well as it was perfectly a whisk. Our thought and emotion when functioning as thought and emotion are transcending at the very moment and not at a later time. Baijang in question form was expressing these contradictory simultaneous aspects of their nature.

"After an interval the Patriarch hung the whisk on a corner of the meditation seat and continued to keep silent." Why "After an interval"? Matzu was giving Baijang time to make sure he deeply understood what he was understanding in the spur of the moment. Even rain after drought had better know the need of soaking deep into the soil. "Deep" means to universalize our personal experience by reflecting on it. Matzu then "hung the whisk on a corner of the meditation seat and continued to keep silent." "Hung the whisk on a corner" and "continued to keep silent" and "transcending thought and emotion" are synonymous. When we transcend our thought and emotion, or when we put away our tools, or when we are meditating (= truly living) with no aim of any particular thing to do, we are not functioning and at once we are fully functioning.

There are cases when transcending our thought and emotion has power while our engaging in thought and emotion has power. There are also cases when transcending our thought and emotion has power while our engaging in thought and emotion has no power. There are also cases when transcending our thought and emotion has no power while our engaging in thought and emotion has no power. There are also cases when transcending our thought and emotion has no power while our engaging in thought and emotion has power. Important is that our ability to use the turn of our mental hinge in good timing in every case depends after all on how much we can transcend our thought and emotion.

The rest of this episode is a confirmation of the contradictory nature of being, which is the contradictory nature of our thought and emotion, and it is a confirmation of the grave confirmation that is of our use of such natures for helping other creatures.

> Then the Patriarch asked me in return, "In the future, by speaking, how will you help people?"
> I took and raised the whisk.
> The Patriarch said, "It is detaching itself while fulfilling its function."
> I returned the whisk to the corner of the meditation seat.

> The Patriarch gave a thunderous shout.
> I was instantly deafened and for three days I could not hear.
> Huangbo unconsciously stuck out his tongue in amazement.

Baijang takes exactly the same behavior (= I took and raised the whisk" and "I returned the whisk to the corner of the meditation seat") as his teacher Matzu did,…as Nanyue did, as Sixth Patriarch Hueineng did,…as Bodhidharma did,…as Sakyamuni Buddha did. All of them all go hand in hand in the world in which they transcend their thought and emotion. Not only they did, for we all are the same. When one of them is peaceful beside a pond with flowering lotus, we all are peaceful. When one of them is shivering beside an icy stream, we all are shivering.

Even though Baijang understood to raise the whisk and also to return it, Matzu gave a thunderous shout. This shout was to confirm that what Baijang understood was the very content of the Dharma transmission, which started from Sakyamuni Buddha and went down the lineage. So with this meaning too the patriarchs all go hand in hand.

By this episode the Dharma transmission was perfected from Matzu to Baijang. It must have been a solemn experience for Baijang, expressed as "deafened and for three days I could not hear." Baijang thereafter could live as transmitted Dharma rather than as an individual person. So in this sense, deafened for three days means for all his life, and it also means what exists in the world is nothing other than the transmitted Dharma. Huangbo was amazed at Baijang's ability to be thus deafened (to be thus blinded). They each directly confronted the total exposure of the contradictory nature, that is, the world of rupa as well as the world of sunyata, and such could be used and manifested as their function of thought and emotion. For this confrontation, their reactions were each different, rather unique. Matzu gave a thunderous shout, Baijang was deafened for three days, and unconsciously Huangbo stuck out his tongue. Although they all saw the same contradictory nature by transcending thought and emotion, each was resurrected to his own unique form, that is, to his own thought and emotion. Matzu always went on with a positive and active way of life, Baijang was reflective and considering, and Huangbo kept everlasting sensitivity, appreciating all good things.

For instance, Baijang was the one who made the first monastic rules in China. His rules were to allow his community to survive by a self-sufficient religious life. Fortunately the rules were made by one who knew the totality of transcending thought and emotion. Baijang is well known for his words "One day of no work is one day of no meals." For him "work" meant the life of transcending thought and emotion, and "no meals" meant no life. He had experienced being deafened and for three days unable to hear. Evidently his deafness didn't last only three days.

In later life Huangbo must also have been remembering his experience of being introduced to Baijang's "Studying from Matzu for the Second Time." His words were recorded by his good lay student Peishiou and given the title *Chuanshin Fayau* (Essence of the Dharma of transmitting the Mind):

> It is better to serve a person of no mind who is unavailable than to serve all Buddhas in the Ten Directions. No mind means not having any mind. The body of suchness is like a piece of wood, like a stone, inside and out, and does not move, does not turn. Inside and out it is like the void, not choked, not blocked. It has no division of being, no active or passive side, no difference between here and there, no looks, no form, no gain, no loss.
>
> The people when they confront it dare not enter. They fear that if they follow this truth they will fall into a void. Believing that they will there have no place to dwell, they dreamingly look to the far borders and resume their ordinary life.

The first paragraph describes Baijang's life, the second describes the many pious people who believe in any religion. Further, shouldn't we say the first paragraph describes the world of transcending thought and emotion, and the second describes the world of thought and emotion? This is an example of Huangbo's sensitivity. Yangshan (Yangshan Hueiji, 803-887) quoted Ananda, who said, in the *Surangama-sutra*, on hearing Buddha's sermon, "With this deep mind I will devote myself to serving all Buddhas of numerous countries. This is the true way of returning thanks to Buddha. Note: "deep mind" means, "to seek Bodhi upwards and to be always helpful for sentient beings downwards."

Yangshan, student of Kueishan, to Kueishan was quoting Ananda when they were studying the episode of Linji's arriving at Huangbo's summer session, which will follow below after this Huangbo/Linji pine-planting episode:

> Huangbo asked Linji when Linji was planting pine seedlings:
> "In the depths of these mountains for what are you planting so many seedlings?"
> Linji: "First, to make a nice environment for the temple, and second, to make an example for later comers," and with his mattock he thrice struck the earth.
> Huangbo: "Though you be so, you have already received my staff's thirty beatings."
> Linji again thrice struck the earth with his mattock as he produced the sounds of slow exhaling.
> Huangbo declared: "My teaching will prosper well in your generation." (*Linji lu*, also in *Chuandeng lu*, vol. 12)

Huangbo when opening dialogue by his question was already sensitively seeing that Linji was forgetting thought and emotion. Linji was intent on planting seedlings. It is the good fortune of students to have so sensitive a teacher. Parents enjoy seeing their children fully absorbed beyond thought and emotion and worry over them unsettled by thought and emotion. Without this sensitivity, scholars often misinterpret the pivotal meaning of the sutras and the patriarchs' records. Without this sensitivity, Huangbo's last saying that his teaching will prosper well in Linji's generation will be no different from the avaricious prediction of a founder of franchise stores. Worldly success wasn't the point. We have already studied that Baijang's "One day of no work is one day of no meals" isn't about energy efficiency, such as is a worldly concern today. Here, Huangbo's "will prosper well" means "There will be many more people who will enjoy the benefit of transcending their thought and emotion in their acts."

Likewise, Linji's "First, to make a nice environment for the temple" did not mean for a tourist business or for gardeners and horticulturists. He meant that among all sites, the temple is where Dharma produces Dharma, pines produce pines, and our thought and emotion will be buried in such Dharma recycling. Naturally, "Second, to make an example for later comers" does not mean his determination was to be an unabashed example of a hard-working creature in a poor community on the earth's surface. He meant, like Sakyamuni, here an example of the happiest human life, which is to transcend thought and emotion and to participate in Buddha's deeds. Linji got an unshakable confidence for this way of life, regardless of other human views, including his teacher's, and he showed it in his gesture of continuing on with his work planting seedlings.

However, Huangbo knew Baijang's "Studying from Matzu for the Second Time," and the opportunity to teach Linji "for the Second Time" came soon:

> Linji came up Mt. Huangbo in the middle of a summer session and found His Reverence [Huangbo] reading a sutra. Linji said, "I have been regarding you as the very person, but now I see only a reverend oldster pecking at black beans."
>
> A few days later, as Linji was leaving, Huangbo said, "You are violating the monastic rule, coming in the middle of the session and now leaving before completing it." Linji said, "I came only to pay homage to Your Reverence."
>
> Huangbo finally struck him and sent him off. Linji as he walked away some distance came to reconsider the matter and he returned to complete the session. (Ibid.)

If Linji was really mastering how to transcend his thought and emotion he could go along with the thought and emotion of anyone else. Huangbo says again in his *Chuanshin Fayau*:

> Most ordinary people do not acknowledge emptiness, for they fear falling into a void. They do not know their mind is empty from the beginning. Fools try to remove the problems of life and do not remove their mind. The wise remove their mind and do not remove life's problems. A Bodhisattva's mind is like the empty sky: Abandon everything all at once and behave without adherence to any virtues.

Indeed we must know that when we transcend our thought and emotion we are also transcending the void and we won't even be conscious of our transcending. The mind "empty from the beginning" doesn't mean the void or absence of any being. It means the mind has no eternal fixed nature.

> Linji after completing the session at Huangbo visited various other masters. One of his earliest visits was to the Reverend Ping.

Linji came to Mt. Sanfeng. There the Reverend Ping asked, "From where did you come?"
Linji: "From Huangbo."
Ping: "What sort of words had he?"
Linji: "The golden bull entered a smelting furnace without trace even to this day."
Ping: "The golden breeze plays the jade flute. Who can appreciate it?"
Linji: "[He who hears] decisively penetrates a million barriers and even in the blue sky doesn't dwell."
Ping: "Your saying is quite arrogant."
Linji: "The dragon birthed a baby phoenix that breaks through the blue sky."
Ping: "Well, for now, sit down and have a cup of tea."

(*Linji lu*)

Being asked what words had Huangbo, Linji answered "The golden bull entered a smelting furnace without trace even to this day." Ping's "words" in "What sort of words" means thought and emotion. Linji is saying Huangbo is a golden bull that has melted away with no trace of thought and emotion. Huangbo's response to Linji transcended words, thought, and emotion, whether he actually spoke or not. The point is, Ping asked Linji what were Huangbo's words. As his best understanding of Huangbo, Linji in place of Huangbo is responding to Ping. For Linji, Huangbo has mastered how to transcend words (thought and emotion). So Huangbo, whether or not he actually spoke, completely transcended words (= golden bull melted away). Linji is thinking Ping isn't recognizing Huangbo's achievement and thus is asking what were his words. It is silly to ask "What sort of words had he?" about a person who has transcended words. There are two truths: 1) Huangbo spoke actually, so he didn't speak true words actually, and 2) Huangbo didn't speak actually, so he spoke true words actually.

Ping is admiring Huangbo, likening him to a jade flute producing a wonderful melody in the autumn wind. Ping then checked Linji: "Who can appreciate it?" The sense of Linji's answer is "The one who could hear Huangbo's flute is none other than I who am before your very eyes. Blind man! Out of compassion I will show you evidence I am one who understands Huangbo's teaching. One who truly understands will understand all by a single incident ("decisively penetrates a million barriers"). And more, such a one doesn't stay at the same level as his teacher ("even in the blue sky doesn't dwell"). Ping's response is "Your saying is quite arrogant." We know what Linji's teacher Huangbo said and did in a similar circumstance: "'With what kind of understanding of this place are you fondling such a relative idea as rude versus gracious?' and he again slapped him [Dajung]." Linji free of thought and emotion says "The dragon birthed a baby phoenix that breaks through the blue sky"—"dragon" Huangbo, "baby phoenix" Linji. This is Linji kindly restating what he has already stated as "decisively penetrates a million barriers and even in the blue sky doesn't dwell."

The world where Huangbo is educating people is "the blue sky." Linji was a person of Henan, South of the Yellow River, but he was going to Hebei, in the North, to where no influence of the Fifth and Sixth Patriarchs had ever set in.

Ping invited Linji to sit down for tea. It was to calm Linji's highly risen spirit, but Linji was no longer a person who makes a division between rest time and working hours. He wouldn't have enjoyed tea and chat with Ping. He must have just simply left.

There are many interesting points in this episode. But for our itinerary on to the conclusion of this essay, we need only "The golden bull entered a smelting furnace." "The golden bull" was Huangbo (according to Linji's confident view at least). It must be a great thing to be modified as "golden," and very great, "entered a smelting furnace without trace even to this day." We can already understand by the sentence structure that "golden bull" was Huangbo's words, thought and emotion. For a Mahayana Buddhist there can be a thing more "golden" than the Bodhisattva's vow to help all sentient beings with wisdom and patience. Huangbo was already transcending even such a vow.

Here in comparison with "golden bull" and "without trace even to this day" we like to study "a pair of bulls made of mud" and "I have never seen them since."

> Dungshan [Dungshan Liangjie 801-869] together with Uncle Sengmi arrived at Mt. Lungshan and bowed from the waist.
> The old monk [Tanjou Lungshan, ?-?] asked him, "This mountain has no path. How did you come here?"

> Dungshan said, "Put aside there being no path, how did Your Reverence come?"
> The old monk said, "I am neither cloud nor water."
> Dungshan: "How long have you been in this mountain?"
> The old monk: "It has nothing to do with spring and autumn."
> Dungshan: "Which was the first to dwell here, this mountain or Your Reverence?"
> The old monk: "I do not know."
> Dungshan: "Why do you not know?"
> The old monk: "I came from neither the heavenly world nor the human world."
> Dungshan: "Your Reverence, what kind of truth did you see to make you come to dwell in this mountain?"
> The old monk: "I saw a pair of bulls made of mud enter the ocean as they fought and I have never seen them since."
> Dungshan only then made a dignified prostration.
>
> (*Dungshan lu*, entry 24)

At the beginning Dungshan bowed from the waist in the normal manner. Only at the end did he make a dignified prostration. We are going to focus our telescope on this prostration. But first we can study an outline of the episode.

Lungshan asked Dungshan, "This mountain has no path. How did you come here?" Indeed the mountain had no path for people. A different source (*Chanyuan mengchiou*) for the same episode describes:

> The Teacher when advancing with Uncle Sengmi saw a vegetable leaf in a creek. He said, "Why is there a vegetable leaf in the deep mountain where no one is dwelling? If we follow up the creek, maybe we will meet a trainee." So they decided to go along the creek, pushing aside the grasses. After walking some five or six miles, they saw a strange-looking very lean person. This was the Reverend Lungshan.

Dungshan was just then arriving at Lungshan, so what he wanted to know was how Lungshan had come: "Put aside there being no path, how did Your Reverence come?" It is interesting to note that the reason Linji traveled was to express who he was, according to the preceding episode, and to many other examples not quoted here, whereas Dungshan's motive, according to these passages, as well as to many more examples not quoted here, was to deepen his understanding of who he was.

Lungshan replied to Dungshan "I am neither cloud nor water." He had to take a righteous path to come here, for he was not a cloud and not water. Dungshan on hearing this must have felt the blood in his body flow rapidly through his past and his present.

Dungshan then asked "How long have you been in this mountain?" Lungshan: "It has nothing to do with spring and autumn." He wanted to say "I am not one to make a calendar after settling on an island like a destitute castaway. I am a blessed Buddhist who came here neither for recreation nor to escape a depressing society. Chronological time is not my concern." Dungshan saw his fault in asking about a mere phenomenal concern. So he asked more theologically "Which was the first to dwell here, this mountain or Your Reverence?" Lungshan to that curtly replied he didn't know. He was pointing out the sterility of metaphysical curiosity. But Dungshan wanted to know what was wrong with fondling metaphysical curiosity, so he asked "Why don't you know?" Lungshan was kind enough to say "I came from neither the heavenly world nor the human world." It means all heavenly and human beings are the subjects of thought and emotion, which have no substance, and yet they have the nature of leading us to dualistic valuation. So there is the sense "I dwell here in the mountain, which has no dualistic valuation. Even if I can say I was born from this mountain, I'd rather not say I came from neither the heavenly world nor the human world."

Dungshan then put forth a careful question: "Your Reverence, what kind of truth did you see to make you come to dwell in this mountain?" Did he suppose an answer like Linji's "The golden bull entered a smelting furnace without trace even to this day"? By Linji's answer, Dungshan might have finished the dialogue and descended the mountain. But Lungshan answered "I saw a pair of bulls made of clay enter the ocean as they fought and I have never seen them since."

It is said country folk made bulls out of clay to offer at spring festival. Those clay bulls were fired so they wouldn't dissolve in water. Here Lungshan is using them to represent klesa, which is thought and emotion dreadfully fighting, entering the ocean as they fight. We must well exercise our sensitivity here too. An eagle may carry a jewel in its beak.

Lungshan didn't say the pair of bulls entered the ocean and dissolved. Indeed, no. His meaning was, they entered the ocean and he never saw them again. However, there is no assurance he won't ever see them again. Any moment they might show up, so he must keep watch as a trainee in active service.

This is the reason Lungshan came to live in the mountain. The mountain is transcending thought and emotion. In other words, he kept studying as well as transcending his thought and emotion, a totality of rupa and sunyata, the totality of his life. Dungshan understanding Lungshan and seeing his own past, present, and future "only then made a dignified prostration." In later life he asked a monk:

> What is the utmost suffering?
> The monk said, "Hell."
> Dungshan: "Wrong. Not clarifying life-death even though having put the kasaya upon ourselves."
>
> (*Dungshan lu*, entry 105)

Life-death is our thought and emotion as well as our transcending our thought and emotion. This study isn't the thing completed. The study continues on and on. For the continuous study Dungshan made his prostration, not for its completion.

In *Dungshan lu*, entry 105, Shyuefeng appears in the summer training season under Dungshan. It is said in any monastery where he visited he volunteered to be cook monk, bearing the hard and responsible work for the health of all monks.

> When Shyuefeng was sorting the rice, Dungshan asked him, "Are you sorting out sand from the rice, or sorting out rice from the sand?
> Shyuefeng: "I am at the same time sorting out both."
> Dungshan: "Then what will the monks eat?"
> Shyuefeng covered the rice tray.
> Dungshan said, "It will be good for you to study from Deshan."

Sand signifies klesa (thought and emotion), rice signifies Bodhi (transcending thought and emotion). Both are the same thing (rupa, sunyata). Here Dungshan is testing Shyuefeng's understanding by asking him dualistically in the presence of actual rice and sand. It is more like asking a little child which he would prefer, dying under a ton of iron, or dying under a ton of cotton. Shyuefeng made no mistake of falling into the trap of materialistic dualism. However, he made the mistake of falling into philosophical dualism, into the void. He was vigorous and passionate in his response "I am at the same time sorting out both," meaning in his world there was neither klesa nor Bodhi. It is like a stout farmer saying "I care nothing about either pollution or the environment."

So Dungshan quietly asked "Then what will the monks eat?" It was to ask "What is human life if we remove both thought and emotion and transcending thought and emotion?" For this, Shyuefeng covered the rice tray, covered the source of the issue. But that isn't the way to solve any problem. Dungshan saw Shyuefeng's eager, passionate, practical, and highly physical character and was going to introduce him to Deshan, a more suiting master than himself. Dungshan loving mountains, waters, and literature was more tender than Deshan.

Anyway, this episode hints to us that transcending thought and emotion doesn't mean going into a different space or dimension. Buddhist transcendence should be attained at the same standpoint as bondage. Therefore Buddhist transcendence shouldn't have a time lapse between the time of exercising thought and emotion and the time of transcending thought and emotion. Buddhist transcendence is more like lightning, if thought and emotion are likened to thunder. There are those who think "We should after all go beyond love and hate, so it is better to give back goodness when receiving evil." This is a nice attitude, but not the words of true Buddhists.

Dungshan's teaching was detailed and sensitive:

> While fording the river with Yunjyu [Yunjyu Daying, 835?-902], the Teacher asked:
> "How deep is the water?"
> Yunjyu: "So shallow it's not wetting my feet."
> "Insensitive fellow," Dungshan replied.
> Yunjyu: "Please teach me."
> Dungshan: "It will never be dry."
>
> (*Dungshan lu*, entry 46)

Yunjyu was thinking only of crossing the river. Though told he was insensitive, he couldn't have been so coarse as to take the water as simply physical water. After all, Dungshan was asking him so as to teach him. Yunjyu must have then understood Dungshan's concern was about the depth of klesa. The river is our life, a hard thing to cross from shore to shore. Because of our klesa, we can easily drown and fall into hell, or into the world of hungry ghosts or the world of beasts.

    Sakyamuni Buddha taught us The Eight Right Ways to cross the river of sufferings. He then asked his followers each to become a sangha (monk), to become a ferryman, a bridge, to help all sentient beings cross from this shore to the other shore. Huangbo reproached the monk ahead crossing a swollen river as if it were a plain field. Linji's temple was beside the river Hutsuo; "Linji" meant literally "to help people to cross the river." Yantou when only around age twenty met the Great Destruction of Buddhism in China and he actually became a ferryman. He hung a board at either side of the lake so people could strike it whenever they wanted a crossing. He'd ask "Where do you want to go?" and after a while, flourishing a pole, he'd appear from the reedy thickets. (In Hinayana Buddhism, sangha meant monks more than three or four. In Mahayana Buddhism it defined three kinds: 1) sangha as the harmony of reason, and even one person can be a sangha; 2) sangha as the harmony for performing the ceremonious life, with monks more than three; and 3) sangha as the harmony of a social element, with monks more than four, five, ten, or twenty.)

    Yunjyu's "So shallow it's not wetting my feet" disappointed Dungshan, who couldn't help but sharply express "Insensitive fellow."

    Yunjyu at least immediately asked "Please teach me." Dungshan decisively showed the totality of the world in his teaching "It will never be dry." This water of klesa won't ever dry. Don't have a fantasy in which there is life without klesa (thought and emotion). There will never be such a time when we can enjoy a sustained peace of no devastating and internally scorching thought and emotion. Therefore Vimalakirti said he was sick because all suffering sentient beings are sick, and Hippocrates diagnosed a visiting patient, "You are ill for the shortage of this," and he gave coins.

    Dungshan's "It will never be dry" at the same time means the water is Dharma water, which will never dry. Simultaneously klesa water (thought and emotion) is Dharma water (transcendence of thought and emotion) with no change of time or change of form. This is Buddhist transcendence, Buddhist transition.

The following episode should also be understood in the same way. Dachyuan (?-894) was the inheritor of Dungshan's temple.

> Dachyuan asked, "What is the essential point of transcending the worldly world?"
> Dungshan answered, "The smoke is rising under your feet."
> Dachyuan immediately understood and he never again made a training pilgrimage.
> Yunjyu spoke in place of Dachyuan: "I will never betray Your Reverence, for the smoke is rising under your feet as well."
> Dungshan said, "A person who practices at each step is a person of total virtue." (*Dungshan lu*, entry 64)

This "smoke" is referring to a metaphor in the Lotus Flower Sutra:

> There is no peace in The Three Worlds. They are like a burning house, filled with many fearful sufferings such as living, aging, illness, and death. These fires are furious, endlessly burning. The Tathagata has already transcended the burning house of The Three Worlds.

Dungshan's comment "total virtue" means "harmony in the contradiction between klesa and Dharma, between suffering and transcending." This episode above and *Biyan lu* Case 43 "Dungshan's No Cold or Heat" are the same. So is *Dungshan lu*, entry 73:

> The Teacher [Dungshan] said in his sermon at the end of the term: "Brothers all, a summer has ended and an autumn has come. Go east or west at your free will. But by any means go where there is not a single stem of weed in a million miles." After a period of silence he added, "But how will you go to such a place where there is not a single stem of weed in a million miles?"
> Later someone narrated this sermon to Shyshuang [Shyshuang Chingju, 807- 888]. Shyshuang said: "As soon as we go out the gate there are weeds."
> Dungshan hearing of this comment said, "Throughout all Great Tang how many are as great as he?"

In my case this year somehow I couldn't use any motored tools such as grass cutter and lawnmower. With a single pair of shears by squatting I had to cut all grasses within the property—north and south yard, west and east slope, around the pond, around the vegetable gardens, surrounding the vice chief's house, and all the meandering driveway. Morning after morning I cut the grasses. Each morning I sharpened the shears before cutting. Morning and evening I did stretching exercises for my limbs, back, neck, and fingers. I had to be cautious for the penetrating sun, bee stings, and chigger bites.

If we talk about efficiency, shouldn't we say anyway we all have important tasks to carry out, and more enjoyable works to engage in? There may be. I will do gladly when they come and I must know nothing lasts forever. And after all, most afternoons and evenings I could engage in studying the sutras and the patriarchs' sayings, and, for instance, write this essay. There isn't much to complain about. My only wish is that I can be little more helpful and useful for a few more people.

September 4, 2008

To Understand *Biyan lu*, Case 3:
Matzu's "Sunface Buddha, Moonface Buddha"

The great master Matzu was gravely ill.
The chief administrator monk came to pay his respects: "Your Reverence, these days how are you?"
The master replied, "Sunface Buddha, Moonface Buddha."

Yuanwu introduces Case 3 with "The great function manifests itself naturally, unlimited by fixed rules." The subject of "the great function" is the universal life innate in the particular life of us each. Universal life is "unlimited by fixed rules" of course because universal life is the father of fixed rules. But universal life is limited by fixed rules of course because fixed rules are the son of universal life.

In this Case 3 we must see Matzu's great compassion as well as the great compassion of every phenomenon. It is said "Dharma-kaya has neither appearance nor disappearance, but out of compassion shows us appearance and disappearance. (This means Dharma-kaya appears as Nirmana-kaya.) Our birth and our death are appearance and disappearance and they are the Dharma-kaya's compassionate figure. But ignorant people see our birth and death as suffering, which is an upside-down view from Buddha's viewpoint. So Dogen says:

> Our birth and death are travel kits for Buddha and the patriarchs, utensils for Buddhas.
> (*Gyo butsuyigi* [Practicing Buddha's noble deeds])

Great patriarchs use their birth and death as well-used tools and at any rate won't be used by them. How do they attain such a remarkable attitude? Shyuedou says in his gatha for

Case 3:
> For twenty years I have had fierce struggles,
> how often descending into a dragon's cave for you!

Matzu guided his students by simple words, "The mind is Buddha." Dogen admires it:

> What all Buddhas and patriarchs without exception have been preserving and practicing is only "The mind is Buddha." Therefore under the Western sky there is no "The mind is Buddha." It appeared in China for the first time.
>
> (*Sokushin zebutsu* [The mind is Buddha])

As we studied, "The" of "The mind is Buddha" is Buddha, "mind" of "The mind is Buddha" is Buddha, "is" of "The mind is Buddha" is Buddha, and "Buddha" of "The mind is Buddha" is Buddha. In other words, every phenomenon is Buddha. If it is so, when the phenomenon appears, Buddha disappears; and when Buddha appears, the phenomenon disappears. So Dogen says "Therefore under the Western sky there is no 'The mind is Buddha.'" That means when it is a phenomenon, which is "under the Western sky," there is no "The mind is Buddha," which is Buddha. As for "It appeared in China for the first time," when "The mind is Buddha" appears, there should be no presence of China. It will be an anya-tirthya's view if Buddha (sunyata) and phenomena (rupa) were to appear at once in the same dimension. For the true Buddhist view, Buddha (sunyata) and phenomena (rupa) shouldn't appear at the same time in the same dimension. So Dogen says "What all Buddhas and patriarchs without exception have been preserving and practicing is only "The mind is Buddha." To be like that is a difficult achievement, and Shyuedou says "For twenty years I have had fierce struggles."

To appreciate Matzu's "Sunface Buddha, Moonface Buddha," we must know what kind of "twenty years" Matzu had been living in his training days.

For the first time after some ten years studying under his teacher, Nanyue (Nanyue Huairang, 677-747), Matzu wanted to once visit his native land, Shyfang.

> When he came halfway, then and there he turned about, went back, and offered incense and paid worship to his teacher.

Nanyue instantly composed a gatha:
> I advise you not to return to your native land.
> Return to the native land and the Way is not practiced.
> The old crones in the row houses
> will call you by your native name.
>
> *(In Gyoji* [Endless training], vol. 2)

If we have to live apart from our native land, we generally feel nostalgia because the native land is the place and time to be given birth by compassionate parents and where childhood is spent in generally warm circumstances. This nostalgia comes from our imperfect perception, inaccurate thought, sloppy memory, and sourceless imagination about that place and time as well as about our career of how we spent our time there. We must understand Matzu once wanted to return to his native land after some ten years of solitary training life.

Then, how should we understand that he quit proceeding to his native land and that he turned and went back to his training temple? It was his voluntary choice, but with what thought? Did he foresee his nostalgia wouldn't be satisfied by visiting there? Did he sense his geographic native land wasn't the true native land for his life? Did he feel ashamed of his desire to see his native land, whereas a million others could never satisfy their same desire? Or did the Dharma want him to be the Dharma power to promote the Dharma function instead of his becoming a mere consumer of the Dharma?

Anyway, he decided to return to his training life, and he lit incense and paid worship to his teacher to renew his vigor for training. He must have realized his life wasn't his but belonged to the Sangha. It means he determined to come to realize he must be the Dharma as well as Buddha. This part is figuratively described, simply as "He came halfway."

After all, Sakyamuni Buddha at birth lost a core of his native land, which was his mother. When his determination became brimful, he left his family and his native land. Mahakasyapa determined to leave family to become a great father of all orphaned children, that is, to promote the Sangha function. Naturally Dungshan refused to see his mother when she finally found him at his monastery. Huangbo lost his blind mother in a flooding river by consequence of his hiding from her reach.

Ejo was a responsible monk to observe monastic rules and had already consumed his allowed permissions to take temporary leave. Urgent messages twice came from his dying mother and he presented the matter to the officer monks. All encouraged him to go, saying "Monastery rules can be kept many years. Comfort to your mother at her deathbed is possible only once." Ejo concluded not to go. Prior to Ejo's decision, a senior monk reported to the master Dogen how the monks' discussion was proceeding. Dogen said "He will not go."

After all, priests are public utensils. So Nanyue's advice in his gatha first line "I advise that you not return to your native land" is advice to everyone, every creature, every being, because all beings are possible to be addressed as "you." There isn't a being unsuitable to be addressed as "you." All in the Ten Directions are "you." The Ten Directions is the life of the kasaya-donning monk, which is "I." Now, we must know in detail what is "you" in order to understand Nanyue's gatha.

We will see *Biyan lu*, Case 1:

> The Emperor then spoke to Jygung about this.
> Jygung: "Do you actually not know who he is?"
> The Emperor: "I do not know."
> Jygung: "He is the Bodhisattva Avalokitesvara, bearer of Buddha's Heart Seal."
> Greatly taken with regret, the Emperor longed to send for Bodhidharma.
> Jygung said, "No use in that. Even if all the people of your country go, he will not turn back."

Why didn't Bodhidharma (?-528?) turn back? "Bearer of Buddha's Heart Seal" he was said to be. For the sense of true Buddhists, "bearer of [something]" means one who is that something and it doesn't mean one who is a carrier of it. So Bodhidharma was Buddha's Heart Seal. Coming to this understanding, we should realize we human beings, or just beings, are bearers of Buddha's Heart Seal, and it means each of us beings is Buddha's Heart Seal. Bodhidharma is another name of Sakyamuni Buddha, or of Mahakasyapa, or of Matzu Dauyi (709-788). So, Shyuansha (Shyuansha Shybei, 835-908) said:

Bodhidharma never came to this Eastern land and the Second Patriarch never went to the Land under the Western Sky. (*Chuandeng lu*, vol. 18)

Understanding Bodhidharma who doesn't turn back, or Buddha's Heart Seal, or "you," is to keep up the Seventh Primary Precept, Neither admiring oneself nor depreciating others:

> All Buddhas and patriarchs present the Great Body at one time and in the sky no distinction exists between inside and outside. At another time they present Dharma-kaya and not an ounce of soil exists on earth. (*Kyoju kaimon*)

The body of a Buddhist isn't five feet eight inches tall, weighing a hundred thirty-five pounds. The body of a Buddhist is the entire entity of beings in The Whole World in the Ten Directions throughout past, present, and future. This body is called "The Great Body." This Great Body is "you." We often call it simply Buddha nature. Buddha nature anyhow doesn't return to Buddha nature. So, the first line of Nanyue's gatha, "I advise you not to return to your native land" is read as expressed, but it should be understood as "I admire you for not returning to your native land, because you are already in your native land and always are."

Every inescapable multi-pound statement ("advice") pressing us down should be understood as an exclamation in recognition of the positive and wonderful nature of the content of "Every inescapable multi-pound statement pressing us down." "Do not return" isn't an order.

> Return to the native land and the Way is not practiced.

"The native land" is Buddha nature, or the Unsurpassed Way. There, there is contrasting existence, such as the person who practices the Way, and the Way. So, it is said "the Way is not practiced." This is the ultimate function of Buddha nature, though it is expressed as a negative. In the bald-mountain-like meditation there are three virtues: thought, thinking the unthinkable, and beyond thought. This "beyond thought" is "the Way is not practiced."

> The old crones in the row houses
> will call you by your native name.

Buddha nature, or the Unsurpassed Way, appears as mountain, river, great earth, also as "the row houses." "The old crones" are every Buddhist matter, such as training and realization, study and devices, theological study and devotion in practice, temple care, practice of the Way, and so forth. In this gatha these are called "The old crones in the row houses." In other words, these Buddhist matters are Buddha nature. "Not an inch of weeds in a million miles" means "As soon as we go out from the gate there are weeds," and also "There are weeds even without going out from the gate." "The old crones in the row houses" is phenomena, and "Return to the native land and the Way is not practiced" is the True Form.

So, in total, this Nanyue gatha is describing the true human being in the Ten Directions. Matzu on hearing this gatha reverently received it, and then and there the transmission of raising a flower and a wink of the eye and breaking into a smile was perfected. Ever after, Matzu never returned to his native land because he was native land itself (Buddha nature) and his body was The Whole World in the Ten Directions.

Again, what is the meaning of "not returning to the native land" and "returning to the native land"? Our every conduct should be "not returning to the native land" because we are already in the native land. In such case, why should we choose, prefer, a particular conduct, such as to return to the native land? For great heroic persons, such as the patriarchs, after all there is no trifling distinction between returning and not returning to the native land. It can be a returning from one aspect and also a not returning. This is the true description of the world and is well expressed in the Ninth Primary Precept, Not Angering:

> Not regressing and not advancing, not true and not false, everywhere the ocean of bright clouds, the solemnly ornamented ocean of clouds. (*Kyoju kaimon*)

The Whole World in the Ten Directions is the native land. The native land is The Great Compassion. The Great Compassion is The Great Endurance. The Great Endurance is another name of Sakyamuni Buddha. In the world of The Great Endurance there is no difference between returning and not returning, no difference between regressing and advancing, and no difference between true and false. All worlds, all phenomena, are one body of Buddha. Whatever we do, we are doing after all within ourselves. When we return to the east, the whole of us, which means the whole world, is returning to the east, and so there's no east. When we return to the west, the whole of us, which means the whole world, is returning to the west, and so there's no west. When we go to heaven, the whole of us, which means the whole world, is heaven, and so there's no conflict between heaven and hell. When we anger, the whole of us, which means the whole world, is angering, and so there's no anger.

Returning to the native land means we devote ourselves to anything in daily life with the whole of our body and mind. When we "Return to the native land," "the Way is not practiced." It is because the Way is already being practiced with full combustion. Not practicing the Way is returning to the native land. Returning is not practicing the way. If so, not practicing the Way is not practicing the Way, and returning is returning. Then, not practicing the Way is absolutely unrelated with the Way. This is non-alternation, which is the extremity of alternation.

The third and fourth gatha lines contain a difficult subject we must study. They are not saying "The old crones in the row houses" "will call you by your native name," but saying "The old crones in the row houses will call you by your native name." In other words, the third and fourth lines aren't a combination of two independent ideas. It is one idea indivisible, sunyata-rupa, instead of sunyata and rupa. We must be extra careful not to divide one thing. Once divided, it cannot return to healthy perfect no matter how skillfully we join the parts. Training and realization shouldn't be divided in two.

"The old crones in the row houses" is phenomena or all beings, and it is another name of the Unsurpassed Way. If so, instead of saying it is the Unsurpassed Way, we had better call it by each of its names, such as mountain, river, grass, tree, tile, pebble, etc. We don't call each of them by their "native name." We call each of all phenomena by its individual name, and the True Form we call the True Form. A mountain is fine as a mountain, a river is fine to be called a river (= non-alternation).

"The old crones in the row houses will call you by your native name" is alternation as we can see also in the following thirty-one syllable poem by Dogen:

> The color of the peaks, the echoes of the valley,

all are the voice and figure of our Sakyamuni Buddha.

Thus the third and fourth lines of Nanyue's instantaneously-composed gatha are only repeating the meaning of the first and second lines, with a little more concrete figures.

In everyday talk, how could Nanyue spell out this sort of profound Buddhist truth? How he could is that he was daily practicing the Unsurpassed Way. In everyday talk, how could Matzu hear this sort of profound Buddhist truth? How he could is that he was daily practicing the Unsurpassed Way. So, Nanyue is Matzu, Matzu is Nanyue. For instance, when we say Nanyue, Matzu is hidden in Nanyue, and when we say Matzu, Nanyue is hidden in Matzu. We have no need to say "Nanyue and Matzu." "Nanyue" is sufficient, or "Matzu" is sufficient. Some households must say "he and she" (wife and husband) as if they are a good couple. It is very far from being a truly good couple. If a truly good couple, "he" or "she" is sufficient. From Buddha's side if we express it, Sakyamuni Buddha transmitted the Dharma to Sakyamuni Buddha. If expressed from Mahakasyapa's side, Mahakasyapa transmitted the Dharma to Mahakasyapa. This is the Buddhist transmission and the Buddhist realization. Buddhists see this transmission as the standard of how the relationship should be between people and any environment they are in.

How can we attain such a relationship and practice it all the time, or at least once in a while? Anything that appears with a devilish character we grab, squeeze, and cook until we find the throughway to this relationship. Anything appearing with human character we grab, squeeze, and cook until we find the throughway to this relationship. Anything appearing with Buddha character we grab, squeeze, and cook until we find the throughway to this relationship. This grabbing, squeezing, and cooking is the content of the transmission of true Buddhism and it is expressed as "practicing sitting meditation."

After receiving this transmission, Matzu was practicing such meditation day by day whether or not rainy, windy, or snowy.

This practice is beautifully described in Dogen's *Fukan zazen gi* (Recommendation for the protocol of sitting meditation):

Even now we can hear the resonance of the nine years of

facing the wall practiced by the transmission of Buddha's Heart Seal, in Shaulin.

This practice of sitting meditation is the core of Buddha's teaching and it is thoroughly studied by the episode "Nanyue's polishing a tile":

During the era of Kaiyuan there was a priest called Dauyi (that is, Great Teacher Matzu), who dwelled in Chuanhua Temple, and he was always practicing sitting meditation. The Teacher [Nanyue], understanding he was a Dharma talent, approached him and asked,

"Your Reverence, what are you hoping for by your practice of sitting meditation?"

Dauyi replied, "I am hoping to become Buddha."

Then the Teacher picked up a tile and began to polish it on a stone in front of the cottage.

Seeing this, at last Dauyi asked, "Your Reverence, what are you doing?"

The Teacher: "I am polishing a tile."

Dauyi: "What is the use of doing that?"

The Teacher said, "I am fashioning a mirror."

Dauyi: "By such polishing can we fashion a mirror?"

The Teacher: "By practicing sitting meditation can we become Buddha?"

Dauyi: "Then what is right?"

The Teacher: "It is like a person is riding on a cart. When the cart does not advance, is it right to whip the cart, or to whip the cow?"

Dauyi made no response.

The Teacher further said, "If you are studying sitting meditation, you are studying sitting Buddha. If you are going to study sitting meditation, meditation is beyond sitting or reclining. If you are going to study sitting Buddha, Buddha has no certain form because there is no preference in the Dharma of no dwelling. [This "because there is no preference in the Dharma of no dwelling" is a complementary phrase found only in *Chuandeng lu*.] If sitting Buddha is what you are, then you are killing Buddha. If you adhere to the form of sitting, you cannot reach the truth."

For Dauyi, hearing the teaching was like drinking lassi.[1]

He bowed and asked further, "How should I be to fit

with non-form samadhi?"

The Teacher said, "Your studying the Dharma of the field of the mind is like sowing seed, and my preaching the essence of the Dharma is like the benefits of heaven. When your indirect cause accords, you will see the Way."

Again Dauyi asked, "The Way is beyond color and form. How can I see it?"

The Teacher: "The person who sees the Way with the mind of forming and ruining and gathering and scattering does not see the Way. Listen to my gatha:

> The field of the mind contains all variety of seeds
> all of which sprout when they receive heavenly
> benefits.
> The flower of samadhi has no form,
> by any means it does not ruin and does not form.

Dauyi cleared up his ignorance and came to understand the Mind and his mind rose above the clouds. He attended the Teacher ten more years, deepening his understanding.

(Chuandeng lu, vol. 5)

The posthumous name of Matzu Dauyi is Daji ("great quietude"). This name already shows the meaning of the episode "Nanyue's polishing a tile." Now we will study in detail line by line:

> "Your Reverence, what are you hoping for by your practice of sitting meditation?"

Teacher Nanyue is respecting his disciple Matzu and addressing him as "Your Reverence."

In Nanyue's question, this word "hoping" is itself a word deeply dyed with worldly desire, which should be transcended by Buddhists. So we shouldn't understand the question in a worldly manner as if Nanyue were asking Matzu what he was lacking and wanting to gain. One of Dogen's disciples, Senne, interpreted Nanyue's question in his memoir *Okikigaki*:

> "What are you hoping for" is the same rhetoric appearing in Yaushan's episode: "What should we think when we meditate like a bald mountain?"

To Understand Matzu's "Sunface Buddha, Moonface Buddha"

This thinking is not our intellectual speculation. In the practice of sitting meditation there are the three virtues that are thought, the unthinkable, and nothing to do with thought. Thought means controlling our body, the unthinkable means controlling our mind, and nothing to do with thought means to enter Buddha's Way.

Upagupta at age fifteen attended the Third Patriarch, Sanavasin. At seventeen he left family.

> His Reverence asked, "Is your body going to leave family, or is your mind going to leave family?"
> Upagupta: "Truly my body is going to leave family."
> His Reverence: "How does the wonderful Dharma of all Buddhas bind body and mind?"
> Upagupta then came to the great realization. He became the Fourth Patriarch.
> (*Denko roku*, vol. 1 [Transmission of the Light])

Upagupta determined to control his body first (and in the next stage control his mind). But suddenly he came to greatly realize his body and mind were shedding themselves.

So "What are you hoping for" means "thinking the unthinkable" and is "nothing to do with thought." With this annotation we must quietly understand Nanyue's question, understand through our body, through our mind, and in our practice, which is beyond thought.

When we practice "sitting meditation" there is no better "thought" (life) than practicing "sitting meditation." Therefore meditating with some hope, however great it might be, isn't true Buddhist meditation. There is no better thought outside the practice of "sitting meditation." Practicing "sitting meditation" is also "thinking the unthinkable" and also "nothing to do with thought." Practicing "sitting meditation" has these three virtues. "What are you hoping for?" is rhetoric to express 1) the three virtues come simultaneously and 2) yet each is an entire independent totality. So when engaging in any one of them, you are fulfilling the two others.

> Dauyi replied, "I am hoping to become Buddha."

As we already studied, "hoping" is "thought" and in this "thought" there are the two other virtues. The wisdom of Manjusri is "thought." The compassion of Samantabhadra is "thinking the unthinkable." Both fully combined is Buddha and is "nothing to do with thought." Dauyi (Matzu) responded that he was hoping to become this Buddha. When we practice sitting meditation we are hoping to become Buddha. It means practicing sitting meditation is (becoming) Buddha.

This practice of sitting meditation is practice and not simply mental activity. It is the life of Buddhism, our true life. So it is said:

> Sitting erect in the ring of purity,
> not moving so little as an inch,
> even for the duration of
> three-thousand-particles-of-dust kalpas. (*Hungjy lu*)

The patriarchs who thus understood their life could establish their peace instead of fearing their death. This establishing of peace is "I have taken refuge in Buddha, Dharma, and Sangha." Dogen expressed the same establishing in the following way:

> Preaching the Dharma and listening to the Dharma, body after body, life after life, means listening to the Dharma generation after generation. It means, anew in this generation listening to the Dharma, which formerly was rightly transmitted. Because we are born in the Dharma and die in the Dharma, we listen to the Dharma life after life and practice body after body by rightly transmitting the Dharma in all ten directions. Because we perfect the Dharma with our life, life after life, and perfect the Dharma with our body, body after body, we grasp both dust and the Dharma world and make both dust and the Dharma world realize the Dharma.
>
> (*Jisho zanmai* [Samadhi in self-realization])

This is "I have taken refuge in the Dharma," which is Unsurpassed Bodhi.

> When one is a person of Unsurpassed Bodhi, one is called Buddha. When Buddha is Unsurpassed Bodhi, it is called Unsurpassed Bodhi.
>
> (*Yuibutsu yobutsu* [Buddha to Buddha])

Here there are "I have taken refuge in Buddha," "I have taken refuge in the Dharma," and also "I have taken refuge in the Sangha." In Buddhism, understanding theology means to practice this virtue of the Three Treasures. The meaning of "hoping (to become Buddha)" is to practice the Three Treasures.

"To become Buddha" means to be made into Buddha by Buddha. It is so because we ignorant human beings can't make ourselves into Buddha. We may think we can make ourselves into Buddha, or that we can "become Buddha" by taking refuge in or paying homage to the Three Treasures, or by practicing "sitting meditation." But come to think of it, while we are behaving as humans, we have no way to take refuge in or pay homage to the Three Treasures or to practice sitting meditation. While we are human we will do everything other than this conduct. No human being can practice "sitting meditation." Only after we shed our human selves can we practice "sitting meditation." So it means only Buddha can practice "sitting meditation," only Buddha can make Buddha, only Buddha is able "to become Buddha."

Only Buddha can make Buddha. This is the Buddhist formula, equation, for the relationship between cause and effect. A sculptor is unquestionably a human being who can make Buddha by carving wood. A true Buddhist, who isn't a human being but is Buddha, can't make Buddha out of wood, because wood is already Buddha. A true Buddhist can only make Buddha out of Buddha.

We are already Buddha, but if we don't raise Bodhi mind, practice, come to an awareness of the realization, and accomplish Nirvana, we can't become Buddha. The time when we engage in one of these four Buddha deeds is called the season Buddha meets Buddha. This is paying homage to Buddha, or taking refuge in Buddha.

> 1) Being made into Buddha by Buddha
> = the seeds for becoming Buddha appear from causation
> = think the unthinkable.
>
> 2) To become Buddha or to make Buddha
> = causation appears from the seeds of Buddha
> = thinking is the unthinkable.

This 1) and 2) look like two different things. Actually they are one. In our meditation these two aspects are simultaneously satisfied. Moreover, our meditation by not adhering to either of them is satisfying the third virtue, "nothing to do with thought." In Matzu's response "hoping to become Buddha" there are as much as the three virtues, yet none of them is taking over in a fixed way. Each is "paying homage to Buddha," so they are entangled, hard to be discerned from one another. This is the positive meaning of the expression "entangled ivy and wisteria."

Now we understand practicing sitting meditation is to become Buddha, or Buddha is practicing sitting meditation. We also understand Buddhist cause perfectly equals Buddhist effect. Living with this understanding of causation or paying homage to Buddha is to keep the First Primary Precept, Not killing:

> Life cannot be killed: Buddha's seed keeps increasing.
> The life of Buddha's wisdom should be continued, so do not kill life. (*Kyoju kaimon*)

"Do not kill life" means to know Buddha nature, which is always existing through past, present, and future. "Keeps increasing" shouldn't be understood as change in relative volume or value. When we understand such life as cannot be killed, for the first time we can transcend our problem of life-death:

> Free and forget body and mind. Cast them into Buddha's house and let Buddha act. Follow his act, then with no use of force, no exertion of mind, you will graduate from life-death and become Buddha. (*Shoji* [Life-death])

This is the total meaning of Matzu's answer "I am hoping to become Buddha" to Nanyue's question "What are you hoping for by your practice of sitting meditation?"

> Then the Teacher picked up a tile and began to polish it on a stone in front of the cottage.
> Seeing this, at last Dauyi asked, "Your Reverence, what are you doing?"
> The Teacher: "I am polishing a tile."
> Dauyi: "What is the use of doing that?"
> The Teacher: "I am fashioning a mirror."
> Dauyi: "By such polishing can we fashion a mirror?"
> The Teacher: "By practicing sitting meditation can we become Buddha?"
> Dauyi: "Then what is right?"

To Understand Matzu's "Sunface Buddha, Moonface Buddha" 129

It seems Nanyue is recommending to Matzu (Dauyi) that he practice mental rather than physical meditation because physical meditation is only troublesome with no good effect to become Buddha. However, that would be an incorrect and shallow reading. Buddhism doesn't divide mind and body, and further, Buddhism doesn't divide a person and a person's environment, nor divide training and realization.

> When we view the world of training with awakened eyes, no shadow enters our eyes, so even if we endeavor to see any shadow, there is not, not even white clouds a million miles away.
> When we lift our training feet to walk up the stairway of realization, no dust adheres to our feet. So when we walk, the earth is infinitely apart from heaven.
>
> (*Gakudo yojin shu* [Advice on studying the Way], entry
> The Buddhist way to enter the Realization is by practice.)

Cross-legged sitting meditation is the noblest posture for Buddhists. (So too is hands joined flat on the chest in standing meditation; so too is reclining with head north, face west; so too is walking, regularly alternating feet, eyes lowered to see the ground six paces forward.) Only cross-legged sitting meditation can transcend the utmost teachings of Buddha and the patriarchs.

Cross-legged sitting meditation is Taking Refuge in Buddha, offering one's entire body and mind to Buddha. Cross-legged sitting meditation is also to keep up the Sixth Primary Precept, Not speaking of faults:

> *Kyoju kaimon*: In Buddha's Dharma there is the one same Way, same Dharma, same Realization, same Practice. Make no one speak of faults, no one disturb the Way.

Anya-tirthyas seek only their own profit. Therefore their cross-legged sitting meditation is only speaking of others' faults and disturbing the Way. Great Bodhisattvas practice sitting meditation for the sake of practicing their great compassion, not for their own sake. Dogen describes beautifully the world of our meditation:

> When one even temporarily stamps Buddha's seal on one's body, mouth, and mind [Three Karmas] and sits serene in samadhi, all the Dharma world becomes Buddha's

seal and all vastness is realization. Hence all Buddhas, or Tathagatas, increase their primordial Dharma enjoyment and renew the solemnity of the path of realization.

(*Bendo wa* [Essay on studying the Way])

Dogen here says one person even temporarily meditating has the power to characterize the vast and abstract Dharma world as a physical, enjoyable, serene world. "Buddha's seal" means awesome concrete form, and "Dharma" of "Dharma enjoyment" is an adjective usage of "Dharma," meaning "wonderful," "orderly," or even "Buddha-like."

Here after all Dogen is saying training and realization are one. When we say "realization" there isn't "training," when we say "training" there isn't "realization." When we say "tile" there isn't "mirror," when we say "mirror" there isn't "tile." Matzu is The Treasure Repository Housing the Eye to See the Right Dharma. When we say The Treasure Repository Housing the Eye to See the Right Dharma, there is no Matzu. So when we practice cross-legged sitting meditation, there isn't (becoming) Buddha, and when there is (becoming) Buddha, there isn't cross-legged sitting meditation. Matzu and (becoming) Buddha aren't two things, they are truly intimate. This intimacy is expressed as "fashioning a mirror (by polishing a tile)."

"Tile" is Matzu's life, "mirror" is (becoming) Buddha. So there is no mirror without tile, mirror is tile. When we say Matzu, there isn't (becoming) Buddha. When we say (becoming) Buddha, there isn't Matzu. So when (polishing) a tile becomes a mirror, we say Matzu becomes Buddha. Then are there two? Not two, merely different names for the same thing. The time Matzu becomes Buddha is when Matzu becomes Matzu. The time Matzu becomes Matzu is when tile becomes tile.

This relationship between "'polishing a tile' and 'fashioning a mirror'" and between "'Matzu' and 'becoming Buddha'" are the same as the relationship between "'Not Falling into Causation' and 'Causation is inevitable'" developed by Baijang's Wild Fox episode.

"Not Falling into Causation" is transcending the law of causation. "Causation is inevitable" is severe evidence of the law of causation. Polishing a tile is cause, fashioning a mirror is effect. Between there isn't a nano-second or a micro space,

just as there's no gap between cause and effect. Matzu is cause; (becoming) Buddha is effect. This is alternation.
 The same must be studied from non-alternation. Matzu is cause; (becoming) Buddha is effect. $3 \times 3 = 9$. And yet, $9 = 9$. Cause is 9 and effect too is 9. So $3 \times 3 = 9$ means only 9 becomes 9. Matzu himself is (becoming) Buddha; (becoming) Buddha itself is Matzu. It means Matzu becomes Matzu, or (becoming) Buddha becomes Buddha. Here there is no causation. It is "Not Falling into Causation." It means not being effected by causation. It means not following causation. Small 3×3 doesn't become a bigger thing. 3×3 becomes only the same value, 9. It isn't following causation, for 3×3 becomes only $3 \times 3 = 9$ becomes only 9; tile becomes only tile, mirror becomes only mirror, and there, there's only transcending causation. It is odd even to say "becomes." Causation isn't applicable. So we say, transcending. This transcending is called "Not Falling into Causation." This is non-alternation.

 Seeing this, at last Dauyi asked, "Your Reverence, what are you doing?"

 "What" here is the same as "what" in "What should we think when we meditate like a bald mountain?" and in "What are you hoping for by your practice of sitting meditation?"

 Buddha's Dharma is "What is this 'thus come'?" Manifestation or coming to real existence of "no self nature" is expressed by Dauyi as "what are you doing?" When we lean rightward, there is the "self nature" of being "right side," when we lean left, there is the "self nature" of being "left side." When we say "female," there is the nature of being "female," when we say "male," there is nature of being "male." Instead of saying a female "person" or a male "person," if we say a "person," there will be no particular nature of either male or female. Whenever there is self nature, there will be a contrasting nature. When there is a contrasting nature, we won't be free, because we will be bound by the nature of contrast. When we kill our own individual nature, Buddha for the first time will appear.

 When Buddha nature appears in an individual, that individual is to the full extent an individual. Now, "what are you doing?" is no self nature. So "what are you doing" can become "thought," can become "think the unthinkable," can become "nothing to do with thought." When we polish a tile, a tile can become a mirror. Also, when we polish a tile, a tile can become a tile.

> When all dharmas are Buddha's Dharma, there is delusion and realization, there is training, there is life, there is death, there are all Buddhas, and there are sentient beings.
> (*Genjo koan*)

This is thought (abundance).

> When there are no million dharmas with us, there is no delusion, no realization, there are no Buddhas, no sentient beings, and no life and no death. (Ibid.)

This is the unthinkable (poverty). It is the world of True Form. When the total reality including all nature and human affairs throughout all time past, present, and future is, as Dogen is saying, not "with us," it means they are not ours. The meaning of "the unthinkable" ends up the same as the meaning of "thought." But by going through this poverty, abundance now appears as different from what it was as mere abundance.

> Buddha's Way from the beginning transcends abundance and poverty. (Ibid.)

Here, with "transcends," Dogen is destroying the base of recognition relating to being and non-being, or eternal existence and the extinction of existence (denial of the value of the epistemology of ontology). Because all things have no self nature, they can become anything, they can transcend both abundance and poverty. This is expressed as "what are you doing?"

> Let a million dharmas exist upon the Realization, and practice One Suchness upon the path of departure. When each dharma and realization are shed and transcend the border, minor principles and particulars are irrelevant.
> (*Bendo wa*)

This "are shed and transcend the border" is "what are you doing?" It is the totality of Buddha's Dharma, and this totality is cross-legged sitting meditation, and it is the tile. Therefore "polishing a tile" is "what are you doing?" In Matzu's thus asking, Matzu's meaning is the positive statement "Your

To Understand Matzu's "Sunface Buddha, Moonface Buddha"   133

Reverence is in the midst of doing what."
Seeing "polishing a tile" in this manner is the way all patriarchs see. They all know how to fashion a mirror by polishing a tile. Even in having meals they aren't simply having meals, they are practicing "what are you doing?"

>By the first spoonful sever all evil.
>By the second spoonful do all good.
>By the third spoonful help all sentient beings.
>By all spoonfuls attain Buddha's Way.
>
>>(Gatha of Three spoonfuls,"*Zenrin Nikka*
>>[Zen Monastery Manual])

The behavior of the patriarchs is far beyond the understanding of ordinary people. They are so in their donning robes, having meals, using the washroom, talking and meeting, in all use of their six senses.

>a tile being polished becomes a mirror
>= thought = alternation
>
>a tile being polished becomes a tile
>= the unthinkable= non-alternation
>
>= what are you doing?
>= it has nothing to do with thought

In "what are you doing?" there is the truth of thought and also the truth of the unthinkable. Simultaneously there are two contradictory truths. Therefore "it has nothing to do with thought" and it is "what are you doing?" All these truths are universal whether in Sakyamuni Buddha's Saha World, or in the East World of Medicine Buddha, or in the South World of Excellent Treasure Buddha, or in the West World of Amita, or in the North World of Sakyamuni Buddha the Fearless Tathagata. It means all these truths are presented by one Buddha. This phenomenon exists in every household, village, town, in every social unit. The name could be different, but the content is the same "what are you doing?" and "nothing to do with thought."

>think the unthinkable = Dharma-kaya
>thought is the unthinkable = Nirmana-kaya
>how to think the unthinkable = Sambhoga-kaya

These three are the Tathagata who is one but contains three bodies (kaya), and each is practicing sitting meditation, polishing a tile.

Confucius was also polishing a tile:

> The Teacher practiced four Do not's: Do not guess, Do not conclusively assume, Do not be obstinate, and Do not be selfish. (*Lunyu*, IX-4)

This "polishing a tile" is to decisively believe there is religious truth in every phenomenon not only to decisively understand that one's own view isn't a perfect view. In every phenomenon, in one's every doing, there is the great truth of polishing a tile. Great persons see a mountain and make it their body. Heavenly persons see water and think it is lapis lazuli, hungry ghosts see water as fire, whereas fish regard water as their home.

> The Teacher: "I am polishing a tile."
> Dauyi: "What is the use of doing that?"
> The Teacher: "I am fashioning a mirror."
> Dauyi: "By such polishing can we fashion a mirror?"
> The Teacher: "By practicing sitting meditation can we become Buddha?"
> Dauyi: "Then what is right?"

For Matzu's "Your Reverence, what are you doing?" Teacher Nanyue, responded "I am polishing a tile." We studied the meaning of Matzu's question. Therein were two truths, polishing a tile to fashion a mirror and polishing a mirror to fashion a tile.

> rupa is no different from sunyata
> = polishing a tile to fashion a mirror;
>
> sunyata is no different from rupa
> = polishing a mirror to fashion a tile

So,
> tile is mirror, and mirror is tile = alternation

However,
> Rupa is sunyata and sunyata is rupa. Rupa is rupa and sunyata is sunyata.
> (*Shobogenzo*, vol. 2: *Makahannyaharamitsu* [*Mahaprajnaparamita-sutra*])

Therefore,

> polishing a tile to fashion a tile, and polishing a mirror to fashion a mirror = non-alternation

When we combine this alternation and this non-alternation, it becomes "what are you doing?" Now put aside non-alternation. Focus on alternation. In the ordinary way of thinking, polishing a tile to fashion a mirror is by any means odd. A tile has no way to become a mirror. So, here the words we need are only "polishing."

Mere sitting on the floor doesn't become "polishing." Practicing cross-legged sitting is "polishing." It is to place right foot on left thigh and left foot on right thigh.

> This sort of study is done in case 1: Devil becoming Buddha. By grasping and defeating the devil in us we make ourselves Buddha; in case 2: Buddha becoming Buddha. By grasping Buddha in us and hoping to become Buddha we make ourselves Buddha; and in case 3: Person becoming Buddha. By grasping and training the person in us we make the person in us Buddha. We must study that in our very act of grasping there is a throughway. (*Sanjushippon bodaibunpo* [Thirty-seven divisions of highest wisdom])

"In our very act of grasping there is a throughway." When we grasp our ego and sever the root of our thought, we can defeat our own mind. Then our entire self becomes Buddha. For this phenomenon the sutra says "Indeed there is no place to dwell, yet the mind rises." We must grasp our thought and emotion. We must grasp our Buddha also. We are primordially Dharma-kaya, we are innately Buddha. Then why should we train? The balance of being innately Buddha and practicing our own training is the "throughway." We must become Buddha because we are innately Buddha, and we must practice Buddha's deeds. "Defeating the devil" is describing our polishing a tile and fashioning a mirror.

Nanyue said "I am fashioning a mirror." His very act of polishing is fashioning a mirror. So we must understand there is no "mirror" outside "polishing." It means there is no (becoming) Buddha outside of cross-legged sitting meditation. This time, place, and our action is described in the following manner by Dogen:

> Now make human skin-flesh-bone-marrow full cross-legged posture, and in so doing make king-of-samadhi full cross-legged posture. This is the season wherein Buddha sees Buddha, the very time sentient beings become Buddha.
> (*Sanmai o sanmai* [Samadhi among samadhis])

The days of practicing our polishing are here called "season."

The act of polishing, or practicing cross-legged sitting meditation, is itself called "mirror" and this mirror isn't the achievement after polishing or after meditating. Polishing is mirror. It doesn't mean when we polish a material called "tile" it can become a mirror. It is a metaphor for a truth polishing itself is Buddha, or it is a metaphor for the greatness and deep meaning of "grasping." There are many ways of "grasping."

> Once there was an old woman who for twenty years had been serving the master of a hermitage. She always had a maiden deliver and serve his meals to him.
> One day she made the maiden embrace him and ask him how he felt being embraced.
> The master said, "A dead tree devoid of warmth the last three winters leaning by a cold cave." The maiden reported this to the old woman, whereupon the old woman said, "Twenty years I have been serving this worldly man!" She then chased him away and burnt down his hermitage.
> (*Wudeng hueiyuan*, vol. 6)

The master said "A dead tree devoid of warmth the last three winters leaning by a cold cave." In the Three Inclusive Vows, the first is:

> Do no evil. *Kyoju kaimon*: Do no evil is the cave and the root of the Dharma of all Buddhas.

It means to see all of oneself and one's environment as sunyata. This master of a hermitage was practicing to see the metabolism of his life, the old woman's life, the maiden's life, and all surrounding lives with the eyes transcending perception and thought, that is, he was practicing to see them with Buddha's eyes. There are Dogen's poems describing the vow Do no evil:

> The red dust from the worldly world does not drift
> into the thatched hut on a snowy night

> in the deep mountains.
> The moon cannot be a companion of this mountain
>   dweller,
> fated as it is to call upon the worldly world.
> I will not approach the creek to see my image reflected,
> for the creek flows down to appear in the worldly world.

With this thorough perfection of Do no evil, the master left the hermitage without grudge or excuse, left as if nothing was the matter. He went on to Inclusive Vow 2: Do all good.

> Seeking no thanks or reward, we share our power and are driven only by beneficial acts.
> (*Bodaisatta shishoho* [A Bodhisattva's Four Embracings])

In the state "devoid of warmth the last three winters," it is possible to be beneficial to others without seeking reward. First of all in this episode we must see the master's profound power to exist in such a state. It is the power of his last twenty years' polishing. This power to turn the practice Do no evil to Do all good is clearly shown by the Sixth Patriarch, Dajian Hueineng:

> By nature Bodhi has no tree,
> Bright mirror has no stand.
> Buddha nature is ever pure.
> No place for dust to land.

The Sixth Patriarch destroyed both the Bo tree and the mirror. With that power he could enter either Buddha or Devil. If we are insufficient in polishing, even if we are able to enter Buddha, we are incapable of entering Devil. If insufficient in polishing, we won't act anywhere other than where the sun shines.

> When we intellectually understand Bodhi as Bodhi, we are bound by our intellectual understanding.
> (*Gyo butsuyigi* [To practice Buddha's deeds])

This is the fault of intellectual understanding. Intellectual understanding divides one thing into dual values and tries to take only the good part. We have to study the Third Primary Precept, Not having incorrect sex:

> Because the Three Wheels are pure, there is nothing to be hoped for. All Buddhas go the same way. (*Kyoju kaimon*)

In the annotations *Shobogenzo sho* it is said:

The Three Wheels are body, mouth, and mind, or greed, wrath, and ignorance. These should be pure. Although the word "pure" is used here, it should by no means be understood to equal lower-level pure. This pure is also different from pure as used by Bodhisattvas, Sravakas, Pratyeka-Buddhas, Celestials, and human beings. Hence this is Buddha's fruit. You must understand not attaching to purity is pure.

After all, "polishing" means to kill one's own ego. With this training of killing our ego we can enter either Buddha's world or Devil's world according to our situation. With this power we can on any occasion express words equal in value to Buddha and the patriarchs. The power of polishing a tile, of practicing cross-legged sitting meditation, creates the words that can dislodge a person from a stuck situation. The power of practicing cross-legged sitting meditation appears through our body, mouth, and mind. So, sitting meditation is no different from (becoming) Buddha, and (becoming) Buddha is no different from sitting meditation. Sitting meditation is (becoming) Buddha, and (becoming) Buddha is sitting meditation. Therefore sitting meditation is sitting meditation and (becoming) Buddha is (becoming) Buddha. Polishing a tile is polishing a tile. In all the world of heaven and earth there is only polishing a tile. There is no fashioning a mirror there. The essence of Buddhist life is to pour our energy into what appears to be socially useless affairs.

Dauyi: "By such polishing can we fashion a mirror?"

Hereafter, non-alternation is the focus. Non-alternation distinguishes differences and rank. But these discriminations produce no complaints because they are surely backed up by alternation, which is sameness. So, polishing a tile is polishing a tile and there's no problem in being a tile. This is the meaning of "being dissatisfied" in the episode wherein Huangbo studies from an old woman:

> Later he visited Shangdu, and there he parted from the group. He came to the gate of a house and asked for an offering of lunch. From behind the wall, an old woman said, "Your Reverence is greatly dissatisfied." Hearing this, and detecting some deep meaning, he asked, "I am not yet given lunch, why do you accuse me of being dissatisfied?"

To Understand Matzu's "Sunface Buddha, Moonface Buddha"   139

> The old woman said, "Just being like you, isn't it dissatisfaction?" Hearing and considering this, he smiled.
> The old woman at the sight of his abnormally tall and stately figure invited him in and gave him lunch. When he finished, she sincerely asked about his training career. He couldn't conceal and told her. The old woman resumed her talk and in a whisper taught him the Wonderful Dharma. He then instantly understood the profound gateway and he widely opened up and he doubly thanked her and he wished to inherit her Dharma teaching.
> The old woman said, "I am a body of five obstacles, not a Dharma talent. I have heard of a great teacher, Baijang, in Jiangshi, who is an excellent carpenter in the Dhyana forest and supreme among the peaks. You had better visit him and inherit from him. My only wish is that in the future you will become teacher of heaven and the human world and that you will not slight the Dharma." Later it was said when young she studied from National Teacher Nanyang.
> <div align="right">(<i>Tzutang ji</i>, vol. 16)</div>

Huangbo understood her words "Just being like you, isn't it dissatisfaction?" He must have been the tile, a perfect stately figure. Yet he voluntarily wanted to train himself tirelessly and endlessly. So she commented "Just being like you, isn't it dissatisfaction?" Her power was to detect Huangbo's positive dissatisfaction. Huangbo was a perfect stately figure, such as to be called "an iron man" in the Zen records. He had no shortage, so he had no need of borrowing the power of others. He was "In all the world of heaven and earth I alone am respectable."

So too was Matzu (Dauyi). He said "By such polishing can we fashion a mirror?" It means he had no need of becoming a mirror. He had no complaint being a tile. He is a perfect tile and will continue to practice being a tile. And this continuing to practice is being a mirror. In short, it isn't that the tile first should be polished for a certain time duration and finally becomes a mirror. It is that the tile by being a tile is already simultaneously a mirror. This mechanism carries the positive sense of such sayings as "Mistake upon mistake," "Seeing the master and regarding him as the master," "Seeing a thief and regarding him as a thief," and "Seeing a child and regarding the child as a child."

> The Teacher: "By practicing sitting meditation can we become Buddha?"

Here Nanyue is stating that practicing sitting meditation isn't for the purpose of becoming Buddha. Tile is tile, mirror is mirror. So practicing sitting meditation is practicing sitting meditation, and becoming Buddha is becoming Buddha. Because practicing sitting meditation is becoming Buddha, practicing sitting meditation and becoming Buddha needn't alternate. Practicing sitting meditation and becoming Buddha are in the most intimate relation. Therefore practicing sitting meditation rejects becoming Buddha, and becoming Buddha rejects sitting meditation. An old Chinese proverb describes how a saloon madam must act: "Courtesy to the first comer, rejection of the frequent comer." A more important way of understanding than this old proverb is Dogen's declaration:

> There is totality in Mt. Sumeru and totality in a mustard seed.
> (*Gyoji* [Keeping up the priestly acts]).

Both are the True Human Body in all the ten directions. It is sad if a frog swells its belly in competition with a cow. A mustard seed doesn't compete with Mt. Everest. Father is father, son is son, rank and order distinguished. Sitting meditation has no outrageous desire to become Buddha. Sitting meditation and becoming Buddha are absolutely unrelated. This is Lungshan's white cloud:

> The white cloud is around all day long,
> though the green mountain doesn't know it at all.

Therefore we shouldn't be so foolish as to respect only what is far away and slight what is near. There was a guy called Yegung Tzygau in the BC age who loved dragons and collected paintings and sculptures of them. A heavenly dragon heard tell of this and thought there would be a welcome by visiting him. So the dragon came down to earth and peered in the window. Yegung noticed and jumped in surprise and lost his function of memory. Respecting becoming Buddha and slighting practicing meditation and being told that practicing meditation is indeed to become Buddha, one such as Yegung will jump in surprise and lose even memory function.

> Non-alternation = turning illusion to illusion, and turning realization to realization.
>
> Alternation = turning illusion to realization, and turning realization to illusion.

To Understand Matzu's "Sunface Buddha, Moonface Buddha"

So, in non-alternation,

> Realization upon realization, and illusion upon illusion.

But we needn't say "polishing a tile is polishing a tile," or "fashioning a mirror is fashioning a mirror." "Polishing a tile" or "fashioning a mirror" is sufficient. This is the meaning of Matzu's following words,

> Dauyi: "Then what is right?"

Matzu Dauyi's words seem a question, but actually it's a positive statement meaning "Whatever is right." In other words, he is expressing "becoming Buddha," "fashioning a mirror," or "thinking the unthinkable" while expressing "practicing meditation," "polishing a tile," or "thinking." Whenever we talk about sunyata, we are inevitably talking about rupa. When we talk about our life-death, "the life of no birth" is always backing it up. When we say "death," "the death of no death" is always backing it up. They shouldn't be separately observed, because the truth is that the eternal life throughout the past, present, and future keeps repeating life and death.

"The Realization" of "Let a million dharmas exist upon the Realization" is True Form (which is the life that doesn't die, which is the Dharma existing always throughout the past, present, and future). The eternal Dharma is making a million dharmas possible to exist. One of a million dharmas is our life, our death. This inevitable nature is like the relationship between wave and water. When we say right foot there is always left thigh. So, thinking is okay, and not thinking (= the unthinkable) is also okay. Because this thinking is transcending both wealth and poverty, it can become either thinking or not thinking, and therefore either is okay. And yet, it is never only one of them at a time. Phenomena always become substance, and yet substance is always in phenomena. Life is the life of no birth, death is the death of no death, and when the totality of both is fully acting, life and death are transcended. Because life and death are transcended, it is expressed as "Then what is right?"

> "But the flowers are soon gone" = poverty
> "To our annoyance the grasses increase" = abundance
> "Buddha's Way from the beginning transcends abundance and poverty."

Therefore Matzu's "Then what is right?" carries the same sense as his previous words "Teacher, what are you doing?" Practicing sitting meditation and becoming Buddha are intimate friends. When intimate friends meet, which is which is hard to distinguish.

Tsyming [Shyshuang Chuyuan, also known as Tsyming, 987-1040] moved to Dawu, and then to Shyshuang. Yangchi followed and helped him by tending to the temple affairs.

Though thus spending many years, Yangchi could not come to the realization...[here Seikan's abbreviation].

Whenever he had surplus time amid the temple affairs, he kept asking his teacher.

Tsyming said, "You must be busy in the office, go back. In the future your disciples will spread throughout the world. What is the use of caring [about the Way] at a busy time?" So saying, Tsyming went down to have tea with an old woman acquaintance at the mountain foot.

There came a sudden rain shower. On the narrow path Yangchi secretly waited for Tsyming. When he appeared, Yangchi said, "Old Man, today you must explain about the Dharma to me or I will beat you."

Tsyming said, "If you understand that much, you should be at ease."

Yangchi worshipfully prostrated himself on the mud and asked, "What should I do when I meet you on narrow path?"

Tsyming replied, "Move aside! I must go there."

(*Shyu-Chuandeng lu*, vol. 7)

"What should I do when I meet you on narrow path?" is the intimate meeting of "the temple affairs" with Unsurpassed Bodhi on a narrow path. So Yangchi's question "What should I do" is a positive statement: "When the temple affairs and Unsurpassed Bodhi meet on a narrow path, they are what."

Tsyming: "Move aside! I must go there."

The "temple affairs" are coming out from this "there." Martha's cooked meals should be coming out from Mary's "good part" (cf. Luke 10). Any people however they estimate they are worthless are each coming forth from Buddha nature.

How wonderful! All sentient beings without exception possess the Tathagata's wisdom and virtue. One Buddha is all sentient beings, and when such a Buddha sees the Dharma world, all sentient and insentient beings are together simultaneously sentient beings. (Avatamsaka Sutra)

In Linji's words, each of us is "the true man of no rank." What we lack is only our believing we are as Linji said.

What made Yangchi speak "Old Man, today you must explain about the Dharma to me or I will beat you"? What is the vigor to seek the Dharma? The temple affairs and Unsurpassed Bodhi are really intimate friends. We must notice this intimate relationship in whatever we do in daily life. When we become aware of this relationship, we are able to prostrate ourselves the same as Yangchi, who "worshipfully prostrated himself on the mud." Then, when it is Unsurpassed Bodhi there are no temple affairs, and when it is temple affairs there is no Unsurpassed Bodhi. So it becomes "Move aside! I must go there."

Becoming Buddha is the intimate friend of practicing sitting meditation, and practicing sitting meditation is the intimate friend of becoming Buddha. This is the relationship between our body and our mind.

> The thing comes to the mind, and the mind goes to the thing. (*Tenzo kyokun* [Kitchen officers' principles])

Therefore it is "Then what is right?"

> We must know we establish our training in the illusion and obtain the evidence before our realization. Then for the first time we will know yesterday's dream, which was a boat and a raft, and we will forever extinguish such an old view as wisteria and snake. This is not because of Buddha forcing us. It is due to the turning around and around of the function. Naturally what our training invites is the evidence. One's own treasure does not come from outside. What the evidence uses is the training. Why does the activity of our mind not freely move both ways?
> When we view the world of training with awakened eyes, no shadow enters our eyes, so even if we endeavor to see any shadow, there is not, not even white clouds a million miles away.
> When we lift our training feet to walk up the stairway of evidence, no dust adheres to our feet. So when we walk, the earth is infinitely apart from heaven. Here by withdrawing we leap into Buddha's land.
>   (*Gakudo yojin shu* [Advice on studying the Way], entry:
>   Buddhists should always enter the evidence by their practice)

"Our training" invites "the evidence" is "our practicing

sitting meditation" invites "(becoming) Buddha." But when one side surfaces, the other is hidden. So when the evidence surfaces, the training disappears like "not even white clouds a million miles away"; and when the training surfaces, the evidence disappears, as is said, "the earth is infinitely apart from heaven." Then when both training and evidence are transcended, it will be "nothing to do with thought" or "Here by withdrawing, we leap into Buddha's land."

It can therefore be said,

> When all dharmas are Buddha's Dharma, there is delusion and realization, there is training, there is life, there is death, there are all Buddhas, and there are sentient beings.
> (*Genjo koan*)

And also it can be said,

> When there are no million dharmas with us, there is no delusion, and no realization, and there are no Buddhas, no sentient beings, and no life and no death. (Ibid.)

The same is expressed in the Brahma's Net Sutra (*Brahmajala-sutra*):

> When our body and mind speak false words, we say we see when we do not see, and we say we do not see when we see.

The whole world in the ten directions is called "speak false words," in contrast to the world of thinking the unthinkable, which is "not speaking false words."

> Nanyue: "It is like a person is riding on a cart. When the cart does not advance, is it right to whip the cart, or to whip the cow?"

Here rupa, which is "tile," is expressed as "whip the cart," and "mirror" espressed as "whip the cow." Now, the relationship between "whip the cart" and "whip the cow" is such that "whip the cart" isn't different from "whip the cow," and "whip the cow" isn't different from "whip the cart." "To whip the cart" is "to whip the cow," and "to whip the cow" is "to whip the cart." In such case, "to whip the cart" is "to whip the cart," and "to whip the cow" is "to whip the cow." So it is unnecessary to say "to whip the cart" is "to whip the cart" for it would become redundant. Thus we will say "whip the cart" is right, and likewise "whip the cow" is right.

More, there is always the cart does not advance, backed by the cart does advance. This "does not advance" is the Dharma, which is forever existing throughout past, present, and future. Because of forever existing, it is said "does not advance." This is our true life.

> The Way as its nature is perfectly open; why should we depend on our training to bring forth the evidence? The vehicle of the religious truth is free; of what need is endeavor? Moreover, the totality is far beyond all dust; why should we believe we must keep cleaning? The totality is not apart from here; of what use are the legs of the mendicant trainee?
> (*Fukan zazengi* [Recommended protocol for sitting meditation])

This "Way," or "the totality," is "True Form." Therefore it doesn't "depend on our training to bring forth the evidence." Both "training" and "the evidence" are other names for "The Way." Because they are one, neither depends on the other. Because "The Way as its nature is perfectly open," there is no need of "endeavor." "The Way" is "endeavor," so there is no need to endeavor.

Our body is the Unsurpassed Way. Therefore our body is fated to practice cross-legged sitting meditation (devoting our total life, body and mind, and living the life that transcends dualistic valuation). Practicing cross-legged sitting meditation is called the Unsurpassed Way. So there is no need of endeavor. This is said from the standpoint of True Form. It is the world of "no delusion, and no realization, and there are no Buddhas, no sentient beings, and no life and no death." This world is rhetorically mentioned as "one's original face before one's parents were born," or the world of the Sunyata King. This world is also called "the cart does not advance," or in another episode, "the water does not flow."

"The cart advances" or "the water flows" are the world of "thought" and "oneself, now, here." This is the world of "delusion and realization, there is training, there is life, there is death, there are all Buddhas, and there are sentient beings."

> Donning the robes and having meals is donning the robes and having the meals of Dharma nature samadhi. Dharma nature is manifested by the Dharma of donning the

robes, Dharma nature is manifested by the Dharma of having meals. In not donning the robes, not having meals, not talking, not confronting, not utilizing the six sense organs, in not acting by doing thus, there is no Dharma nature samadhi. (*Hossho* [Dharma nature])

This cart of Nanyue's "like a person is riding on a cart" is the cart pulled by the Great White Cow, not a cart pulled by goat or deer. (Source, *Sutralankara-sastra*, translated to Chinese by Kumarajiva, 350-409.) The cart pulled by the Great White Cow is the Dharma Flower (Lotus Flower), symbol of True Form. People are going to ride on this cart (Dharma). Therefore person and Dharma are one. Anyone riding on this cart means anyone practicing cross-legged sitting meditation, and cart pulled by the Great White Cow means to become Buddha. So, riding on this cart means "practicing sitting meditation is (becoming) Buddha" and "(becoming) Buddha is to practice sitting meditation"; that is, practicing sitting meditation and (becoming) Buddha are one.

Therefore Nanyue's words to Matzu "If you adhere to the form of sitting, you cannot reach the truth" doesn't mean if we are attached to sitting form we can't reach True Form, which is the Great White Cow pulling the cart.

> When the cart does not advance, is it right to whip the cart, or to whip the cow?"

This "When" is "If the time has come"

> If one would like to know Buddha nature, one had better know Buddha nature is the time, in other words, causation. "If the time has come" means "Already the time has come." There is no doubt about it.
> (*Bussho* [Buddha nature])

So, this "When" expresses time throughout past, present, and future. Therefore Nanyue's words "When the cart does not advance" isn't a conditional phrase, but a statement: "The cart already (primordially) does not advance."

Here we must correct our misunderstanding based on everyday common sense.

> "If you adhere to the form of sitting, you cannot reach the truth."

We misunderstand this saying to be "If we are possessed

by practicing sitting meditation, we cannot reach the truth, a tile cannot become a mirror however much we polish it, and we wrongly conclude we must practice mental meditation, which is intellectual thinking." Continuously we misinterpret this "When the cart does not advance" as "When Buddha's wisdom is not opened," and we conclude that whipping the cow (intellectual thinking) is better than whipping the cart (practicing physical meditation). We must know there is no way to whip the cow except by whipping the cart.

Koun Ejo (1198-1280) had been studying Yamato Zen (Linji lineage transmitted to Japan from China, briefly prospering in a narrow area called Yamato, now called Nara, where they studied Zen through koan study—episodes of former patriarchs on how they came to the realization). Now, Ejo had been studying from the Zen master Kakuan (details unknown). So he asked Dogen: "How about if we open Buddha's wisdom by studying the manuscripts while simultaneously practicing sitting meditation?" Dogen replied:

> We cannot understand Buddha's Dharma while with our mind we are figuring it out, even if a million kalpas and a thousand lives are spent. We can understand when we abandon our mind, when we abandon our intellectual views and understanding. Even "studying the mind and clarifying the mind, hearing the teachings, and realizing the Way" too is attained only through our body. Hence, if we thoroughly abandon our thought and intellectual views, and if we just practice sitting meditation, we can be intimate with the Way. Attaining the Way can thus be done through our body. So, regard sitting meditation and single-heartedly endeavor at it.
>
> (*Shobogenzo zuimonki* [Ejo's records of the Master's talks])

There are cases when we can open Buddha's wisdom by studying the manuscripts. But it isn't actually owing to our reading the manuscripts. The power of practicing sitting meditation is appearing on reading the manuscripts.

Yet if we abandon studying through our intelligence, we will end up studying through practicing sitting meditation because they are intimate friends. Anyway, this "When the cart does not advance" shouldn't be mistaken as the teaching of pointing out the fault of practicing sitting meditation.

The cart does not advance = the unthinkable

= right foot→ right foot on left thigh

= let a million dharmas exist upon the realization

= think the unthinkable = phenomena in True Form.

The cart advances = thought

= left foot → left foot on right thigh

= practice One Suchness upon the path of departure

= thought is the unthinkable = True Form in phenomena

"The cart advances" and "the cart does not advance" are Yaushan's "Think the unthinkable" and his answer to "How to think the unthinkable?"

When the Teacher [Yaushan] was sitting, a monk asked: "What should we think when we are singularly sitting?"

The Teacher: "Think the unthinkable."

The monk: "How to think the unthinkable?"

The Teacher: "Beyond thought."

(Chuandeng lu, vol. 14)

So, whichever, whatever, is okay. This is "It has nothing to do with thought." This "It has nothing to do with thought" is "When each dharma and realization are shed and transcend the border, minor principles and particulars are irrelevant" (*Bendo wa*). When we lose this harmony, we say "There is no grandma's kindness." So, whipping the cart is right and whipping the cow is also right.

Bald mountain-like cross-legged sitting meditation has those three virtues: thought, the unthinkable, and nothing to do with thought. The same can be said about the water flows and the cart advances, and the water does not flow and the cart does not advance.

Bald mountain is the pairs ① and 1., ② and 2., ③ and 3., etc.

To Understand Matzu's "Sunface Buddha, Moonface Buddha" 149

① Thought = ② sitting meditation = ③ polishing a tile= ④ sitting meditation = ⑤ cart advances

1. Unthinkable = 2. hoping to become Buddha
= 3. fashioning a mirror = 4. becoming Buddha
= 5. cart doesn't advance

= ⑥ whipping cart = ⑦ bridge flows
= ⑧ studying sitting meditation
= ⑨ studying sitting Buddha
= ⑩ studying sitting Buddha

= 6. Whipping cow = 7. water does not flow
= 8. studying sitting Buddha = 9. dhyana is not sitting
= 10. no certain form

= ⑪ Sitting Buddha = ⑫ attaching to sitting form
= ⑬ body's training

= 11. Killing Buddha = 12. does not reach the truth
= 13. the mind's evidence

"The cart does not advance" is backed by "the cart advances"—it isn't the absence of "the cart advances." To keep seeing this hidden "advances" contributes to form a humane Buddhist character.

"The cart does not advance" is no birth and no ruin = eternity. "The cart advances" is birth and ruin = transition. These two aspects are also expressing the relationship between "silence" and "reflection."

> Sitting coldly in absolute solitude at Shaulin,
> fully exposing the right order in deep silence.

This is "thought" and "the unthinkable"; and "right order" is cross-legged sitting meditation.

> In the clear autumn the moon turns the frost ring,
> the Milky Way is faint, and the Dipper offers down its night handle.
> (Hungjy's gatha, in *Tsungrung lu*, Case 2)

This is "It has nothing to do with thought." And "the Dipper offers down its night handle" is transmission of the Dharma.

In "the cart does not advance" there is the training of "the cart advances." So in "the cart advances," "the cart does not advance" is included.

"The juniper there in the garden" is the entire juniper, which has nothing that exists other than it. (in *Jaujou lu*, entry 12)

> "What is the meaning of the Patriarch's having come from the West?" (positive statement in question form) = "the cart does not advance."

> A monk asked Jaujou, "A million dharmas return to One. To where does One return?
> Jaujou replied, "When I was in Chinjou I made a hemp under-robe. It weighed seven pounds."
>
> (*Biyan lu*, Case 45)

"One" will be hidden in "a million" and "a million" will be hidden in "One." The size of "a million" is the size of the whole world, and the size of "One" is also the size of the whole world. They therefore don't appear at the same time. Shyuedou's gatha for this case tells us we should go beyond both One and a million:

> Now I have tossed it into Lake Sihu
> Returning downstream,
> with whom can I share the pleasant breeze?

"With whom," or an anonymous person, whoever has shed dualistic values, such a one can receive "the pleasant breeze."

When to use "the cart advances" and when to use "the cart does not advance" depends on timing.

> A dead tree remains beside a dreary forest,
> With no change of mind,
> though many springtimes come.
> (first half of gatha by Damei Fachang, 752-829)

"With no change of mind, though many springtimes come" doesn't mean Damei feels no joy at the coming of spring. He dons winter robes in winter, summer robes in summer, and enjoys spring and autumn. Going along with change of environment is here expressed as "With no change of mind, though many springtimes come." It is possible because our nature hasn't a fixed nature.

We can study Jyujy in *Biyan lu*, Case 19:

To Understand Matzu's "Sunface Buddha, Moonface Buddha" 151

> Thereafter, for every monk who came to study, Jyujy only raised one finger and preached in no other way... To his followers he said when he was going to pass from this world, "Ever since I received the dhyana of one finger from Tianlung, I have used it all my life and I have never used it up," and so saying, he died. (*Chuandeng lu*, vol. 11)

We shouldn't take his words literally. He didn't actually mean he raised one finger to whomever, to whatever question. His "one finger" means the Six Paramitas, and a million Buddhas' deeds. It means "Indeed there is no place to dwell, yet the mind rises."

> It is like a person is riding on a cart. When the cart does not advance, is it right to whip the cart, or to whip the cow?

Whipping the cart is right. Whipping the cow too is right. They are the same. But also they are not exactly the same. In the worldly world there is no Dharma of whipping the cart. In Buddhism there is the Dharma of whipping the cart. Studying this Dharma is the core of studying Buddhism.

Practicing sitting meditation is fine, and (becoming) Buddha too is fine. The name changes according to timing. Whipping the cart is fine, and whipping the cow is also fine. This truth is expressed as follows:

> Dauyi: "By such polishing can we fashion a mirror?"
> The Teacher: "By practicing sitting meditation can we become Buddha?"

This means "polishing a tile is polishing a tile," and "fashioning a mirror is fashioning a mirror." Both are the same, but the timing is different. The reason the tile doesn't fashion a mirror isn't that the tile is imperfect. The reason the tile doesn't fashion a mirror is that it's perfect.

There is the Dharma of whipping the cart and also the Dharma of whipping the cow. When whipping the cart there's no whipping the cow, and when whipping the cow, there's no whipping the cart. Body and mind are one. So there is the time that whipping the cart and whipping the cow are equal and also the time that they are not equal.

> There is primordially the training inseparable from the realization. We have fortunately already received the pure transmission of one segment of the Wonderful Training. The

initial study of the Way is a matter of naturally obtaining one segment of the True Realization. We must know that in order not to pollute the realization, which is inseparable from the training, Buddha and the Patriarchs frequently taught us that we should not relax our training. When we go beyond the Wonderful Training, the True Realization is brimful in our hands. When we come out from the True Realization, the Wonderful Training is practiced throughout our whole body. (*Bendo wa*)

"We have fortunately already received the pure transmission of one segment of the Wonderful Training": "Wonderful training" is an abbreviation of "True Realization-Wonderful Training." It means "The training that is being practiced because of the evidence, or realization." If there is hardship as a Buddhist trainee, it is the evidence that the trainee is amid the realization. "One segment" is "the totality" because the Buddhist unit of measurement is always endless.

"We must know that in order not to pollute the realization, which is inseparable from the training, Buddha and the patriarchs frequently taught us that we should not relax our training": This "not to pollute" is defined in the following episode:

> The Sixth Patriarch asked Zen Teacher Dahuei, "Is there the need of training to practice the realization?"
> Dahuei replied, "There may very well be the need of training to practice the realization, but practice and the realization should not be polluted."
> The Sixth Patriarch said, "This non-pollution is the concern kept up by all Buddhas. You must also do likewise. I also do likewise." (*Senjo* [Purification]) [2]

"When we go beyond the Wonderful Training, the True Realization is brimful in our hands": The Wonderful Training is the training practiced in the True Realization. Yet, if we go beyond being conscious of this training, the True Realization will be brimful inside and outside our body. This is the stage, describing psychologically, that we are loving to train. Not loving to train means to be pulled in by worldly valuations and it doesn't mean being discouraged to continue the training because of physical or mental fatigue consuming our energy.

"When we come out from the True Realization, the Wonderful Training is practiced throughout our whole body":

To Understand Matzu's "Sunface Buddha, Moonface Buddha" 153

The True Realization can be achieved by training. However, the truth is such realization has always been innate in us. If we abandon (come out from) such true realization, our body becomes a training body without our being conscious of training. Our practicing sitting meditation is "whipping the cart." This practice of sitting meditation is "(becoming) Buddha," and Buddha is one who is always preaching the sutras that have been spelled out and the sutras yet to be spelled out, and this preaching is named "whipping the cow." The following illustrates:

> Yaushan had a long time been delivering no sermons.
> The head monk said, "The monks are longing for your sermon. Your Reverence, please would you give them a sermon?"
> Yaushan ordered that the bell be struck, and the monks assembled.
> Yaushan stepped up to the lecture chair, and after sitting there a while, he stepped down and returned to his residential quarters.
> Following him, the head monk said, "Your Reverence, you granted their request for a sermon, why then did you utter no word?"
> Yaushan said, "For the sutras there are sutra teachers, for the theologies there are theology teachers. How can you suspect this old monk?" (*Tsungrung lu*, Case 7)

"Yaushan ordered the bell to be struck": This bell is such as here described:

> It is not mere training during sitting meditation. It is much more like the wonderful sound that keeps ringing before and after the stroke. (*Bendo wa*)

"After sitting there a while": This is a demonstration of practicing sitting meditation. Practicing sitting meditation is the headquarters of Buddha's Dharma. There all sutras that have been spelled out, and all sutras that have yet to be spelled out are expressed.

"How can you suspect this old monk?": This old monk was "whipping the cart" and it was the Unsurpassed Bodhi. By using this special pronoun "this old monk," Yaushan is expressing himself as Unsurpassed Bodhi, universal being, as well as a particular being. This universal being is eloquently preaching all the time. Every being is "practicing sitting meditation," and is ceaselessly preaching the Dharma, like a wind bell resonating, regardless of wind direction, wind speed, and temperature.

> Buddha's mouth speaks in daily life throughout time.
> (*Kenbutsu* [To see/become Buddha])

The same truth is pointed out also by Confucius:

> The Teacher said: "Do you think I conceal from you or I do not? I have no act I do not do together with you. That is my way." (*Lunyu*, VII-24)

This means he is always practicing sitting meditation because sitting meditation is another name for preaching the Dharma. Only when we understand preaching in this way is it possible for us to practice the Sixth Primary Precept, Not Speaking of Faults.

> The Teacher [Baijang Huaihai, 749-814, disciple of Matzu] one day had finished his sermon and the monks were leaving the lecture hall. He summoned them back. They turned back. The Teacher said, "What is this?"
> (*Chuandeng lu*, vol. 6)

This episode is also telling us the importance of listening to the preaching beyond our lips. We must know, who "turned back"? Yaushan admiringly called this episode "The phrase of Baijang leaving the lecture hall." After all, as long as we keep whipping the cart, the wind bell keeps resonating whether or not there is wind.

Whipping the cart and whipping the cow are the same thing. But because they are the same, when we say whipping the cart, whipping the cow won't at all appear, and when we say whipping the cow, whipping the cart won't at all appear. Because they are extremely intimate, they don't care about each other.

> No one has ever known that sitting is sitting, and of course no one has kept up Buddha's Dharma as Buddha's Dharma. (*Sanmai o sanmai*)

Buddhist whipping the cow is "to become Buddha." Whipping the cart and whipping the cow are the same. For the worldly world there is only the truth of whipping a work cow and no truth of whipping a cart.

In Buddhism there is the truth of whipping the work cow, whipping the iron cow, and whipping the mud cow. Even in the way of whipping there are many ways, with a whip, with the whole mind, to the extent of scattering the marrow, and with the bare fist.

Nanchyuan was the first to introduce whipping the work cow. Kueishan also promoted it.

> Jaujou [Jaujou Tsungshen, 778-897] asked Nanchyuan [Nanchyuan Puyuan, 748-834], "Where does one who understands this matter go?"
> Nanchyuan: "One who understands will become a work cow at the layman's house over there."
> Jaujou: "Your Reverence, thank you for your guidance."
> Nanchyuan: "Last night at eleven the moon shined in the window." (*Jaujou lu*, entry 3)

How can we (work cow) become like the late-night moon without expectation of reward? There is Buddha's compassion or protection, but it is triggered to function only when we can act like that. If we wish for the well-being or benefit of others by our Buddha deeds, we should act like that. At any rate, to be thus able, we must have great confidence in our being already Buddha in "the world where all sentient and insentient beings are accomplishing the Way."

We must be thankful but also must be aware of the danger of being thankful for the sake of our egoistic satisfaction.

> Dakuei [Kueishan Lingyou, 771-853] said in his sermon, "A hundred years hence I will go to a layman's house at the foot of this mountain and become a work cow. On its left side will be five letters: 'a certain monk from Mt. Kuei.' If one then addresses it as 'a certain monk from Mt. Kuei,' it will be a work cow, whereas if one addresses it as 'a work cow,' it will be 'a certain monk from Mt. Kuei.' Now tell me, what is the right way to address it?"
> Yangshan [Yangshan Hueiji, 803-887] stepped forward and paid worship. (*Chuandeng lu*, vol. 9)

Yangshan satisfied these two contrasting aspects, monk and cow, by paying worship. We must satisfy them by devoting ourselves to becoming either the monk or the cow.

Again it is impossible without great confidence.

> I [Fujou Daan, 793-883] stayed thirty years on Mt. Kuei. There I ate Kueishan's food, used Kueishan's lavatory, but I did not study Kueishan's Chan [Zen]. I only tended a cow. Whenever she strayed from the path into the grasses, I pulled her back on, and whenever she invaded the crops of others, I whipped her into obedience.
> With the passing of many years, she grew lovable and came to understand human language. Now in front of me she has turned into a white cow that needs no rope, and all day she enjoys her leisure and does not go away even if I chase her off. (Ibid.)

In this metaphor we must know the meaning of straying from the path into the grasses, and also the meaning of invading the crops of others.

"All day she enjoys her leisure and does not go away." This too is a metaphor. It doesn't mean she doesn't sense the change of the four seasons, the cold or heat, nor mean she doesn't get old age or illness. Nor does it mean she doesn't experience frustration, depression, and hardship. It means she faithfully goes through all such changeable but hard circumstances. In her going through, she is establishing her peace and the meaning of her life, "All day she enjoys her leisure and does not go away."

Whipping the iron cow can be seen in *Biyan lu*, Case 38: Fengshyue and the Patriarch's Dharma Seal. Before being adopted as his name, "Fengshyue" was a mountain with a cave formed by the wind (*feng shyue*) over a long period of time.

Yuanwu introduces this case from the viewpoint of how we should see our life and the world. Our life and the world are always perceived by us as all sorts of endless dualistic valuations, and we are often stuck on one side of a dualistic valuation, and we mostly don't directly see the true virtue of our life and the world. So Yuanwu says:

> Now, how about when one uses neither the gradual nor the sudden method? A word is sufficient to the wise, as is the flick of a whip to a fine horse.

We mostly perceive the flick of a whip as a suffering. It is hard to be thankful for the flick of a whip. We should experience such flicks ten times a day, it could be a hundred times a day. But instead of being able to appreciate them, we regard them as "enemies," and when in a good mood we say love your enemies as well as your friends.

The high level of understanding of suffering and our life and the world cannot be attained by the level of studying psychology and practicing moral codes and social laws. This high level of understanding is possible only when we see the true nature of our life and the world. So this Case 38 presents:

> CASE: Fengshyue took the high seat in the government office of Yingjou and said: "The Dharma Seal of the Patriarch is like the iron cow's spirit. When the seal is withdrawn, its impression appears; when not withdrawn, its impression does not appear. Now, if we neither withdraw it nor keep it pressed down, is it impressed or not?"
>
> Then a senior monk, Lupo, stepped forward and said: "I have the iron cow's spirit. I ask that you not pollute it."

"The iron cow's spirit" is "The Dharma Seal of the Patriarch," and this is our life and the world. The senior monk, Lupo, was right and courageous to step forward and say "I have the iron cow's spirit. I ask that you not pollute it." This "I have" should be the meaning of "I am." Then can he be thankful and appreciate all sufferings in his everyday life? This is the theme of the case. Fengshyue is a kind person. He presents the "life and world" to Lupo. In other words, here Fengshyue is universal truth as well as a particular phenomenon.

> Fengshyue said, "Long I have been trying to catch a whale in the great ocean. Now I rather see a horse mired in muddy water."

Fengshyue with endless empathy saw Lupo to be such a horse. From this empathy his helping devices, shouts, and strikes innately came forth. Are his empathy and beneficial conduct the same as those of the worldly world or not?

> The governor said, "Buddha's Dharma is the same as the emperor's law."
> Fengshyue asked, "Why do you say so?"
> The governor: "When punishment is called for,
> punishment should not be neglected, or one invites trouble."

Buddha's Dharma is on the surface the same as the emperor's law. The emperor's law suggests to nip the evil in the bud because the emperor's law fears evil will act more frequently and more viciously in the future. (Buddhists don't fear such future troubles. Buddhists know that the content of the world or life is trouble upon trouble. For Buddhists, frequent and vicious visits of trouble are assumed to be daily affairs.) But Buddhists fear the budding of Buddhist evils, so without waiting for its physical appearance, we must nip any evil as soon as it begins to form in our mentality. Seeing a pine tree as a pine tree is already a budding of Buddhist evil because it is not a pine tree. On the other hand, to see a pine tree as Buddha nature is already a budding of Buddhist evil because it is a pine tree and not Buddha nature. We shouldn't be intoxicated. We fear what we should fear and don't fear what we shouldn't fear. Here we see the sameness and difference between Buddha's Dharma and the emperor's law, as is said, "The moon in the clear sky is the same for everyone, but the valley where we stand is for each a different valley." So,

> Fengshyue descended from the lecture seat.

We must try to understand Fengshyue's mind as he was descending. Lupo couldn't understand his teacher's device, and was far from understanding every phenomenon is Buddha's device, though such a horse there is that can go even at the sight of the shadow of the whip. So Lupo was likened to a horse stuck in muddy water.

About whipping the mud cow, we study from Lungshan (Tanjou Lungshan, ?-?)

> When on a pilgrimage, the priest Dungshan Liangjie [801-869] lost his way and arrived at that mountain. When he paid worship, the Teacher [Lungshan] asked him, "This mountain has no path. How did Your Reverence come here?"
>
> Dungshan said, "Put aside there being no path, how did Your Reverence come?"
>
> The Teacher said, "I am neither cloud nor water."
>
> Dungshan: "How long have you been in this mountain?"
>
> The Teacher: "Spring and autumn have nothing to do with me."
>
> Dungshan: "Which was first to dwell here, this mountain or Your Reverence?"
>
> The Teacher: "I do not know."
>
> Dungshan: "Why do you not know?"

The Teacher: "I came from neither the heavenly world nor the human world."

Dungshan again asked, "Your Reverence, with what truth you obtained did you decide to come to dwell on this mountain?"

The Teacher: "I saw two bulls made of mud entering the ocean as they fought and they even to this day have never shown up." (*Chuandeng lu*, vol. 8)

When Lungshan was asked "How did Your Reverence come here?" he answered, "I am neither cloud nor water." Here he is confessing he has human thoughts and emotions. He was asked "Which was the first to dwell here, this mountain or Your Reverence?" In his reply "I do not know" there is his conscious effort to repel all irrelevant and shallow questions and answers. Dungshan pursuing with his second question "Why do you not know?" wanted to know exactly how much Lungshan had perfected his Buddhist humanity. Lungshan first declared he was "neither cloud nor water." But this time he said "I came from neither the heavenly world nor the human world." He is declaring that even though he is an organic human being, he has transcended the reincarnation of transmigrating through the Six Worlds, including the heavenly world and the human world. Reincarnation is possible to exist only for the consciousness or discrimination of the human brain. So he could attain the state of putting down or transcending his thought and emotion while perfectly preserving his humanity.

For Lungshan's remarkable achievement, Dungshan naturally wanted further to ask "Your Reverence, with what truth you obtained did you decide to come to dwell on this mountain?" In other words, Dungshan wanted to know Lungshan's causation. But Lungshan's causation must be Buddhist causation. Buddhist causation is cause and effect are absolutely equal. For Dungshan's question, Lungshan replied "I saw two bulls made of mud entering the ocean as they fought and they even to this day have never shown up." "Two bulls " is cause, called "training." At the same time they are effect, called "realization." So the bulls called "training" and the bulls called "realization" were fighting and they entered the ocean of perfect freedom.

The Way as its nature is perfectly open; why should we depend on our training to bring forth the evidence? The vehicle of the religious truth is free; of what need is endeavor? Moreover, the totality is far beyond all dust. Why should we believe we must keep cleaning? The totality is not apart from here. Of what use are the legs of the mendicant trainee? (*Fukan zazengi* [Recommended protocol for sitting meditation])

Lungshan could see his phenomena as training because of his innate realization (Buddha nature), and realization is in his daily phenomena. Thus the conflict between whipping the cow and whipping the cart is melted into the ocean. This "whipping" is the same as the "polishing," of "polishing a tile to fashion a mirror." It is also the same as "grasping."

Devil becoming Buddha = work cow
Buddha becoming Buddha = iron cow
Person becoming Buddha = mud cow

All these are Buddhas and patriarchs. Because they are Buddhas and patriarchs, they practice cross-legged sitting meditation. Now we will study about how to whip.

"Whipping with a whip" means our karmic power is causing our practice of meditation:

Miraculously we each happen to have a human body and mind owing to the power of our studying the Way from eons ago (*Butsudo* [Buddha's Way])

Confirming the nature of the cause of our present life is important in order to establish our peace. We realize that the Samadhi King of samadhi is practicing the Samadhi King of samadhi through the Samadhi King of samadhi. This is the whole world is whipping. There is the whipping that is the whole mind is whipping. In such case, the Three Worlds are only the mind. There is "whipping to extent of scattering the marrow."

Jaujou said to his monks, "Mahakasyapa transmitted to Ananda. Tell me, to whom did Bodhidharma transmit?"
Question: "What if I tell you the Second Patriarch obtained the marrow?"
Jaujou: "Do not depreciate the Second Patriarch."

(*Jaujou lu*, entry 93)

"Mahakasyapa transmitted to Ananda": When Mahakasyapa transmitted the Dharma to Ananda, Mahakasyapa was hidden in

To Understand Matzu's "Sunface Buddha, Moonface Buddha"   161

Ananda's body and there was no Mahakasyapa. (This is the horizontal prostration side by side in the ordination ceremony.) When Ananda received the Dharma transmission from Mahakasyapa, Ananda was hidden in Mahakasyapa's body. (This is the vertical prostration head to head in the ordination ceremony.) This transmission is called "self-realization without a teacher." (It is not the same as literally having no teacher.) In this right transmission there is no division between teacher and student, so such student is called "to whom," as Jaujou expresses. Thus Jaujou is making a positive meaningful statement in question form.

To respond to such depth of Jaujou's question, his monk gave a rather deliberate question instead of a fast answer. In his response there is his acknowledgement of the historical sense that the Second Patriarch received the transmission from Bodhidharma, and more, his sense that the true transmission was done when the particular personalities, such as of Bodhidharma and the Second Patriarch, were completely denied. Jaujou responded "Do not depreciate the Second Patriarch." It means approval of his monk's response, saying "You are right. The true Second Patriarch is such a being that cannot be depreciated." Jaujou and his student were truly loving their daily life because they could respect universal nature.

> Jaujou continued: "Bodhidharma said the one who is outside obtains the skin, and the one who is inside obtains the bone. Now tell me, what does the one who is more inside obtain?"
> Question: "What is the underlying truth in obtaining the marrow?"
> Jaujou: "Just obtain the skin. Where I am there is no specific marrow."
> Question: "So, what is the marrow?"
> Jaujou: "In your way you will not obtain even the skin."
> (Ibid.)

"Just obtain the skin": Short is a short Dharma-kaya, long is a long Dharma-kaya. Buddhists must transcend such value judgment as skin, flesh, bone, and marrow.

> Question: "Your Reverence, from whom did you receive the Dharma transmission?"
> Jaujou: "I received it from Tsungshen."
> (*Jaujou lu*, entry 230)

This "Tsungshen" is "to whom" as in Jaujou's question to his monks, "Tell me to whom did Bodhidharma transmit?" Tsungshen is also Jaujou's first priest's name. There is whipping with bare fist. This means bare fist whips bare fist. So, even the conduct "whip" is "bare fist." There is no (becoming) Buddha outside of practicing sitting meditation. Practicing sitting meditation and (becoming) Buddha are the same thing, so without mentioning practicing meditation, "(becoming) Buddha" is enough, singularly exposed.

Practicing sitting meditation is whipping the cart, and (becoming) Buddha is whipping the cow. When it is whipping the cart, we don't say about whipping the cow. By saying "whipping the cart," it becomes explanation of "whipping the cow." It after all means only talking about (becoming) Buddha. So, there is only the Dharma of (becoming) Buddha. This mechanism is expressed as "Fist whipping fist." Thus the Buddhist "fist" is different from the worldly fist. It is the same as to say the Buddhist cow. For the Buddhist cow, cow is cow, whip is cow, and even the conduct to whip is cow. So the worldly words "We whip a cow" can become everything for Buddhists, "cow cow cow cow." A great patriarch can convert any worldly sentence to "Buddha nature Buddha nature Buddha nature," repeating as many as the original sentence parts, that is, the abstract noun Buddha nature can become any sentence part—noun, verb, adjective, adverb, etc. This is the content of one of Buddha's most famous sayings: "In all the world of heaven and earth I alone am respectable."

> The Teacher: "It is like a person is riding on a cart. When the cart does not advance, is it right to whip the cart, or to whip the cow?"
> Dauyi made no response.

We shouldn't be sloppy here to understand Matzu (Dauyi). His no response is "The person who has no tongue understands the language very well." In alternation, Matzu is Buddha and Buddha is Matzu. It means there is no Buddha without practicing sitting meditation. Whipping the cart is okay, and whipping the cow is okay. Therefore there was no response. It can be said that it is practicing sitting meditation, but can also be said that it is (becoming) Buddha. So there is no way to

To Understand Matzu's "Sunface Buddha, Moonface Buddha"   163

respond except to nod.

> The Teacher [Confucius] said, "Tsan [=Tzengtzy], my way has one thing that runs right through it."
> Tzengtzy said, "Yes."
> The Teacher left the room.
> A junior disciple asked, "What did he mean?"
> Tzengtzy said, "Our teacher's way is to be sincere with himself and with others. (*Lunyu*, IV-15)

This "Yes" is the same as Dauyi's no response. It is hoped that we will understand the great eloquence in this kind of response.

> Kueishan summoned the head administrator, and the head administrator came.
> Kueishan said, "I summoned the head administrator. What is the use of your coming?"
> The head administrator did not say a word.
> (*Chuandeng lu*, vol. 9)

"The head administrator" is not only a certain monk. "The head administrator" is existing throughout past, present, and future. So the coming of a certain monk is of no use. This head administrator, a certain monk, well understood, so he had no way but to keep silent. For him the universal, head administrator, and the particular, a certain monk, are one. "The head administrator" is a certain monk. If they are one, what is the need of "is" or "="? "The head administrator" is perfect, enough, or "a certain monk," utterly enough. If he says "I am head administrator as well as a certain monk," he is falling into the secondary level of communication, which is reasoning instead of the truth presenting itself. When we need sugar, what's the use of bringing its chemical formula? In this context, in his saying not a word, we see the tremendous power of his accumulating training. After all, this episode is saying that practicing sitting meditation and training and becoming Buddha are the same thing.

> Tzygung said, "We can understand our teacher's protocol and his rules of music by hearing his teaching, but we cannot understand his character and Way by hearing his teaching. (*Lunyu*, V-13)

By saying "but we cannot understand," Tzygung is expressing his joy in coming to understand the character and

Way of the teacher through years of following him.

> The Teacher said, "Huei [Yanhuei] does not assist me by filling in where I lack. He cherishes whatever I say."
>
> (*Lunyu*, XI-3)

The total body of Yanhuei is becoming the Way of Confucius (= to do everything with one principle = "one thing that runs right through it"). Assisting the teacher is the life shining by the light coming from outside, and cherishing the teacher's words is the life shining by the light within oneself.

> The Teacher [Nanyue] further said, "If you are studying sitting meditation, you are studying sitting Buddha."

Practicing sitting meditation is acting like Buddha:

> This is the season wherein Buddha sees Buddha, the very time sentient beings become Buddha.
>
> (*Sanmai o sanmai* [Samadhi among samadhis])

It is not like "to become Buddha" after practicing sitting meditation. Practicing sitting meditation itself is practicing Buddha's deeds. Turning each scoop of soil is a deed of Buddha.

> Pile even one more speck of dust on the mountain of good deeds. Do not waste even a drop of the ocean of virtue.
>
> (*Tenzo kyokun* [Kitchen officers' principles])

This is a practical matter, so we can understand how right it is only when we practice it.

When we practice sitting meditation, we are already Buddha before we understand the dynamics of how sitting meditation can be Buddha.

> A monk asked, "What is the essence of Buddha's Dharma?"
>
> The Teacher [Lingyun Shichin, ?-?] replied, "Before the donkey affairs have left, the horse affairs have arrived."
>
> (*Chuandeng lu*, vol. 11)

Lingyun, a disciple of Kueishan, came to a great realization at the sight of peach blossoms. Before illusion has left, true form has arrived. Before Matzu (Dauyi) has left, (becoming) Buddha has arrived. Before "studying sitting meditation" has left, "studying sitting Buddha" has arrived.

To Understand Matzu's "Sunface Buddha, Moonface Buddha" 165

Before cold water has left, hot water has arrived. Before anxiety has left, a solution has arrived. After all, this is describing the relationship between phenomena and True Form. When we talk of True Form we don't talk of phenomena, when we talk of phenomena we don't talk of True Form, for they are the same thing. By studying this relationship, we are trying to perceive Buddha nature, which is already existing throughout past, present, and future.

Even if for the first time we are practicing sitting meditation, the content of our meditation is transcending the division between first and last time because the content is (to become) Buddha. Likewise, even if we practice sitting meditation a short while, the content is forever. Likewise, we can transcend our causation, or phenomena, by practicing sitting meditation. When we begin to be aware of such profound power of practicing sitting meditation, we can begin to sense that our practicing sitting meditation is an effect of great causation of eons ago.

> [The Teacher further said:] "...If you are going to study sitting meditation, meditation is beyond sitting or reclining.

It seems the Teacher (Nanyue) is saying meditation has nothing to do with such form or conduct as sitting or reclining. But here first of all we must understand that the "if" of "If you are going to study sitting meditation" is used to mean "already." It is because time has no division between past, present, and future. Therefore, second of all, we don't practice sitting meditation in order to gain Buddha's wisdom by severing our klesa. The relationship between sitting meditation and attaining Buddha's wisdom isn't a relationship polluted by preference or dualistic valuation. So "meditation is beyond sitting or reclining" doesn't mean denial of sitting or reclining. It means "meditation is transcending sitting or reclining."

In order to understand the denial sentence as the transcending sentence, there is one good example in the Brahma's Net Sutra:

> The light of the precepts issues from the mouth. Because the truth is not that there is no cause but only effect, the light of each light is not blue, not yellow, not red, not white, and not black. The truth is that there is not color [= not rupa] and not Mind [= not sunyata]. The truth is that there is not being

> [= not rupa] and not non-being [= not sunyata]. The truth is that there is no causation. This truth is the origin of all Buddhas and the root of practicing the Bodhisattva's Way.

This "not" of "the light of each light is not blue, not yellow, not red, not white, and not black," and "The truth is that there is not color and not Mind," and "The truth is that there is not being and not non-being"—each is an example of the case that this "not" is not a denial. This "not" means "transcending" the state of the following noun. So the quoted lines should be understood as "the light of each light is transcending being blue, transcending being yellow, transcending being red, transcending being white, and transcending being black," and "The truth is there is (something) transcending the state of color and transcending the state of Mind. The truth is there is the state of transcending being, and the state of transcending non-being."

The Fifth Primary Precept, Not Buying or Selling Intoxicants, is explained in *Shobogenzo sho* (Annotations to the Zen precepts):

> "The light of the precepts issues from the mouth. Because the truth is not that there is no cause…" "This truth is the origin of all Buddhas and the root of practicing the Bodhisattva's Way." By only listing the sentences in this manner, the sutra is not saying we should detach from the Dharma above listed, nor saying we should abandon it, nor saying we should lose it. By saying simply "not," the concept of relativity is forever shed. We should not say although we lost yesterday we are today brightly penetrating. Not saying or thinking so is the wisdom of only Buddha to Buddha.

If we sit erect "putting right foot on left thigh, left foot on right thigh, leaning neither left nor right, bending neither forward nor back," our form is sitting but we are actually transcending sitting, we are practicing cross-legged sitting meditation. With this meaning, Teacher Nanyue said "If you are going to study sitting meditation, meditation is beyond sitting or reclining." Now we understand "beyond sitting" means "transcending sitting." How about "reclining"?

Just as sitting transcends sitting, reclining transcends reclining. In Buddhism, "reclining" means with head positioned north, face west, right-side body down. It is said to be the way a lion reclines.

> Reclining thus = the right position
> = Winter = Repository
> = Nirvana = The Way as its nature is perfectly open
> = The Vehicle of the Essence is free
> = The totality is far beyond all dust
> = the unthinkable = before our parents were born
> = All Buddhas are always residing here and do not appear in any perception and recognition in any direction.

Then this reclining is accomplishing Bodhi, Buddha's fruit. (East is cause, spring is to raise Bodhi mind. South is summer, training. West is autumn, Bodhi, fruiting season.)

This reclining is the Tathagata, which is Sambhoga-kaya. When Dharma-kaya (the unthinkable) acts fully in Sakyamuni Buddha, which is Nirmana-kaya, Sakyamuni Buddha becomes a Tathagata, which is Sambhoga-kaya. So, this reclining is as virtuous as cross-legged sitting meditation, and it is meditating in the form of reclining by shedding reclining.

Whatever affairs we engage in, if we engage with the mind of practicing cross-legged sitting meditation, we can shed each affair and each affair will become Zen.

This Zen (dhyana) is intoned by Yungjia (Yungjia Shyuanjyue, ?-713):

> Walking is also dhyana, sitting is also dhyana. Within is tranquil in every act of speaking and of keeping silent, and in moving and in keeping still.
> (*Jengda ge* [Hymn to verify the Way])

This state is expressed:

> It is unnecessary to engage in burning incense, prostrating in worship, chanting Buddha's name, confessing, and reading the sutras. Just practice sitting meditation.
> (Said by Dogen's teacher, Tiantung Rujing, 1163-1228)

This doesn't mean priests needn't engage in burning incense, prostrating in worship, chanting Buddha's name, confessing, reading the sutras. Each of these is shedding itself and becoming practicing sitting meditation. It means before the affair of burning incense has left, the pure meditation has come. Daito (National Teacher Daito: Shuho Myocho, 1282-1337) says in his Admonition: "You monks are gathering your heads in this mountain for the sake of the Way. Do not live for the sake of dress and food." He means shed dress and food.

So, "meditation is beyond sitting or reclining" means transcending sitting or reclining without reforming the form of sitting or reclining. Likewise when blue, yellow, red, white, and black each shed, each sheds without nullifying its color. This shedding happens only when blue, yellow, red, white, and black each thoroughly devote to being each. When one devotes to oneself, one sheds oneself and the true virtue of being oneself will come to real existence. Flesh sheds flesh and becomes the virtue of practicing sitting meditation. Even a worn-out gunstock can be converted to a Buddha image by a good sculptor's hands.

After understanding shedding, we further must understand that sitting meditation is sitting meditation and not mere sitting or reclining. This is because, as we have been studying, sitting meditation is sitting or reclining, and sitting or reclining is sitting meditation. Then sitting meditation is sitting meditation, and sitting or reclining is sitting or reclining. So, sitting meditation isn't mere sitting or reclining. So it is said "meditation is beyond sitting or reclining." In short, the true nature of "sitting or reclining" is "meditation." This should be said of each of our acts; each is a variation of "meditation," or Buddha nature.

> Jaujou in his youth accompanied his first teacher on a mendicant tour. They came to Nanchyuan. After his first teacher finished his greetings, Jaujou was going to offer his.
>
> Nanchyuan was by then already reclining in his residential quarters.
>
> Seeing Jaujou, he asked, "From where did you come?"
>
> Jaujou: "I came from Rueishiang Temple."
>
> Nanchyuan: "Did you see the Rueishiang [Beautiful Buddha Statue]?"
>
> Jaujou: "I didn't see the Rueishiang, but I now see a reclining Tathagata."
>
> Nanchyuan got to his feet and asked, "Acolyte, are you an acolyte who has a master or not?"
>
> Jaujou replied, "I am an acolyte who has a master."
>
> Nanchyuan: "Who is he?"
>
> Jaujou: "It is cold, though it is spring. I humbly wish Your Reverence good health."

To Understand Matzu's "Sunface Buddha, Moonface Buddha" 169

> Nanchyuan summoned the reception monk and said, "Place this acolyte on a special seat."
>
> (*Jaujou lu*, section *Shingjuang*)

Nanchyuan was one of Matzu's important disciples. Jaujou at age eighteen had the eye to see that reclining is shedding reclining and shedding reclining is the Tathagata.

In *Biyan lu*, Case 24,

> Liou Tiemo [dates unknown] visited Kueishan
> Kueishan said, "Old Cow, have you come?"
> Liou said, "Tomorrow there is the great prayer ceremony at Mt. Wutai. Will you be going?"
> Kueishan lay down and took his ease.
> Liou left.

"Kueishan lay down and took his ease." His reclining is the practice of sitting meditation, putting right foot on left thigh, left foot on right thigh, leaning neither left nor right, bending neither forward nor back. It is practicing Middle Way, and the Middle Way is to shed. When reclining sheds reclining, it becomes Compassion, Zen, Buddha. At such a time the Great Earth is gold, the Great River is lassi, and the meditation is cherishing to be itself.

When itself cherishes itself, no effect of dualistic thought invades. So sitting meditation is sitting meditation and reclining is reclining, each thoroughly utilizing the Dharma world.

> [Teacher Nanyue:] "...If you are going to study sitting Buddha, Buddha has no certain form because there is no preference in the Dharma of no dwelling." [3]

Earlier Nanyue said "If you are going to study sitting meditation, meditation is beyond sitting or reclining," and we studied the relationship between sitting meditation and mere sitting or reclining. Now he is saying "If you are going to study sitting Buddha, Buddha has no certain form." Here we study the relation between "sitting Buddha" and "has no certain form."

"Has no certain form" should be understood as "having no-certain form." In other words, "no" isn't a negative particle, as in "no certain form." Buddhists take this having no-certain form "no" as a positive particle.

In the Diamond Sutra there is the passage "If one sees all form as no-form, one can see the Tathagata." This is the early Mahayana traditional way of reading. But the same passage can be read "If one sees all phenomena and no-form, one can see the Tathagata." This suggested second way of reading deepens to the extreme the meaning of the Diamond Sutra passage. This is the destination of Mahayana development, which reached to the point of denying even Mahayana (which was denying Hinayana).

In the annotations *Gosho* (by Kyogo, a disciple of Senne, who was one of Dogen's direct disciples who wrote *Okikigaki* [Memo of responses to questions]), the following is said:

> When one faces forms, if one understands that forms are no-form because all forms are Buddha's body and all Buddhas are Tathagatas, then one's view is profound in comparison to what was one's former view that forms are forms only. Hence there comes such approval as "Your study is good within its narrow reach." However, those who are of the Bodhidharma line do not give their approval of this way of seeing Buddha, because the mind presented in Buddha's expression is not like that. Seeing all forms as no-form is a relative view that has a subject and an object and it is not seeing Buddha intimately. If we understand "all forms—no-form" [phenomena and no-form], then we are free of that relative view and this "no-" is not a negation.
>
> (*Shobogenzo sho*)

"Right and wrong," if taken as two separate things, is dualistic relative valuation. Combined as "right-wrong" is Buddha's view. Sakyamuni Buddha with thirty-two virtuous features is an "all-forms Tathagata," and an earthworm is a "no-form Tathagata." The point of this positive particle "no-" is to go beyond dualistic valuation.

So Nanyue's words "no certain form" means "no-certain form Tathagata." Therefore, "If you are going to study sitting Buddha, Buddha has no certain form" means "Already you have studied sitting Buddha and Buddha is no-certain form." This no-certain form is on a certain form. There are no-certain forms on all certain forms, the same as to say no-forms are on all forms.

One day Matzu asked a monk to visit the Teacher [Damei Fachang, 752-829] with a question.

To Understand Matzu's "Sunface Buddha, Moonface Buddha" 171

> So the monk went and asked the Teacher, "Your Reverence, when you studied from Matzu, what truth did you attain that led you to come and live on this mountain?"
> The Teacher said, "Matzu told me 'The mind is Buddha.' I straightaway came to live here."
> The monk said, "Nowadays Matzu differently presents Buddha's Dharma."
> The Teacher asked, "How so?"
> The monk said, "He says 'No mind, no Buddha.'"
> The Teacher said, "There's no end to that old man's confusing people. Let 'no mind, no Buddha' be. As for me, solely it is 'The mind is Buddha.'"
> The monk reported this all to Matzu.
> Matzu: "The apricot [*da mei*] has ripened."
>
> (*Gyoji*, vol. 1)

Damei well understood that "the mind is Buddha" and "no mind, no Buddha" are the same thing. So he said "As for me, solely it is 'the mind is Buddha.'" Buddha is prefixed sometimes by "the mind" and sometimes by "no mind." It is like the English "in" and "at." The meaning of "in" is contained in "at" and the meaning of "at" in "in." It is said light is particle as well as wave. In Buddha there are the two virtues "the mind" and "no mind."

> For those who are to be helped by the body of Buddha, he [Avalokitesvara] shows Buddha's body and preaches the Dharma; for those who are to be helped by the body of Pratyeka Buddha body, he shows Pratyeka Buddha's body and preaches the Dharma; and for those who are to be helped by the body of a prime minister, he shows a prime minister's body and preaches the Dharma.
>
> (Lotus Flower Sutra)

Avalokitesvara is free, and thus has many virtues. On "certain form" there is "no-certain form." How does Avalokitesvara attain this freedom? By graduating from all intellectual distinctions, as we studied in *Biyan lu*, Case 1: Bodhidharma's "Vacancy and no Holiness." When we see this "vacancy and no holiness," we are graduating from discrimination between an earthworm and the Tathagata, between ignorant persons and sages. Emperor Wu was showing his full discrimination in asking "Who stands before me?" Bodhidharma's response was "I do not know," not a negation, it means transcending or shedding. Bodhidharma was graduating from his common senses, his intellectual distinctions. The first principle of the holy teachings will be manifested when we are free of our intellectual distinctions, dualistic valuations.

By one sentence Nanyue remarkably expressed this compound truth: "If you are going to study sitting Buddha, Buddha has no certain form."

All who practice sitting meditation are great because their sitting meditation contains both form and no-form. There is freedom upon bondage. Upon cross-legged sitting meditation the perfect Way is manifesting itself and is beyond all dust. So our sitting meditation (a certain form) is innately activating "no certain form" = more clearly expressed as "no-certain form." Without practicing sitting meditation, no-certain form won't begin to act. No-certain form is the true face of certain form. No-certain form is Buddha's face, Buddha's form.

The Fourteenth Patriarch, the Venerable Nagarjuna [c. 150 – 250 AD] was from West India. Nagarjuna in Sanskrit means Dragon Tree, Excellent Dragon, or Fearless Dragon, in the language of Tang. When he went to South India he found most of the inhabitants believed in the work that brings happiness. The Venerable Nagarjuna preached the Wonderful Dharma. Those hearing said among themselves, "We have work that brings happiness, and that work is most important. He talks of Buddha nature in vain. Who has ever seen it?"

His Reverence addressed them: "If you wish to see Buddha nature, first you must get rid of your pride, your self."

The people questioned, "Is Buddha nature big or small?"

His Reverence said, "Buddha nature is neither big nor small, wide nor narrow, joy nor misery, death nor life."

Hearing this excellent reasoning, they all raised Bodhi mind.

Then while sitting, His Reverence showed his own free body, and it looked like the full moon. The entire gathering could hear only the Dharma sound and no longer saw his figure.

Among them was Kana-deva, son of a rich man. He spoke to the gathering: "Can you make sense of this figure?"

The gathering responded with "Now what we see we never saw, what we hear we never heard, and what we think we never thought, and our bodies have no place to dwell."

Kana-deva said, "His Reverence is showing us the figure of Buddha nature. How can we know it is so? It is so because the Samadhi of No-form is the essence of Buddha nature, which is like the full moon vacant and bright." Just then the figure of Kana-deva disappeared and Nagarjuna reappeared as before, and he said in a gatha:

> The body shows the figure of the full moon.
> Thus it shows the body of all Buddhas.
> The Dharma Preaching has no form.
> Eloquence is not sound and color.
>
> (*Bussho* [Buddha nature])

Here Nagarjuna said "Buddha nature is neither big nor small, wide nor narrow, joy nor misery, death nor life." Not a negation, it means "big is Buddha nature as it is, small is Buddha nature as it is, wide is also, narrow also, joy, misery, death, life, all are Buddha nature as they are."

Then Nagarjuna "showed his own free body, and it looked like the full moon." Kana-deva interpreted this happening as "His Reverence is showing us the figure of Buddha nature." This means Nagarjuna was practicing cross-legged meditation and Kana-deva saw in that meditation "the figure of Buddha nature." In short, the episode is describing that cross-legged sitting meditation has no-certain form. Because having no-certain form is Buddha nature, and because practicing sitting meditation (= a certain form) is no-certain form, Buddha nature and practicing sitting meditation are inseparable. The Teacher [Nanyue] further said, "...because there is no preference in the Dharma of no dwelling."

"The Dharma of no dwelling" means the Dharma isn't a fixed thing that can be expressed by "nature" (attribute), "body," that is, "no-certain form." If we lean left or right, there are places to dwell. If we sit erect and serene, there is no place to dwell. In erect and serene there are two simultaneous virtues, the Buddha of no-certain form and the Buddha of acertain form. So we are unable to prefer one or the other. Both are the virtue of the bold-mountain-like sitting. Not being Buddha is the unthinkable, being Buddha is the thinkable. But when we talk about the unthinkable Buddha, there is only the unthinkable Buddha in the whole world and there is no thinkable Buddha. Likewise, when we talk about the thinkable Buddha, there is only the thinkable Buddha in the whole world and there is no unthinkable Buddha. Before we are going to practice our preference for a certain form, that certain form is already shedding itself. Before we are going to practice our preference for no-certain form, no-certain form is already shedding itself. Then what will remain? What will remain is sitting Buddha.

> Jaujou spoke to the assembly: "The Ultimate Way asks of us no difficult training but rejects our preferences. With but a word, either preference or clarity may arise. This old monk does not live in that clarity. Do you long to live there?"
> Then a monk asked, "If already you do not live there, what's to long for?"
> Jaujou: "Neither do I know."
> The monk: "If you do not know, how can you say you do not live there?"
> Jaujou: "To ask is good enough. Now make your bow and retire." (*Biyan lu*, Case 2)

"The Ultimate Way asks of us no difficult training" is the same as "It is vacancy and no holiness." As soon as our words refer, we fall into dualistic values, such as preference or clarity. The truth will then be divided into delusion and suchness; and then "Whipping the cart is right and whipping the cow is right" will become a question sentence as to which is right; and practicing sitting meditation and becoming Buddha will become conflicting terms. When the question sentence becomes the positive statement, the conflicting terms are resolved. The world of this no conflict is as we studied, "Buddha nature is ever pure."

> By nature Bodhi has no tree,
> Bright mirror has no stand.
> Buddha nature is ever pure.
> No place for dust to land.

This is "This old monk does not live in that clarity," that is, "Put right foot on left thigh, left foot on right thigh, which is neither preference nor clarity. It is transcending both right foot and left thigh. This is "no-certain form," that is, "no-certain form Buddha." The monk didn't understand this and was regarding clarity as the most important matter. So he asked "If already you do not live there, what's to long for?" So Jaujou said "Neither do I know." Jaujou is entering into samadhi and thus doesn't know. This not knowing is Matzu's (Dauyi's) "no response." The "no-certain form" or "no-certain form Buddha" is appearing. But Jaujou's monk continues his inquiry. Jaujou urges him to transcend his intellectual and dualistic inquiry: "To ask is good enough. Now make your bow and retire." This is "there is no preference in the Dharma of no dwelling." We must understand by the way of not understanding.

> [Teacher Nanyue:] "...If sitting Buddha is what you are, then you are killing Buddha." There is more virtue in sitting meditation, that is, in sitting Buddha, which we should be acquainted with. Sitting Buddha is "killing Buddha." This killing isn't worldly killing; it means there's nothing other than Buddha. In other words, when we are sitting, there's only Buddha and nothing else exists:
> This is the season wherein Buddha sees Buddha, the very time sentient beings become Buddha.
>
> (*Sanmai o sanmai*)

At this time whether we say sentient beings or Buddha, there is no difference, and:

> Going straightaway beyond the whole world and being most respectable in the house of Buddha and the patriarchs is full lotus posture. Trampling on the heads of anya-tirthyas and devils and becoming a person in the depths of the hall of Buddha and the patriarchs is full lotus posture. This and nothing else is the Dharma, which enables us to master the extremity of Buddha and the patriarchs and still go further. Therefore Buddha and the patriarchs engaged in this and had no time to be involved in anything else. (Ibid.)

Also,

> When one even temporarily stamps Buddha's Seal on one's body, mouth, and mind and directly sits in samadhi, all the Dharma world becomes Buddha's Seal and all vastness becomes realization. Hence all Buddhas, or Tathagatas, increase their primordial Dharma enjoyment and renew the solemnity of the path of realization. (*Bendo wa*)

When we practice cross-legged sitting meditation, we can

go beyond big and small, beyond ourselves and our environment, and all the world becomes one Buddha. Therefore "If you are sitting Buddha, you are killing Buddha." This is "being most respectable." In the theology this is known as the Vairocana Tathagata. It is "a person in the depths of hall of Buddha and the patriarchs," and for such a person there is no need of Buddha.

> The Third Primary Precept, Not having incorrect sex: Because the Three Wheels are pure, there is nothing to be hoped for. All Buddhas go the same way. (*Kyoju kaimon*)

This "pure" is not pure in our dualistic valuation. It is purity beyond purity. It is annotated in Kyogo's *Shobogenzo sho*:

> Receiving Buddha's precepts means Buddha nature receives Buddha nature. Therefore the body, mouth, and mind of a man and a woman, now presented, are also made by Buddha nature. Therefore "The Three Wheels are pure" means, to purify body, mouth, and mind. Purifying body, mouth, and mind means, to purify body with body, mouth with mouth, and mind with mind."

Dogen's teacher, Tiantung, "abandoned theological study at age nineteen and attended the seat of Bodhidharma, and threw himself into the assembly of Shyuedou [Shyuedou Jijian, 1109-1192], where he had already spent a year. Normally he was excellent in practicing sitting meditation."

When he first met his Zen Teacher Shyuedou, Shyuedou asked him, "What is your name?" This statement in question form is "observing body" (the first of the Four Earnest Observations), which is transcending pure and impure. When it is beyond pure and impure, there is no noun to call it, so it is said "What is your name?" It is whoever is "going straightaway beyond the whole world and being most respectable....Trampling on the heads of anya-tirthyas and devils and becoming a person in the depths of the hall of Buddha and the patriarchs...."

Tiantung responded "My name is Rujing [to purify]." Everything including Rujing is such a being that transcends pure and impure, but he answered "Rujing." Shyuedou challenged him: "Nothing is ever polluted, what are you going to purify?" This was the start of Tiantung's serious study.

One day he [Tiantung] expressed the wish to be appointed to the work of lavatory cleaning. Shyuedou asked, "How can you purify a place never polluted? If you can answer, I will appoint you." Tiantung could not answer. Two or three months passed and he still could not answer.

At a certain time Tiantung visited him in his quarters. The Teacher asked, "Can you answer?" Tiantung tried to say something. Then the Teacher said, "How can you purify a place never polluted?" Tiantung still could make no response.

After a year and some months, the Teacher again asked. Tiantung still could not answer. Then the Teacher said, "If you can get out of that old cave, everything will turn out to be so convenient for you. Why can you not answer?" Tiantung gained power and further intensified his will to study.

One day his realization suddenly came. He went up to the Teacher's quarters and said, "I can answer!" Then the Teacher said, "This time you can answer?.."

Tiantung: "Actualize the place never polluted." Before Tiantung finished speaking, the Teacher struck him. Tiantung shed sweat and paid worship. (*Denko roku*, vol. 2)

"Two or three months passed and he still could not answer": Day after day he continued his earnest study and still he saw pure and impure. It is said "Buddha nature is ever pure." Yet Tiantung saw filth and tried to purify it. Illusion upon illusion. He couldn't come to the awareness that pure and impure both come from "Buddha nature is ever pure."

"If you can get out of that old cave, everything will turn out to be so convenient for you." If we keep endeavoring, we're never polluted. Then we're bright and clean from the beginning. Then what's there to purify? This is "everything will turn out to be so convenient."

"Actualize the place never polluted": Still keep on going, then we will not have such view as pure and impure throughout the twenty-four hours. This is expressed as no pollution. Yet, there are eyes to see pollution, eyes to make use of purifying devices. So Tiantung spent a year and some months and he then could shed his own skin, his own body and mind, and could say "Actualize the place never polluted." Yet there is one stain in his awakening itself. Therefore "Before Tiantung finished speaking, the Teacher struck him." Then for the first time "Tiantung shed sweat and paid worship." This is truly his abandoning his body, and really he understood the original bright pure unpolluted world. With this experience he later always said in his teaching, "Studying Zen is to shed body and mind."

Thus the very time of our sitting Buddha is the time of our "killing Buddha." The figure of "killing Buddha" is Vairocana, that is, the form of sitting Buddha. So the word "killing" is here used very differently from the worldly world.

> Killing Buddha does not mean murder. It means being zealous. It means, there is not only no second person to be met but also not even a first. (*Shobogenzo kyakutai ichijisan* [*Shobogenzo* translated to Chinese with annotations])

"Zealous" is Dungshan's word (Dungshan Liangjie, 801-869), meaning "be truly kind" (intimate with).

> A monk asked, "Among the Tri-kaya [Three Bodies of Buddha], which does not fall into any concept?"
> The Teacher [Dungshan] replied, "About that I am always zealous." (*Dungshan lu*, entry 101)

Dharma-kaya, Sambhoga-kaya, Nirmana-kaya, these are the theological Three Bodies of Buddha. In the sutra *Vimalakirti-nirdesa* (part 3, Disciples, chap. Ananda) it is said: "Buddha's body is not contrived and does not fall into any concept." Not contrived (Skt. *asamskrta*) means free of causation, beyond rise and fall, beyond time, existing always as absolute being. It is Nirvana by another name, indicating absolute, unlimited being beyond phenomena. Practically speaking, it is the way of living freely with no hindrance, no contrivance, no trace of behavior like fish in water, birds in the sky. With this understanding, the monk asked Dungshan. Sitting Buddha and killing Buddha are really with each other intimate.

Sitting Buddha is thought, is the unthinkable, and is nothing to do with thought. Sitting Buddha is killing Buddha. Sitting Buddha can be anything.

So,

> Fashi [Fashi Lingtzun, ?-?] at Mt. Chingping in Ejou asked Tsueiwei [Tsueiwei Wushyue, ?-? Dharma heir of Danshia Tianran, 739-824], "What is the essential meaning of the Patriarch's coming from the West?"

To Understand Matzu's "Sunface Buddha, Moonface Buddha" 179

> Tsueiwei: "I will tell you when no one is around."
> Fashi after a while said, "Now there is no one. Please say."
> Tsueiwei left his meditation seat and took Fashi into the bamboo garden
> Fashi said again, "Here there is no one. I beg you, please explain." Pointing to the bamboos, Tsuewei said, "This bamboo is quite tall, and that bamboo is quite short."
> (*Sanbyaku soku* [Three hundred cases], vol. 1-71)

This "essential meaning of the Patriarch's coming" is The Treasure Repository Housing the Eye to See the Right Dharma, and Nirvana, Wonderful Mind. It is described in the Diamond Sutra as "no self, no person, no ignorant people, no form having life duration." The Patriarch's coming isn't a matter of the human world, it is a matter of Buddha's world in the Ten Directions. So Tsueiwei said "I will tell you when no one is around." Further, he pulled the monk to the bamboos and said one was quite tall, another quite short. This way of nature has absolutely no presence of any person. It is the figure of The Treasure Repository Housing the Eye to See the Right Dharma. Tsueiwei taught the monk in a highly concrete manner: tall bamboo is tall Dharma-kaya, short bamboo is short Dharma-kaya. The one tall is shedding tall body and is tall Dharma-kaya, the one short is shedding short body and is short Dharma-kaya. When we speaking of the meaning of the Patriarch's coming, every phenomenon is the meaning of his coming, and at such a time there are no phenomena. This is killing Buddha. In other words, at such a time, every phenomenon is an expression of killing Buddha.

Kueishan and his disciple Yangshan are deepening this same subject:

> One day together with Kueishan cultivating a field, he asked, "Teacher, here is low there is high, what should we do?"
> Kueishan said, "Water levels things."
> Yangshan said, "Your Reverence, there's no need to rely on water, here is level at its height, there is level at its height."
> Kueishan gave his approval. (*Chuandeng lu*, vol. 11)

High sheds high without distorting high, low sheds low without distorting low. There is equality in rank and rank in equality. In sitting meditation there is (becoming) Buddha, and when sitting meditation becomes Buddha it kills Buddha. So Yungjia said,

> Without leaving this very place, we are always tranquil.
> By searching, we understand you cannot be found.
>
> (*Jengda ge*)

All mountains, rivers, and earth are Spiritual Recognition, the sum total of original nature, everywhere the appearance of the totality. Yet we can't see it because our function of seeing is Spiritual Recognition, that is, original nature. Spiritual Recognition or original nature is True Form. It hasn't form, doesn't become the object of our recognition. About this mechanism the Sixth Patriarch said:

> The nature of Spiritual Recognition is detached from every form. We therefore cannot gain it. It is also directly related with all dharmas. We therefore cannot lose it.
>
> (*Lioutzu fabau tanjing* [Sixth Patriarch Sutra]).

There is no Buddha other than ignorant people and no original nature other than phenomena. Original nature doesn't see original nature.

> Buddha and the patriarchs in their past were we ignorant people, and we in the future ought to be Buddha and the patriarchs.
>
> (*Keisei sanshoku* [Sound of the valleys, color of the mountains])

Buddha and ignorant people are equal in the past, in the present too, in the future too. There are all sorts of forms or occurrences of "sitting Buddha," so we must come to the awareness that we are Buddha. Otherwise we will see only forms or occurrences different from Buddha. If there is "killing Buddha," there is "not yet killing Buddha." We must kill (= shed) Buddha, sentient being, Three Worlds, One Mind, all dharmas, True Form, Realization, life, death, every noun and concept. Jaujou's "No (Buddha nature in a dog)" means, to shed itself. So Jungfeng Mingben (1263-1323) asked us to read his eight no's in a meaningful way:

> No, no, no, no, no, no, no, no.

Everything every day should be done with this shedding

mind.

On this shedding or "killing Buddha" there is 'killing ignorant people'; and also on "killing Buddha" there is 'not yet killing Buddha,' and also 'not yet killing people.' On "certain form" there is "no certain form." On "the mind is Buddha" there is "no mind, no Buddha." It is said in Bodhidharma's One Mind Precepts:

> One's original nature is marvelous. Not killing means to hold the view that death is not the end of existence, for the Dharma is eternal.

"Not killing" means to understand the Dharma always existing. Our life is Buddha's life. Buddha's life is the Unsurpassed Way. The Unsurpassed Way is always existing throughout past, present, and future. If we understand this Dharma, then "Buddha's seed" keeps increasing. In the Dharma world, Buddha nature will become brimful. The totality of the world becomes fully the Dharma or Buddha nature, Buddha's life. Buddha's life is eternal through past, present, and future. When we practice cross-legged sitting meditation, Buddha's life will continue. When we quit cross-legged sitting meditation, Buddha will die. Having wisdom (prajna), keeping the precepts (sila), and practicing sitting meditation (dhyana) are all the same thing. It is the meaning of the First Primary Precept, Not killing, as we studied.

> [Teacher Nanyue:] "...If you adhere to the form of sitting, you cannot reach the truth." For Dauyi, hearing the teaching was like drinking lassi.

This adhering isn't negative attachment, it is intimacy, to become the form of sitting itself and nothing else exists, only cross-legged sitting meditation exists in the whole world.

> The Way as its nature is perfectly open; why should we depend on our training to bring forth the evidence? The vehicle of the religious truth is free; of what need is endeavor? Moreover, the totality is far beyond all dust. Why should we believe we must keep cleaning? The totality is not apart from here. Of what use are the legs of the mendicant trainee?
>
> (*Fukan zazengi* [Recommended protocol for sitting meditation])

This is the state of what we should do, what we can do,

and what we want to do, all at the same time achieved. Because we enjoy our training, "why should we depend on our training to bring forth the evidence?" Because we enjoy our training life, we are "of what need is endeavor?" In other words, when we are enjoying our training (practicing sitting meditation) there is only training and there is no "Way." So it is said, "If you adhere to the form of sitting, you cannot reach the truth." Adhering to the form of sitting (practicing sitting meditation) and reaching the truth are the same thing, intimate. Therefore when adhering to the form appears, reaching the truth is hidden. It is the dynamics that when one appears, the other is hidden.

> Lutzu [Lutzu Bauyun, ?-?] faced the wall as soon as any monks came to visit him. Hearing of that, Nanchyuan said "I always tell him if we don't nod in assent before the kalpa of formation, if we don't understand before Buddha's birth, we won't obtain even one or half of one person. In his way he will satisfy himself only when the Year of the Donkey comes.
>
> (*Tsungrung lu*, Case 23)

Nanchyuan and Lutzu were Dharma brothers. Nanchyuan saw through Lutzu. Lutzu was adhering to sitting form and for him there was no "training for the purpose of realization." When he was single-heartedly practicing sitting form, there was no truth of nodding "in assent before the kalpa of formation," no truth of "if we don't understand before Buddha's birth." When we single-heartedly practice sitting meditation, we are already attaining the truth itself. In what kind of time are we single-heartedly practicing sitting meditation? It is when we are graduating from endeavoring, habitually practicing without being conscious of it.

This is the life of the master rather than the life of the earnest apprentice. It is like a master sportsman always naturally assuming the right form for any action, thanks to a long career of engaging in right form. We must build up our mind and body to be a Buddhist patriarch so we can unconsciously practice Buddhist life, and in this stage we will be blocked by Buddhist conduct from doing un-Buddhist conduct. It is like a normal good mother who by her baby is blocked from any other unreflective conduct. Whether a sweltering day or with much else to do, she can't ignore or push away her baby.

Being blocked and adhering are the same thing. If we must be addicted to anything, be addicted to Buddhist life. If we thus practice sitting meditation, we can't be anything other than "adhering to the form of sitting." When we aren't anything other, then our form of sitting is "cannot reach the truth." This is the truth of rupa is rupa and sunyata is sunyata. In this adhering to the form of sitting, there is the true shedding of our body. The whole world will be the virtue of adhering to the form of our sitting, and this form of sitting is the content of the truth, experienced only when we practice sitting meditation and at no other time. So it is said:

> Abandon all affairs, do not stir up millions of matters, nor think good or evil, right or wrong. Stop your streaming consciousness, stop all thought and judgment, do not hope to become Buddha, nor attach to sitting or reclining.
>
> (*Fukan zazen gi* [Recommended protocol for sitting meditation])

Nanyue's sitting Buddha is "thought," Matzu's becoming Buddha is "the unthinkable." Nanyue's sitting Buddha sheds sitting Buddha, Matzu's becoming Buddha sheds becoming Buddha. Teacher and student combined have "nothing to do with thought." All these meanings are in Matzu's last words "Sunface Buddha, Moonface Buddha."

It is Buddha upon Buddha whether we are in the native land or in another, whether sick or well, at ease or stressed. However, we can confirm this truth only when zealously training.

February 24, 2009

Jaujou's Weed Stem

Jaujou said: "This old monk at one time grasps a weed stem and uses it as the Twelve-foot-high Golden Buddha, and at another time grasps the Twelve-foot-high Golden Buddha and uses it as a weed stem. Buddha is klesa and klesa is Buddha."
Question: "For whose sake does Buddha suffer klesa life?"
Jaujou: "For the sake of everyone."
Question: "How can we escape from the suffering of klesa?"
Jaujou: "What is the point of escaping from klesa?"

(Jaujou lu, entry 77)

Yuanwu uses Jaujou's first saying in his lecture on Case 4 and in his introduction to Case 8 of *Biyan lu*:

> One who understands sometimes makes a weed stem stand for the golden body twelve feet tall, and sometimes makes the golden body twelve feet tall stand for a weed stem.

Dogen too uses Jaujou's first saying with the same meaning after minor modifications in his "Instructions for Kitchen Officers."

> Grasp a vegetable stem and make the Twelve-foot-tall body. Invite the Twelve-foot-tall body and make a vegetable stem.

Putting aside how Jaujou's saying was popularly appreciated, we would like to understand his entry 77 fully and correctly. Shortages of understanding result in our enervation, misunderstanding blocks our throughways, and before we are aware of it we are minimizing the words of the great patriarchs.

1. Why did Jaujou say his second saying "Buddha is klesa, and klesa is Buddha" after his first "This old monk at one time grasps a weed stem and uses it as the Twelve-foot-high Golden Buddha, and at another time grasps the Twelve-foot-high Golden Buddha and use it as a weed stem"?

His second saying is a summary of the well-known Mahayana theology about the relationship between klesa and Bodhi. (In the Hinayana teaching, klesa and Bodhi are regarded as definite opposite values, the distance between as far as between heaven and earth, and not convertible. Sixth Patriarch Hueineng [638-713] in his *Lioutzu tanjing* was the first to clearly say "Ignorant people are Buddha, and klesa is Bodhi.")

Many people understand Jaujou's first saying almost as only a more concrete expression than his second saying; that is, the relation between his first and second sayings is a kind logarithm: a weed stem is klesa and the Twelve-foot-high Golden Buddha is Buddha; and a weed stem is the Twelve-foot-high Golden Buddha because klesa is Buddha. So the totality of his words is understood as "Our klesa, which is like a weed stem, is humble, a trifle, a negative value, but Jaujou uses it as Buddha, which is noble, majestic, and a positive value, the Twelve-foot-high Golden Buddha, and vice versa."

But Jaujou didn't intend his two sayings as a kind of logarithm, that is, he didn't bring his second saying just to make a parallel with his first. He wanted to show the vast difference between his first saying and his second; his second, the traditional and theological saying. This second saying is an equality of idea, which is not placed in human daily life. The first saying is a vigorous approval of the truth of the second saying. The theological truth can be proved in human life only through our religious training, which is expressed here with the rhetoric "grasps" and "uses." Into these words Jaujou poured his life experience of how to manage his klesa, that is, his thought and emotion, such as anger, greed, and ignorance. These two words, "grasps" and "uses," are keys for him to live up to his given human life within the total worlds of sunyata and rupa. The total world, which is the Dharma world for

Buddhists, can be enriched when the part of it that is human beings takes mastership in Buddhist training. This human honorable participation in the Dharma world is the teaching Jaujou wanted to be shared with his monks.

2. "For whose sake does Buddha suffer klesa life?" The monk almost understood his teacher Jaujou's intention, and he wanted to make sure about the relationship between human training and the Dharma world. For that, he needed to know the relationship between Buddha and klesa or sunyata and rupa.

3. Jaujou: "For the sake of everyone." Here we shouldn't imagine a powerful saint or any leader preaching to a mob. For Jaujou, Buddha and "everyone" aren't conflicting entities. For Jaujou, Buddha exists when each of us "grasps" and "uses." Otherwise Buddha exists nowhere in relation to us and at any time in the whole universe. (This is one example where we shouldn't minimize the words, for instance "grasps" and "uses.")

Therefore "everyone" too isn't a numerical collective noun. Jaujou means everyone who "grasps" and "uses." This was the meaning of Sakyamuni Buddha's declaration "In all the world of heaven and earth, I alone am respectable." His "I" was allowed and recommended to be recognized in every being in every direction, and it is Jaujou's meaning of "everyone."

Worldly "everyone" can't form and comprise the whole world. Ones who "grasps" and "uses" can form and comprise the Buddhist whole world, as Jaujou himself says, "This old monk grasps a weed stem and uses it as the Twelve-foot-high Golden Buddha." So, Buddhists can create the whole world, which is Buddha, on a weed stem, which is klesa. This is the most important content of Buddhist compassion. In Jaujou's whole world, everyone is accomplishing Buddhahood.

4. "How can we escape from the suffering of klesa?" Immediately after being told such an honorable idea as Buddha suffers klesa life for the sake of everyone, the monk doesn't wish to escape from such a compassionate life. He wishes only to know how to bear the suffering of klesa life, which sometimes occupies all his vigor, with loss of poise, which makes him sometimes wail in pain and frustration. Jaujou too must know the monk's wish to make his suffering more bearable. He too is bearing up under all sorts of klesa

sufferings, and of course he isn't opposed to relieving our klesa sufferings. He eats when hungry, drinks when thirsty, covers with more blankets when cold. He knows reliefs and comforts are natural needs for humans as long as we have our naturally given sense organs and perceptions. Before our self-encouragement for endurance and assiduity, we are already seeking relief and comfort, as we see in babies naturally seeking warmth and milk. So Jaujou asks:

5. "What is the point of escaping from klesa?" As we studied in 4., the meaning of this question in response to the monk's question is that there's no point in endeavor, because we have already acquired the skill, could master it naturally. Escaping from klesa shouldn't be a noble kasaya-donning monk's concern. The very concern should be how to make Buddha out of klesa. The episode ends here seemingly abruptly. But the ending is actually reasonable. Jaujou is telling the monk to return to the first saying: "This old monk at one time grasps a weed stem and uses it as the Twelve-foot-high Golden Buddha, and at another time grasps the Twelve-foot-high Golden Buddha and uses it as a weed stem."

Our point isn't to devote ourselves to the study of how to reduce the pain of klesa and isn't to increase the comfort of klesa. It is how to "grasp" our klesa and "use" it. As all good episodes should be, this episode is a cyclical, self-perfected, self-recycling manifestation of one truth.

Now how to "grasp" and "use"? Only True Buddhism knows. First we must believe all rupa, including klesa, is Buddha's compassionate devices to make us attain unsurpassed Buddhahood. Next we must figure out how all klesa concerns can be Buddha's compassionate devices. Each time we must make the connection of Buddha's compassionate devices in the endless cycle of our Buddhist training, to raise Bodhi mind, to actually practice, to recognize Bodhi, and to attain Nirvana. The validity of Buddha's compassionate devices is maintained only by Buddhist training and not by any other cultural values.

* * *

A weed stem isn't a trivial matter for Buddha's Dharma, and also isn't a newly invented allegory. There is in a weed stem the right attitude and great attainment to change our self or to change our world.

> The World Honored One walking with followers pointed to the earth and said, "Here a temple should be built." Indra plucked a weed stem, stood it on the earth and said, "A sacred temple is built."
> The World Honored One gave a smile.
>
> (Tsungrung lu, Case 4)

In this Indra episode also, "a weed stem" is given significant meaning as we studied it in *Jaujou lu*, entry 77. Here too it must be used to mean our klesa. But in this episode the place "here" is given additional important meaning by the World Honored One.

"Here" isn't "there," "then," "that," "others," "other shore." "Here" is "a weed stem." "There" must be not "here, "now," "this," "oneself," "this shore." It is "the Twelve-foot-high Golden Buddha."

"Here" was specifically said in the situation "The World Honored One walking with followers." "Here" means Sakyamuni Buddha was living the same life with his followers, enjoying the same joy, suffering the same difficulty. Yet he was regarding their well-being, hoping they will understand they are dwelling in a temple no matter what their circumstances.

"Temple" is always where the Dharma is practiced without pollution, that is, without exercising any dualistic notions. It is the world of no division between "here" and "there" as we listed above, but most of all it is the world of no causation or mortality. As usual, we must be careful that these no divisions don't mean absence of any being. Buddha's Dharma is built on being and not on non-being, and no division means that each being is transcending itself while satisfying its being.

Indra (likely an actual disciple with the same name as Sakra Devanam Indra, God of Lightning in the Vedic age, later by Buddhism adapted as a guardian), this "Indra" without delay "plucked a weed stem" and "stood it on the earth," with his colligated judgment, "A sacred temple is built." This episode is regarded as substantially identical with the following:

> The Tathagata when he was Prince Sumedha in the era of Dipankara-buddha spread his hair over the muddy pathway to make way for him.
> Dipankara-buddha said, "Here a temple should be built." The Prince plucked a weed stem and stood it on the earth, saying "A sacred temple is built."
> *(Abhiniskramana-sutra*, vol. 4)

This episode is in the sutra *Jataka*, telling how Sakyamuni trained as various Bodhisattvas so as to attain his Buddhahood. Naturally emphasized in this episode is his practice of Bodhisattva deeds or personal virtues, such as dana, sila, and ksanti (endurance). To Buddha he gave up his personal pleasures and desires and as a token of total devotion he offered (seven flowering lotus stems and then) his own hair, regarded as a most precious personal possession. His offering to pave the mud is an allegorical expression, to purify the polluted and suffering world.

The area he could cover with his hair wasn't such a measurable area as three feet square. It is everywhere in the Ten Directions past, present, and future. The Buddhist world is called "the Ten Directions" because it exists in every being endlessly extending in the Ten (countless) Directions. Even on the head of an ant is such an endless world.

The area Sumedha could cover with his hair is the quantity (unlimitedness) and quality (compassion of no division) of the temple that Dipankara-buddha recommended to be built. There Sumedha's practice of dana or ksanti, for instance, was backed up by his sure understanding of prajna, wisdom. This "temple" was the prajna world on the muddy ignorant world.

In this Prince Sumedha episode we see the great change of environment caused by his training under Dipankara-buddha. We can assume Indra's environment must also have changed greatly in his building a temple, though it wasn't directly referred to in that episode. Its main issue is how Indra could attain such a mentality as to see "here" as "there," to convert "a weed stem" to "the Twelve-foot-high Golden Buddha," to change his klesa to Buddha nature, and to change his suffering life to satisfactory Nirvana. On this point the Indra episode is highly similar with Jaujou's "grasp" and "use."

In the Indra episode there wasn't muddy land. What he had to gather was the power to "grasp" and "use." Those words describe the active and positive conducts of those with no doubt of their confidence and responsibility in managing their life as well as their circumstances. They manage their given occasions and situations, their daily doings, even in suffering and crying, just as Linji strongly recommended to us: "At any rate do not be influenced by any human delusions. Master yourself. Then the world wherever you stand immediately becomes the truth itself." (*Linji lu,* lectures 13 and 17)

This mastership in Buddha's Dharma shouldn't be messily confused with such worldly phenomena as to attain a superior position in conflicting or competing relations or to acquaint with such skill to attain a certain standard repeatedly. This mastership can include such attaining too but includes also the failing of attaining. It is the delightful recognition and exercise that our life is the Dharma life, and that the peak of the total Dharma is surfacing through each individual life.

Linji (?-867) was slightly senior to Jaujou, and Jaujou once visited Linji. (See *Linji lu,* Dialogue 40) It is easy to see that Jaujou must have well mastered Linji's teaching before he had the opportunity for such an episode with the monk as we saw in *Jaujou lu,* entry 77. We can assume he studied these other episodes, Sumedha, and Indra, though it isn't so easy to detect how sensitively he did. But he certainly studied the relationship between person and environment.

Of course Sumedha and Indra were dwelling in the same Buddha's Dharma. The sameness of the two episodes is more obvious when we think that Prince Sumedha in the Dipankara era became the World Honored One in our era. But we shouldn't over-simplify, saying that they are all the same. The Sumedha episode focuses on change of environment, Indra on change of self.

We are made from Dharma-kaya, so too is our environment. So these two episodes are about the same subject, but with different nuance, different way of approaching the Dharma. We'd like to activate the Dharma more and wish to use it more efficiently. We should be intimate with Dharma instead of strangers to it. So we should be sensitive in understanding the sameness and difference.

* * *

Su Dungpo (known also as Su Shy, 1036-1101) is one of the most important poets throughout Chinese entire history and he was the best prose writer in the Sung dynasty. We are thankful for his studying the Dharma and clarifying it through his writing.

> One day the Teacher [Foyin Liauyuan, 1032-1098] invited each student to his room for Zen interview. The layman Su Dungpo promptly appeared to the very front of his face.
> The Teacher said: "Here has no meditation seat. Layman, what will you do here?"
> Dungpo: "I will borrow the Four Elements of Foyin to use as a seat."
> The Teacher: "I have a question for you. If you can answer, you can sit down. If not, you must give me your belt with its ornamenting gems."
> Dungpo said with delight, "Please ask."
> The Teacher: "You say you will borrow my Four Elements to use as a seat. They are essentially empty and the Five Gatherings are no being. Where will you sit?"
> Dungpo could not respond. At last he handed over his belt with ornamenting gems.
> The Teacher in turn gave him a kasaya.
> (*Liandeng hueiyau*, vol. 5)

Dungpo's belt was ornamented with gems so precious it would be designated a national treasure if it survived to this day. This donation in exchange for a kasaya reminds us of Sumedha's behavior.

Dungpo later visited Dunglin Changtzung (1025-1091) at Mt. Lu and was told the topic of the preaching of insentient beings. The next morning he came to a great realization, made the following poem, and his understanding was approved by his second teacher, Dunglin.

> The sound of the brook is Buddha's eloquent preaching.
> The figure of the mountain is nothing other than the figure

of pure Dharma-kaya.
Eighty-four thousand gathas are delivered since last night.
How to tell of it to people in the coming days? (*Pudeng lu*, vol.23)

Su Dungpo now could see mountain as pure Dharma-kaya, could hear the sound of the brook as Buddha's preaching, or as the preaching of insentient beings. This mountain means everything that has form. So it isn't only a geological mountain but includes our body too. It is every being, so it isn't simply considering all beings on this planet or in this solar system. Sumedha could turn mud to temple with a weed stem; Indra could with a weed stem build a temple. Su Dungpo in one night could change all ten directions and all beings to Buddha's body or Buddha's preaching.

"Since last night" is his euphemistic expression to extinguish the fire of his klesa, human value judgment. By his extinguishing, all nature, causations, mortals, and meaningless repetitions began to act as Dharma-kaya, or Buddha. It seems his extinguishing made mountain and river able to function as Buddha instead of their being continuously ignorant and instead of making himself an able man who can "use a weed stem as the Twelve-foot-high Golden Buddha."

Should we become able persons who can control their klesa? Yes, it is hoped so. Should we become ordinary persons blessed for being surrounded by Dharma-kaya mountain and Buddha-nature water? Yes, it is hoped so. We with our klesa are made from Buddha nature, and our surroundings too are made from Buddha nature. It is reasonable if we help our surroundings to act as Buddha nature and if we control our klesa to behave as Buddha nature. All are made to help one another.

Who are we and what are our surroundings if Su Dungpo was one who could hear only the preaching of sentient beings and was unable to hear the preaching of insentient beings?

Mountain and river will be more beneficial than harmful in areas where periodic wind causes typhoon or hurricane, because the periodic wind brings heat and moisture for the birth and growth of life. In such areas good people are those who are thankful for the gift of nature, and who cooperate to secure recycling benefits.

On the other hand, mountains and rivers will be more

harmful than beneficial in areas with no periodic wind. Mountains and rivers are dry oceans of sand, gravel, or rock for those who live in such hot and dry areas. There good people are those who steal some good from nature and who labor together to control nature.

In either case, their view about their surroundings can't avoid being polluted by human desire, klesa, and nature will remain just as geographic mountains and rivers as long as we keep our dualistic view. Besides, nature showing as geographic mountains and rivers isn't the true nature of mountains and rivers.

Shiangyan (Shiangyan Jyshian, ?-898) is another great example. Nature nursed as Dharma-kaya by him helped him to realize he was Dharma-kaya:

> When Shiangyan Jyshian was studying the Way in the assembly under Zen Teacher Dakuei Dayuan, Dakuei said to him, "You are bright and learned. Express to me one phrase for the world before your parents were born, but do not depend on your memory of any gathas or annotations."
>
> (*Chuandeng lu*, vol. 11)

The guiding of Dakuei (=Kueishan Lingyou, 771-853) was highly intellectual, fair enough to respect a student's ability to be universal, in contrast to leaders who promote an ethical obligation.

> Shiangyan several times tried to express, but could not. He deeply condemned his own body and mind, opened the books he had been keeping for years, and was lost. Finally he took all those books he had gathered over the years, set them on fire, and said, "Painted cakes cannot relieve hunger. I vow I will not wish to understand Buddha's Dharma in this life. I will simply become a priest who serves meals to other monks." Thus he spent some years and some months.
>
> After the passing of many years, Shiangyan visited the trace of National Teacher Dajeng [Nanyang Hueijung, ?-775] on Mt. Wudang and there he built and dwelled in a thatched hermitage. (Ibid.)

This is an intellectual way to "grasp" and "use" our klesa, or "weed stem." Klesa is given ample opportunity to exercise its best ability and is almost voluntarily transcending itself: "I vow I will not wish to understand Buddha's Dharma in this life.

I will simply become a priest who serves meals to other monks."

To quietly spend his remaining life, Shiangyan chose the best place we can hope, the trace of National Teacher Nanyang. Nanyang was the first to advocate the importance of hearing the preaching of insentient beings.

Shiangyan planted bamboo for companionship. In the lonely life with no sight of any human beings, bamboo most resembles animal life among plants. The new shoots are like animal cubs. The wind passing through their leaves is like a human whisper, and the moon rising above their grove reminded him of the sky of his native land.

> One day as he was sweeping the path, a bit of tile was thrown and it struck a cane of bamboo. At the sound of the resonance, he suddenly attained the great realization. (Ibid.)

Who has no experience of a bit of tile or a pebble striking a bamboo, just as who has no experience of hearing the sound of a brook and seeing a mountain peak? Shiangyan "suddenly attained the great realization." It is more suitable to say he was helped in attaining the great realization by the bamboo and bit of tile.

Could this fortune have occurred if he had happened to dislike bamboo and tile? Even if disliking, he could easily have heard their physical sound, but their physical sound wouldn't have been the preaching of insentient beings that are the Dharma-kaya. Who gave power to the bamboos and tile to make Shiangyan realize? What he engaged in was rather not to "grasp" and "use" his klesa. He was sharing time and space with them with mutual love, trust, and respect. He made a gatha:

> One strike made knowing forgotten
> with nothing further to correct.
> Clearing the old path in daily conduct
> without falling into inactivity.

He forgot his klesa and physical environment. There is "nothing further to correct" once we understand that our klesa and environment are not klesa and not environment, but are Dharma-kaya. The life of such a Dharma person is in full combustion in proving that everything for that person, both internal and external, is Dharma-kaya. By one's own life one is directly proving one's life will never cease even in rest time. Self-proving is another name of Dharma activity.

One of Shiangyan's Dharma brothers was Lingyun (Lingyun Shichin, ?-?). Lingyun was one day climbing the slope of a village settlement. When he came up to a little hill, all of a sudden there was a peach orchard in full bloom. What kind of hand care did it take to nurse such a peach orchard that could gave him the confidence of Dharma life?

Later he reflected on this experience and made a simple gatha, so simple we must be cautious not to wander into a byroad, but must go directly to the core of his reflection, the core of Buddha's Dharma:

> A passenger was searching thirty years for his lost sword.
> So many times leaves fell and branches budded.
> From the moment of the single sight of flowering peach,
> no rise of doubt.

By the first couplet he regrets he spent half a lifetime in ignorance and is saddened he couldn't fully appreciate the true kindness and beauty of the surrounding nature. In the second he enjoys his having attained the same wisdom and compassion as Sakyamuni Buddha, and in his "no rise of doubt" there is the determination to help those who are not yet coming to the same awakening.

"A passenger" is referring to a fool in the Country of Chu who from a moving boat dropped his sword into a harbor, and marked the location on the gunwale so as to later search for his sword. Lingyun, like that foolish passenger, was seeing only surface phenomena. The phenomena were tediously and meaninglessly repeating their rise and fall, causing him pain and relief, leaves falling, flowers blooming. Not finding the right way to find his sword, which is the spirit of phenomena, is to practice the wicked view that results in devaluating one's surroundings and oneself, even though Yunjia (Yungjia Shyuanjyue, ?-713) had cautioned us: "If you do not wish to create cause to enter the endless hell, do not devaluate the Tathagata's continuous turning of Right Dharma Wheel." (*Jengda ge*).

But by "the single sight of flowering peach" Lingyun

could see the profound Truth, the True Cause underlying the surface cause and effect. It was as if seeing in the disturbing waves the water. He was seeing the endless universal flowering season. Spring wasn't limited to any particular region, season, and person. He realized it was even in winter, even at the back side of the moon, even in jail, even in this saha world. Such spring exists everywhere, every time, in every being, whether sage or ignorant, sentient or insentient. This spring exists even in the klesa of anger, greed, and ignorance. Once he saw this spring he must have felt "Why would I grasp and use a weed stem? By seeing endless spring, a weed stem is already the Twelve-foot-high Golden Buddha!"

This spring is universal existence in all ten directions past, present, and future. In India "flower" meant lotus; in China, peach; in Japan, cherry. For Lingyun, flowering peach was Sakyamuni Buddha's raising a stemmed lotus flower; he was like Mahakasyapa, who smiled in understanding what Buddha meant. Buddha was raising a stem of wisdom to see wisdom as well as compassion as universally and equally innate, in every being, every phenomenon.

Until Lingyun saw the flowering peach orchard he couldn't by himself prove Buddha's teaching. He was seeing peach only as a horticultural fruit tree, an effect of phenomena. His life was that of a mere mammal and his klesa was negative, not grasped by him and used for a good purpose.

So did his klesa bring his realization? Unless his klesa was not Dharma-kaya, how could it make him see it as Dharma? Did the flowering peaches help his realization? Unless they were not Dharma-kaya, how could they help him to see them as Dharma-kaya? Here there is reason we must widen and deepen our definition of Jaujou's "grasp" and "use." Jaujou said: "This old monk at one time grasps a weed stalk and uses it as the Twelve-foot-high Golden Buddha, and at another time grasps the Twelve-foot-high Golden Buddha and uses it as weed stem." Later Lingyun said: "Before the donkey affairs leave, the horse affairs have arrived."

* * *

We began to understand that "a weed stem" is the "Twelve-foot-high Golden Buddha." Both are active figures of Dharma-kaya. We also began to understand that we and our surroundings whether they are "a weed stem" or the "Twelve-foot-high Golden Buddha" are also Dharma-kaya. In other words, both our inside and outside are Dharma-kaya. Our conducts, to "grasp" and to "use," are also the activity of Dharma-kaya.

Changsha (Changsha Jingtsen, ?-?) is Jaujou's Dharma brother under their teacher Nanchyuan (Nanchyuan Puyuan, 748-834). They must have received the same education, but Changsha was more expressive than Jaujou about the relation between us and our surroundings, or the relation between Dharma-kaya and phenomena. We hope we can study by the deeper underlying mechanism what Jaujou meant in his "grasping" and "using" by following Changsha. In his formal lecture he said:

> The whole world in the ten directions is the one eye of the sramana [trainee, monk, pure attitude], the whole ten directions are the sramana's daily words, the whole ten directions are the sramana's whole body, the whole ten directions are the light of the sramana's self, in the whole ten directions there is no one who is not theサsramana's self.
> (*Chuandeng lu*, vol. 10)

Changsha proposed five standard understandings about the triangular relations between Buddha, the World, and each trainee. "Sramana" is a friendly way of addressing Sakyamuni Buddha, though here it is used as ideological Buddha instead of historical Buddha. There is a tendency in the patriarchs to give their subject more gravity by the use of more concise words. So some precise study is needed.

*   *   *

1. The whole world in the ten directions is the one eye of the sramana: This "whole world," as we have already studied a certain amount, is the Buddhist worlds. It is the astronomical universe if we think of its largeness, but it has no limit in size or time span, so there's no beginning and no end. It is in a subatomic particle too if we think of its smallness and yet it has no limit to its extent. It is in any being and function, including material sentient and insentient, including even our notion and word. Each is endless in its extent and yet they each don't disturb one another. Therefore each of "the whole ten directions" is infinite, and the totality of "the whole ten directions" is also infinite.

So Changsha says any of "the whole ten directions" or all of "the whole world in the ten directions" ("any " and "all" end up the same) are the one eye of Buddha transcending dualistic view, hence called "one eye." This "one eye" is the wisdom and compassion accomplished by Sakyamuni Buddha, and is already mentioned when Lingyun's peach was flowering. So Changsha gave trainees a Buddhist standard here, which is that any trainee must be able to see in any being and any affair "the whole ten directions," and it should be discerned as Buddha's wisdom and compassion. For example, when we face our own or others' anger we must be able to see in it Buddha's wisdom and compassion.

Facing others' anger doesn't mean to see an angel face floating on a furious face. It also doesn't mean if someone strikes you on the cheek, to turn the other also. This isn't about psychological and social solutions. Whether we are raging or another is raging, our gut will tighten, our internal secretions and emotions greatly disturbed. But here our concern is eternal being, the eternal spring underneath our phenomena. The world of phenomena is the world influenced by causation, and the eternal being underneath our phenomena sheds causation. We must gradually realize that our life belongs to this world of no causation rather than to the world of causation with its transitory and partial manner.

This "one eye" is transmitted from patriarch to patriarch ever since transmitted from Sakyamuni Buddha to Mahakasyapa. It can be transmitted to only those who lose their life in their teacher's life and when the teacher loses his life in his disciples' life. When we lose our ego, the surrounding nature sheds itself and begins to show the Buddhist whole world in the ten directions.

2. The whole ten directions are the sramana's daily words: The daily words of the Buddhist trainee must be speaking truths and not speaking untruths. It is because not speaking untruths is the figure and the nature of the whole world in the ten directions. The truth in the whole world in the ten directions keeps telling (=preaching) the world of no causation, eternal spring, the life of the Dharma-kaya, which is the true life of us each.

So here "truth" means the underlying fact of phenomena, and it doesn't mean the truth that is a concept contrasting with untruth, falsehood, or lie, in the phenomenal world. For the Buddhist, every being and behavior within phenomena is called an untruth, whether or not it is a social, legal, historic, aesthetic, scientific, or any other dualistic truth. Only such a world as is described in the *Prajnaparamita-hrdaya-sutra* as not being born, not going to ruin, not pure, not impure, not increasing, and not decreasing is regarded as the truth. It doesn't mean the phenomenal world is only negative in its values. To be born as a human being in the phenomenal world, which is the whole ten directions, is as rare as the sand under one fingernail compared with the sand of all macrocosms. Actually the phenomenal world is the device to understand the world underlying phenomena. "Underlying" doesn't mean the phenomenal world and the world transcending the phenomenal world exist in a double layer. It means the phenomenal world is the very world transcending the phenomenal world.

Now Changsha gave us the second standard, to live the trainee's life in which we always detect the true words in our every gesture, behavior, and notion, each of which is the ten directions. Each word and act of the trainee should agree with the words of the ten directions. In short we must go along with causation.

Then we are like Su Dungpo, Shiangyan, or Lingyun, who could hear the preaching of insentient beings. It is a tragedy if the side telling and the side hearing are not in perfect accord.

3. The whole ten directions are the sramana's whole body:

The size and function of great persons like Buddha and the patriarchs are equal with the size and function of the whole world in the ten directions. They don't divide the worlds from themselves. So when they see any world, it isn't the mere geographic world but is the Buddhist world, that is, in the ten directions. Naturally in each of their ten directions there is Buddha. Thus their world is Buddha's worlds, just as Sakyamuni Buddha pointed to both heaven and earth. This "heaven" and "earth" aren't merely two areas, just as "ten directions" doesn't mean any literal ten directions. They are endless areas and endless directions, and they don't divide themselves apart. This is the fundamental reason we can possibly see Buddha in any world and Buddha can possibly help all sentient and insentient beings in the past, future and present world. Wherever Buddha dwells is called Pure Land. Pure Land doesn't exist without Buddha. That is to say, the vital condition to see Pure Land is to understand this third standard of Changsha. Pure Land is neither at such a distance as another galaxy nor at such a near distance as our psychological spot.

4. The whole ten directions are the light of the sramana's self: Here Buddha nature (=sramana's self) is compared to sunlight spread equally all over the world. Buddha nature is also a universal and formless existence, which can be detected only through materialistic existence as if light can be sensed only as heat. Changsha here says the whole ten directions, which are the worlds seen through the Buddhist trainee, are the universal light of Buddha (and the same should be said of the Buddha nature of each individual trainee). The usage of the word "light" was to refer to such attributes of Buddha nature as being rather than non-being, positive and active rather than negative and passive, bright and direct rather than dark and indirect. In sum, wonderful Buddha nature is universal in the whole ten directions, and the wonderful whole ten directions are Buddha nature.

It seems as if to say there is (universal) Buddha nature in the whole ten directions. But actually it isn't true. Buddha nature is the whole world in the ten directions, and vice versa. Buddha nature and the whole world in the ten directions are same thing. However, when we see the whole ten directions we don't see Buddha nature, and when we see Buddha nature we don't see the whole ten directions. Because they are same thing, we see only one of them at one time. If we happen to see both at one time we are actually not seeing them really but are seeing only concepts or shadows of them.

They are the same thing, so it is possible to have such a relation as when we can say "I take a bath, and the bath takes me," or "I tend to the plants, and the plants tend to me." Because they are the same, Su Dungpo was helped by the mountain brook and the mountain brook was helped by him. Lingyun was helped by the flowering peaches and the flowering peaches were helped by him.

They are same thing so it is impossible to see them both at one time. For instance, a furious flare of klesa is Buddha nature, yet we can't see Buddha nature in it and see only its furious flare (which is the ten directions.) When Buddha nature takes a form, we can't see its nature, we see only its form. The earthquakes or hurricanes that steal thousands of lives and a million happinesses are the whole ten directions for Buddhists, the light of Sakyamuni Buddha or the Buddhist trainee, Buddha's wisdom as well as Buddha's compassion. We can see only the form of Buddha nature, and unfortunately cannot see Buddha nature. There is the path for the Bodhisattva to go in this gap between formless existence and form existence of Buddha nature.

Primarily our eyes and the objects of our eyes, our ears and the objects of our ears, our nose and the objects of our nose, our tongue and the objects of our tongue, our tactile sense and the objects of our tactile sense, and our mental function and the objects of our mental function are the same, made by the same Buddha nature, and yet it is a pity that we often see them as if in hostile relations. Here there is the bottomless depth of our ignorance and there is the un-exposable height of Buddha's compassion. We are better off to go on studying the meandering way, on and on.

5. In the whole ten directions there is no one who is not the sramana's self: "Sramana's self" is Buddha nature. Here Changsha is saying Buddha nature is every trainee's nature. This is the same as Buddha's declaration that all sentient and insentient beings innately possess Buddha nature. To sum up

his five articles in one list of synonyms:

> The whole world in the ten directions = Buddha's eye
> = trainee's daily words = Buddha's Body
> = light of Buddha nature = trainee's nature.

Changsha hoped his followers through their monastic life would gain confidence in these five standards. Mostly they engaged in meditation and garden work. For them the opportunity to ask the teacher directly about their meditation subject was an exciting event.

> A monk: "How can one make mountain, river, and the great earth return to oneself?"
> The Teacher: "How can one make oneself return to mountain, river, and the great earth?"
> The monk: "I do not understand."
> The Teacher: "The region south of the Lake is fertile to sustain its denizens, rice is cheap, firewood ample, in all four quarters."
> The monk had no words.
> Then the Teacher made a gatha:
>> Who is asking to return mountain and river?
>> Mountain and river return to whom?
>> Freely they come and go and there are no two sides.
>> Dharma-kaya has no place to return.
>
> (*Chuandeng lu*, vol. 10)

As long as the monk's "oneself" is the biological and psychological self, such "oneself" and a geographic mountain will never have any relation, they are absolutely foreign to each other. We think we fight against mountain, conquer, and tame, but such thought is a mere one-sided view. Mountain isn't fighting with us. Mountain, river, and the great earth shed their geographic features and act as Dharma-kaya when we forget our ego, our one-sided hostile relation.

At such time when we and our surroundings are Dharma-kaya, we having meals and the rice we eat can be the same. One of the Buddhist practical teachings is "not to worry about foods, care only about the Dharma." In Jaujou's "grasping" and "using" this way of understanding, we and our surroundings are hidden. Then, we would like to know, what are the Buddhist mountain, river, and great earth?

Langshie (Langshie Hueijyue, ?-?) was a contemporary with Shyuedou (Shyuedou Jungshian, 980-1052) and in that period they were admired as two great amarta. The dialogue between Langshie and Changshuei (Changshuei Tzyshyuan, 1038-?) was adapted as the final case, one of the most important cases, in *Tsungrung lu*:

> A monk asked the Reverend Langshie, "Being pure is the primary state. How do mountain, river, and the great earth immediately arise?"
> Langshie replied, "Being pure is the primary state. How do mountain, river, and the great earth immediately arise?"
> (*Tsungrung lu*, case 100)

The monk, Changshuei, belonged to a different sect, the Huayan sect, established on the teaching of the Huayan Sutra (*Mahavaipulya-buddhavatamsaka-sutra*). At the time he brought this question, he was making annotations on the *Surangama-sutra*, a sutra unfolding Buddha's dauntless Samadhi. He had advanced his annotation up to volume 4, where there is Purna's question "If all six sense organs, six objects of six sense organs, and the worlds consisting of these six sense organs and six objects are Tathagata-garbha [= Buddha nature], how do all beings such as mountain, river, and the great earth take form, change sooner or later, finally end their existence, and all over again begin each to take form?"

To Purna's question, the sutra records the response "Analyze it and you will understand it. The Body of Awakening is primordially wonderment. Ignorance is primordially empty. Mountain, river, and the great earth are like illusory forms in the air. When we are lost, we carelessly divide ourselves from our objects. As soon as we artificially awaken our mind, such minute forms rise in our mind and the four preceding stages of the earth's formation are germinated."

The theology is only analyzing the process of phenomenal transition. It isn't challenging us to see the fundamental cause beneath the surface mutual relations and phenomenal cause (which is indirect cause, not direct cause). Nor is it suggesting how from urgent reality to find the answer. Buddhist trainees under overwhelming governance of theology are sad because they suppressed their creativity and expected to make themselves inured to think in such an indecisive manner utterly contrary to the way Sakyamuni recommended to us.

Changshuei was a righteous person and couldn't annotate or skip what he couldn't clarify. Indeed he didn't understand the meaning of the repetitious change of the environment causing sorrow, ugliness, and suffering. Buddha repeatedly said the environment and everything else is Buddha nature. Yet, it seemed mountain, river, and the great earth were causing torture for creatures in collusion with too much or too little water, fire, and wind, and soon they invite warfare, plague, and starvation.

So, Changshuei asked Langshie: "Being pure is the primordial state. How do mountain, river, and the great earth immediately arise?"

In asking, he was indeed dividing himself and his environment just as the theology analyzed. With divided mind if we see a mountain we can see it only as a geographic mountain. In response Langshie just repeated what Changshuei asked: "Being pure is the primordial state. How do mountain, river, and the great earth immediately arise?"

This parroting was Langshie's remarkable educative skill, and because of this turning power of human attitude, triggering human intellectual rebirth, this episode was placed at the end of *Tsungrung lu* to begin afresh. Right off, Changshuei understood a million differences in the sameness, and which difference he should see was utterly his choice. Teacher Langshie "grasped" and "used" every available circumstance in order to awaken one more person on this earth. Truly Changshuei has been "grasped" and "used" by phenomena or by Buddha nature.

From then on, he was able to freely "grasp" and "use" his surroundings. His virtue to make his fortunate realization come true must have been very high and vast. (This is the nature of the Buddhist mountain, "high" because the bodhisattva keeps seeking *anuttara-samyak-sambodhi* in any given situation and "vast" because the bodhisattva with attained wisdom is determined to help all sentient and insentient beings. Thus the Buddhist mountain isn't staying still but is constantly moving.) Changshuei kept believing Buddha's teaching that all sentient and insentient beings, mountains, rivers, and the great earth, are at once accomplishing Buddhahood, and he trusted a teacher of another sect. He was a decent person. Without hesitation he asked what he didn't understand, though it should have been the matter he was at home with.

Shyu-Chuandeng lu, volume 7, records how this dialogue concluded:

> The Teacher [Changshuei] came to full realization, and he said in thanks, "Grant my wish to be your attendant."
> Langshie told him, "A long time it has been since your sect declined. Devote yourself to saving it in returning your thanks for Buddha's love. You had better not change your sect."
> Changshuei obeyed the teaching and left Langshie after offering the repeated homage.
> Later, having the opportunity to lecture to the assembly, he said, "The Way can be attained outside the words, and the Zen can be understood beyond intellectual inquiries. There is no different destination when the mind is grasped and the origin is known."

Whether we "grasp" or not, "use" or not, first we must understand that as soon as we see mountain, river, and the great earth as geographic beings, they hide their primordial state of purity. Exactly the same can be said of all natural phenomena, earthquake, lightning, flood, drought, severe heat and cold, illness, aging, and death. The same can be said of every social phenomenon—poverty, discrimination, hate, sorrow.

By any means we mustn't cast the shadow of our desires on them. We had better believe mountain, river, and the great earth are Buddha nature. If they aren't Buddha nature, then Venus didn't help Gautama to be awakened, there is no preaching of insentient beings, and there will be no glimpse of beauty of any objects for our sense organs, and there will be no love, trust, and respect among human beings. Most of all, there will be for us no suffering.

Not casting the shadow of our desires on our surroundings means to respect the Dharma more than we respect ourselves. Believing Buddha nature means to rely on oneself, after all.

Didn't Sakyamuni say as his last teaching to Ananda, "Make yourself like an island in the ocean and depend on yourself. Make the Dharma your torch and rely on it, rely on nothing else."

May to July 2009

The Meaning of the Eighth Primary Precept, Not Being Stingy

It is not easy to understand the Eighth Primary Precept: Not being stingy with the Dharma and the Treasure, or the Dharma, that is, the Treasure.

First of all, we are soaked with the worldly definition of stingy and we naturally understand this precept as a recommendation to be generous in giving. But the Buddhist meaning seems obviously different from such worldly virtue. In the transmission of Bodhidharma's One Mind Precepts it is said:

> One's original nature is marvelous. Not being stingy with the Dharma and the Treasure, or the Dharma, that is, the Treasure, means not to raise any concept of any particular form, for universal Truth pervades the Dharma.

Here "One's original nature" isn't one's nature attained after birth by mutual relations. Rather, it is the same as to say one's original nature is the nature of the whole world in the ten directions throughout past, present, and future. So Buddhists view the precept Not Being Stingy from the standpoint of the nature of the world rather than from the standpoint of the human being. We must study Buddha's view rather than investigate human views.

For Buddha's view, raising any concept of any particular form is already a violation of this precept, because any form is different from any other form and becomes cause of being stingy to the effect of depreciating the nature of the world.

When we cannot transcend difference of form, we have great difficulty to practice the Compassion. Discriminating between different forms, we inevitably exercise our investigation and calculation and thus limit our understanding of other.

We have Bodhidharma's gatha made on the occasion of his transmission of the Dharma:

> The primary reason I came to this land
> was to transmit the Dharma to help confused sentient beings.
> If one flower opens with five leaves
> the fruits will naturally form. (*Chuandeng lu*, vol. 3)

Bodhidharma is reflecting on his main reason for being born into this world. It wasn't just to make a big geographic travel but was to transmit the Dharma to help confused sentient beings. The fundamental meaning in transmitting the Dharma is to enable sentient beings to see the abstract Dharma in concrete phenomena (that is, in Dungshan's rhetoric, "to see with our ears and hear with our eyes).

So Bodhidharma said "...the Dharma and the Treasure, or the Dharma, that is, the Treasure..."

Indeed when we raise any concept of any particular form between forms, and between the abstract Dharma and concrete phenomena, we are forced to be stingy in the task of helping confused sentient beings, including ourselves.

Dogen's annotation to this Eighth Primary Precept, Not Being Stingy, accords with this understanding, as expected:

> Not being stingy means to study that there is no self and no others.

"There is no self and no others" means no distinction between this person and that person, and further, no distinction between the Dharma and concrete phenomena. Buddhists study this truth through the relationship between teacher and disciple until no distinction exists between teacher and disciple, which means, as is said, "self realization without a teacher," or "self realization without a self."

By now we can begin to understand the Buddhist precept Not being stingy with the Dharma and the Treasure, or the Dharma, that is, the Treasure. (This "Treasure" must mean "concrete phenomena" in our usage of the words.) Now, here is Dogen's *Kyoju kaimon* (Transmitted Essence):

> One phrase, one gatha, a million forms, a hundred weeds. One Dharma, one Realization, all Buddhas, all

The Meaning of the Eighth Primary Precept, Not Being Stingy 209

patriarchs. Never have they been stingy.

With the help of Bodhidharma's One Mind Precept, we can rewrite *Kyoju kaimon* in ordinary prose:

> The content of any phrase, any gatha, expressing the Nature of the world, is not different from any physical form, any physical weed. Any Dharma, any Realization, is not different from any Buddha, any patriarch. Never have they been stingy.

After all, this *Kyoju kaimon* is stating there is no distinction between Dharma and concrete phenomena. The statement content is Buddhist wisdom, prajna. So it is said in the *Maha-prajnaparamita-hrdaya-sutra*:

> Rupa is not different from sunyata, sunyata is not different from rupa. Rupa is sunyata, sunyata is rupa.

Now we can move our interest from understanding what the Eighth Primary Precept means to how to practice it. In the *Maha-prajnaparamita-sutra*, volume 172, it is written:

> Sakyamuni Buddha said: "Sariputra, all sentient beings should serve, respect, and regard this prajna-paramita as the living Buddha. Why should they serve, respect, and regard it as the Bhagavad [World Honored One]? The reason is that prajna-paramita is not different from Bhagavad, and Bhagavad is not different from prajna-paramita. Prajna-paramita is Bhagavad, Bhagavad is prajna-paramita. Why so? Sariputra, the reason that all Tathagatas and all Nirmana-kayas come out from this prajna-paramita. Sariputra, the reason is that all Bodhisattvas, Pratyeka Buddhas, Arhats, Srotapannas, Sakradagamins, and Anaagamins come out from this prajna-paramita. Why so? Sariputra, the reason is that all Ten Good Deeds of the worldly world, Four Dhyanas, Four No-form Dhyanas, and Five Divine Powers come out from this prajna-paramita.

This is the source of the Eighth Primary Precept, Not Being Stingy. At any rate, when we don't divide self (Dharma) from other (concrete phenomena), we can keep this precept. The figure of not dividing is described in this sutra as serving, respecting, and regarding. In other words, if we sincerely wish to practice not being stingy and not dividing our self from others, we should engage in such deeds, serving, respecting, and regarding. The meaning of Regarding is to think as Buddha thought:

> Always thinking thus: How should I enable sentient beings to enter the Unsurpassed Way and to attain Buddha's body?
> (*Dharmapundarika-sutra* [Lotus Flower Sutra], chap, The Tathagata's Life Duration).

The meaning of Respecting is to join one's palms, prostrate with brow to the ground, and receive Buddha's feet on one's hands. Joined palms symbolizes not dividing Buddha, which is right hand, from ignorant sentient beings, left hand. Prostrating and receiving Buddha's feet is physical expression of taking refuge in Buddha, Dharma, and Sangha, and when we become one with Buddha, Dharma, and Sangha, we can prostrate ourselves as Huangbo did: "Thus I always pay worship to Buddha, Dharma, and Sangha, seeking nothing."

> Bodhidharma pitied Hueike standing in the snow all night long: "You have long been standing in the snow, what do you seek?"
> Hueike replied, "Your Reverence, I beg of you, please open the gate of sweet dew, Compassion, everywhere to help sentient beings." (*Chuandeng lu*, vol. 3)

This wish of Hueike's is Serving. His wish and Bodhidharma's primary reason for coming to this land become splendidly one. This is the moment when seeking the Wisdom changes to practicing the Compassion, which is to say, according to *Kyoju kaimon*, "One phrase, one gatha, a million forms, a hundred weeds. One Dharma, one Realization, all Buddhas, all patriarchs." When our interest turns from the Wisdom to the Compassion, we will realize that nothing has ever been stingy.

In detail if we study Hueike's case, it is said he severed his left arm and Bodhidharma accepted him as a disciple, saying "All Buddhas at the start of studying the Way forgot their body for the sake of the Dharma." Whether or not a historical fact, Hueike's severing his arm can be taken as abandonment of worldly powers, arm symbolic of power in the East and West even now. According to Buddhism, right arm symbolizes sunyata, the Dharma; left arm symbolizes rupa, the worldly world.

What were his worldly powers? In *Chuandeng lu* and other

records it is said:

> Hueike's parents, yet childless, thought they were diligent in philanthropy but not blessed with child...
>
> From infancy his spirit was beyond compare. Staying in the capital city he read every sort of book and took no part in the family business. He loved mountain and water. Always he lamented, "The teachings of Confucius and Dau are only regulations of manners, the writings of Juangtzy and Yi not yet the ultimate truth..."

According to such records, Hueike's worldly powers must have been family economic wealth and social status and high intellect and learning. Facing Bodhidharma, he severed those worldly powers. He asked after Bodhidharma accepted him,

> "I beg of you, please put my mind at peace."
>
> The Teacher: "Bring me your mind and I will put it at peace."
>
> Hueike: "I have searched and searched and cannot obtain it."
>
> The Teacher: "How can your mind be a thing you can search for and obtain? Now I have put your mind at peace."
>
> [Hueike kept silent]
>
> The Teacher: "I have put your mind at peace, do you not see so?"
>
> Hueike came straightaway to the great realization.

This time the source is an earlier record, *Tzutang ji*, vol. 2. Here Hueike is asking for his own sake after saying "Your Reverence, I beg of you, please open the gate of sweet dew, Compassion, everywhere to help sentient beings" and after severing his left arm. It illustrates how difficult it is to sever worldly powers, or worldly concerns, that is, to enter the mode of practicing the Compassion instead of only satisfying an intellectual interest in the Wisdom.

To appreciate Hueike's greatness, we must intimately understand how hard it was for him to shed his desires, his worldly powers, worldly concerns, here as he expresses "I beg of you, please put my mind at peace." This "my mind" isn't a leisurely abstract idea, it is his concrete, painful daily state. What was troubling his mind? No one has a proper record, but we must intimately understand.

Dogen says in his *Gakudo yojin shu* (Cautions for

practicing Buddha's Way), entry 4: Buddha's Dharma should not be practiced with the mind to get something:

> When our purity does not match the Way, our body and mind are not at ease. When not at ease, our body and mind are not at peace. If not at peace, thorns grow on the way to proving the Way.
> Then, how should we live to make our purity match the Way? Our mind should have no preference, no desire for name and profit. Practicing Buddha's Dharma should not be done for the sake of the person. Nowadays the mind of trainees is far from the Way. Without people's respect and admiration, trainees do not practice even if it is the Right Way. How painful! You all, for a trial, must be quietly self-observant. Is your mind Buddha's Dharma or not?

Dogen's caution came long after Hueike, but Hueike's mind was not at peace and he appealed to Bodhidharma as he did, and then, "I have searched and searched and cannot obtain it." "How can your mind be a thing you can search for and obtain? Now I have put your mind at peace." The moment Bodhidharma said so, Hueike could understand we can't obtain the mind of past, present, or future, for everything is passing in time. The chronological future never comes but keeps advancing; in chronological time there is no present, for the present belongs to the past or the future.

Everything passes, so our objects keep changing. In this context Hueike couldn't possibly put his mind at peace, and neither can we, for sensing chronological change rather contributes to our agony and frustration. Before long, what we believe we have obtained will pass, our youth turns to senescence, our health deteriorates, and our life turns to death. So even if Hueike gained some relief in realizing his mind too would pass, it must have been a minor relief and not Bodhidharma's wished effect.

Therefore out of great kindness Bodhidharma said again "I have put your mind at peace, do you not see so?" We must carefully hear his tone, this second time unlike the first. Then, as recorded: "Hueike came straightaway to the great realization." Now he understands: the reason he couldn't obtain his mind or anything else wasn't because of the chronological character of time. The reason was that the character of time denies time itself. In other words, Hueike could now understand his mind denies to be his mind and all else likewise denies each to be itself. Hueike and all things change to Buddha nature. Now realizing rightly that he couldn't grasp his mind or anything else, he "came straightaway to the great realization." *Kyoju kaimon*: "One phrase, one gatha, a million forms, a hundred weeds. One Dharma, one Realization, all Buddhas, all patriarchs." The content of Hueike's great realization was to understand the dynamics of the Eighth Primary Precept, Not being stingy.

Then, even Heike's great realization wasn't the end of his training life. It was the start. We can understand the importance and deep-rooted hardship of putting his mind at peace if we consider he spent the rest of his life devoted to reconfirming his great realization. As was written:

> After transmitting the Dharma to Sengtsan (Jianjy Sengtsan, ?-606), he said, "I have accumulated karma. I will now clear it away." He then went to Yejou and spent his last thirty years lecturing on occasion to gatherings of the four kinds of people and mingling among the commoners without revealing his priest identity. Sometimes he showed up in the pleasure quarters, sometimes in the slaughterhouse. Sometimes he chatted with the people on the street, and sometimes he engaged in carrying night soil.
> Someone asked him, "You are a Trainee, why you do as you do?" Hueike said, "I am putting my mind in order, and it has nothing to do with you." (*Denko roku*)

By this episode we must deepen our understanding of Hueike's uneasy mind. He is practicing to put his mind at peace, practicing what he intellectually understood in his earlier life. Obviously his difficulty came from all sorts of discrimination dividing him from others, and he was now practicing the life in which discrimination doesn't appear as visible obstacle to cause unease of mind.

Discrimination is a Buddhist's fundamental subject, and the solution to discrimination is a Buddhist's notable teaching. Sage and ignorant are not two but one, mind and body, life and death, wisdom and compassion, study and practice, cause and effect, not two but one. Discrimination is the very concern of the Eighth Precept, Not being stingy. We will study about such discriminations and the way to solve them through Hueike's earlier training under Bodhidharma. Hueike after severing his arm was accepted as Bodhidharma's disciple, and eight years he attended Bodhidharma.

> One day he asked, "By hearing, can we obtain the Dharma Seal of all Buddhas?" The Great Teacher replied, "The Dharma Seal of all Buddhas cannot be obtained from another person." (Ibid.)

This a denial of difference between a person having and a person not having the Dharma. The Dharma Seal cannot be obtained from another person and no one should attempt to give it. Here Buddhism recognizes universal truth, not particular truth.

> One day the Great Teacher instructed: "Stop all outer affairs, and within, do not pant. Make your mind like a fence or wall and enter the Way." (Ibid.)

By this teaching, Bodhidharma was hoping Hueike would make no distinction between his outer and inner mind. More important, he hoped Hueike would understand that all human beings, all beings, are stopping all affairs and not panting over anything whether assiduously endeavoring or not, whether impressively coming to the realization or not. The example of this "whether...or not" is here said as "like a fence or wall," and it is "the Way."

In detail, we shouldn't be careless in our understanding of "Make your mind like a fence or wall." It obviously isn't recommending that we become a material fence or wall. It also obviously isn't recommending that we imitate them with a figure in a still state, as we may imagine a quietly seated posture to be. Bodhidharma isn't particularly respecting fence or wall as phenomenal material. His regard is the highest regard for them, recognized as Buddha's view. Buddha sees them without discrimination, sees them as the Dharma.

The Dharma is unaffected by discriminative values or by any causation of phenomena. It can exist from the beginningless beginning and freely extinguish and resurrect itself. Further, it can be any concrete phenomenon. Bodhidharma wished Hueike would understand it was his life.

> About Mind, Nature, the Great Teacher was always clarifying to Hueike. But Hueike could not come to a perfect accord with the Truth. (Ibid.)

Always clarifying about Mind, Nature, is the Buddhist tradition. The Mind, Nature, of the Dharma is always clarifying about Mind, Nature. It is hoped we will also keep clarifying.

The same source, *Denko roku*, records an episode transmitted only in intimate interview between teacher and student:

> One day when Hueike was attending the Great Teacher to climb Shaushy Peak, the Great Teacher asked, "In which direction should we go?" Hueike replied, "Your Reverence, just go straight on." The Great Teacher said, "If we go straight on, we cannot advance even a step." Hueike came to an understanding.

For Buddhists, "go straight on" doesn't mean physical or even ethical straight. However, even the veteran trainee is often tinged with worldly definitions of "straight," which illustrates how hard it is to get rid of the influence of form or concept. Here Hueike must have been starting to understand that whatever is established straightness could bind him, that he ought to be able to freely create straightness, and that the concept of straight or bent was irrelevant to describe his life or the world. Going on the established straight way isn't necessarily to go straight on. In front of his eyes any frontier hadn't an established way. So going straight on or not highly depends on how we are, not how the way is. There is the truth that the way makes us, but there is the more important truth: we make the way. Hard for us is that we can study about the Dharma but the Dharma we can understand is not the Dharma.

> Hueike one day told Bodhidharma, "For the first time I have stopped all affairs."
> Bodhidharma said, "Are you forming a nihilistic view?"
> Hueike said, "I am not forming a nihilistic view."
> Bodhidharma said, "How do you prove it?"
> Hueike said, "Brightly, clearly, I always know. It cannot be referred to by words."
> Bodhidharma said, "This is the very body and mind all Buddhas proved and there is no further doubt."
> (*Chuandeng lu*, added chapter on Bodhidharma)

From the early stage of Hueike's training, Bodhidharma was always clarifying about Mind, Nature. Now for the first time Hueike understands what Bodhidharma was trying to make him understand. "All affairs" are our mental functions uniting the six objects of our six sense organs—eyes, ears, nose, tongue, sense of touch, and cognition. Bodhidharma had said "Stop all...affairs...and enter the Way." Unlike what appears as his words, stopping all affairs and entering the Way are not two stages. The state of stopping all affairs is the very Way. Who knows this is the Way and cherishes it?

Moreover, stopping all affairs doesn't mean to abandon all personal, domestic, and social care and abandon the study and practice of all Buddhist virtues. It means to transcend while performing all these acts and virtues.

> When at Tiantung...this mountain monk [Dogen is referring to himself], on the way of going to the refectory, noticed a cook monk drying mushrooms before the Buddha Hall. He had a bamboo cane but no hat. The sun was scorching, the earth was hot. He was heavily sweating as he assiduously spread the mushrooms. He looked pained, his back bent like a bow, his eyebrows like the crests of cranes. This mountain monk approached and asked him his age.
> "Sixty-eight," he said.
> "Why are you not using a lay worker?"
> "He is not me."
> "So much you are according with the Dharma, but the sun is now very hot."
> "When is a good time?"
> This mountain monk closed inquiry and quietly departing along the corridor understood the core function of the cook monk. (*Tenzo kyokun* [Kitchen discipline])

This cook monk devoting to his work is the figure of "Stop all affairs." It is the figure of taking refuge in Buddha, Dharma, and Sangha. In the Diamond Sutra there are important revealing words:

> All Buddhas and anuttara-samyak-sambodhi come out from this sutra.

"This sutra" means wherever we devote ourselves carefully and kindly to performing our engagements, expecting nothing other than to perform. This is presenting the world of not being stingy and is the life Hueike began to enjoy:

> Brightly, clearly, always I know. It cannot be referred to

by words.

And Bodhidharma:

> This is the very body and mind all Buddhas proved and there is no further doubt.

They are confirming exactly what is described in the Lotus Flower Sutra:

> Buddha told Sariputra: "...All Buddhas, World Honored Ones, appear in this world only for the most important matter. Sariputra, what does it mean that all Buddhas, World Honored Ones, appear in this world only for the most important matter? All Buddhas, World Honored Ones, appear in this world to enable sentient beings to open Buddha's view, to enable them to attain purity. They appear in this world to show Buddha's view to sentient beings, appear in this world to enable sentient beings to understand Buddha's view, appear in this world to enable sentient beings to enter the Way of Buddha's view. Sariputra, this is the reason we say All Buddhas, World Honored Ones, appear in this world only for the most important matter."
> (Chap. *Upayakausalya* [Devices])

In other words, the Lotus Flower Sutra describes a highly human intellectual achievement rather than one process in the biography of a particular sage. Buddhists are interested in universal Truth, without grave interest in individual phenomenon.

They are confirming what is said in Bodhidharma's gatha transmitting the Dharma:

> The primary reason I came to this land
> was to transmit the Dharma to help confused sentient beings. (*Chuandeng lu*, vol. 3)

In other words, the purpose of this gatha wasn't to explain why he came to the East from the West but to describe the wonderful achievement of human intelligence.

This human intelligence can intuitively understand that any tangible weed is one phrase, one gatha, that any Buddha, any patriarch, is the Dharma, the Realization. In a sense, seeing the Dharma in any phenomenon is the one most important matter, or Bodhidharma's primary reason for coming. The Dharma is such a being to be thus seen by us and is also such a function to enable us to see it. This is the essence of the Eighth Precept, Not being stingy. Baijang calls this Dharma "a wild fox." But before studying Baijang's Wild Fox we must further clarify about Mind, Nature, as Bodhidharma did for Hueike. For this, *Dungshan lu*, entry 33, gives the best episode:

> When the Teacher [Dungshan] was traveling with Shengshan, he pointed to a little auxiliary temple and said, "There behind, a person is clarifying about Mind, Nature."
> Shengshan said, "Who is he?"
> Dungshan: "Being asked by you, he has perfectly died."
> Shengshan: "The one clarifying about Mind, Nature, is who."
> Dungshan: "Got the life in death."

According to Dungshan's words, it sounds as if someone is behind the temple clarifying about Mind, Nature. That isn't so. This episode is clarifying about Buddha's Dharma. When we say "behind," the whole world is behind.

> When we say "behind," all skin, flesh, bone, and marrow are "behind."
>
> (*Shobogenzo*, vol. *Katto* [Ivy and wisteria])

How then should we understand the size of the little auxiliary temple? The whole Dharma world is whole little auxiliary temple, boundless in size, with no front or behind. For Buddha Mind, Buddha Nature, there is no difference between front and behind. Both are Buddha Mind, Buddha Nature. Dungshan said "...a person is clarifying." This "person" is also Buddha Mind, Buddha Nature; and "is" of "a person is clarifying" is also Buddha Mind, Buddha Nature. All beings, all functions, are clarifying about Buddha Mind, Buddha Nature. Dungshan meant the whole world is Buddha Nature by his saying "There behind, a person is clarifying about Mind, Nature."

The same is said simply by Linji:

> See through the puppets, a person behind is working the strings. (*Linji lu*, section Lectures)

Here "puppets" means phenomena, "person" means the Dharma. It doesn't mean there are two things, puppets and person. Puppets are person, person is puppets. It is said "When we comprehend Mind, there is not an ounce of soil on earth."

The little auxiliary temple is the whole world, such temple, whole world, is Mind.

Every time is the appearance of Mind. For instance, one o'clock is the appearance of Mind. So, about this Mind we can say one o'clock's Mind, likewise two o'clock's Mind, and so on. Thus the whole of our life is Mind. Each human behavior, going, staying, sitting, reclining, each natural phenomenon, wind, rain, is clarifying Mind. Each always keeps clarifying Mind, Nature, throughout past, present, and future. There isn't any time not clarifying Mind, Nature, because there isn't any time of not existing as phenomenon. Thus throughout past, present, and future, throughout the ten directions, every being, thing, every affair, all are clarifying Mind, Nature. So it is said "This Dharma is equal, there is no higher and no lower."

What we are talking about, in another way, is Buddha nature. So Buddha nature means every clarification. When the whole world is Buddha nature, we can say there is no Buddha nature in the whole world. It means no Buddha nature is every clarification. Buddhists must therefore keep studying about Buddha nature. Buddhists must keep studying about clarification. We believe Nature is clarification. So, for Buddha's Dharma, being and clarification are one, not two. Clarification means Buddha is clarifying the Dharma, and whoever understands the Way is clarifying Buddha. In short, only Buddha nature is turning the Wheel of the Wonderful Dharma, and it means to raise Bodhi mind, to practice the Bodhisattva Way, to realize Buddha's Wisdom, and to attain Nirvana. In this endless clarification there is no birth, no death, no cause, and no effect.

Now, Dungshan said "a person is clarifying about Mind, Nature." It is a dualistic view if we shallowly understand his saying. The truth is that the very existence of "a person" is already "clarifying about Mind, Nature." The existence of a person and a person's function aren't two different things, they are one same thing. Therefore it is said "There is not a single Dharma to obtain," the words of one of Bodhidharma's four disciples, Dauyu, and "There is not a single Dharma to give," the words of Deshan Shyanjian (780-865).

Anyone whose existence is already clarifying was called by Linji "a true man of no rank." Not "a true man of rank." What Dungshan is proposing in his saying "There behind, a person is clarifying about Mind, Nature" is indeed Linji's "true man of no rank." The person indicated by Dungshan isn't supposed to be any *Homo sapiens*, not even a priest or sexton.

Shenshan said "Who is he?" "Who" is the name for the nameless thing. It is "What is this" or "What is it that comes thus." Auxiliary temple isn't an auxiliary temple, it is the Dharma. There behind isn't there behind, it is the Dharma. A person isn't a person, a person is the Dharma. All are the Dharma, the Dharma function clarifying Mind, Nature. So when asking "Who is he?" Shenshan is positively stating in question form: "The person there behind clarifying about Mind, Nature, is who."

It is easy to say a pine tree isn't a pine tree, it is the Dharma. However, not easy to say is that oneself is not oneself, oneself is the Dharma. It took Hueike eight more years to understand that he wasn't he, that he was the Dharma. In this context "he is the Dharma" means Hueike hid himself in Bodhidharma, he became Bodhidharma. So when Shenshan said "Who is he?" everything, including himself and Dungshan, was hidden in "who," which is "a person," which is the Dharma, which keeps clarifying Mind, Nature. When we successfully hide ourselves in the Dharma, we for the first time gain our true life. Then, what is the life of exercising all our perceptions or recognitions before we hide ourselves in the Dharma? It is said in Buddha's teaching in the *Surangama-sutra*, vol. 1 (*Taisho-zo*, vol. 19):

> Buddha told Ananda, "[such a life] is dust, false images. You have been losing the true Nature. Ever since the beginningless beginning you have been recognizing the thief as your child. You have lost the primordial endless Truth and have been receiving reincarnations."

We remember Chuantzy's words when transmitting the Dharma to Jiashan (Jiashan Shanhuei, 805-881):

> The Teacher [Chuantzy, ?-?] said: "After trial of fishing all around the harbor, I for the first time could meet a golden fish."
>
> Jiashan covered his ears.
>
> The Teacher said, "Like that, like that," then said, "Hereafter extinguish trace of where you hide yourself and do not hide yourself where you extinguish your trace. Thirty

years I stayed in Yaushan to clarify this matter."
(*Sanbyaku soku*, vol. 1, entry 90)

Saying "Who is he?" Shenshan was hiding every phenomenon, including himself, in "Who." Dungshan could detect Shenshan's great power to convert phenomenal life to Dharma life. Shenshan could condense "a million forms, a hundred weeds" to "one phrase, one gatha." Dungshan said in admiration:

"Being asked by you, he has perfectly died."

Every phenomenon is perfectly hidden in "who." So even "he" who is "a true man of no rank" will also be hidden in "who." This "who" is the totality of purely and only clarifying Mind, Nature. Here Shenshan and Dungshan together succeeded to present that the whole world and the whole function of the ten directions throughout past, present, and future are clarifying Mind, Nature and are doing no other thing. Isn't it evidence of "Never have they been stingy"?

Shenshan: "The one clarifying about Mind, Nature, is who."
Dungshan: "Got the life in death.

Everything is the totality of clarifying Mind, Nature, and this truth is expressed by Shenshan as "Who is he?" Now Shenshan is saying "he" is "who." In other words, the totality of Mind, Nature, is each such thing as "behind," "auxiliary temple," "person," etc. If we sum up as a theological chart, Shenshen's first "Who is he?" is universal Truth, and "he" is "who" is a particular truth:

Who is he? = rupa is returning to sunyata
= universal Truth

= true man of no rank = Dharma
"he" is "who" = sunyata is returning to rupa

= particular truth
= true man of rank = weeds

Delighted and with admiration Dungshan said "Got the life in death." His words aren't referring to the life and death of

organic metabolism through the medium of water. He is describing the whole world in the ten directions, the True human body. "Death" is describing the sunyata aspect of the

True human body, and "the life" is describing the rupa aspect of the True human body. The truth contained in "he is who" is beautifully put in a thirty-one syllable poem by Dogen:

> The shape of the peaks, the resonance of the valleys,
> all is the voice and the figure of our Sakyamuni Buddha.

To fully activate 'a true man of no rank,' we must fully wipe out our own 'true man of rank.' This was the difficulty of Hueike's training and Hueike devoted his life to practice this truth in his life. In other words, he became the most respectable sample of practicing Bodhidharma's Not being stingy, the eighth of his Ten Primary Precepts in his One Mind Precepts.

January 18, 2010

Baijang's Wild Fox
Buddhist Causation

This episode is about Zen Teacher Dajy (a posthumous name for Baijang Huaihai, an heir of Matzu) at Mt. Baijang in Hungjou.

Whenever the Teacher delivered his lectures, an old man followed the monks to come to hear. When the monks left, the old man left. One day he did not leave.

The Teacher asked, "Who are you who stands before me?"

The old man answered, "I am not a person. In the eon of Kasyapa Buddha I dwelled in this mountain. A student asked me, 'Does a greatly trained person also fall into Causation or not?' I answered, 'Will not fall into Causation.' I have ever after been falling five hundred lifetimes into the body of a wild fox. Your Reverence, I beg you to give me a turning phrase in place of what I answered so I may now shed the body of a wild fox."

He then asked, "Does a greatly trained person also fall into Causation or not?"

The Teacher answered, "Causation is inevitable."

Hearing this, the old man came directly to the great realization, offered worship, and said, "Here now I have shed the body of a wild fox. I will dwell behind this mountain. Please, Your Reverence, perform a funeral in the manner for a deceased monk."

The Teacher asked the officer in charge of chanting to summon all monks and tell them to perform after lunch the funeral for a deceased monk.

The monks inquired among themselves, "All monks are fine, none sick in the Nirvana Hall. How come it is like this?"

After lunch the Teacher led the monks to the foot of a rock at the back mountain and indicated with his staff a dead fox. Then and there they performed the proper cremation. In the evening lecture the Teacher spoke on the subject of that Causation.

Huangbo then asked, "The ancient person gave a wrong turning phrase and fell five hundred lifetimes into the body of a wild fox. Each time if he had not been wrong, what would he have become?"
The Teacher said, "Come here and I will tell you."
Huangbo drew near the Teacher and slapped him.
The Teacher clapped, saying with a laugh, "I thought of the alien's red beard—here is the red-bearded alien!"

This episode can be found in many records compiled from the twelfth century onward. Zen Teacher Dajy, commonly known as Baijang, lived from 749 to 814, but this episode cannot be found in *Tzutang ji* (compiled in 952), *Chuandeng lu* (compiled in 1004), and Baijang's *Guang lu* (in *Sija wulu*, compiled in 1085?). It is treated as Case 8 in *Tsungrung lu* (compiled in 1226).

Wumen (Wumen Hueihai, 1183-1260) treats this episode as Case 2 in his *Wumen guan* (Gateless barrier). Wumen's comment and his following gatha present his view:

"Will not fall into Causation," how come he falls into wild fox? "Causation is inevitable," how come he can shed wild fox? Here whoever attains an eye will know that the former Baijang was cherishing a noble life in five hundred lifetimes.

> Not fall versus Inevitable—
> two faces of one dice.
> Inevitable versus Not fall—
> a thousand mistakes, a million mistakes.

Here Wumen is obviously regarding "Will not fall into Causation" and "Causation is inevitable" as the main issue of the episode. Consequently he thinks that having a wisdom eye determines whether we fall into Causation or transcend Causation. Furthermore, he thinks "Will not fall into Causation" and "Causation is inevitable" are two effects derived from a single origin. One of these two effects enables us to cherish a noble life, the other leads us to a thousand mistakes, a million mistakes.

Wumen is utterly missing the point of this episode. The main issue of the episode is Buddhist training (referred to as "a greatly trained person"). For Buddhists, training means to perform and participate in universal Truth, which is Causation. Buddhist Causation is Great Cause and Great Effect. Great Cause and Great Effect means Cause and Effect are exactly the same: both are Buddha nature.

Indeed if both are Buddha nature, falling into Causation and transcending Causation are irrelevant concerns. Cherishing a noble life or not doesn't depend on our attaining a wisdom eye. The Whole World in the Ten Directions throughout the past, present, and future and throughout the world of desire, the world of form, and the world of no form is filled up with Buddha nature. Even a raccoon with skin disease and a rabid fox, hated by folks for miserable looks and behavior, they too have Buddha nature. And we aren't mere folks. We are descendants of Buddha, Buddha who said "All sentient and insentient beings, including mountains and rivers, weeds and trees, are attaining Buddhahood." In the Buddhist world how can there be "a thousand mistakes, a million mistakes," and how can a wild fox be associated with the concept of mistake?

Baijang and Huangbo are great patriarchs. They don't exercise worldly dualistic valuations. When they say "wild fox" they don't mean a zoological fox. When they say "wrong" they don't mean in the sense of there being a contrasting "right."

Baijang's famous saying "A day of no work is a day of no meals" shouldn't be sloppily understood as a mere diligence in a consumer's material life.

> The Teacher always engaged in the work in advance of the monks. The head monk, unable to endure it, quietly hid the Teacher's tools and asked the Teacher to rest. The Teacher said, "I am a person of no virtue, how can I make others do my work?" and he searched for his tools, couldn't find them, and so skipped his meals. Hence came his words, now well known: A day of no work is a day of no meals.
>
> (*Wudeng hueiyuan*, vol. 3)

The greatness of this episode is that this "work" can also be recognized as the Dharma. "A day of no work is a day of no meals" means a day of no Dharma is a day of no life.

Huangbo, an unusually great patriarch, delivered this renowned lecture:

"All of you are draff-eaters! In your manner of pilgrimage you will never find the day. Do you know there is no Zen teacher anywhere in Great Tang?
A monk stepped forward: "How about those who temper their disciples and preside over assemblies here and there?"
Huangbo: "I do not say there is no Zen. I say only there is no teacher." (*Biyan lu*, Case 11)

When we can see everything inside and outside of us as a Zen teacher, there will be "no Zen teacher anywhere." Zen is another name for wisdom or precept, and with this definition, Zen is another name for Buddha nature, another name for Causation.

Dogen must have regarded Baijang's Wild Fox episode as an important subject. On this subject he wrote two volumes: *Dai-shugyo* (Great training), volume 68 in his 75-volume *Shobogenzo*, and *Shinjin inga* (Deep belief in Causation), volume 7 in his additional 12-volume *Shobogenzo*.

In 1244, when he was forty-five, he wrote *Dai-shugyo*, wherein he denies Causation commonly known as a nice or miserable present life coming by the effect of our past life, and he denies that how we live our present life is the cause of our future life. What is important, he says, is to live the life of training in the world of Buddha nature.

But less than ten years later, he wrote *Shinjin inga* (two years after his death, a clean copy was made by Ejo, in 1255). This later volume strongly emphasizes the importance of not ignoring Causation as was commonly understood. Dogen here says if we disregard Causation as was commonly understood, we trigger an evil Causation because Causation is inevitable. He fortified his view by quoting the words of the nineteenth patriarch in India, Kumaralabdha (AD ?-22); and by quoting the fourteenth patriarch in India, Nagarjuna (c. AD 150–250); and by quoting Yungjia Shyuanjyue (?-713, a disciple of Sixth Patriarch Hueineng). He also negatively criticized a gatha made by Hungjy (Hungjy Jengjyue, 1091-1157), another by Yuanwu (Yuanwu Kechin,1063-1135), and another by Dahuei (Dahuei Tzunghau, 1089-1163).

Given these two volumes contradicting each other makes later comers lost in confusion as if Dogen were presenting an additional wild fox. We don't want to give confusion to others even if we are confused, but on the other hand, giving confusion could be a kindness even if we ourselves aren't confused. After all, phenomena and no phenomena are only the activity of Buddha nature.

Now, Causation has two fundamental aspects, just as Buddha nature has two virtues, its existence as Buddha nature and its existence as no Buddha nature.

> A monk asked, "Does a dog have Buddha nature or not?"
> Jaujou said, "Does not."
> The monk said, "All sentient beings have Buddha nature. Why doesn't a dog?"
> Jaujou said, "The reason is that a dog has karma."
> (*Tsungrung lu*, Case 18)

> A monk asked, "Does a dog have Buddha nature or not?"
> Jaujou said, "Does."
> The monk said, "Why does Buddha nature enter such a skin bag?"
> Jaujou said, "The reason is that it knowingly enters."
> (Ibid.)

The second episode says a dog has Buddha nature. We name this "Buddha nature." The first episode says a dog hasn't Buddha nature. We name this "No Buddha nature." It is more like a plus (+) Buddha nature and a minus (–) Buddha nature.

When a dog has no Buddha nature (– Buddha nature), Buddha nature fully acts as karma. This is the meaning of the vow Do no evil, the first vow of The Three Inclusive Vows. Dogen writes in his *Kyoju kaimon*:

> Do no evil is the cave of all Buddhas' Dharma and the cave of all Buddhas' Restriction and the root of all Buddhas' Dharma and the roof of all Buddhas' Restriction.

All Buddhas and patriarchs do not stay in the state of existence of Buddha nature (that is, "plus Buddha nature"). Remember that the Second Patriarch, Hueike, went to Yejou to help sentient beings.

In the second episode, Jaujou answers that a dog does have Buddha nature ("plus Buddha nature"). It sounds as if the monk then asked "Why does it enter such a skin bag?" Actually the question is hiding the positive statement "By any means Buddha nature must enter such a skin bag in order to help sentient beings." Therefore Jaujou's response was "The reason is that it knowingly enters." In other words, the monk and his teacher Jaujou were together clarifying about the inevitable nature of Buddha nature, that is, Buddha nature can't exist without being beneficial to all sentient beings.

Deeply understanding this "knowingly enters" means to practice the Sixth Primary Precept, Not speaking of faults.

> *Kyoju kaimon*: In Buddha's Dharma there is the same Way, same Dharma, same Realization, same Practice. Let no one speak of faults, let no one disturb the Way.

Therefore plus Buddha nature or minus Buddha nature are not what is important. What is important is that we shouldn't avert our eyes from Buddha nature. The content is more important than the appearance. Likewise, "Will not fall into Causation" or "Causation is inevitable" aren't what we should focus on. We should always keep observing Causation.

Causation is Buddha nature: Cause is Buddha nature, Effect too is Buddha nature—two names, but for only one Buddha nature. Causation is True Form, Causation is *anuttara-samyak-sambodhi*.

Buddha nature is already Buddha nature, so Buddha nature has no way to become Buddha nature. This is "Will not fall into Causation." Cause is Buddha nature, Effect too is Buddha nature. The expression "Will not fall into Causation" reveals Causation's universal character, that is, Causation doesn't change according to the passing of time. Buddha nature always exists throughout past, present, and future. So Kasyapa Buddha in the past is Buddha nature, Sakyamuni Buddha in the present is Buddha nature, and Maitreya Buddha in the future is Buddha nature. (They are three names for one same Time.) Buddha nature also extendingly exists in space, so an earthworm is Buddha nature, a bucket also, a nandina shrub also.

Here a gatha by Damei Fachang (752-829) describes this universal Buddha nature:

> A dead tree remains beside a dreary forest,
> With no change of mind, though many springtimes come.
> Even a woodsman gives it no heed,
> No use to any craftsman. (*Chuandeng lu*, vol. 7.)

"A dead tree remains" is "Body is the Bodhi tree, / Mind is like a bright mirror on its stand. / Keep cleaning time after time,

/ So no dust will land." This is Do no evil.

"With no change of mind, though many springtimes come" means no moving mind. For Buddhists the meaning of no moving mind is to become spring when spring comes, autumn when autumn comes. Dauntlessly trying to become whatever comes is Right Effort, *samyag-vayayama*. In the natural world this Buddhist right effort is constantly practiced with no time lapse. So The Whole World in The Ten Directions is *samyag-vayayama*, and trying to go along with The Whole World in The Ten Directions is the Bodhisattva Way.

Dogen says:

> At a certain time it stands on the summit of an extremely high peak, at a certain time it walks on the bottom of a deep ocean, at a certain time it becomes Three Head Eight Arms, at a certain time it becomes Sixteen or Eight Feet Tall, at a certain time it becomes the priest's staff or whisk, at a certain time it becomes an exposed pillar or lantern, at a certain time it becomes the third son of Jang or the fourth son of Li, and at a certain time it becomes the Great Earth or the Void.
>
> (*Yuji* [A Certain (which is Existing) Time])

"A certain time" means in normal usage a particular but unspecified time. However, Dogen adds the meaning "the time of an existing matter." His usage comes from an understanding that Time doesn't exist apart from an existing phenomenon.

"At a certain time it stands on the summit of an extremely high peak, at a certain time it walks on the bottom of a deep ocean" is originally Yaushan's expression. Yaushan's "a certain time" obviously means "when the time comes in a certain situation and sometimes."

For Yaushan the subject of the verb "stands" or "walks" is a great trainee. So the meaning of Yaushan's expression is that great trainees stand on or walk in such a place where nobody can see them. It doesn't mean they go to a secret geographic place, it means they transcend human thought and emotion.

However, for Dogen the subject of "stands" or "walks" is Time, that is, Time becomes a great trainee, becomes Raga-raja (Three Heads Eight Arms, a symbolic figure for klesa), becomes Buddha (Sixteen or Eight Feet Tall, the height of Buddha standing or seated. By listing Buddha after Raga-raja, Dogen is suggesting klesa is turning to realization, that is, klesa is the essential preceding stage for Compassion).

"The priest's staff or whisk" is used by priests, thus they symbolize the compassionate Sangha (one of The Three Treasures as well as one aspect of Buddha). "Exposed pillar" and "lantern" were common items for temple or monastery residents, so they represent ordinary things, affairs, occurrences. It is interesting that Dogen placed in association with daily items those teachers who used the staff or whisk when they lectured about the Dharma. That is to say, the Way exists near around us, whereas things that exist far apart....

"At a certain time it becomes the third son of Jang or the fourth son of Li and at a certain time it becomes The Great Earth or The Void": A great trainee or Time sometimes becomes an ordinary person and sometimes becomes a heroic person who behaves as the Great Earth or as the Void.

What Dogen is saying is that such various things as he lists become Time (= Causation, Buddha nature. The duration of our shifting our concern from one thing to another is Buddhist "transition," that is, the duration of shifting a certain Buddha nature to another certain Buddha nature. In contrast, worldly "transition" is the duration of shifting from a certain chronological time to another certain chronological time). Each of such various things is Buddha nature. So we can say Buddha nature becomes Buddha nature. It means "Will not fall into Causation."

On the other hand, Buddha nature becomes such variety of things as a great trainee, Three Heads Eight Arms, Sixteen or Eight feet tall, a priest's staff or whisk, an exposed pillar or lantern. Here "Causation is inevitable," and Buddha nature becomes each of such variety of things (which are Buddha nature).

Now we can study the episode of Baijang's wild fox in detail, phrase by phrase.

This episode is about Zen Teacher Dajy (heir of Matzu, priest's name Huaihai) at Mt. Baijang in Hungjou.

> Whenever he delivered his lectures, an old man followed the monks to come to hear. When the monks left, the old man left. One day he did not leave.

In this essay Zen Teacher Dajy will hereafter be referred to by his well-known name Baijang. Baijang's experience of

vivid realization is put forth in *Biyan lu*, Case 53:
> Great Teacher Matzu and Baijang as they were walking saw wild ducks take wing.
> The Great Teacher asked, "What are they?"
> Baijang said, "They are wild ducks."
> The Great Teacher: "Where have they gone?"
> Baijang: "To somewhere they have flown away."
> The Great Teacher after all twisted Baijang's nose.
> Baijang yelped.
> The Great Teacher said, "What? They didn't fly away."

Time flies fast as wild ducks. Chronological time that flies is the Dharma taking phenomenal form. Time hidden in chronological time that doesn't fly is also the Dharma. Difficult to understand. Here Matzu wanted to make Baijang understand time that doesn't fly. When we understand the Dharma that doesn't fly, we for the first time can establish our peace, that is, be free of change, phenomenal causation.

"Baijang yelped." We are almost misguided to understand his yelp was from having his nose twisted. What teacher would give additional physical pain to a caring disciple enough suffering over life? We had better understand Matzu's twisting as only a gesture. Baijang yelped by realizing Time doesn't pass, the Dharma isn't influenced by causation. Seeing universal life, Baijang yelped in astonishment.

Because of this realization about the Dharma, Baijang later encouraged his disciple Kueishan (Kueishan Lingyou, 771-853) to recognize the universal Dharma.

At age fifteen Kueishan left his parents, at twenty-three he arrived at Baijang's temple. It is said that at first glance Baijang straightaway allowed Kueishan to study intimately from him, and soon Kueishan became head of the monks.

> One day Kueishan stood in attendance. Baijang voiced "Who is it?"
> Kueishan responded, "Lingyou."
> Baijang said, "Check to see whether the coals are hot."
> Kueishan stirred the brazier. "No fire," he said.
> Baijang rose, stirred the ash, found a small hot coal and showed it. "Isn't this?"
> Kueishan came to a realization, expressed his thanks, and offered his view. Baijang said, "Only arrived at a fork in the road. A sutra says 'If one would like to see Buddha

nature, one must truly observe Causation. When the time has come, delusion turns to realization, no thought rises, as if forgotten, and one reflects on one's own innate being and there's nothing to obtain from another.' Therefore the Patriarch said 'Complete realization is the same as no realization. No mind obtains no Dharma. There are no falsehoods. Ignorant and sage are equal. From the beginning, Mind and Dharma are self-sufficient whether we realize it or not.' Now you are so. Keep it well."

(Chuandeng lu, vol. 9)

Baijang found a small hot coal and asked wasn't it fire. Kueishan then came to a realization. He and his teacher Baijang weren't seeing the possibility of small Buddha nature growing large like a small tomato growing large according to time. By seeing "a small hot coal" they were seeing Buddha nature equal in size with The Whole World in the Ten Directions. This "small" is absolute small, not relative small paired with large. Naturally Kueishan "expressed his thanks."

Even so, Baijang said "Only arriving at a fork in the road." Kueishan understood his life was the same size as Buddha nature, which is the same size as the Whole World. His understanding would disappear like frost under sunlight if he wasn't going to keep practicing his understanding. Therefore these words came from Baijang.

But Baijang soon says in closing his teaching, "Now you are so. Keep it well." His "Only arriving at a fork in the road" must therefore have a second meaning. "A fork in the road" doesn't mean halfway, it means on the very Way. The surface meaning of these words is somewhat paradoxical. The deeper sense is the process is the goal, the goal is the process.

This double meaning will be again considered by Baijang's quoting a sutra: "If one would like to see Buddha nature, one must truly observe Causation. When the time has come…" This passage can be found in the Nirvana Sutra *(Mahaparinirvana-sutra),* volume 28. When the time comes, the sutra says, milk turns to butter or cheese. This is one meaning, describing the character of chronological time or phenomenal causation. The second meaning is milk is butter or cheese, cheese or butter is milk. Therefore, though saying "When the time comes," the sutra means "The time has come." This is a reasonable way of understanding, because Time has no division of past, present, and future, so any certain time mentioned can be indicating the totality of Time. For instance, even when we say AD 1253, we righteously can't avoid thought of all time past, present, and future.

However, Time doesn't exist as past, present, and future put like computer thumbnail images, nor overlap like computer windows. So when we say "At a certain time it stands on the summit of an extremely high peak," there is only "stands on the summit" in The Whole World in the Ten Directions and there is nothing else. When we say "At a certain time it walks on the bottom of a deep ocean," there is only "walks on the bottom" in The Whole World in the Ten Directions and there is nothing else.

Therefore this kind of time, standing on the summit or walking on the bottom, isn't time in our idea. It is absolute dynamic indisputable Time actually existing. This kind of time is existence with the truth that existence exists in the Dharma rank. It is also called Samadhi of Self-cherishing, that is, to be content in just being, not depending on any object or aim.

This absolute Time is the topic of *Biyan lu*, Case 26, Baijang Sits on the Great Sublime Peak:

> A monk asked Baijang, "What is the most wonderful thing?"
> Baijang replied, "To sit alone on the great sublime peak."
> The monk paid worship.
> Baijang struck him.

To the monk's question, Baijang was replying with the deepest true meaning: "To sit alone on the great sublime peak." This "great sublime peak" is not only Mt. Baijang (*bai* = 100, *jang* = 6 ft, *baijang* = a mountain 600 ft high).

It is Baijang's body and mind, his life. Because he mastered the way to live the absolute Time, his reply without premeditated calculation accorded with Buddha's words "In all the world of Heaven and Earth, I alone am respectable."

The monk though he paid worship was struck. Was it Baijang's approval or negative criticism? It is the problem of whether his paying worship was worship as The Whole World in the Ten Directions, or instead a particular chronological behavior.

Now we will return to Baijang's Wild Fox text: "Whenever he delivered his lectures, an old man followed the monks to come to hear." This "old man" is Buddha nature. Buddha nature, according to whatever the time, becomes anything, including a person or a fox. So Buddha nature is attending Baijang's lectures. ("Lecture" means clarifying Mind, Nature, or Dharma.) This "old man" is us. It doesn't mean in us there is Buddha nature. Buddha nature is shedding Buddha nature and becoming the realistic and absolute present of us each. Buddha nature reincarnates in the Six Worlds and becomes anything. Thus it can become a wild fox for five hundred lives.

> Yaushan many days did not ascend to the lecture seat. The temple head respectfully said, "The monks wish to be guided. Your Reverence, please lecture to them."
> Yaushan asked an officer monk to strike the bell to summon the monks. Yaushan ascended to the lecture seat, sat meanwhile there, then descended and returned to his residential quarters.
> Following in attendance, the head monk asked, "Your Reverence, you agreed to lecture to the monks. Why did you not speak even a word?"
> Yaushan said, "There are sutra teachers for the sutras, theologians for the theologies. Why do you suspect me of being so?" (*Tsungrung lu*, Case 7)

Yaushan (745-828) and Baijang (749-814) were contemporaries. Yaushan in this episode asked an officer monk to ring the bell. We in the context of studying the Dharma must be able to hear this bell ringing on and on from eons ago. Of course it's not the sound we can hear with our physical ears or with our intellectual imagination.

Yaushan "ascended to the lecture seat, sat meanwhile there, then descended and returned to his residential quarters." His meanwhile sitting there was a direct presentation of the Samadhi of Self-cherishing. Every being whether sentient or insentient has Buddha nature and is practicing the Samadhi of Self-cherishing.

Yaushan "returned to his residential quarters." Yaushan is returning to the life of phenomena.

Yaushan's Samadhi of Self-cherishing is "an old man" in Baijang's Wild Fox episode. In other manuscripts "an old man" is identified as a changeless "ancient person." Either expression indicates Buddha nature, which is "True Form," in contrast to the expression "a young man" ("a student" in Baijang's Wild Fox episode), which is a presently progressing phenomenon.

So "a young man" and "an old man" are two aspects of one body, though what surfaces is always only one of the two aspects. Even though either of the two aspects is becoming True Existence, the other is always backing it. Therefore the text narration says "an old man followed the monks to come to hear. When the monks left, the old man left." We can say "an old man" (and "a young man") repeatedly surface and submerge, come and go.

It is true that "an old man" comes and goes. However, as in the context of Shyuansha's expression, he does not come and go:

> Bodhidharma does not come to China, the Second Patriarch does not go to India. (*Chuandeng lu*, vol. 18.)

This "old man" always stays throughout the past, present, and future. Even though we each die, our death is a part of the changeless existence of Buddha nature. We must realize that this Buddha nature is our true life. So it is said "One day he did not leave."

> The Teacher asked, "Who are you who stands before me?"
> The old man answered, "I am not a person. In the eon of Kasyapa Buddha I dwelled in this mountain. A student asked me, 'Does a greatly trained person also fall into Causation or not?' I answered him, 'Will not fall into Causation.' I have ever after been falling five hundred lifetimes into the body of a wild fox. Your Reverence, I beg you to give me a turning phrase in place of what I answered so that I may now shed the body of a wild fox."

Baijang asked the old man "Who are you who stands before me?" This is the positive statement in question form. This "old man" is Buddha nature and can become anything, any person, can become Mt. Baijang, ocean, any building too. Yet its substance always exists without any change. Such contradictory dynamics beyond our thought are called here "who," as in "you are who."

The old man answered, "I am not a person. In the eon of

Kasyapa Buddha I dwelled in this mountain." We understand "I am not a person" also as this "who" instead of our imagining a kind of mysterious creature. The old man's saying "this mountain" is not simply Mt. Baijang, it is The Whole World in the Ten Directions. If we practice our sensitivity to appreciate the Buddhist literature, we will understand this Mt. Baijang is the old man's body and the old man's body is Mt. Baijang. With this sensitivity we must understand Dogen's vow made on September 10, 1248, at his age forty-nine:

> Hereafter into the endless future this old man in Eihei will be always in the human world and not leave these precincts day or night. He vows never to leave this mountain even if by Imperial command asked to leave. Why? Because of the wish to be diligent in practicing both sitting meditation and walking meditation. Thus he may increase the virtue to save all sentient beings, enable them to see Buddha, enable them to hear the Dharma, and enable them to fall into the cave of Buddha and the Patriarchs. Then he may sit under the Buddha Tree and destroy Papiyas, complete the most important matter, and attain the Unsurpassed Realization.
>
> (*Kenzei ki*, vol. 1 [Kenzei's memo])

According to a biographic record, Dogen left Eihei to be carried all the way to Kyoto to receive medical treatment. It was about half a month before he there died. If we don't exercise our sensitivity, we will give negative criticism for the difference between his vow and the fact of where he died. His life is Mt. Eihei, no, it extends beyond the solar system.

So "this mountain" is the old man's body and more, it is the past Kasyapa Buddha's eon, the present Sakyamuni Buddha's eon, the future Maitreya Buddha's eon, and The Whole World in the Ten Directions. All are the old man's body. This much truth is expressed as "I dwelled in this mountain."

> Now, there is this sort of causation of being born in this Saha world as a consequence of our vow. Shouldn't we enjoy being able to see Sakyamuni Buddha?
>
> (*Kenbutsu* [To see Buddha, that is, to become Buddha])

When we accord with this truth that everything is Buddha nature, and thus vow to be reborn as a Bodhisattva, the nature of the world and the nature of our vow will blend and we can be reborn as a Bodhisattva. To this old man, a student (young man) asked, "Does a greatly trained person also fall into Causation or not?" On the surface of the sentence there is evident nuance that even a greatly trained person can't escape from the yoke of phenomenal causation, and it means a negative valuation of the training of true Buddhism. But that isn't the right way to read the text. First of all, the training of a greatly trained person is Buddha nature. We said at the onset of this essay, training too means to live according to Causation. Buddhist Causation is Great Cause and Great Effect. Great Cause and Great Effect are the same thing, Buddha nature. So training means to live with Buddha nature in the world of Buddha nature. Naturally the training of a greatly trained person is Buddha nature.

In Buddha nature there are those two aspects, not falling into Causation and the inevitability of falling into Causation. In the saying of this student these aspects are neatly stated: "Does a greatly trained person also fall into Causation or not?" It means 1) a greatly trained person also falls into Causation (inevitable), and 2) a greatly trained person does not fall into Causation. In one sentence these contradictory aspects are expressed. Therefore this is expressing about the "who" of "Who are you...?" and also of "You are who."

The old man answered to the student: "Will not fall into Causation." He was answering only one of these two aspects. The reason is one has already the other.

He has been falling five hundred lifetimes into the body of a wild fox. Thus the surface linguistic meaning of the saying is that he became a wild fox in each of those five hundred rebirths. Buddha becomes Buddha from Buddha: There's no way to fall into Causation. Hence comes the reply "Will not fall into Causation." Being born repeatedly like this, Buddha (equal to Bodhisattva in this context) works to help sentient beings, as is said:

> Always thinking thus: How should I enable sentient beings to enter the Unsurpassed Way and attain Buddha's body?
> (Lotus Flower Sutra, chap. The Tathagata's life duration)

So, what is "a wild fox"? It is the reincarnation of Buddha and the patriarchs in every possible world. Every diversity of form of the old man is called "a wild fox." This is the confidence or matter of fact for a Dogen type of zealous Buddhist trainee.

> After raising Bodhi mind, even if one is reincarnated in the Six Worlds with the Four Kinds of Birth, all cause and effect of reincarnation become the practice of Bodhi.
>
> (*Keisei sanshoku* [Sound of the brook, color of the mountain])

Dogen's rhetoric is filled with abstract idea. We will be lost in the world of emotional idea unless we devote the whole of our body and mind to the work without regarding efficiency or achievement. If for some reason left with only the function of one's toes, one must steadily function patiently, carefully, and devotedly, thus coming to understand what Dogen meant. (This is the practice of the Samadhi of Self-cherishing. The point is to make such a world with no division between self and other come to be lived by us in our daily life.)

No matter how much Buddha nature changes to all sorts of forms to help sentient beings, after all Buddha nature is becoming only Buddha nature. Therefore it is said "Causation is inevitable." However, Buddha nature is already Buddha nature. Therefore Buddha nature has no way to become Buddha nature. Therefore Buddha nature "will not fall into Causation." But only adopting "Will not fall into Causation" and not living in accord with Great Cause and Great Effect only triggers a negative causation. Therefore it is said "Your Reverence, I beg you to give me a turning phrase in place of what I answered so I may now shed the body of a wild fox."

By the way, this old man's saying "I have ever after been falling five hundred lifetimes into the body of a wild fox" proves this isn't a mere zoological wild fox. Zoological wild foxes have no way to know "five hundred lifetimes." According to the episode, this old man (wild fox) is asking Baijang for a turning phrase so he can shed the body of a wild fox. It means even at his very moment of asking, he is living with the body of a wild fox. In short, he isn't finishing even his present one life. Yet, he knows "five hundred lifetimes." The ability to know lifetimes he hasn't yet lived, in addition to past lifetimes he must have lived, is the ability of only Buddha and the patriarchs. We normal human beings, and of course zoological foxes, can't even dream of having such an ability. This wild fox in the text episode repeats five hundred lifetimes living the life of "how to make sentient beings attain the Unsurpassed Way and accomplish Buddha's body." That is, this wild fox is Buddha and the patriarchs, who well clarified "Causation is inevitable."

Sakyamuni Buddha told the monks,

> "The life duration I have attained by formerly practicing the Bodhisattva's Way is not exhausted even now; it rather is doubling the fore-mentioned kalpas."
> (Lotus Flower Sutra, chap. The Tathagata's life duration)

Buddha's life is Causation. Causation is life continuing to the present Sakyamuni Buddha since five hundred kalpas ago, and that life is "how to make sentient beings attain..." Now we can see why the words "five hundred lifetimes" came up in association with five hundred kalpas. In other words, the wild fox here is Buddha's life, which is Causation, which is Time, which is Being.

Buddha and the patriarchs can know five hundred lifetimes of this quality. We can know the greatness of Buddha and the patriarchs. But we can't know five hundred lifetimes, because we can't tell when one lifetime begins and ends. It is traditionally said why we can't know five hundred lifetimes is because we forget everything by our suffering of birth. So some of us can understand if told by Buddha and the patriarchs.

It is clear a mere wild fox can't know five hundred lifetimes, but this old man can know, and also he somehow knows a mere wild fox can't know. In short, he knows the world of knowing and also the world of not knowing. Therefore he can say he has been "falling five hundred lifetimes into the body of a wild fox." Because he has been so doing, he can say "so that I may now shed the body of a wild fox." In other words, he knows both the falling and the shedding. Knowing them both, the "Will not fall into Causation" and the "Causation is inevitable," is evidence of being Buddha and the patriarchs and not the dream of a mere wild fox.

> He then asked, "Does a greatly trained person also fall into Causation or not?"
> The Teacher answered, "Causation is inevitable."

Buddha doesn't stay as Buddha. Buddha becomes old man,

becomes wild fox, becomes whatever thing, and thus "Causation is inevitable." However, old man is Buddha nature, wild fox too, anything is Buddha nature. In that sense, however much Buddha becomes anything else, it is only Buddha becoming Buddha. But when a thing becomes the same thing, we don't say it "becomes," just as we don't say Buddha becomes Buddha. In Buddha is becoming Buddha, there is no Causation; thus Buddha is becoming Buddha is Will not fall into Causation. In other words, there are two seemingly contradictory aspects in the virtue of Causation, even though the two aspects, "Will not fall into Causation" and "Causation is inevitable," are the same thing.

 Hearing this, the old man came immediately to the great realization. He offered worship and said,
 "Here now I have shed the body of a wild fox. I will dwell behind this mountain. Your Reverence, please, I ask you to perform a funeral in the manner for a deceased monk."
 The Teacher asked the officer in charge of chanting to summon all monks and tell them to perform after lunch the funeral for a deceased monk.
 The monks inquired among themselves, "All monks are fine, none sick in the Nirvana Hall. How come it is like this?"
 After lunch the Teacher led the monks to the foot of a rock at the back mountain and indicated with his staff a dead fox. Then and there they performed the proper cremation.

 This wild fox indeed wasn't a zoological wild fox. It was Buddha nature. "Monk" (Sangha) is Buddha nature. So the old man said "I ask you to perform a funeral in the manner for a deceased monk."

 Baijang isn't performing a funeral for a mere wild fox as if it were for a deceased monk. Baijang was the patriarch who for the first time compiled the monastic rules for Mahayana Buddhism. He could finely distinguish the protocol for a wild animal from the protocol for a monk.

 A monk has a monk's career after leaving family. A monk has the fundamental matter that is always a monk's concern. Therefore even an emperor or a president or even Indra or any others who haven't left family, even if they ask that their funeral be performed in the manner for a monk, it can't be granted. Not understanding this grave distinction means ending up not understanding what a monk is, which is "Appearing in bodily form, explaining the Dharma, and serving as a pier for the world" (in *Kyoju kaimon*, from The Tenth Primary Precept, Not devaluating The Three Treasures: Buddha, Dharma, and Sangha).

Unable to understand the virtue of a monk and therefore unable to keep The Tenth Primary Precept is fatally sad because this precept is the precept from which the other primary precepts stem. This sadness comes from the misfortune of not understanding that The Whole World in the Ten Directions is The Treasure Repository Housing the Eye to See the Right Dharma; that is, Nirvana, as well as Wonderful Mind. At the same time this sadness comes from the misfortune of not understanding the virtue of a monk.

Dogen says in his volume *Dharani*:

> The Second Patriarch in olden times thrice offered his worshipful prostration to the First Patriarch whenever he expressed his view. To develop the figure of The Treasure Repository Housing the Eye to See the Right Dharma, worshipful prostration should be thrice offered.
>
> We had better know such offering of worship is The Treasure Repository Housing the Eye to See the Right Dharma. The Treasure Repository Housing the Eye to See the Right Dharma is Dharani....As long as this offering of worship exists in the world, Buddha's Dharma exists. If this offering of worship disappears, Buddha's Dharma will come to ruin.
>
> In offering our worship to the teacher who transmits the Dharma, we do not choose any particular time, nor consider where we offer it. We offer it whenever we go to bed, whenever we have meals, whenever we go to the lavatory. At any certain time we offer our worship beyond fence and wall, beyond mountain and river, beyond the kalpas waves, beyond life and death, beyond coming and going, beyond Bodhi, beyond Nirvana.

When receiving the transmission we must be greatly delighted to have even one chance to offer our worship. Without this attitude, we won't be able to use the virtue of meeting a thousand Buddhas even though we are surrounded by them. "Monk" means Buddha and the patriarchs receiving and transmitting the Dharma at any time.

Baijang "indicated with his staff a dead fox." We must know from where he pulled out a dead fox. There is a difference between falling into the body of a wild fox (rupa) and shedding the body of a wild fox (sunyata). Even though there is a difference, both falling and shedding are the Causation of the wild fox. This kind of wild fox who knows both shedding and falling doesn't come out from behind a physical rock. The old man who knows this kind of wild fox doesn't fall into Causation even if he says "Will not fall into Causation." In the great training there is the truth "Will not fall into Causation." Therefore "Causation is inevitable." It means the virtue of training is true and not false.

In the evening lecture the Teacher spoke on the subject of that Causation.

Baijang spoke on the events of the day. He is a great patriarch. Such a one can narrate an event precisely with no exaggeration, devaluation, careless observation, distortion of fact, and so forth. For instance, when he narrated the words "five hundred lifetimes" was it a counting unit for ordinary human beings, for wild foxes, or for Buddha and the patriarchs? The Buddhist way of counting this five hundred lifetimes means from endless past to endless future.

Like that, a wild fox or an ordinary person sees a wild fox or an ordinary person. But the patriarch Baijang sees the patriarch Baijang. The text said "Whenever the Teacher delivered his lectures, an old man followed the monks to come to hear. When the monks left, the old man left. One day he did not leave. The Teacher asked, "Who are you who stands before me?" It means the teacher Baijang saw the old man as Baijang seeing Baijang. If Baijang were a Mafia member, he would have seen the old man as a Mafia member. Baijang was Buddha and the patriarchs, so when he saw the old man (a wild fox), he saw him as Buddha and the patriarchs. Naturally in this episode "a wild fox" means Buddha and the patriarchs, not a wild fox. So as a natural conclusion, Baijang performed a funeral for a wild fox in the manner for a monk. There is an episode suitable to study here:

> King Prasenajit asked the Reverend Pindola, "I have heard Your Reverence intimately saw Buddha. Is it true or not?"

In response His Reverence with his fingers raised his eyebrows. (*Asokavadana*, vol. 3)

The Reverend Pindola was one of Buddha's direct disciples, historically counted as one of the sixteen Arhats. Said to have overused divine powers, he was scolded by Buddha and ordered to remove himself to the western region. Later he was forgiven and he returned to the capital, Janbudvipa, and there he helped people after Buddha's death.

This episode is very difficult to understand unless we exercise the truth that Buddha sees Buddha, patriarch sees patriarch. The king's question can possibly contain the weight of regal authority. So as king, all the more this king was eager and sincerely wanting to know. He asked "Is it true or not?" Then the Reverend Pindola by pulling up his eyebrows acted like Buddha. This is a truth that only Buddha can see Buddha, and Pindola's response was much more authoritative than the authority of King Prasenajit. (Of course Pindola's response has more truths to it, which are Pindola is Pindola, Pindola is not Buddha. Further, Pindola is neither Pindola nor Buddha; Pindola is what. To express the whole truth, Pindola responded without words.)

Baijang could see Buddha, could see Baijang, see Causation, see The Treasure Repository Housing the Eye to See the Right Dharma, and see the wild fox. Therefore he was very able to give the turning phrase. What the turning phrase is, is Bodhidharma's coming from the West: "The primary reason I came to this land was to transmit the Dharma to help confused sentient beings."

So, as his concrete achievement, what did Baijang turn? He turned the body of a wild fox, that is, the body of Baijang. Turning means to shed. So he shed the body of a wild fox, the body of Baijang. This is the shedding of the phenomenal body. He shed "I am not a person," which is The Whole World in the Ten Directions. Thus everything becomes a variation of Buddha and the patriarchs, thanks to Baijang's turning phrase.

By now we can understand Baijang's turning phrase wasn't about the language issued by the human mouth. It is nonsense to think the old man could shed the body of a wild fox by hearing a turning phrase issued by a human mouth. A human mouth is a particular phenomenon; and every turning phrase coming from a human mouth is also a particular phenomenon. Any particular phenomenon hasn't power to shed the body of a wild fox for five hundred lifetimes. It is because any particular phenomenon hasn't the power to change five hundred kalpas of causation.

Therefore it is wrong to think the old man by misguiding the trainee fell five hundred lifetimes into the body of a wild fox. Even incorrect words or even malicious words have no such power to change five hundred kalpas of causation.

Baijang's turning phrase came from the mouth made out of The Whole World in the Ten Directions, which is Causation.

> The whole body is like a mouth hanging in the empty sky regardless of winds from east, west, south, and north.
> Always it is clarifying prajna,
> di ding, dung liau, di ding, dung liau—
> (*Mahaprajna-paramita*, a volume of *Shobogenzo*)

This gatha by Dogen's teacher, Tiantung (Tiantung Rujing, 1163-1228), describes, by borrowing a wind bell, this Baijang's mouth.

Huangbo then asked, "The ancient person gave a wrong turning phrase and fell five hundred lifetimes into the body of a wild fox. Each time if he had not been wrong, what would he have become?"

The Teacher said, "Come here and I will tell you."

Huangbo said "The ancient person gave a wrong turning phrase." This "gave a wrong" doesn't mean a misguidance. As we have been studying in this Baijang's Wild Fox episode, there is no sense of worldly wrong or right. By giving a wrong answer if the teacher must become a wild fox, this world would by now be filled up with wild foxes, with no space left for any human beings or any others to dwell.

"Gave a wrong" means Avalokitesvara who attained the realization loses the realization in order to help sentient beings. This is the meaning of Huayan's couplet:

> A broken mirror never again reflects.
> A fallen flower never returns to the bough.
> (*Chuandeng lu*, vol. 17)

Huayan's teacher Dungshan when he was young had

occasion to help his training companion Shenshan about the same subject:

> When traveling together, the Teacher and Shenshan saw a white hare dash away. Shenshan said, "How alert, and agile!"
> The Teacher: "Why so?"
> Shenshan: "It is like a talented commoner raised to the rank of cabinet minister."
> Dungshan: "You attained a good old age and yet you talk like that!"
> Shenshan: "How about you?"
> Dungshan: "It is like a man who having inherited the rank of prime minister has for a duration been demoted."
>
> (*Dungshan lu*, entry 30)

Baijang didn't say "wrong," nor did the old man. Huangbo didn't mean "wrong," though he used the word "wrong." He used it in the sense of "non-alternation." He said "Each time if he hadn't been wrong, what would he have become?" which means "What would he have become in non-alternation?" which means "Buddha nature stays as Buddha nature," which means "Causation is inevitable," which is the same as shedding the body of a wild fox, which can be understood as $5 \times 5 = 5 \times 5$.

Alternation means Buddha nature becomes the old man, Baijang, and the body of a wild fox. It means "wrong answer," and "falling into the body of a wild fox." It means $5 \times 5 = 25$.

Thus there are these two aspects of Causation, as we have studied, and this compounded truth can be expressed by the one phrase "what would he have become?" This is also positive statement in question form. In Huangbo's statement there are both truths, alternation and non-alternation. This "what" is "Who is he who comes thus?"

The person who can express or detect this contradictory dynamics in one word, one phrase, in one thing, in one activity, is the excellent patriarch. Only a person well-acquainted with the Buddhist Great Causation is able to do so.

Even though Huangbo's question is a positive statement, it must be decently answered. Huangbo detected the motive and the true content of Baijang's wild fox narration. Baijang could detect that Huangbo detected his motive and true content. So he said "Come here and I will tell you." Then the conclusion of this episode comes: "Huangbo drew near the Teacher and slapped him." Here Huangbo understood that his teacher Baijang understood that he, Huangbo, understood the motive and content of Baijang's lecture. "The Teacher clapped, saying with a laugh, 'I thought of the alien's red beard—here is the red-bearded alien!'"

In the Huangbo and Baijang dialogue, we wish to detect the following meaning: Huangbo asked "Each time if he hadn't been wrong, what would he have become?" and Baijang answers "Come here and I will tell you." Baijang's words contain three answers: 1) You know. He would have become you. 2) Even if he hadn't been wrong, he would have become you. 3) Asking about him, you are talking about you, so he would become you.

> Huangbo drew near the Teacher and slapped him.
> The Teacher clapped, saying with a laugh, "I thought of the alien's red beard—here is the red-bearded alien!"

Huangbo drew near. This Huangbo is a splendid wild fox. Therefore he is the one who is most respectable in all of heaven and on earth.

For him there is no Baijang, Sakyamuni Buddha, or Maitreya. There isn't even Huangbo, but only a wild fox. So there's even no falling into Causation, that is: "Will not fall into Causation."

Huangbo "slapped" the Teacher. This is Huangbo's way to become a wild fox: He became his teacher. Huangbo from his youth had the talent to express concisely by both his words and his conduct. So he was admired as "a natural-born Zennist."

Similar response from Huangbo is recorded in *Chuandeng lu*, volume 9:

> One day Baijang asked Huangbo, "What have you been doing?"
> Huangbo: "Picking mushrooms in the lower area of Mt. Dashung" [= Mt. Baijang].
> Baijang: "Did you see a tiger?"
> Huangbo made the sound of a roaring tiger.
> Baijang gestured as if to slice it with his ax.
> Huangbo instantaneously slapped Baijang and grabbed him.
> Brightly laughing, Baijang returned to his residential quarters.

In his lecture he told the monks, "There is a tiger in the lower area of Mt. Dashung. You all had better see it well. Today I intimately met up with it."

"I thought of the alien's red beard—here is the red-bearded alien!" are Baijang's words of admiration.

    Baijang = "alien's red beard" = "ancient person" (old man)
    = "Will not fall into Causation" = "body of a wild fox"
    = "wrong turning phrase" = Dharma-kaya = sunyata
    = vicinity of Aksobhya-buddha.

    Huangbo = "red-bearded alien" = Baijang (young man)
    = "Causation is inevitable"
    = "shedding the body of a wild fox"
    = "Each time if he hadn't been wrong"
    = Sambhoga-kaya
    = rupa = everyday life.

In order to understand "I thought of the alien's red beard—here is the red-bearded alien!" there have been many interpretations since old times. Why so many is that Baijang's saying is clear enough for us to visualize the image, but his meaning is awfully ambiguous. His saying is crisp, concise, and very suitable to end the episode, but as we are at a movie's THE END, we are left with only our vague emotion and no rise of any intellectual words.

One meaningful interpretation is that "the alien's red beard" needs nothing else to exist with it (because it is presenting sunyata). It can exist aloof, independent of all else (for instance, the number 5 exists independent of all other numbers). In contrast, "the red-bearded alien" needs others to exist with itself (because it is presenting rupa). It can exist because of the existence of all else (for instance, the number 5 can't exist without 4, 6, or any other numbers).

Then the point of the aforesaid interpretation is that "the alien's red beard" and "the red-bearded alien" are different, but not so different after all, because either is only half of the total truth, and we shouldn't recognize only one or the other.

There is another meaningful interpretation of Baijang's words. It is that they are suggesting the view of Eternity in contrast to the view of Mortality. Eternity is the concept that all sentient beings will be reborn into an endless succession of lives, that is, the body dies but the soul leaves the body and survives, acquiring in each life a new body. The view of Eternity accords with Causation is inevitable. The view of Mortality is that all beings when they die return to the void, hence no Causation, no past, present, or future life. Buddhists do not accept either view. Baijang's final saying in this episode should be understood in the context of the episode's main flow, which is about Great Causation, that is, Cause is Buddha nature, and Effect too is Buddha nature. We would like to know how to live after learning about this Great Causation. Therefore in Baijang's words there must be the meaning.

The true human body of Buddha and the patriarchs is The Whole World in the Ten Directions, as is said, "These three worlds are all my possession, and sentient beings within them are my children." When we are in the mode of the phenomenal world, that is, "the red-bearded alien," there are objects, which have risen by Causation. Bodhisattvas must do their best for whatever are their objects for only the reason that their objects are presenting themselves as sad beings. Bodhisattvas doing their best must often go where they don't want to go, must often do what they don't want to do. Yet they shouldn't detach themselves from whatever are their objects and must closely go along with them. This is known as "Going along with the behavior of alien species." In the phenomenal world, the diversity of quality freely rises and a bodhisattva must go along with it naturally.

Phenomena expose their numerous diversities, which demands that bodhisattvas follow the orders and guidance of phenomena. But bodhisattvas while patiently, painfully following will realize they are only meeting themselves. Thus when seeing and hearing nature, mountain and river, azaleas on rocks, water dripping from mossy stones, then too they will know they themselves are unfolding.

So Shiangyan could come to the great realization by hearing a pebble hitting a bamboo. Lingyun seeing peach flowers could come to no further doubt. Mahakasyapa broke into a smile. They were not realizing until just then that The Treasure Repository Housing the Eye to See the Right Dharma was nothing other than their own life.

This is called "self-proving." This is the Dharma with no division between self and other. Bodhisattvas practice their training only for the sake of this Dharma. Here Cause accords with Effect, so Causation spontaneously sheds Causation. This is "the alien's red beard."

February 18, 2010

Essays on Jaujou's Twelve Hours Verses

Jaujou's Twelve Hours Verses

Two O'clock Cock's Crow

I rise and am distressed seeing my shabby dotage.
No priestly robes nor skirts have I,
though still there is my kasaya, even if crumpled.
Threadbare my sash, drawers so worn
I know not where to step in.
Much as my scalp is layered with a bushel of greenish lime,
I once desired to train myself and free the sufferers of this
    world.
Who could foretell I would become this very sort of sluggard?

Four O'clock Morning Twilight

Indescribable is this run-down temple
in a devastated village.
Not a single grain for gruel
makes me face in vain the window and the dust there gathered.
Commotion of sparrows, no presence of anyone.
Leaves often fall as I sit alone.
Who said leaving family is for severing love and hate?
Before my notice, my scarf is wet with tears.

Six O'clock Sunrise

Purity turns and becomes klesa,
the virtue of artificial merit goes moldy.
So I never cleaned my boundless field.
My eyebrows many times frown, few suit my fancy.
Unbearable is that black yellowish peasant
of the neighboring east village.
Without ever donating, he brings his donkey
to graze before the Buddha Hall.

Eight O'clock Mealtime

Futilely seeing the cooking smoke
of the neighbors in the four directions.
A year ago we made buns and steamed bread.
I swallow my saliva in vain.
Right thought I rarely have, I often sigh.
In a hundred households no good person.
Those who come only ask to be served tea.
If not offered, they depart with anger.

Ten O'clock Morning

Ordained by the shaving of the head.
Why has it come to this?
I became chief priest in this village,
invited for not much reason.
Hungry, humiliated, almost better off dead.
Those guys Hu, Jang, Hei, and Li
never have shown me any respect.
Abruptly they appear at the gate, "Lend paper and tea."

Noon

Not provided with rice and tea,
I must repeatedly ask.
Arrived at a north house after a south house.
As expected, not welcomed.
Bitter sandy salt, fermented barley,
rice with millet, vinegared cutting lettuce.
The host said offerings should not be slighted
priests should keep firm faith and strict practice.

Two O'clock Sun Declining

No more walking the land
with light and shade.
Once satiated, never hungry, it is said.
This old monk's life today is the very example,
not studying Zen, not discussing theology.
Napping on a frayed straw mat.
Even in Tusita Heaven there could not be
such pleasure as to bask in the sun.

Four O'clock Afternoon Tea

There are those who come to worship
with offerings of incense,
five old women, three of them each with a goiter,
two with cracked cheeks.
They bring flaxseed for tea, indeed precious.
Deva Kings, ease your muscles.
If only I could give a coin to Rahula
next year at the harvest of mulberry leaves and wheat.

Six O'clock Sunset

Nothing to maintain except a desolate scene.
Noble trainees have never come.
Immutable are those acolytes
who visit temple after temple.
No unprecedented words issue from my mouth.
Descendant of Sakyamuni I am in vain.
Here is a coarse staff used to beat a dog,
not only to climb a mountain.

Eight O'clock Nightfall

Sitting alone in a dark vacant room.
Shimmering and torchlight are never seen.
In front of my eyes is like lacquer produced in Jin.
Without hearing the bell
I spend the day in vain.
Only the sound of scurrying mice.
How do I have the mind
to think about paramita?

Ten O'clock Settling

Who cherishes the moon before the gate?
Indoors my concern is how to sleep.
No upper or lower bedclothes, no covers.
Odd are Liou, the regulations monk,
and Jau, who keeps the Five Precepts.
With their mouth they preach the morals,
even though my bag has become empty.
Never do they understand whatever I ask.

Midnight

How does my mind cease even a moment?
Come to think of the monks in this world
dwelling in temples,
how many can be like me?
Earthen bed, unraveled bamboo mat,
a long time using an elm pillow without a cover.
For Buddha no benzoin in the incense burner.
Only the smell of cow dung.

Essays on Jaujou's Twelve Hours Verses

Two O'clock Cock's Crow

I rise and am distressed seeing my shabby dotage.
No priestly robes nor skirts have I,
though still there is my kasaya, even if crumpled.
Threadbare my sash, drawers so worn
I know not where to step in.
Much as my scalp is layered with a bushel of greenish lime,
I once desired to train myself and free the sufferers of this world.
Who could foretell I would become this very sort of sluggard?

*　　*　　*

    A shortage of clothing is distressful in a cold climate, and a shortage of heated water makes a difficulty of keeping clean. But because Jaujou exaggerates that his dandruff amounts to a bushel, no one believes he hasn't enough clothes. He is poor, but not eager for what he doesn't have. Rather, he is relieved to have no more than enough, and here he uses worn-out clothes as a metaphor.
    From the beginning of history it has been positively said that there are definite differences between mankind and animals. We use tools, fire, language, and so on. Jaujou makes a topic of another difference: we use clothes by stealing the lives of animals, which no animal does. In this context, few clothes is better than many.
    Jaujou is concerned more about our mental clothes, or concepts, than about material clothes. This concern formed his most important lecture:

The Teacher [Jaujou] said in his lecture: "A metal Buddha will not survive a smelting furnace, a wooden Buddha will not survive fire, and a mud Buddha will not survive water. The true Buddha is in the depths of the Hall. Bodhi, Nirvana, Tathata, and Buddhata all are decorative robes, and are called klesa. There is no klesa if you do not ask. Where are you going to place a mental state such as True Ultimate Existence? 'Only if one's mind is not born do all phenomena have no problem.' Meditate in seeking Reason for twenty or thirty years and cut off the head of this old monk if you are not yet going to arrive at the understanding.

"'Trying to grab a dream, a phantom, and a flower in the air is to try in vain.' If our mind does not oppose [primary mind], all phenomena will also not oppose.' [The Dharma] cannot be obtained from outside. Then what's to care for? What good is it to put whatever you pick into your mouth like a sheep? When this old monk met Yaushan, he was told by Yaushan 'Anyone who asks me will just be made by me to shut his doggy mouth.' I also will say just shut your doggy mouth. 'Recognizing the existence of oneself is filth, and not recognizing the existence of oneself is purity.' You are like a hunter's dogs wishing to put things in their mouth for no reason. Where are you attempting to put Buddha's Dharma? The thousand and ten thousand people are all those who are seeking Buddha, and among them there is not a single trainee. If you wish to become a disciple of the King of Sunyata, you had better not be taken ill in your mind. Such illness is most difficult to be cured.

"There has always been this nature from before the world came to exist and it will not be destroyed even when the world is annihilated. Once you see this old monk, you are no one else, you are a master. Such a being you are, so what is the point of seeking outward? Do not replace your head, your face. [Watch out,] you will lose it easily."

(*Jaujou lu*, entry 209)

The first paragraph of this Jaujou lecture directly relates to our topic, but by translating the remainder it becomes clear that not having any mental clothes is in itself the goal of training. Nor is it necessary in becoming a master to acquire anything before putting them on or after taking them off.

From the Indian third patriarch, Sanavasin, we have an enviable example of having no such clothes:

The Teacher [Sanavasin] was born in Mathura. His name means "natural clothes." He was born clothed. Since then his clothes became cool clothes in summer and warm clothes in winter. When he raised Bodhi mind, his layman's clothes became his kasaya. (*Denko roku*, vol.1)

Mathura was the name of central India in those days and from there Buddhism began to prosper. The meaning is not that Sanavasin was born literally clothed. It is that from infancy he knew his body was Buddha nature and that he should therefore live according to its nature. Our physical mother gave us Buddha nature within us. Jaujou says we shouldn't put on additional clothes. When Sanavasin became a monk, it is said his clothes turned to kasaya. This means that although he was born with Buddha nature, he had to activate Buddha nature and actually practice it by means of behaving as a sangha in order to function as Buddha nature.

Jaujou with this understanding says "though still there is my kasaya, even if crumpled."

The descriptions "neither priestly robes nor skirts have I....Threadbare my sash, drawers so worn I know not where to step in" could be hiding more detailed metaphors. For instance, "drawers so worn I know not where to step in" could mean Jaujou won't be involved in any dualistic valuation because such relativity in his life is well gone like a vanished mist.

Yaushan (Yaushan Weiyan, 745-828) was one generation earlier than Jaujou, and he impressed Jaujou, as we have studied in Jaujou's lecture above.

> He [Yaushan] said to himself, "Man should be able to be pure without depending on precepts. Why should I care about such trivia as the bits and hems of robes and sash?"
> Then he visited Shytou and understood the profound meaning.
> One day when he was sitting, Shytou came to him and asked, "What are you doing here?"
> Yaushan replied, "I am not doing anything."
> Shytou: "If so, you must be killing time."
> Yaushan: "If so, it is one kind of doing something."
> Shytou: "Tell me, you say you are not doing anything. What are you not doing?"
> Yaushan: "The thousand sages too do not know about that." (*Chuandeng lu*, vol. 14)

According to this Yaushan episode, Jaujou in his verse could have meant graduating from the precepts by his words "robes" and "sash." Anyway, in the earliest hour of the day he renews his determination not to be used by human concepts. Though he was around a hundred years old when he wrote these twelve hours verses, he had the vigor to live life directly without putting any buffer between himself and his life. This direct life he mentions in his lecture by such expressions as "There is no klesa if you do not ask" and "Just shut your doggy mouth."

The middle lines of the verse are in concert, expressing Jaujou's messy and even unclean looks. But they are hiding in contrast his ideal priestly life, and they are going to lead us to the concluding couplet.

The line "though still there is my kasaya, even if crumpled" shows Jaujou is living the life of a kasaya-donning monk. "Kasaya-donning monk" means to study what Buddha taught and to go the way that Buddha recommended. In essence each monk should become a Buddha. So Sakyamuni Buddha taught us "Make yourself a light, rely on yourself, and do not depend on anyone else. Make the Dharma your light, rely on the Dharma, and do not depend on any other place." In Buddha's time, saving oneself was regarded as the main feature of being a monk.

But when Mahayana Buddhism began to rise, helping others, all sentient and insentient beings, became the main issue of being a monk. So the Mahayana sutras emphasize "All Buddhas including Sakyamuni came into this world only for one cause: to enable all beings to accomplish Buddhahood" (*Saddharmapundarika-sutra*), and "I made all beings enter Ultimate Nirvana, I saved them, saved unlimited unbounded numbers of beings with none left unsaved" (*Vajracchedika-prajnaparamita-sutra*). All Mahayana sutras dwell only on this subject no matter how much diversity they have in expressions and devices.

So the first Chinese patriarch Bodhidharma will say in his gatha of transmission of the Dharma:

> The primary reason I came to this land
> was to transmit the Dharma to help
> confused sentient beings.
> If one flower opens with five leaves
> the fruits will naturally form. (*Chuangdeng lu, vol. 3*)

The first half of the gatha expresses the exact same religious truth as what Buddha stated in the sutras. "I came to this land" says Bodhidharma. He means first, the meaning of the life for which he was born on this earth, and second, the reason he risked that life in coming from India to China, and third, the "I" who is every being, every phenomenon, and every function that can be expressed by the first person singular.

"Five leaves" means an endless number of leaves, and one of the "fruits" is Jaujou. Jaujou's lines "though still there is my kasaya, even if crumpled," and "Much as my scalp is layered with a bushel of greenish lime" are only a variation of the first half of Bodhidharma's gatha.

Why is his kasaya "crumpled" and why should his scalp be "layered with a bushel of greenish lime"? Jaujou understood the Way at age eighteen. It was like a Hinayana monk (*bhiksu*) who achieves the right wisdom, right precept, and right dhyana for his own benefit.

In order to become a Mahayana monk (*sangha*), Jaujou asked his teacher Nanchyuan what he should do after understanding the Way. Nanchyuan told him to become a work cow. To become a work cow means in this context that Jaujou doesn't stay in the status of understanding the Way. He must deny what he understands and put himself in "a bushel of greenish lime," which is the difficulty of living with worldly people.

It is said in the Chinese-made Brahma's Net Sutra:

> Not being conscious of rightly keeping the precepts and also not having an evil mind is called keeping the pure precepts.

Among all beings, only human beings can be conscious of rightly keeping the precepts. It is hard to help others if we happen to be conscious of our own right doing.

"Kasaya" has many meanings. One of them is the color that is not being born. All visible colors are born or produced. The person who intuitively understands the color that is not being born can be a kasaya-donning monk, and it is a natural consequence that the color that is not being born will not die. The occasion when Sanavasin received the Dharma transmission from Ananda clarifies the nature of the life that is not being born as well as the nature of being compassionate for other lives:

> Venerable Sanavasin asked Venerable Ananda: "What is the nature that is the origin of all phenomena and is not being born?"
> Ananda indicated a corner of Sanavasin's kasaya.
> Sanavasin asked once more: "What is the primary nature of the Bodhi of all Buddhas?"
> Ananda pulled the corner of Sanavasin's kasaya.
> Sanavasin then came to a great realization.
> *(Denko roku*, vol.1)

Everything is produced by something preceding it. Sanavasin asked about the origin that is not produced by anything. It is said God made the world, or the Big Bang made the universe. Sanavasin is asking who made God and what made the Big Bang. Ananda indicates a corner of Sanavasin's kasaya. As we studied, kasaya is the color that is not being born. Anything with color cannot be kasaya. So the nature that is the origin of all phenomena and is not being born also cannot be seen as having any color. In short, we can't know with our eyes, with our intelligence. The reason is that we are not on the side produced by the origin but are on the side going to produce all sorts of phenomena.

In order to know "the nature that is the origin of all phenomena and is not being born," the best we can do intellectually is just to keep denying any defined form (= Brahma's Net Sutra's "Not being conscious of rightly keeping the precepts"). For instance, what is "kasaya"? Not a cloth, not cotton or silk, not a discarded rag, etc. While we keep applying the best description we have, shedding each form and color, we are engaging in the content of the form. So Sanavasin asked "What is the primary nature of the Bodhi of all Buddhas?"

Sanavasin wanted to make sure about the origin of compassion. Ananda instantaneously pulled the corner of his kasaya. First Sanavasin saw no form or color or beginning or end of life through the kasaya. Then he returned to form and color and beginning and end of life. Sanavasin's seeing no color was, for Jaujou, an understanding of the Way, and Sanavasin's coming back to color was, for Jaujou, becoming a cow. This all is the coming and going of the truth "Indeed there is no place to dwell, yet it keeps rising." For Buddhists, wisdom means to see no form, and compassion means to see form. A patriarch is perfectly acquainted with this free coming and going. Therefore Jaujou says here at the start of the day, "though still there is my kasaya, even if crumpled."

The actual figure of "Not being conscious of rightly keeping the precepts" is "Much as my scalp is layered with a bushel of greenish lime."

To have one's head covered with worldly judgments, requests, abuse, blame, disregard, and suspicion isn't an enjoyable life. For self-centered persons clever for their own benefit these all are unbearable. Each morning amid showers of worldly venom, Jaujou renews his determination to live his life for the benefit of others. His greatness is beyond admiration. His teacher Nanchyuan taught him:

> [Nanchyuan] often said in his sermons: "Nowadays there are many Zen teachers, but I cannot find even one who is an idiotic dullard. Don't any of you misuse your mind! If you wish to master this matter, you must directly go to the time before Buddha came to this world, where there are no nouns, and act there in the manner in which no one discerns your hidden functions and your fathomless transactions. If you do, for the first time you will be truthful, somewhat.
>
> Therefore I will say Buddhas and patriarchs do not know being, whereas rat-catchers and bullocks know. Why do they know? They know because they haven't emotional and measurable judgment.
>
> Therefore even calling it "suchness" is already calling it something different from itself. You should directly enter the beasts' life.

Under the Fifth Patriarch [Huangmei Daman Hungren, 601-674] there were five hundred ninety-nine monks who all understood Buddha's Dharma. The only one who didn't understand was the trainee Lu [later named Dajian Hueineng, the Sixth Patriarch, 638-713]. He just understood the Way.

> So even if all Buddhas were to come to this world, what they would do is make you understand the Way and they would do nothing else. (*Tzutang ji*, vol. 16)

Jaujou must have been thankful for Nanchyuan, who loved Jaujou so much that Jaujou lived every day the life Nanchyuan recommended. Ananda loved Sanavasin, and his love enabled Sanavasin to live a wise and compassionate life. Predecessors enable later comers to live as kasaya-donning monks.

According to Buddhism, people suffer from their own ignorance, which is a kind of autointoxication. So the primary job for a kasaya-donning monk is to remove the negative influence of self-made emotions and thoughts. Nanchyuan loved Jaujou more than anyone else ever could, so Jaujou now lives like Nanchyuan, where no one notices.

Dogen also noted the importance of the transmission of love:

> To train in Buddha's Dharma, one must always inherit the core teaching of one's predecessors and not use one's own private interpretation. Buddha's Dharma cannot be understood by either the mind or the absence of the mind. Buddha's Dharma can be understood only by the practice of not being polluted.
>
> Don't you see that all tiny insects and beasts alike raise their young and go through mental and physical hardship? After pain and toil their young finally grow up, but after all there are no benefits to the parents. About this, the behavior of even small creatures resembles the thought of all Buddhas toward sentient beings.
>
> The wonderful Dharma of all Buddhas is not simply compassion alone. The wonderful Dharma of all Buddhas universally presents all sorts of gates because the origin of the wonderful Dharma is like this.
>
> (*Gakudo yojin shu* [Advice for studying the Way], entry 4)

Now it is clear that in the beginning of the day Jaujou is quietly relieved that his life took no other course.

He is content to be "an idiotic dullard."

> I once desired to train myself and free the sufferers of this world.
> Who could foretell I would become this very sort of sluggard?

Four O'clock Morning Twilight

Indescribable is this run-down temple
in a devastated village.
Not a single grain for gruel
makes me face in vain the window and the dust there gathered.
Commotion of sparrows, no presence of anyone.
Leaves often fall as I sit alone.
Who said leaving family is for severing love and hate?
Before my notice, my scarf is wet with tears.

* * *

According to the conclusion, the essential concern of this verse is about our thought and emotion. The figure of the person with thought and emotion is visible, but the content of the thought and emotion is ambiguous. Making the content clear is necessary to appreciate this verse.

Forms at twilight appear dim. Then just as sunyata turns to rupa what shows up is "this run-down temple in a devastated village." The destructive storm against Buddhism instigated by Emperor Wu of Tang was raging in 845 when Jaujou was sixty-seven and on the way of mendicancy. We can assume he was avoiding it, walking away from the capital, Changan, and heading north.

With a weakened central government, the local military cliques kept fighting for hegemony. Jaujou when around age eighty settled in Hebei, protected by military cliques lead by Jauwang (Jauwang Wangrung, 873-921) and Yanwang (Yanwang Likeyung, 856-908). It is said these two protectors also fought each other for survival during Jaujou's residence in the temple receiving their support.

Special mention is given in entry 6 of his biography, in *Jaujou lu*:

> Throughout his forty years' residence as chief priest of the temple, he [Jaujou] never once sent a letter [of request] to his protectors.

The reason he never did must have great relation with the major part of the content of his thought and emotion.

Political, economic, and military power over weak creatures is so dreadful as to almost extinguish any self-sufficient culture wherein we depend least on other lives for our own enjoyment and satisfaction.

Jaujou wets his scarf with tears. He is sad for the many victims tortured by those hegemonic powers, and he is feeling anger toward those who can't properly guide their own illusory desires to the extent that they make innocent rupa sinful. Yet those very powers are his protectors. He can't become entirely independent of them, nor simply hate them, and is in the position to be beneficial to their well-being.

So he says:

> Indescribable is this run-down temple
> in a devastated village.

It is not difficult for the poetically talented Jaujou to describe the surface looks of where he is, shallow as a newsreel or realistic novel. Here he isn't expressing a shortage of descriptive ability but rather saying he won't go in the direction of describing such phenomena because it would be a negative act, stimulating more fighting. He knows fighting won't cease unless one side or the other just stops without making any demands.

More inward he turns his gaze, from the problems related with human ethical behavior to the ontological subject characteristic of any being. There he finds not a single grain of rice. Cultivated foods are a luxury. He and his monks gathered chestnuts, sawtooth oak nuts, and such. But the purpose of this verse isn't to express his skimpy food. Yunmen (Yunmen Wenyau, 864-949) is helpful for understanding the meaning of "a single grain":

> If there is a mind, heaven and earth are miles apart. Not even fire can burn him who has mastered. Even if he preaches all day long, he will have no teeth or lips and will utter not so much as a word. All day long, even if he dons the robe and eats meals, he will not touch so much as a grain or a thread. Even if thus he is, it merely belongs to the level of device. Only when we actually practice will we for the first time understand. (*Chuandeng lu*, vol. 19)

Yunmen is introducing us to the life that cannot be burnt by fire, cannot be controlled by causation, and cannot be separated by space and time. It is obvious that when we don't divide ourselves from our environment we will "not touch so much as a grain" even if we regularly eat meals. Jaujou wishes us to have such a morning without a single grain to eat.

This life of no division doesn't mean being unconscious of the relation between us and a single grain. Though we are conscious of our separateness, we must understand intuitively that we are one and that such a time is when we have no thought and emotion. Thought and emotion are produced in us only when we are observers of life. Only observers can produce thought and emotion. When we are participants in life, we are thought and emotion itself and thus are unaware of our thought and emotion.

In other words, the oneness of us with our environment isn't simply describing our psychological state. It is highly describing our shift of interest toward ontological participation and away from indulging in concerns over our human ethical behavior. This ontological participation is Right Dhyana and is called the practice of cross-legged meditation, under the heritage of the first patriarch in China, Bodhidharma.

Now it becomes clear what Jaujou means by "not a single grain." It is his determination to live this day too in the practice of his meditation.

Naturally he faces "in vain the window and the dust there gathered." "In vain" doesn't mean his thought and emotion aren't functioning. It means he is participating in the life of such beings as the window and the dust.

As for thought and emotion, "not a single grain" reminds him of his incompetence in managing the materialistic aspect of life, and that such a time is the very time every being surrounding him, window, dust, will begin to expose its meaning of being rather than its meaning as function. Likewise, a being such as dust, regarded as useless in daily life, will begin to show its intimacy with a human being.

When Jaujou takes the part of the same life with the window and the dust, they haven't physical space and chronological time. So they are actually the ones who are becoming Jaujou's life. It is the time Jaujou enriches his life because his life is amalgamated with them. This is the dynamism in which Dharma-kaya takes Jaujou's life and acts as Nirmana-kaya, as is said: "Indeed there is no place to dwell, yet it keeps rising."

> Teacher Tsaushan asked the senior trainee De, "Buddha, the true Dharma-kaya, is like the vacant sky, and the way it presents its form according to causation is like the moon on the water. How do you describe this truth?"
> De replied, "It is like the well-pulley seeing down the well."
> Tsaushan said, "Your expression is quite good, but to the degree of eight out of ten."
> De asked, "Your Reverence, how do you yourself say?"
> Tsaushan replied, "It is like the well seeing the well-pulley above." (*Sanbyaku soku*, vol. 2, Case 25)

This episode is important to understand, for it reveals to us the unbounded life. The relationship between Nirmana-kaya and Dharma-kaya, our concrete limited life and abstract universal life, is here likened to the relationship between moon and water.

Tsaushan asked the senior trainee De to describe the essential character innate in the relationship between Nirmana-kaya and Dharma-kaya. If we haven't a complete understanding of the essential character, we can't use the relationship effectively, beneficially. De replied, "It is like the well-pulley seeing down the well." Inorganic matter is seeing inorganic matter. In this relationship there is the absolute absence of our thought and emotion. Even so, Tsaushan gave no complete approval to De. However, Tsaushan's answer was merely the reverse. So his answer alone must be also only "good, but to the degree of eight out of ten." The secret of the perfect answer is in both directions going simultaneously: well-pulley to well, well to well-pulley.

After all, there is no room in any phenomenal relationship, including the relationship between our particular life and our universal life, to insert our thought and emotion, and therefore we each and our environment are cherishing boundless life.

For instance, between us and a pine tree there's no room to insert our thought and emotion, regardless of content. This is true even if we actually plant a seedling or cut with a chainsaw. This relation is universal in every relation possible to exist. Boundless life is therefore in everything, everywhere.

Boundless life because it is universal is even in the midst of our thought and emotion and even outside of our thought and emotion. Even if we don't shed our thought and emotion, our boundless life will never be influenced by our thought and emotion. With this understanding, meditation under the First Patriarch Bodhidharma is to see the nature of being, and as to this, there is no purpose in correcting our ethical behavior.

However, the relation between boundless life and our thought and emotion is a simultaneous flow in both directions, as we have studied. The theme of Jaujou's following lecture is about this and not anything else:

> The Teacher said in his lecture: "This matter is like a bright crystal orb in one's palm. If a foreigner comes, a foreigner appears, and if a native comes, a native appears."
>
> (*Jaujou lu*, entry 76)

It is an extremely short lecture. So we must figure out the meaning of the episode by studying the totality of *Jaujou lu* and by our own reflection. This metaphor isn't expressing the accuracy of an optical reflection of any figure on a bright mirror. "This matter" means "the most important matter for our life."

The depth of the episode is in its mention of the relationship between phenomena and Buddha nature. A foreigner and a native are likened to phenomena, and a bright crystal orb is likened to Buddha nature. What we should attend to is "This matter" is "in one's palm."

Buddha nature produces Buddha nature whether the figures it takes appear to be ignorant beings or Buddha and the patriarchs. In our palm is the authority and responsibility to decide which appears, and the metaphor of a bright crystal orb in our palm is valid for only this much. The place where a foreigner or Buddha and the patriarchs appear isn't on the crystal orb. There's no such special breeding place for Buddha nature to produce phenomena. If we don't see Buddha nature in phenomena, there's no place we can see Buddha nature.

> Commotion of sparrows, no presence of anyone.
> Leaves often fall as I sit alone.

Jaujou sees the window and its dust, which are inorganic, and they reveal no more than what they are. In meditation as time passes, he hears the sound of sparrows and falling leaves. They give some comfort through his ears, but soon he becomes aware of the distance between his life and theirs. The reason they comfort is only that they resemble some similarities with the human figure and behavior. So the more intimate he becomes with things inorganic, and with animals and plants, the stronger is his wish to contact with actual human beings.

Our tragedy is that only when we give up hope of meeting our ideal person on this earth can we have the possibility of meeting such a one at least in our spiritual life, and if we meet such a one on this earth, of course we won't have much possibility of meeting such a one in our spiritual life. Jaujou says "no presence of anyone" in either his spiritual life or on this earth. What's the good of it? It is not a matter of good or bad. Always he starts from reality:

> Who said leaving family is for severing love and hate?
> Before my notice, my scarf is wet with tears.

Here he simplifies all emotions and desires into the one phrase "love and hate." Since old times, analytical study of our emotions and desires has been well advancing, while study of how to cope with them has been assigned to the slowest of snails. The seven emotions are joy, anger, pleasure, fancy, sadness, fear, and surprise. The six desires are desire for food, sex, wealth, stability, power, and nobility. In the conclusion of this four o'clock verse, we are going to see how Jaujou copes with his thought and emotion.

Evidently the topic of thought and emotion was a basic topic he concerned himself with all his life. It is squarely dealt with in *Shinshin ming*, and related discussions from varying angles are four times given in *Jaujou lu*; and the discussions were inherited by Shyuedou in his One Hundred Gathas (later becoming *Biyan lu*, by Yuanwu).

> The Ultimate Way asks of us no difficult training
> but rejects our preferences.
> It exposes itself explicitly, in detail, and in totality
> when we free ourselves from love and hate.
> *(Shinshin ming)*

It is strange that love and hate are flatly denied here in *Shinshin ming*, whereas Jaujou openly states "my scarf is wet with tears." (In those days and society Jaujou's behavior would have been scorned as feminine. So we can detect an evident emphasis in his statement.) *Shinshin ming* was written by the Third Patriarch, Sengtsan. Jaujou can be counted as the Tenth.

Expecting consistent Dharma transmission, we cannot help being perplexed by Jaujou's contradictory behavior. Carefully we must again read *Shinshin ming*.

Shinshin ming is telling us the Ultimate Way "rejects our preferences." It isn't saying we should reject them. The Ultimate Way is sunyata, and sunyata is rupa, which is "preferences." It means the Ultimate Way (sunyata) and "preferences" (rupa) aren't two different things. So when sunyata exists, rupa doesn't at the same time exist. Likewise the time when the Ultimate Way "exposes itself explicitly" is the time when we are free of our "love and hate." So *Shinshin ming* is describing the relationship between sunyata and rupa.

Jaujou well knows this relationship, but his interest is to bring out rupa from sunyata rather than stay with the concern of *Shinshin ming*, which is that is rupa is returning to sunyata. So making his scarf wet with tears is the very appearance of the Ultimate Way. His thought and emotion is thus backed up by the Ultimate Way, with no inconsistency between him and Sengtsan, even if there is advance from Sengtsan to him.

The reason we can claim advance is that Jaujou discovered a synergistic effect in the dynamics of sunyata turning to rupa, if we make an active choice in taking a particular form of rupa instead of merely observing with resignation the natural transition of sunyata turning to rupa or rupa to sunyata. As a concrete example, we have the choice to act as a "foreigner" or as a "native" in this rupa world, whatever they may mean. These two terms aren't classifications made by an immigration office of a local government in any country. Here they are interesting terms for how to accept our life in this rupa world. Anyway, Jaujou is saying rupa naturally comes out from sunyata. But in its transition if we willingly chose to be a "foreigner" or a "native," the meaning and influential power of being a "foreigner" or a "native" will be much more than just going along with the natural dynamics between sunyata and rupa. The synergistic effect will be exercised as the beneficial acts of a Bodhisattva. With this hidden meaning, Jaujou concludes his verse Four O'clock Morning Twilight, the beginning of the day's activity.

With the eyes of a mother, he is seeing all suffering creatures. So he says:

> Who said leaving family is for severing love and hate?
> Before my notice, my scarf is wet with tears.

When "leaving family" (sunyata=Buddha nature) surfaces, "love and hate" submerges, but "love and hate" should keep coming up daily, renewed with our best choice. It means we help Buddha nature, and Buddha nature helps us.

> Question: "Does a dog have Buddha nature?"
> Jaujou: "No, a dog does not have Buddha nature."
> Question: "It is said all Buddhas upwards and all ants downwards have Buddha nature. Why not a dog?"
> Jaujou: "Because a dog has karma."
> (*Jaujou lu*, entry 132)

This dog is a Buddhist dog and has chosen to live a dog's life. So the dog can activate Buddha nature. For Buddhists this activating is karma.

> Question: "Does a dog have Buddha nature?"
> Jaujou: "Each road before each house leads to Changan."
> (*Jaujou lu*, entry 363)

The point of the episode is telling us that because every road leads to Buddha nature, it is best that we choose a beneficial road for creatures.

> Question: "What is Dharma-kaya?"
> Jaujou: "It is Nirmana-kaya."
> Question: "I am not asking about Nirmana-kaya."
> Jaujou: "Care single-mindedly about Nirmana-kaya."
> (*Jaujou lu*, entry 133)

Jaujou practices what he teaches and says:

> Before my notice, my scarf is wet with tears.

Six O'clock Sunrise

Purity turns and becomes klesa,
the virtue of artificial merit goes moldy.
So I never cleaned my boundless field.
My eyebrows many times frown, few suit my fancy.
Unbearable is that black yellowish peasant
of the neighboring east village.
Without ever donating, he brings his donkey
to graze before the Buddha Hall.

* * *

It must be difficult for those estranged from Jaujou's greatness to appreciate this verse. Here Jaujou seemingly expresses the common complaint of the less well–to-do, while the appeal of the verse appears to be the unexpected humorous frankness of a dignified master.

To appreciate this verse, we must know Jaujou's essential great ability, which is his quickness to become one with whatever thing when it appears. He first becomes one with his image as a temple master, second he becomes one with a "black yellowish peasant," and third he becomes one with the total environment where there is a temple master and a peasant.

This triple oneness is the core of this verse. It hides well the truth that purity is klesa and klesa is purity.

The ability to become one comes from practicing to see the nature of every phenomenon and not to insistently attach to the form and concept. When we are attached to form and concept, we divide ourselves from other, and then difference and conflict rise, and this mechanism is the basic cause of our suffering and unhappiness. The state of our being controlled by this mechanism is called *avidya*, or ignorance. We can't escape from destined misery unless we learn how to control our attachment to form and concept (and control our detachment from form and concept). So it is said in Bodhidharma's One Mind Precept:

> One's own nature is wonderful. Do not drink alcohol means Do not raise ignorance in the Dharma, which is primordially pure.

Bodhidharma is as sad as Sakyamuni Buddha to see us suffering, and is trying to guide us to see our original nature, which is primordially free of suffering. Our confused and deluded mental state is here likened to alcoholic intoxication.

Buddha assures us of boundless happiness when we free ourselves from form and concept:

> The people who have no perception of form of self, of person, of people, of those who have life duration, of Dharma form, and of No Dharma form gain the boundless happiness.
>
> Why is it so? The reason is that only those who obstinately regard form are attached to the form of self, of people, of those who have life duration. Likewise, when they obstinately regard the form of Dharma, they will be attached to the form of self, of person, of people, and of those who have life duration.
>
> Even if they obstinately regard No Dharma form, they will be attached to the form of self, of person, of people, and of those who have life duration. Therefore Dharma should not be obstinately regarded and, likewise, No Dharma should not be obstinately regarded.
>
> The Tathagata has always been preaching to you bhiksus: The Dharma I preach is like a raft. Even the Dharma should be abandoned [after making use of it], and much more No Dharma should be abandoned.
>
> (*Vajiracchedika-prajnaparamita-sutra* [Diamond Sutra], chap. 7, Rare True Belief)

Kyoju kaimon emphasizes mental alcohol more than material alcohol, and also more emphasizes conceptual form:

> 5. Not buying or selling intoxicants. *Kyoju kaimon*: Do not violate that which has not yet been brought. Not violating is Great Brightness.

Anything involving value judgment, such as honor and profit, is an intoxicant. Intoxicants not yet been brought aren't materials but are metaphysical values such as Sage, Realization, Buddha's Wisdom, Right Precept. Actually every value added to phenomenal materials and functions is an intoxicant not yet been brought.

> The reverend priest Yanyang asked Jaujou, "What will you say to me who am not bringing even a thing?"
> Jaujou: "Abandon it."
> Yanyang: "Not bringing even a thing—what should I abandon?"
> Jaujou: "In such case, go on carrying."
>
> (*Chuandeng lu*, vol. 11)

Dungshan says:

> Fastening our mind is violating the precepts. Having taste is breaking the purity. (*Dungshan lu*, entry 75)

These extreme teachings tell us that actual practice isn't in the form of our conduct. The actual practice is highly in our understanding of Dharma nature and is the time when our conduct confines our consciousness in the depths of function.

In this verse, as daylight increases, Jaujou begins to see a variety of forms, and his thought and emotion also begin to rise like wisps of smoke. So he says in the first line,

> Purity turns and becomes klesa,

Our vision stimulates our dualistic valuation to the effect that negative thought and emotion smoke inside and outside our life. Even exercising our prudence often brings us only worries. We wish to live with our lungs open to purity instead of suffocating with the moldy air of klesa. Klesa means a depressing suffering, and purity means the ease or pleasure beyond awareness of ease and pleasure. We are told by Buddha and the patriarchs that our nature is pure and that we are free of suffering. Then what is this gloom? Many days of a month are suffocated with depression, and many hours of the day are hooked with some sort of worry. The time free of gloom can be a rarity like seeing minnows in a city ditch.

Jaujou is a great master. He can cherish his purity even while he frowns with his eyebrows. He is like a gourd springing back up when it is pushed into the water. He is like a lotus in the fire—mere phenomena, mere human beings, cannot burn it. He must be watching our pure nature and trying not to avert his eyes, or he enough knows our nature is universal and cannot avert his eyes while everywhere is our pure nature.

> Question: "How can we achieve the state of clarity even though we are not pure and are in the state of mixed in even though we are not polluted?"
> Jaujou: "Be neither pure nor polluted."
> Question: "How to be like that?"
> Jaujou: "Cherish your own life."
> Question: "How can we gain the freedom throughout past, present, and future as well as in all the ten directions?"
> Jaujou: "Abandon Diamond samadhi."
>
> (*Jaujou lu*, entry 395)

Jaujou answers "Be neither pure nor polluted." It is the same teaching as that of the *Prajnaparamita-hrdaya-sutra* [Essence of the Great Prajna Sutra]. The distinctive feature of the Mahayana teaching is that it keeps describing the nature of the world, or of being, or of phenomena, instead of recommending to us how to behave by particular conduct. Therefore the monk's second question, "How to be like that?" is irrelevant. So Jaujou replies, "Cherish your own life," hoping if the monk squarely cares about his own life instead of about his conceptual thought and emotion he will resolve his doubt. The nature of life is innately neither pure nor polluted.

The monk, yet unable to free himself from his conceptual worry, asks the third question: "How can we gain the freedom throughout past, present, and future as well as in all the ten directions?" This is a seemingly big question, but any trifling being is living such a life free of time and space because any trifling being is itself the very figure of time and space even though seemingly doomed by time and space.

Diamond samadhi (*vajra-dhyana*) is the most powerful meditation to clear up any devil and klesa. But Jaujou here tells the monk to abandon Diamond samadhi. Jaujou well perceives the monk is thinking he needs to practice Diamond samadhi in order to gain freedom from time and space. But every phenomenon, every being, including our filth and suffering, is Diamond samadhi. All are the figure of Diamond samadhi. We are wretched for our dislike of klesa, which is Diamond samadhi, time and space, Buddha nature, purity. We are really free only when we are free even of ourselves, who are Diamond samadhi.

Buddha taught these Four Earnest Observations (*smrtyupasthana*):

    1. Observing that our body is filth
    2. Observing that what we perceive is our suffering
    3. Observing that our mind is not permanent
    4. Observing that all dharmas have no self

Hinayana and popular Buddhists' understanding of these observations may serve to not increase our misery, but from our misery it doesn't free us. True Buddhist understanding frees us and also enables us to actively and positively construct Buddha's culture. Jaujou solid with these Earnest Observations is like the trunk of a big tree.

He observes our body as filth, observes all beings, every phenomenon, as filth. There isn't a single pure being. So the whole world in the ten directions in the past, present, and future is filth without exception. Thus there is no existence of impure filth. This is Jaujou's power to rise from the bottom of the valley. This observation is possible when he doesn't divide his mind from his body nor divide himself from others.

He observes that what we perceive is our suffering. Our objects, our perception, we, others, our past, present, and future, everything is our suffering. Forests, oceans, all are our suffering. Suffering is also our suffering. A murderer is his suffering, the murdered are their suffering, and the gun that kills is also its suffering. Our world, so to speak, is a giant diamond of suffering and nobody can enter into it and nobody can go out from it. So Jaujou "shuts his doggy mouth."

Our mind is not permanent, he observes. As was said by Sixth Patriarch Hueineng, the thing that is not permanent is Buddha nature. Our previous mind is not permanent, our present mind is not permanent, and our later mind is not permanent. Our previous mind is Buddha nature, our present mind is Buddha nature, and our later mind is Buddha nature. So our mind is forever Buddha nature from the beginningless beginning to the endless end. Our mind to observe is Buddha nature and the mind to be observed is also Buddha nature. Our mind is the whole world in the ten directions, and there is not a thing that is not our mind, not a thing that is not Buddha nature. Further, our mind is not permanent but changeable, transient, a particular being never repeating its existence. Therefore it is beyond all our words, definitions, and understandings. Such a thing is Buddha nature. There is not a thing that is not mind, not Buddha nature.

Jaujou also observes that all dharmas have no self. This dharma can include the aforesaid body, suffering, and mind, but also all remaining other phenomena, beings, and functions. When facing a tree, Jaujou becomes a tree, so there is no dharma tree, when meeting a salamander, he directly becomes a salamander, when pain comes, he becomes pain, when raining, he becomes rain, and when things get insane, he becomes insane. It is possible to do so, because any dharma has no self. There is no self and there is no obstacle. This is the time that Avalokitesvara was freed from all sufferings by practicing the deep Prajna-paramita. When we become one with our object, prajna rises in our environment like rich oxygen in a forest. It is said that all Buddhas and patriarchs dwell in this Dharma and make here the womb for their purity and ease.

So I never cleaned my boundless field.

By now the meaning of this line is clear: Jaujou is continuing to watch Buddha nature in the world of Buddha nature. This continuing to watch Buddha nature is the fodder for Buddhist trainees.

>   Jaujou asked a monk, "How long have you been here?"
>   The monk said, "Seven or eight years."
>   Jaujou: "Do you see this old monk?"
>   The monk: "Yes, I do."
>   Jaujou: "How do you see him when he becomes a donkey?"
>   The monk: "I will enter the Dharma World and see him

there."
>Jaujou: "I have been estimating you as quite something, but actually you have been wasting the meals."
>The monk: "Your Reverence, please could you tell me?"
>Jaujou: "Why don't you say you will see me in the fodder?" (*Jaujou lu*, entry 472)

After all, the kind of food a trainee has is vital. Dungshan says in the fifth of his Five Classifications:

>No one dare make a stanza for the indefinable,
>be it existence or nonexistence.
>Everyone wishes to cross the flow of life and death.
>But after all discontent and compromise, where one settles is before the hearth. (*Dungshan lu*, entry 115)

In the second line is an important ellipsis we are expected to fill in. If we attempt to complete the line, it will be something like this:

>Everyone is wishing to cross the flow of life and death,
>though not wishing to dwell in vacant purity.

Dungshan's "where one settles is before the hearth" is exactly the same for Jaujou:

>My eyebrows many times frown, few suit my fancy.
>Unbearable is that black yellowish peasant
>of the neighboring east village.
>Without ever donating, he brings his donkey
>to graze before the Buddha Hall.

The conspicuous Japanese Zen teacher Hakuin Ekaku (1685-1768) criticized Dungshan's "where one settles is before the hearth" as not being thorough, and he replaced Dungshan's fifth classification by putting there this gatha by Shyuedou:

>Meghasri, old worn-out gimlet,
>how many times came down from Mt. Sumeru?
>He will be called an ignorant sage
>carrying snow to bury the well. (*Tzuing ji*.)

Hakuin wanted to emphasize that Buddhist monks should be passionately compassionate, but here Dungshan was clarifying the relationship between sunyata (nonexistence) and rupa (existence). So Hakuin's criticism is an accusation out of context. Dungshan knew that the quiet study of the relationship between sunyata and rupa is essential for human well-being, because the relationship is the totality of Buddha nature.

We must employ the same careful eye to appreciate the latter half of Jaujou's sunrise verse. We shouldn't hastily say that what Jaujou deals with here is only a relatively minor annoyance. He is not fighting for water or food, not fighting mortgage, cancer, or invader. He is not suffering depression, loneliness, and pains. He is only complaining of his minor annoyance, with some amusement.

We shouldn't be falsely passionate. We often see that those who detest unlawful acts aren't necessarily lawful, and we often hear that those who talk of the need for compassionate acts aren't necessarily compassionate.

Jaujou knows wretched and indescribable problems by his own experience. He confronts them, knows he can't change most of them, and knows the only solution is to change his views, his behavior. We can't change phenomena, and there is no reason to change phenomena when we remind ourselves that all the world is made with Buddha nature. To remind ourselves, we have to fill our abdomen with power and keep observing what is going on in front of our eyes. Then what will happen?

Jaujou tells us that everything, any grave problem inside and outside our life, is possible to be observed by us on the level of the following degree and category, and it is nothing more than this:

> Unbearable is that black yellowish peasant
> of the neighboring east village.
> Without ever donating he brings his donkey
> to graze before the Buddha Hall.

Eight O'clock Mealtime

Futilely seeing the cooking smoke
of the neighbors in the four directions.
A year ago we made buns and steamed bread.
I swallow my saliva in vain.
Right thought I rarely have, I often sigh.
In a hundred households no good person.
Those who come only ask to be served tea.
If not offered, they depart with anger.

* * *

According to legend, the sixteenth emperor, Nintoku, in fourth-century Japan made this poem:

Viewing out from the storied palace,
relieved to see the rising smoke
from the peoples' kitchen ranges.
The world is settled in peace.

Jaujou puts himself in the position of envying others' cooking instead of keeping the position where he can or must care about their welfare. One of the four deeds of a bodhisattva is to put oneself in the same position as other sentient beings. Jaujou's practice exceeds a bodhisattva's standard. A bodhisattva is a Nirmana-kaya, the rupa form of Dharma-kaya. The meaning is that the primary nature of Dharma-kaya is to be beneficial to sentient beings. Jaujou's sure understanding of the primary nature of Dharma-kaya enables him to behave beyond the standard of an ordinary bodhisattva.

There is nothing to eat on his dining table. He casts his vision outward: "Futilely seeing…in the four directions." Indeed he has to see the four gates of the city (= his life).

Question: "What is Jaujou?"
Jaujou: "East gate, west gate, south gate, north gate."

(*Jaujou lu*, entry 99)

This episode is adapted as Case 9 in *Biyan lu* and is there dealt with as if the topic is how smartly Jaujou responds to the fallacy in this complex question coming from a trainee. The question is ambiguous as to whether it is asking about Jaujou's mental state or his environment while "Jaujou" is the name of the city as well as the master's name. Yuanwu comments in his lecture: "Jaujou can decisively judge good and evil, can know how far he should indicate another's faults and how far he should approve, not only detecting a thin strand of autumn hair a thousand miles away"; and Shyuedou in admiration of Jaujou's sure judgment gives a line in his gatha: "The Cakra [diamond] eye has no speck of dust."

The profundity of the episode isn't in Jaujou's smart response to a smart trainee but is in his indication that he and his environment are one, just as he indicates in this verse Eight O'clock Mealtime (where he uses the expression "four directions" instead of "four gates"). He and his environment becoming one doesn't mean they become one in their form like a fantasy in which a transparent person enters an environment such as a wall. It means to understand the nature of the environment is the same as the primary nature of Dharma-kaya, which is to be beneficial to sentient beings. So for Jaujou the city Jaujou is the same as the person Jaujou always engaging in Raising Bodhi Mind, or Actually self-training, or Attaining Bodhi, or Attaining Nirvana, all of which are four aspects of the one Dharma-kaya.

Thus "the Cakra [diamond] eye has no speck of dust" in Shyuedou's verse is Jaujou's state that has no smoke rising from his kitchen ranges.

Not having a sufficient breakfast, Jaujou wishes for a snack and remembers a year ago making buns and steamed bread. Some scholars take "buns and steamed bread" as a metaphor expressing that Jaujou had no miscellaneous theological interests and was single-mindedly devoting himself to cross-legged meditation. Such an interpretation will give us a hard time to understand his following words: "I swallow my saliva in vain."

Better is simply to understand his joy in making and having fresh buns and steamed bread with his disciples. So we can understand his sorrow in being unable to do it this year, expressed as "I swallow my saliva in vain."

At any rate, making "buns and steamed bread" is one of our important daily concerns, which is the ordinary mind. Jaujou's concern is the ordinary mind because it is the very Way. He and his environment are one. His life is the Way, and his environment is the ordinary mind.

An ordinary person's ordinary mind cannot be the Way. For the ordinary mind to be the Way, we must understand this ordinary mind is the mind always existing throughout past, present, and future, and in all the ten directions. The ordinary mind is universal thought, as is stated as Sakyamuni Buddha's thought:

> I should explain the Dharma I have accomplished in three ways by making full use of the devices that were used by all Buddhas. When I thus thought, all Buddhas in the ten directions appeared and with approval they said: "How great, the greatest leader to have accomplished the unsurpassed Dharma. Use every available device of all Buddhas. We also attained the most wonderful first Dharma and divided it into three ways to teach all kinds of sentient beings."

The circumstance of this passage of the sutra is that Sakyamuni was forced to reflect on his initial way of teaching, later compiled as the *Mahavaipulya-buddhavatamsaka-sutra*, because those who heard it were mostly like the hearing-and-speech impaired. For such people his teaching was hard to understand. But rather than blame them for their ignorance, he considered their poor causation and environment, and for the purpose of teaching them, he divided one truth into three stages (Three Vehicles, to carry them all to Nirvana. "Three" symbolizes endless). The wonderful happening is that as soon as Sakyamuni Buddha thought thus, all past Buddhas appeared with approval and naturally helped him to create the necessity devices.

Jaujou understood such thought of Sakyamuni's as universal thought always held by all beings, and he also tried to keep such thought as his ordinary mind, and more, he shared such thought with his monks. His ordinary mind, which is Sakyamuni's thought, which is the Way, is his dauntless, creative help to sentient beings. When personality is built with such ultra-organic dynamics, it is silly to talk of the division between a person and a person's environment. How nice if we can have a sangha with such personalities for the practice of compassion, with such as those not lamenting a shortage of "buns and steamed bread."

> I swallow my saliva in vain.

This is the time any human being shows innocent looks with some air of stupidity, and with some feeling of fatigue too. So Jaujou recreates the vigor of his verse:

> Right thought I rarely have, I often sigh.

With his poetic skill, in the first half of this line he settles his theme dealt with in the lines above, and in the second half he introduces the coming conclusive couplet. Because he sheds his fatigue and renews his vigor, this line is active and positive. He doesn't stay in so-called Right thought. He will be amid the practice of what every Buddha engaged in—in finding and practicing device upon device to be beneficial. Rarely having Right thought is the healthy figure of those who don't divide their understanding from their practice.

"Right thought" means to study equally samadhi and prajna. The term appears in the Nirvana Sutra, chapter Lion's Roar. Samadhi is the composure based on the concentration of our attention. Prajna is to know the nature and dynamic of things. Samadhi and prajna complement each other to perform a beneficial function. In ordinary life it is understandable that we must have composure and wisdom simultaneously, especially when put in an emergency situation.

> A monk asked, "What does it mean, Equal study of samadhi and prajna?"
> The Teacher [Daju Hueihai (?-?), a disciple of Matzu] replied, "Samadhi is the body and prajna is its function. Prajna comes from samadhi and samadhi returns to prajna. They are one thing, like water and wave, with no distinction of which comes first or second. This way of understanding samadhi and prajna is Equal study of samadhi and prajna.
> (*Chuandeng lu*, vol. 28)

This definition exactly follows the declaration of the Sixth Patriarch. According to this definition, Equal study of samadhi and prajna doesn't mean to study them in equal devotion of measurable amount of time and energy as if they were like a pair of wheels. They are two aspects of the same thing. Studying this subject is grave because Buddha nature is definitely manifested when samadhi and prajna are studied equally, as the sutra states.

The more concrete clarification within the actual persons who understood Equal study of samadhi and prajna is in the dialogue between Jaujou's teacher Nanchyuan and Huangbo (Huangbo Shiyun, ?-856). Their dialogue must have been a nourishment for the junior trainee Jaujou.

> The Teacher [Nanchyuan] asked Huangbo, "What is the underlying truth in 'Equal study of samadhi and prajna definitely manifests Buddha nature'?"
> Huangbo said, "Not depending on anything."
> The Teacher: "Isn't what you said the view of Your Reverence?"
> Huangbo: "I dare not deny it."
> The Teacher: "Put aside the meal fee, but who will pay your sandal fee?" (*Tzutang ji*, vol. 16)

Jaujou said in his verse, "Right thought I rarely have," and here Huangbo says in dialogue with Nanchyuan, "Not depending on anything." Both contain the same meaning. If we study this Huangbo with Nanchyuan dialogue well, we will naturally understand Jaujou's saying.

Nanchyuan asks Huangbo how he is daily practicing equal study of samadhi and prajna. Huangbo responds that he doesn't depend on anything at any time anywhere. In the phenomenal world it's impossible to live or exist even a moment without depending on other beings. The fundamental Buddhist view is that all existence is existence in mutual relations and causation.

Even Huangbo must depend on time and space overall, or oxygen, water, sleep, nourishment, mates in detail, just to survive. So he must be seeing them each as Buddha nature, and himself as Buddha nature, and all else too. The cause of how we each come to exist and how came the effect of our existing is also Buddha nature. In such case, Huangbo can say "Not depending on anything," and such a time is only the time we are able to study samadhi and prajna perfectly, equally; and the sutra says only at such a time will Buddha nature be definitely manifested.

There is no higher view than what Huangbo expressed, as to the Buddhist ontological view. So Nanchyuan isn't testing Huangbo by asking "Isn't what you said the view of Your Reverence?" This is admiration, meaning "What you said is the view of all Reverends, not your view only, and in all ten directions throughout past, present, and future, who and what are not Reverend?"

Huangbo understood what Nanchyuan meant and politely responded with "I dare not deny it." So Nanchyuan could admire more with the pleasure of finding this trainee with the same understanding: "Put aside the meal fee, but who will pay your sandal fee?"

It is hard to imagine that a master like Nanchyuan considers charging meal and travel fees or giving a scholarship according to the level of a trainee's understanding of the Dharma.

Here he is speaking of the Buddhist meal fee and the Buddhist sandal fee. The Buddhist meal fee means equally studying samadhi and prajna. The Buddhist sandal fee means definitely manifesting Buddha nature. In short, Nanchyuan is saying "When you put aside Equal study of samadhi and prajna, then Buddha nature is definitely manifested; and when you put aside Buddha nature definitely manifested, then Equal study of samadhi and prajna surfaces. They are two aspects of one thing."

What we must understand is that our study of samadhi and prajna is the definite manifestation of Buddha nature, and the definite manifestation of Buddha nature is our study of samadhi and prajna. Practically speaking, we must by any means believe that every being is Buddha nature without exception. When we believe it, we are children of Buddha and we are parents of Buddha. If we don't believe it, we will have no point in being beneficial to others, and we will have no way of studying samadhi and prajna because samadhi and prajna exist only as utensils to be beneficial to other sentient beings and with no other reason do they exist.

Thus Jaujou says "Right thought I rarely have" because he is amid the practice of samadhi and prajna and there is only the definite manifestation of Buddha nature for his world. But at the next moment he says:

...I often sigh.
Among a hundred households, no good person.
Those who come only ask to be served tea.

Jaujou sighs. No good person visits him. "A hundred

households" couldn't mean his laymen or villagers. He means many traveling trainees that he expects will have a little higher quality of personality than to be asking to be served tea. He sighs, but on the other hand he knows he shouldn't impatiently expect too high, so he is slightly exaggerating: "If not offered, they depart with anger."

His "good person" has no direct relation with social ethics and law. His good person is Yunjyu's "such a person":

> If you wish to accomplish such a matter, you should be such a person. You are already such a person. Why do you care about such a matter? (*Chuandeng lu*, vol. 17)

Yunjyu (Yunjyu Daying, 835?-902) kindly pointed out that cause and effect are the same. The person who wishes to accomplish such a matter is already such a person.

Any phenomena can't be retained by any of our effort. So people say "Yes, any phenomena will slip away like sand from our hand, along chronological change." We aren't talking about such change of form. Buddhists say we can't retain any phenomena because they all change to Buddha nature. Actually every phenomenon reveals its true nature when we "wish to accomplish," and while we don't care, every phenomenon doesn't reveal its true nature and continues to retain its old, tedious, repetitious, meaningless wavy form.

Yunjyu says we are already "such a person." We aren't a private person. We have Buddha nature, which is universal, so we each are a universal person. Yunjyu is saying we are a universal person, and more, saying we shouldn't privately possess ourselves as a universal person. When we return the private person that we wrongly possessed to universal possession, we are accomplishing what we wished to accomplish, that is, to be "such a person," Jaujou's "good person." Jaujou is lamenting that only wrong persons come, persons who believe they are their own possession, who consequently wish to get something from outside themselves in order to accomplish something (= "to be served tea").

Jaujou's life is made with Buddha nature, all visitors too are made with Buddha nature. It is ridiculous to believe this realization can be given like a baked potato, because the realization isn't material, isn't even an object of our intelligence. It is said:

(2) Not stealing. *Kyoju kaimon*: Mind and environment are existing as they are, and the gate to shedding bondage is open.

Our mind as the intelligence of *Homo sapiens* sees our environment as phenomena, which keep changing. The mind and environment described in *Kyoju kaimon* is Buddha's mind and environment. Both are made with Buddha nature, and between them there is no division. With our ego we have no way to go through "the gate to shedding bondage," which, as *Kyoju kaimon* says, is "open."

Jingjau Weikuan (755-817), a Dharma heir of Matzu, couldn't bear to see the slaughter of livestock and at age thirteen he left his family. Each of his words is merciful:

> A monk asked: "What is the Way?"
> The Teacher [Jingjau]: "It is a nice mountain."
> The monk: "Your student is asking about the Way. Why do you say a nice mountain?"
> The Teacher: "You know only a nice mountain, you have not walked the Way."
> Another monk asked: "Where is the Way?"
> The Teacher: "It is in front of your very eyes."
> The monk: "Why can I not see it?"
> The Teacher: "Because you have yourself."
> The monk: "Because I have myself? How about Your Reverence?"
> The Teacher: "Having yourself, myself, now all the more you cannot see it."
> The monk: "If there's no myself or yours, can I see it or not?"
> The Teacher: "Who would wish to see it if there is no yourself or myself?" (*Chuandeng lu*, vol.7)

Jaujou expects us to be not those who seek tea but those who can bring it. Their total life becomes tea, with no division between them and Buddha. They practice what they understand, as is said, "Not knowing is most intimate." It is fish undivided from water, birds undivided from sky, as is said, "Fish make water their life, birds make the sky their life." Avalokitesvara, also making no division, practices the profound Prajna-paramita.

Jauti Hueilang also left family at age thirteen. At twenty he understood Buddha nature and No Buddha nature:

> Jauti after receiving the precepts visited Daji [Matzu's posthumous name] at Mt. Shigung in Kimjou.
> Daji asked, "For what did you come?"
> Jauti: "I came for Buddha's view."
> Daji: "Buddha has no view. View belongs to the devil's world. You came from Nanyue [= Mt. Heng in Hunan]. But you are as if yet unexposed to the essence of Shytou and Tsaushi. You'd better go back."
> Following this advice, Jauti went back, and to Shytou he asked: "What is Buddha?"
> Shytou: "You have no Buddha nature."
> Jauti: "How about all squirming creatures?"
> Shytou: "They have Buddha nature."
> Jauti: "Why don't I?"
> Shytou: "Because you don't approve of it."
> Jauti instantaneously gained his assurance.
>
> (*Chuandeng lu*, vol. 14)

Thereafter, it is said, Jauti didn't leave his precinct for thirty years, and he told whoever came to study, "Get out, you have no Buddha nature."

Buddha nature is universal, so any modification, such as no (Buddha nature) and is (Buddha nature), cannot become significantly important. Caring about universal Buddha nature is fatally important. Otherwise we must seek a particular modification of it outside ourselves, as Jaujou says: "Those who come only ask to be served tea." Reading his verse this far, we begin to understand that his "I often sigh" is neither a complaint nor a low evaluation of the visiting trainees. He is only painfully lamenting they can't cherish their own well-being because of their shortage of understanding Buddha nature.

(3) Not having incorrect sex. *Kyoju kaimon*: Because the Three Wheels are pure, there is nothing to be hoped for. All Buddhas go the same way.

Not having incorrect sex means to make no different value between purity and filth, for both are Buddha nature and each is functioning as Buddha nature according to circumstance. Having Buddha nature or not having Buddha nature is irrelevant; there is no different value for things made with

Buddha nature, and there is not a thing not made with Buddha nature.

> Those who study Buddha's Way should first believe in Buddha's Way. Those who thus believe should always be self-confident, for they are innately on the Way. They are not lost, troubled, or deluded; they do not trip, nor are they increased or decreased, and they are free of error. The practice of raising belief and clarifying the Way is thus essential for studying the Way.
>
> (*Gakudo yojin shu* [Advice for studying the Way], entry 9)

Here Dogen is reflecting on his own case. What he says is reasonable. If we can't believe in Buddha's Way, we can't begin to study it. But Jaujou's visiting trainees would say they came to get such an unshakable belief. Jaujou is unable to offer such tea, so they depart with anger. They may be frustrated, but Jaujou's frustration is larger. He loses even his appetite, and of course hasn't the vigor to make buns and steamed bread.

Dogen writes:

> How trainees are able to clarify the Dharma and accomplish the Way depends on their teacher's power. But by any means they should not expect their view to be the same as their teacher's. If they make it their own, they will not gain the Dharma.
>
> When trainees are going to listen to the Dharma from their teacher, they should purify their body and mind, calm their eyes and ears, then just listen to the teacher's Dharma and bring no other thought.
>
> Idiotic trainees memorize the scripts, accumulate things learned, and strive to have the same view as their teacher's. At such a time they are gathering only their view and the old sayings and not fitting with their teacher's words.
>
> Trainees of another type above all regard first their own view, then check the sutras, memorize one or two words, and believe they are studying Buddha's Dharma. They visit a bright teacher, listen to his Dharma, and judge he is fine if his view coincides with theirs, or judge he is wrong if his view is not their accustomed view. There is no way to walk the right path without knowing how to abandon the evil way. It is a pity such trainees will be lost even as numerous kalpas pass. How sad!

Trainees should learn that Buddha's Dharma is outside of thinking, analyzing, surmising, meditating, imagining, and intellectual understanding. If Buddha's Dharma is in these, how come trainees who think thus are not yet attaining Buddha's Dharma even though they have been fondling such mental activity in such a mental environment? We should not use thought and analysis in study of the Way. It is evident if we examine with our own life. Only the teacher who has attained the Dharma knows intimately how to enter the gate, and it is beyond the knowledge of those who study only words. (Ibid., entry 6)

But instead of crouching, Jaujou keeps standing, beside an eastern hedge, where there is a thin stem of chrysanthemum.[4]

>Futilely seeing the cooking smoke
>of the neighbors in the four directions.

Ten O'clock Morning

Ordained by the shaving of the head.
Why has it come to this?
I became chief priest in this village,
invited for not much reason.
Hungry, humiliated, almost better off dead.
Those guys Hu, Jang, Hei, and Li
never have shown me any respect.
Abruptly they appear at the gate, "Lend paper and tea."

* * *

As the day matures, Jaujou's verse too gets to the core of Buddha's Dharma.

To all human beings Jaujou gives boundless sympathy. Ordained, having a vow, establishing a wish to achieve in one's life, hopeful, and dreaming of the future—there are many who form this sort of ambition, yet how many actually and truly satisfy their wish? By asking himself "Why has it come to this?" Jaujou shares with others all hardship, agony, sorrow, disillusionment. "I became chief priest in this village, invited for not much reason. Hungry, humiliated, almost better off dead." His sympathy is like the mental stage of Buddha when he declared "All sentient and insentient beings, including mountains and rivers, weeds and trees, are attaining Buddhahood."

How then should we understand Jaujou's bitter complaint toward those rude commoners among commoners, Hu, Jang, Hei, and Li, who don't see his intellectual achievement? They seem not even to recognize his physical existence, their immediate material needs being their only concern. They thus represent not only commoners but all mammals, ...horses, donkeys, monkeys....

We had better reread the first line and realize it is hiding a radical reverse of valuation, notably a lamentation for the contrary consequence of Jaujou's youthful ambition.

He got merely the rank of village chief priest instead of a renowned influential position in the capital. But he actually is expressing his relief in having successfully overcome numerous charms and thus is a true man of no rank: "invited for not much reason." Insignificance of career and chance amuses him. For him any great reason is pathetic and laughable, if after all not harmful.

"Hungry, humiliated, almost better off dead." These aren't the words of a clown meaninglessly exaggerating his sad lot for a moment's laugh. With "hungry, humiliated" Jaujou is exposing he is neither a hermit nor an arhat transcending the world. He is a living person, sensitive enough to enjoy food and honor. But he isn't clinging to life or fearing death. He can think fairly "almost better off dead" without longing for death. By this one line "Hungry, humiliated, almost better off dead" he skillfully expresses the Middle Way, the attitude we would like to have toward our life and death.

We are thus bathed by Jaujou's boundless sympathy, but have we yet any beacon lighting up what we should do? Now comes the hidden radical reverse of valuation.

It has to do with the understanding of being ordained, having a vow, establishing a wish to achieve in one's life, being hopeful, and dreaming of the future. In any field this kind of determination is regarded as essential, even encouraged; indeed it is a wonderful passing peak at adolescence. Ironically, in each epochal transition, such as the Renaissance or the Industrial Revolution, the numerous determinations of immature youths is what brought about our present culture. People run and race toward their goal, with the result that most end up lamenting when they perceive the inevitable gap between their determination and their achievement.

Jaujou's case is unusual because he just kept on walking backwards, not toward any goal, but toward the time before his determination began, before he was ordained.

For popular Buddhists, to be ordained means to gain the unsurpassed wisdom upward and save all creatures downward. True Buddhism says there isn't a single Dharma (Truth) to be taught (by anyone), nor a single person (being) to be saved. Indeed when Jaujou visited Nanchyuan he was taught for the first time:

Jaujou asked Nanchyuan, "What is the Way?"
Nanchyuan replied, "The ordinary mind is the Way."
Jaujou: "Should I aim to attain it?"
Nanchyuan: "If you aim, you will be apart from it."
Jaujou: "But if I do not aim, how can I know it is the Way?"
Nanchyuan: "The Way belongs neither to knowing nor to not knowing. Knowing is illusory realization and not knowing is being unconscious. When one truly reaches the Way with no aim, the Way is like the vast void widely vacant, beyond right and wrong."
Hearing this, Jaujou directly understood the profound meaning. (*Jaujou lu*, entry 1)

Jaujou was faithful to the transmission of his teacher Nanchyuan. Can't we indeed with this understanding say he began to walk backward toward the time before he was ordained? If so, then the first two lines "Ordained by the shaving of the head. Why has it come to this?" are not a negative lamentation but an expression of relief and wonder at living an authentic priestly life.

"I became chief priest in this village, invited for not much reason. Hungry, humiliated, almost better off dead" can be sympathy toward others, but just as well a quiet, confident personal statement that shows how we should be, here given by his practical example:

> Those guys Hu, Jang, Hei, and Li
> never have shown me any respect.
> Abruptly they appear at the gate, "Lend paper and tea."

In other words, rather than being Jaujou's bitter complaint toward rude commoners, it is a symbolic description of the time we all cherish before we develop our idea of being ordained, or before we establish our desire. At such a time there is no such dualistic idea as respect for anyone else, because this is the world of practice. In this world our behavior is abrupt and no one schemes or exercises any strategy. Here Jaujou sees in Hu, Jang, Hei, and Li evidence of "All sentient and insentient beings, including mountains and rivers, weeds and trees, are attaining Buddhahood." Jaujou's teacher Nanchyuan also says in his lecture:

Then frequently I will tell you that Buddha and the patriarchs do not know real existence, whereas mountain cats and wild cows know.
Therefore even if we call it suchness as it is, that is already wrong. We must directly become fellows of beasts.
(Tzutang ji, vol. 16, entry Nanchyuan)

In *Chuandeng lu,* vol. 8, there is an episode at first looking almost queer:

A monk arrived when Nanchyuan was residing in a hermitage. Nanchyuan told him, "I am going to work in the mountain. Make lunch when the time comes. After your lunch, bring me my portion." The monk soon finished eating, then abandoned whatever and fell asleep on the floor.
Nanchyuan waited. No one came up. He returned to his hermitage and found the monk asleep. So he also lay down in a corner. The monk got up and just took himself away.
Nanchyuan later recalled this happening and said, "When residing in the hermitage I met a bright trainee. I have never met him since."

If Nanchyuan appreciated that trainee, certainly his disciple Jaujou can appreciate Hu, Jang, Hei, and Li.

Yunjyu [Yunjyu Daying, 835?-902] built a hermitage on Sanfeng Peak and for over ten days he did not go to the Dining Hall. Then the Teacher [Dungshan] asked him, "Why do you nowadays not come here to dine?"
Yunjyu: "A heavenly dweller brings my meals every day."
The Teacher: "I was regarding you as a very person, but still your view is like that. You had better come to see me in the night."
Yunjyu went as he was told. The Teacher invited him in, addressing him through the door, "Hermit Daying."
Yunjyu responded.
Seeing him, the Teacher said, "What is it when you do not think either good or bad?"
Yunjyu returned to his hermitage and there he practiced meditation. The heavenly dweller looked three days for him in vain and then disappeared.
(Dungshan lu, entry 50)

Dungshan isn't teaching Yunjyu for mere ethical or theological interest. He is teaching that he won't be free of suffering, won't be able to establish his true peace, unless he transcends good and bad. Jaujou is a precursor of Dungshan and Yunjyu. From his life they both studied what they should constantly care about, which is the ordinary mind, which is the Way, and not anything else, such as name and profit.

Noon

Not provided with rice and tea,
I must repeatedly ask.
Arrived at a north house after a south house.
As expected, not welcomed.
Bitter sandy salt, fermented barley,
rice with millet, vinegared cutting lettuce.
The host said offerings should not be slighted,
priests should keep firm faith and strict practice.

* * *

A regular income is for us a dream, and a mere disturbance in our daily routine upsets us. We even attempt to insure a major part of our life to be compensated for, in case of change. Jaujou had no settlement even about when and how much he could have the essentials rice and tea. He had to ask every time when in need. Whether or not his request would be granted utterly depended on his parish. He had to exercise his endurance. Role of priest and layman became reversed before anyone noticed, layman preaching to priest and priest having to listen, abasing himself. "Offerings should not be slighted, priests should keep firm faith and strict practice." It is funny that a layman, disregarding spiritual matters and pursuing material matters all his life, can act as if his career was that of a saint.

Jaujou is lamenting his own poor situation, but the point is his lamentation isn't as heavy as the colors of an oil painting of summer flowers, but is as thin as the color of an autumn wind, so to speak, weightless, almost transparent. So he is quietly viewing his status and only states "Not provided with rice and tea, I must repeatedly ask."

"Arrived at a north house after a south house." From house to house his footsteps were quiet. The site where each house stood was also quiet, and quiet it was when, as expected, he confirmed he wasn't welcomed. All food items were quiet, the host's preaching was quiet, and Jaujou quietly listened.

This quiet refers not only to Jaujou's behavior and psychological state. All he describes is quiet. It isn't the material quiet we experience in a deep forest, in meditative calm, or under anesthesia. It is the quiet that must be intuitively understood to exist behind beings, in relations between things, in the process of phenomenal causation, and it is the central theme Jaujou cares to share in his verse "Noon."

The meridian sun is directly overhead. At such a moment no shadows appear, for the sun isn't in the east or the west. The time is exactly midway between sunrise and sunset, not ante meridian or post meridian. Because of this character of no dualistic valuation, Buddhists symbolize noon as the Middle Way, as endless time, as our true Life, and we sense it as quiet because Jaujou describes it as quiet.

Danyuan, a disciple of National Teacher Nanyang, uses noon with this very meaning in his reply to Emperor Sutzung's question in *Biyan lu*, Case 18, National Teacher Nanyang's Seamless Pagoda:

> Emperor Sutzung asked National Teacher Nanyang Hueijung, "A hundred years hence, what may I do for you?"
> The National Teacher replied, "For this old monk, make a seamless pagoda."
> The Emperor: "Please, would you describe its design?"
> The National Teacher meanwhile kept silent. Then he asked, "Do you understand?"
> The Emperor: "I do not."
> The National Teacher: "I have a disciple named Danyuan. To him I transmitted the Dharma Seal. He is well versed in this matter. Please invite him and ask him."

Sutzung was a tragic figure. In the reign of his father, Emperor Shyuantzung, there rose in revolt a local commander, An Lushan. Sutzung while his father was escaping was helped by a eunuch, Li Fuguo, and he succeeded to his father's throne. During his six-year reign, while controlled by these eunuchs, including Li Fuguo, he unsuccessfully fought An's Rebellion. Then in successor fighting his son was ordered to kill himself, and next, at age fifty-one Emperor Sutzung died, just thirteen days after the death of his father, Shyuantzung. National Teacher Nanyang was seeing Sutzung's environment and character and must have pitied him. In one of those days the Emperor asked him:

"A hundred years hence, what may I do for you?"

The mind of National Teacher Nanyang was obviously "You needn't bother for me. Better is to quickly establish your life undisturbed by surface phenomena. Help yourself. The only way is to discover the universal life within you."
Thus,

The National Teacher replied, "For this old monk, make a seamless pagoda."

Emperor Sutzung was too busy caring only about visible matters. So later he had to ask Danyuan:

After the National Teacher went elsewhere to teach, the Emperor invited Danyuan and asked him the meaning.
Danyuan said:

It is located south of Shiang and north of Tan,
where gold abounds, filling the land.
At the hour of shadowless noon,
ferry to the lapis palace and you will not find a teacher.

With this evidence of transmission, we can see how Jaujou was cleanly stating universal life while describing the prosaic phenomenal world. National Teacher Nanyang was a disciple of the Sixth Patriarch and it was Nanyang who said "Klesa is by itself naturally shedding klesa." Just by this verse "Noon," with no theological scent and no elaborate episode, Jaujou is presenting the world where klesa is shedding klesa:

Bitter sandy salt, fermented barley,
rice with millet, vinegared cutting lettuce.

The meal Jaujou was offered satisfied the five basic tastes, salty, sweet, bitter, sour, and pungent (in the vinegared lettuce), and there were two additional: fermented and acrid (vinegared lettuce). Some people may regard as crude and humble this offered meal. But we must know any other foods can't exceed these five tastes plus two more. Jaujou states each item quietly, confidently, with appreciation. Each is transcending its phenomenal being while in the process of its phenomenal life.

The truth here expressed in just such a meal is the very truth Sixth Patriarch Hueineng found in the Diamond Sutra: "Indeed there is no place to dwell, yet it keeps rising." All phenomena issue from what place?—from no place. This "no place" is the world of Noon and is our true life. With such an understanding, Jaujou can hear the preaching of the layman quietly and with no complaint:

> The host said offerings should not be slighted,
> priests should keep firm faith and strict practice.

The layman may believe he is living in the world of give and take, offering and thanks, in the human social world. Jaujou doesn't deny it, but also knows all human behavior is within sunyata and rupa. The layman may fear that a priest not firm in faith and not strict in practice will be unable to cure his own faults and will never attain Buddhahood. Jaujou agrees, but also knows the Wonderful Dharma-kaya is behaving as the Phenomenal Dharma, regardless of our realization and assiduity.

> A monk said to Fayan [Fayan Wenyi, 885-908], "I have heard a sutra says all phenomena rise from the origin that has no dwelling. I ask you, what is that?"
> Fayan: "Form rises from formless, name rises from nameless." (*Tsungrung lu*, Case 74)

The content of the monk's question is exactly "Indeed there is no place to dwell, yet it keeps rising." Here the source is the *Vimalakirti-nirdesa-sutra*. The monk thinks true being is the phenomenal beings he can perceive. But phenomenal beings have no substance; they exist only because of causation, not by their own power, and such existence is mere form and name. True existence exists by itself and has no character to be grasped even by causation. This monk if with Jaujou would be told "Now shall we set forth begging?"

> Yangshan [Yangshan Hueiji, 803-887] asked a monk, "From where did you come?"

Monk: "I came from Youjou."
Yangshan: "Do you remember the place where you were?"
Monk; "I always remember."
Yangshan: "By your subjective mind you remember. The place you remember is the objective environment. Return the mountains, rivers, ground, buildings, people, animals, all, to the place where they belong. Then is there anything in your mind?"
Monk: "In such case I do not see any being."
Yangshan: "You are good as a trainee on the way of ascent, but not enough as a trainee on the way of descent."
Monk: "Please, have you another additional teaching or not?"
Yangshan: "Irrelevant is to say I have or have not. Your view shows you understand only a portion of the profundity. Put on your kasaya and meditate. The time will come to understand." (*Tsungrung lu*, Case 32)

In True Buddhism we don't divide ourselves from the environment. Kindly to this monk Yangshan hinted, "Irrelevant is to say I have or have not" and he recommend that he keep meditating as a kasaya-donning monk. If the monk had been fortunate enough to chance to accompany Jaujou for begging, Jaujou would have said only "Bitter sandy salt, fermented barley, rice with millet, vinegared cutting lettuce."

Two O'clock Sun Declining

No more walking the land
with light and shade.
Once satiated, never hungry, it is said.
This old monk's life today is the very example.
Not studying Zen, not discussing theology.
Napping on a frayed straw mat.
Even in Tusita Heaven there could not be
such pleasure as to bask in the sun.

* * *

Begging, mendicancy, traveling, walking the land with light and shade, such is the conduct of seeking something outside ourselves in the world where we and others are divided. Here Jaujou uses the light and shade produced by the solar system to express man-made dualistic valuation. Buddha said in his last admonition, "Make yourself your light, rely on yourself, do not depend on other. Make the Dharma your light, rely on the Dharma, do not depend on elsewhere." This Dharma light exists in light, in shade, in all places.

"Make yourself your light, rely on yourself, do not depend on other." So Jaujou says "Not studying Zen, not discussing theology," and he is "Napping on a frayed straw mat." He means there is active Zen in his life and profound theology in himself. In his autobiographical life, who taught this way of life?

Napping in the sun is one of the best postures allowed to us for remembrance with thanks and nostalgia. A long time ago Jaujou was young enough to be escorted by his ordination teacher, who acted like a father:

> Jaujou in his youth accompanied his ordination teacher on a mendicant tour. They came to Nanchyuan. After his ordination teacher had finished his greetings, Jaujou was going to offer his own. Nanchyuan was by then reclining in

his residential quarters.
  Seeing Jaujou, he asked, "From where did you come?"
  Jaujou answered, "I came from Rueishiang Temple."
  Nanchyuan: "Did you see the Rueishiang?" [Beautiful Buddha Statue]
  Jaujou: "I didn't see the Rueishiang, but now I see a reclining Tathagata."
  Nanchyuan got to his feet and asked, "Acolyte, have you your master or not?"
  Jaujou replied, "I am an acolyte with a master."
  Nanchyuan: "Who is he?"
  Jaujou: "It is cold though it is spring. I humbly wish Your Reverence good health."
  Nanchyuan summoned the reception monk and said, "Place this acolyte on a special seat." (*Jaujou lu*, entry 3)

To understand to its full extent Jaujou's verse referring to his napping, we must note here Nanchyuan taking the posture of reclining.

Nanchyuan kept on reclining even into the first part of their meeting. He thus could test whether Jaujou was an ordinary acolyte who judges things and people by their form

To Nanchyuan's question "Acolyte, have you your master or not?" Jaujou shows his talent to put what is in his mind into his own words and action without losing a moment.

Nanchyuan surely recognizes Jaujou's talents, to see the Tathagata in any form, and to maintain one's mind, words, and action as a single coordinated whole.

He ordered the reception monk to place him on a special seat. "A special seat" in the guest monks' quarter is where one's back is against the window, not the wall, and near the enshrined Manjusri.

For the young Jaujou, very thankful; Nanchyuan's recognition must have been a really encouraging first recognition of what he was. And meeting such a student not only talented but also showing his devotion to the teacher must have been for Teacher Nanchyuan very thankful, enjoyable. This kind of meeting between teacher and student can be righteously called "to bask in the sun." It occurred when Nanchyuan (Nanchyuan Puyuan, 748-834) was around forty-eight and Jaujou (Jaujou Tsungshen, 778-897) around eighteen.

There could be all sorts of meetings between teacher and student that could be described as a soft blend of apricot and narcissus fragrance, or a reedy field in the dusk beyond a wide river, or a ladybug on a flowering peach branch, and so forth.
Dungshan too chose Nanchyuan as the first master to visit on his pilgrimage to seek the Way.

> In the beginning of his pilgrimage, Dungshan visited Nanchyuan. It was the very occasion that Nanchyuan was performing an anniversary service for Matzu.
> Nanchyuan asked the monks, "Tomorrow we will offer a lunch to Matzu. I wonder whether he will show up." The monks made no response.
> Dungshan stepped forth with a response, "He will show up if there is his companion."
> Nanchyuan said, "You are a later comer, but worthwhile to be refined."
> Dungshan said, "Your Reverence, do not treat a man of good breed as a ill-bred man." (*Dungshan lu*, entry 2)

In Dungshan's response, "companion" is the content of the Dharma which Buddha advised Ananda to rely on. Dungshan is telling that dead and alive and sage and ignorant equally exist in the endless Dharma world. His answer was theologically clever, but if what he said was really true, why did he say "if there is his companion"? Why should we wait for the appearance of a companion? Companion is all over, whether in light or shade. For Buddhists, "light" is the kind of light we can say we are walking in while we have light, as well the kind of light we can say we are walking in even in the dark.
So Nanchyuan couldn't help saying "You are a later comer, but worthwhile to be refined." Yet Dungshan speaks back: "Your Reverence, do not treat a man of good breed as an ill-bred man." For this, Nanchyuan shut his further teaching.
Dungshan (Dungshan Liangjie, 807-869) was fifty-nine years younger than Nanchyuan, and twenty-nine years younger than Jaujou. We don't know exactly when Dungshan met with Nanchyuan, but if Dungshan was about twenty, Nanchyuan was about eighty. Anyway, it was the meeting of a clever young monk with an old matured master, and more like "razor and ax" than was Jaujou's meeting, which was as if "to bask in the sun."

Jaujou in his later age is making a topic of napping, whereas Dungshan in his later age reveals that his meeting with Nanchyuan had a very different nuance: The monk: "Your Reverence, you first met with Nanchyuan. Why do you perform the anniversary for Yunyan?"
> Dungshan: "I do not value the morals and Buddha's Dharma of my teacher. I value only the fact that he did not explain to me." (*Dungshan lu*, entry 11)

Dungshan here is criticizing Nanchyuan for over-explaining.

Now it becomes quite clear that Jaujou wrote his afternoon two o'clock verse in a warm, thankful, nostalgic mood toward his teacher Nanchyuan. His lines focus on the practice of "Once satiated, never hungry," which came to him with Teacher Nanchyuan. It is "The Way belongs to neither knowing nor to not knowing." The Way is the Dharma by Buddha's word. Knowing means to see phenomena (rupa) because what we can know is only phenomena. But knowing phenomena isn't the entire truth. Not knowing means to see Dharma (sunyata). But seeing Dharma by not knowing isn't the entire truth. In our practical acts we should neither attach to nor detach from either phenomena or Dharma.

Therefore Jaujou doesn't spell out Nanchyuan's name, though Nanchyuan is the background of this verse. Nanchyuan is the particular historical teacher as well as universal Dharma. So is Jaujou. It is interesting that when Jaujou is more uniquely Jaujou, Nanchyuan continues to live on more surely. This truth suggests we can transcend Light and Shade only in Light and Shade.

> Even in Tusita Heaven there could not be
> such pleasure as to bask in the sun.

Tusita is one of many heavens. There people are said to be flooded with pleasure and are knowing how to be content except for practicing the Eight Right Ways. Jaujou is comparing his enjoyment. We also bring here the influence of his teacher Nanchyuan. It is said that in the inmost palace of Tusita, Maitreya is residing and will descend to our world to help all creatures left out from the help of our Sakyamuni

Buddha. This will come to be around five billion six hundred seventy million years after the present day.

> Yunjyu asked Dungshan, "Once upon a time Nanchyuan asked a theologian who was lecturing on the Sutra of Maitreya Descending (*Maitreya–vyakarana*), 'When will Maitreya descend?'
> The theologian answered, 'Maitreya is residing now in a palace in Heaven and will descend in the future.' Nanchyuan said, 'There is no Maitreya in heaven nor on earth.'
> "Let me ask you, if there is no Maitreya in heaven nor on earth, who gave him such a name?"
> Dungshan asked this by Yunjyu could only tremble in his chair and say, "Reverend trainee, when I was in Yunyan I asked the same question, and I perceived only the trembling of the hearth. Asked by you today, I sweat all over."
>
> (*Dungshan lu*, entry 49)

The greatness of Nanchyuan is that he clearly denies any authoritative being outside of our mind. Our mind gave something a name, such as Maitreya, and our mind (which gave such a name) is the same something. Giving a name and being given the name are the same our mind, something, or Dharma (by Buddha's calling). We must use our mind, something, or Dharma, before it is given a name, because once it is named we are under a concept and bound by it and not cherishing the real activity of our mind, something, or Dharma.

If something isn't given any name, there's only its function and we won't be polluted by dualistic value of concept and will be amidst Dharma, Dharma in Dharma, and not in the world. Dharma will be in Dharma. We will not suffer illness. Dharma functions in Dharma. We are the ones who make Maitreya, God, illness, suffering, and so forth. They all are Dharma, and the world in the time and place is Dharma upon Dharma. Even this very paragraph is depending on such naming concept as our mind, something, or Dharma. Wishing to avoid polluting anyone when asked "Who gave him such a name?" we can only sweat and tremble in our chair.

There is one more way to answer. It is Jaujou's way:

> Napping on a frayed straw mat.
> Even in Tusita Heaven there could not be
> such pleasure as to bask in the sun.

Now it begins to be clear that "napping" can be replaced by "weeding," "cutting," "cleaning," or any other words that express devotion of our whole body and mind in any situation.

Four O'clock Afternoon Tea

There are those who come to worship
with offerings of incense,
five old women, three of them each with a goiter,
two with cracked cheeks.
They bring flaxseed for tea, indeed precious.
Deva Kings, ease your muscles.
If only I could give a coin to Rahula
next year at the harvest of mulberry leaves and wheat.

* * *

The old farm women after their day's work in the locality visit Jaujou's temple to worship. Routinely visiting the temple is their only available pleasure. They have labored from their girlhood, all year long, all day long, under the strong sun, in the dry cold, often in the rain. Their hard work in the harsh environment is indirectly described:

> three of them each with a goiter,
> two with cracked cheeks.

Jaujou likens them to the five bhiksus (the trainees Ajnatakaundinya, Asvajiti, Bhadrika, Mahanaman, and Dasabalakasyapa) taught by Sakyamuni Buddha as his first disciples. How can we know these old women are being likened to those five bhiksus? The words "worship," "five," "tea," and "Rahula" are enough to understand Jaujou is practicing what and how Sakyamuni taught.

> Seeing a monk who came and offered him worship, Shyuansha said, "Put down your worship. I will then be able to worship you." (*Chuandeng lu*, vol. 18)

The meaning is the same as that in the following episode:

> From the Buddha Hall the Teacher [Jaujou] came by. A monk seeing him offered worship. The Teacher with his staff struck the monk. The monk said, "Offering worship is

a good thing."
The Teacher said, "Having nothing is better than having a good thing." (*Jaujou lu*, entry 513)

Hueike reverently bowed and Bodhidharma said: "You have obtained my marrow." What it means is the very conduct of offering worship is the attainment of the marrow of Buddhist truth; that is, the Treasure Repository Housing the Eye to See the Right Dharma is worshiping the Treasure Repository Housing the Eye to See the Right Dharma. Unfortunately one of the rarest deeds we can witness nowadays is such worship.

Those five bhiksus had already spent six years practicing stoicism, and yet they didn't understand what training is. Buddha thought he should go to Varanasi, where they were. Jaujou's "five old women" had already spent over half their hard life, and yet they didn't know the meaning of their life. Jaujou thought he must go to Varanasi. So Buddha reflected on his way of teaching and determined to use devices to enable those five bhiksus to understand the content of his realization. Then he went to Varanasi (= Mrgadava) to teach them. There his First Turning of the Dharma Wheel was practiced, and that was the first sangha. It is said:

> I could make the group of five trainees understand. When I was teaching two, the three others went out on mendicancy. We six then shared and lived on the food they brought back. When I was teaching three, the two others went out on mendicancy. We six then shared and lived on the food they brought back. (In the Pali *Samyutta-nikaya*, translated to Japanese in *Gautama Siddhartha*, by Hajime Nakamura.)

These trainees were like Gautama before his coming to the great realization, before he was known as Sakyamuni Buddha.

> They age, sicken, and die, they suffered and were polluted, they were troubled by seeing those who age, sicken, and die, who suffer and are polluted. They searched for the unsurpassed peace and comfort that is no-aging, no-sickness, no-death, no-suffering, and no-pollution, and they attained the unsurpassed peace and comfort of no-aging, no-sickness, no-death, no-suffering, and no-pollution.

Then they raised this wisdom and view: "Our having shed is changeless, this is our last life living like this, never again will we live in this changeable life." (Ibid.)

The important process we can become aware of, thanks to Jaujou, is that Buddha reflected on his way of teaching and determined to use devices to enable the five bhiksus to understand the content of his realization. Then he went to Varanasi. In other words, those who reflect on their way of teaching and determine to use devices to enable people to understand are Buddha, instantly in Varanasi with the trainees who formed the first sangha.

The air of Varanasi inside and outside our life is the air of having worship, with no division between the person who worships and what the person worships, and there is no difference between man and woman, as is stated:

> Knowing Buddha nature is called man, and not knowing Buddha nature is called woman.
>
> (*Mahaparinirvana-sutra*)

Bodhidharma went to Shaulin Temple in Northern Wei by crossing the Yangtze River after meeting Emperor Wu in Liang. His life at Shaulin is described by Hungjy Jengjiau (1091-1157):

> Sitting coldly in absolute solitude at Shaulin,
> fully exposing the right order in deep silence.
> In the clear autumn the moon turns the frost ring,
> the Milky Way is faint,
> and the Dipper offers down its night handle.
>
> (*Tsungrung lu*, Case 2)

Here Bodhidharma isn't meditating to put himself at peace. He keeps thinking of device upon device to help sentient beings. He is thus in Varanasi and turning the Dharma wheel for the first time. Hungjy states it as "fully exposing the right order in deep silence." There couldn't be any "right order" by putting aside thinking on and on about device upon device. So Hungjy's second couplet is another expression of his first. The particular act in the first couplet is of equal quality with the second, which is the universal character of every being.

> They bring flaxseed for tea, indeed precious.
> Deva Kings, ease your muscles.

These old women bring flaxseed for tea. It is well known since old times that flaxseed benefits our cardiovascular system. Jaujou truly enjoys having tea with them. He lived in the age of keeping strict prohibitive precepts (vinaya) and monks were disallowed any meal after lunch until a meal next morning.

Deva Kings (Vajradharas) are guardians to protect Buddhism. Their wooden images are enshrined as a pair at the wings of the front gate. Their looks are furious, one directly expressing fury, the other suppressing fury.

Jaujou jokes to them that they can relax their sinuous muscles, for these are good women who bring flaxseed, also for Jaujou, who can at least at such a time drink tea, exempt from the vinaya of proper mealtimes. What kind of content and device upon device at Jaujou's Varanasi can be understood by the following episode:

> The Teacher [Jaujou] asked a newly arrived monk, "Did you ever come here before?" The monk said, "Yes."
> The Teacher said, "Have a cup of tea."
> To another newcomer monk he asked the same. This monk replied, "No, I never did come here before."
> The Teacher said, "Have a cup of tea."
> Later the head monk asked, "Why do you say 'Have a cup of tea' to him who came before and also to him who never did?"
> The Teacher addressed the head monk. The head monk responded.
> The Teacher said, "Have a cup of tea."
>
> (*Jaujou lu*, entry 459)

There is no creature not needing any fluid. Buddhists see tea also as a form, a function, an effect, of Buddha nature. Tea is a daily drink, suggesting the importance of daily practicing Buddha's profound Dharma as a matter of fact.

In general, drinking tea isn't so difficult a matter whether or not one has "ever come here before." It means understanding that sunyata (Buddha nature = our innate nature) is rupa (phenomena = self-training) and rupa is sunyata; and "never did come here before" means practicing such relation between sunyata and rupa instead of staying in the stage of merely understanding. This practice is called "not understanding," and is regarded as a higher stage of training. The importance of practice is emphasized by Jaujou's teacher Nanchyuan:

> Then I will tell you frequently that Buddha and the patriarchs do not know real existence, whereas mountain cats and wild cows know.
> (*Tzutang ji*, vol. 16, entry Nanchyuan)

Jaujou recommends having tea whether or not the monks understand. We base our judgment of whether or not we understand (Buddha's Dharma) on our extremely shallow, dreadfully imperfect estimation, and our judgment is irrelevant for universal truth as well as for particular human life. Jaujou recommends that we just drink tea as long as it makes no problem.

> A monk asked: "Whenever we use language and move our limbs we are going to fall into a net. Teacher, please tell me something that is beyond such bondage."
> Jaujou: "I am not yet having after-lunch tea."
> (*Jaujou lu*, entry 138)

Jaujou drinks such tea with the five old women. Pleasant chat will bring some hope for next spring. They wish for a fine growth of mulberry leaves so the silkworms can make many healthy cocoons. A fine wheat harvest will ensure their noodles, buns, and steamed breads. A surplus harvest might allow them to offer some contribution to the temple, and Jaujou wishes, dreams, and he suppresses his bitter disappointment over the past and now wishes as if for the first time ever:

> If only I could give a coin to Rahula...

Rahula as a proper noun is Sakyamuni's son. He practiced patience and was later regarded as the best among Buddha's disciples to keep in detail the ideal manner and behavior.

> Acolyte Rahula lodged in Buddha's lavatory. When Buddha awoke, he patted him on the head with his right hand and made a gatha:

> It is not because you are poor,
> nor because you lost your wealth.
> Only for the sake of the Way
> a trainee must endure pains.
>
> (*Sarvastivada-vinaya*)

Jaujou sees everyone as having good birth and breeding because of being born from Buddha nature, and he sees that everyone should live the life of a trainee because there is the Way, where we all should keep building, walking, and cherishing. He justly uses Rahula as a common noun for trainee. He wishes to give everyone the chance to understand there is no self in purity, no self in filth, no self in happiness, and no self in suffering.

During the pilgrimage Jaujou started around age sixty,

> He always told himself, "Even by a seven-year-old child if superior to me I will be taught. Even to a centenarian if inferior to me I will teach."
>
> (*Jaujou lu*, Biography, entry 5)

We like to consider the mind of the editor of *Jaujou lu*, who specially wrote: "He always told himself." Anyway, Jaujou's words are famous but have scarcely been correctly understood. People think the point is that in being taught the Way and in teaching the Way, age difference should be ignored, even in a society under strong Confucian influence.

But the pivotal point of Jaujou's declaration is that he will be taught by anyone and will teach anyone, because everyone has Buddha nature, and in the world of Buddha nature being taught and teaching are of equal value; and, although different in form, being taught and teaching are the central forms of Buddha nature. (Jaujou's declaration is Buddha's declaration: "All sentient and insentient beings, including mountains and rivers, weeds and trees, are attaining Buddhahood.")

Thus Jaujou while drinking flaxseed tea is wishing to be able to sponsor trainees.

Six O'clock Sunset

Nothing to maintain except a desolate scene.
Noble trainees have never come.
Immutable are those acolytes
who visit temple after temple.
No unprecedented words issue from my mouth.
Descendant of Sakyamuni I am in vain.
Here is a coarse staff used to beat a dog,
not only to climb a mountain.

* * *

 Any piece of land, whether a temple yard or a commoner's field, is a geography reconstructed by human history and the customs of the related region. History is made by the death of people, custom is made by the survivors. So what a piece of land or landscape contains is neither death nor life, and Jaujou, for that, simply states: "Nothing to maintain except a desolate scene."
 "A desolate scene" isn't where there's a nice variety of well-tended vegetable growth or rich mix of color and height of cultivated garden flowers, and also not where there's fresh trace of hand-to-hand combat, or endless desert. We must admit "a desolate scene" is a rather neutral description among all sorts of descriptions of land. Jaujou therefore says "Nothing to maintain" while actually maintaining "a desolate scene" as the ordinary mind, the Middle Way.
 When I was a monk and serving as a chanting officer, I was told by a senior monk to give the first strike to the evening bell the very instant the lines dividing the roof tiles on the Buddha Hall became undistinguishable. Gazing steadily there made my eyes tearful and before real dusk I lost my clear vision. Besides, for the purpose of telling time, to thus gaze was useless on cloudy or rainy days. With this tradition, what I was expected to see at sunset was the possible world with no

division between light and dark, life and death, and good and bad.

> Noble trainees have never come.
> Immutable are those acolytes
> who visit temple after temple.

"Noble trainees" must have their high and steady resolution, and more than anything else they must have a high adaptability to new situations with no heavy attachment to accustomed objects. Therefore from old times they have been likened to flowing clouds and streams.

But here Jaujou couldn't mean such a stereotypical almost empty definition of "Noble trainees." He is rather assigning such a definition to "those acolytes who visit temple after temple."

In order to avoid slipping from the right understanding of these lines, we must listen reverentially to his strong statements "have never come" and "Immutable are." We are almost going to mistake these lines as an emphatic lamentation from the teacher's point of view. In fact they aren't emphatic rhetoric but are merely universal statements. Because they are universal, and because that is the way the human world works, Jaujou as he states them is calm.

Then for him, who are "Noble trainees"

> Question: "Leaving family is what?"
> Jaujou: "It is one who does not seek fame or decomposing matters." (*Jaujou lu*, entry 197)

Not seeking fame is an orthodox discipline for Buddhist monks. But for Jaujou, the reason we shouldn't seek fame has little to do with any social concern. He is afraid of our wasting our life because of being hooked up by concepts, here called "decomposing matters." What makes our life the same as a dead person's is our being occupied with concepts made by others. Jaujou's severe attitude toward conceptual life is exactly the same as Dungshan's:

> A monk asked, "Among the Three Bodies, which one does not fall into concept?"
> Dungshan: "About that I am always zealous."
> (*Dungshan lu*, entry 101)

Therefore when Jaujou says "Noble trainees have never come," we must agree with him: "Yes, noble trainees have never come because they are content in practicing their own life."

> Noble trainees have never come.
> Immutable are those acolytes
> who visit temple after temple.

Such acolytes are the equivalent of present-day students who go to schools seeking knowledge, acquaintances, how to deal with problems, how to realize their ideas, and to satisfy basic credit and diploma requirements. Eventually what they study is the truth that we each must face life-death. The difference between "Noble trainees" and "those acolytes" is only that the former use their life-death positively and the latter understand it negatively.

> Question: "While living, Buddha and the patriarchs transmitted [the Dharma]. Now after their death, who is transmitting?"
> Jaujou: "That is the work of this old monk."
> Student: "I am unsure, what are you transmitting?"
> Jaujou: "We each must face life-death."
> Student: "But won't Buddha and the patriarchs save us all?"
> Jaujou: "What else do Buddha and the patriarchs transmit?" (*Jaujou lu*, entry 159)

This episode has two subjects. The first is about the relationship between "Buddha and the patriarchs" and Jaujou (or us each). The second is about the content of their transmission.

Jaujou understands "Buddha and the patriarchs" are universal function rather than particular and historical beings. He can therefore say transmitting is "the work of this old monk." With this recognition we can satisfy our life in any situation even if our five viscera and six entrails aren't enough to satisfy us.

Clearly Jaujou states the transmission's content: "We each must face life-death." The student in this episode and "those acolytes" are the same in their passive understanding of life-death. They tend to believe they can solve the problem of life-death by studying life-death, or by following the teachings of Buddha and the patriarchs.

As soon as they start either studying or following, they fail at their aim, because life-death isn't their object but is their life itself. Besides, life-death isn't an abominable thing. It's the very life of Buddha and the patriarchs. For this truth Jaujou says "What else do Buddha and the patriarchs transmit?" This understanding doesn't come no matter how much we study life-death as our study object. Understanding comes only when we live such a life as the very life of Buddha and the patriarchs.

So Jaujou instructs no further. He will accept any acolytes who wish to stay, and he doesn't particularly lament even if they go away. There is no lamentation, and of course no disdain for those acolytes who visit temple after temple. Nobody knows when and by what occasion they will turn into noble trainees, and for a patriarch like Jaujou it is hard to distinguish them from noble trainees, especially in the dusk after sunset.

> No unprecedented words appear from my mouth.
> Descendant of Sakyamuni I am in vain.

Here too Jaujou uses words in contrast. His "No unprecedented words" contrasts with the Eight Styles of Teaching in the Five Epochs, or the Eighty-four Thousand Dharma Gates (not brought to the surface by Jaujou). And "my mouth" contrasts with "Sakyamuni." Seemingly he is contrasting them to reveal how they are different from each other, but it is not the case, for he is contrasting them to actualize they are the same.

So what he means is those who inherit Sakyamuni should indeed be descendants in vain; each shouldn't have a unique self. The sense is "As a descendant of Sakyamuni in vain, I naturally have no unprecedented words coming from my mouth; I live only as I who am the Eight Styles of Teaching in the Five Epochs, or the Eighty-four Thousand Dharma Gates."

Yuanwu says by quoting someone:

> Words are mere vehicles to carry the Way. You must know the saying of an ancient person, that even if you dive

into the phrases, you will not find any grip. It is said: "The Way from the first has no words. We indicate the Way by words and should forget them when we see the Way."
(Lecture on *Biyan lu*, Case 12)

Cases 2 and 59 in *Biyan lu* deal with the relation between the Way and human words:

> Jaujou spoke to the assembly: "The Ultimate Way asks of us no difficult training, but rejects our preferences. With only a word, either preference or clarity may arise. This old monk does not live in that clarity. Are you cherishing that?"
> Then a monk asked, "If already you do not live there, what is to cherish?"
> Jaujou: "Neither do I know."
> The monk: "If you do not know, how can you say you do not live there?"
> Jaujou: "To ask is good enough. Now make your bows and retire." (*Biyan lu*, Case 2)

In this episode Jaujou is hoping for the monks to live in the Ultimate Way and is cautioning how easily we will be apart from it by depending on our words (that is, our thought and emotion). This monk doesn't yet see into the Ultimate Way and believes he can understand it by means of logical pursuit.

The Ultimate Way is universal life causing all phenomena; and for True Buddhists, all phenomena are Words. So human words are words expressed in the midst of Words. From this view, cultivating human words with much sincerity, especially before knowing Words, isn't what we should do, because it will bring us only confusion, like hearing the tenacious echoes and doublings of a defective telephone connection.

So Jaujou clearly points out "Neither do I know," because Words, which are phenomena, the Ultimate Way, don't know phenomena or the Ultimate Way. Why? Because Words are the Ultimate Way itself. We can fully live in the Ultimate Way by not knowing, even as we dream about the Ultimate Way by knowing. Still the monk is in the state of confusion between human words and Words. So Jaujou concludes with "To ask is good enough. Now make your bows and retire." For the monk, no matter when and where he retires there are phenomena, which are Words, which are are the Ultimate Way, awaiting his practice of them.

In this context Jaujou here in his Sunset verse says,

> No unprecedented words appear from my mouth.

He has the quiet confidence of living in the Ultimate Way (in the next line expressed as "Sakyamuni"), and yet he is cautious not to slip away by careless use of words: "With only a word, either preference or clarity may arise." So he says he must keep repeating to himself,

> Descendant of Sakyamuni I am in vain.

If not a descendant of Sakyamuni in vain, he will be ridiculed even by a novice as young as Mokuzu:

> "Master, you must be careful. Nobody doubts you have taken the office of abbot, but some might doubt whether the abbot is you." (ref. *Mind to Mind*, chap. 64)

> Here is a coarse staff used to beat a dog,
> not only to climb a mountain.

The staff was originally a practical tool to support our life. From the time of Matzu, Eighth Patriarch in China, it became an educative tool to indicate Dharma or Buddha nature. A "coarse staff" means the staff unpolluted by later decoration. Jaujou is keeping up his principle of guiding students by direct teaching. Here following is an actual example of a direct teaching that Jaujou witnessed in his youth and it deeply impressed him:

> Jaujou in the Dharma Hall said to his monks, "This matter is very evident. Even a great man beyond compare cannot exceed from here. Once when visiting Kueishan [Kueishan Lingyou, 771-853], this old monk witnessed this:
>
> "A monk asked, 'What is the meaning of the Patriarch's coming from the West?' Kueishan said, 'Fetch me a chair.'
>
> "A true teacher guides with original matter, as you see in this example." (*Jaujou lu*, entry 12)

Making the monk bring a chair, Kueishan demonstrates the actual functioning of Buddha nature. There is no more important matter in Buddha's teaching than our coming to be aware of Buddha nature in every phenomenon, including our conduct. Our conduct is highly particularized by the concrete, absolute reality of now, here, and I. But when we devote ourselves into particularized time, place, and individual, we are entering into anytime, anywhere, and any being, without any destruction of our particularized time, place, and individual. By devoting ourselves we lose ourselves but gain our universal life. Enabling ourselves to come and go freely between particular life and universal life is the most important matter in Buddha's teaching.

The episode continues with another actual demonstration, this time by Jaujou himself with a monk:

> Then a monk asked: "What is the meaning of the Patriarch's coming from the West?"
> Jaujou said: "It is the juniper there in the garden."
> The monk: "Your Reverence, please do not guide me by indicating the environment."
> Jaujou": "I am not guiding by indicating the environment."
> The monk: "What is the meaning of the Patriarch's coming from the West?"
> Jaujou: "It is the juniper there in the garden." (Ibid.)

Here "juniper" is particularized time, place, and individual, and "the meaning of the Patriarch's coming from the West" is universal life, which is Buddha nature. There are four ways of seeing the relation between juniper and Buddha nature:

> Case 1: We see juniper and don't see Buddha nature.
> Case 2: We see Buddha nature and don't see juniper.
> Case 3: We see juniper (with our physical eyes)
>   as well as Buddha nature (with our intuition).
> Case 4: We see neither juniper nor Buddha nature.

Case 4 is unconsciousness and is outside of Buddhist interest. Case 3 is our intellectual understanding of theology and it has no power in the practical field. Case 1 is the life of worldly people, and Case 2 is the life of those Hinayana trainees or theologians. What Jaujou is guiding us into is the life that has no division between Case 1 and Case 2. For such a life, Jaujou gives this verse the title Six O'clock Sunset.

Even so, people love to see a pleasant, beautiful, cheerful scene instead of a desolate scene, and such people may have difficulty finding any great meaning in Jaujou's juniper episode. For them, the conclusion of the verse will be helpful:

> Here is a coarse staff used to beat a dog,
> not only to climb a mountain.

"A coarse staff," that is, Buddha nature, can be used to beat a dog, not only to climb a mountain. For Buddhists, a mountain means any form, but in this context, climbing a mountain is contrasting with beating a dog, so it must mean Mt. Sumeru, where the trainee Sudhana-sresthi-daraka studied the Bodhisattva's Deeds (in the *Mahavaipulya-buddhavatamsaka-sutra*). Bodhisattvas are devoted to benefitting other lives, and it is said in their devoting they can cherish the world of absolute peace beyond thought and word. This mentality is symbolically called "the summit."

Beating a dog is a shabby act. At least in this verse it is understood as such. Why do we beat a dog? Mainly because dogs compete with us for food, bring insects and disease that menace our health, and help us to feel we are superior beings to them. So Jaujou is regarding as "beating a dog" every conduct in which we compete with others in the process of gaining our food, and he is regarding as "beating a dog" every conduct to reject harmful insects and microbes, and he is regarding as "beating a dog" every conduct to gain pleasure from comparison with others. By this definition, most of our present-day social activities given by us a high evaluation can be regarded to be as shabby as beating a dog.

It is said we use the staff to become a bodhisattva and also to beat a dog. The staff is here indicated as Buddha nature, as we have already studied. If we use the staff (Buddha nature) to become a bodhisattva or to beat a dog, then what are we? Here we shouldn't keep using the metaphor of a staff to represent Buddha nature. We are Buddha nature. In short, Buddha nature is becoming whoever climbs up the mountain of Bodhisattva, and also Buddha nature is becoming whoever beats a dog.

Be careful, Jaujou isn't saying whoever beats a dog is shabby, or the bodhisattva who climbs the mountain is noble. He is saying Buddha nature sometimes becomes the bodhisattva who climbs the mountain, and sometimes the same Buddha nature becomes the person who beats a dog.

So we must be aware. When we are a bodhisattva we are a form of Buddha nature, and when we are a person who beats a dog, we are a form of Buddha nature. Whoever we are, and wherever, whatever, and however we are doing, we are Buddha nature. This truth is demonstrated by Jaujou and his monk by using the example of the juniper in the garden. So too, Kueishan teaches us that we and every phenomenon, including a chair and a person who carries a chair, are descendants of Buddha nature. After all, each is unable to exceed Buddha's teaching "All sentient and insentient beings, including mountains and rivers, weeds and trees, are attaining Buddha hood."

So in "Nothing to maintain except a desolate scene," Jaujou starting this verse isn't setting a mode of resignation. He has the confidence of maintaining what he should maintain. We can't decisively conclude a shabby person is a shabby person, a bodhisattva is a bodhisattva. Even being so shabby as to beat a dog, whoever beats, we must know, is functioning as Buddha nature. Such persons haven't good taste, modesty, clean behavior, or deep consideration. Each is a desolate person in a desolate scene.

Not elegant, decent, or noble. But any one of them is a descendant of Buddha nature, so there is no one better in this world. There is no need to stand before a needle's eye like a bulky confused camel. The needle's eye isn't in front of us, it was already behind us when we were born. Just as whoever beats a dog has come from Buddha nature, so has everyone else, every creature. For the Buddhist, all beings, all phenomena, are a form of Buddha nature and all came through the needle's eye eons ago. Even the eye of the needle is a form of Buddha nature.

Buddhists cherish elegance in the Desolate Scene. Thanks to Jaujou we have courage, composure, wisdom, and compassion to see elegance in the Desolate Scene.

Eight O'clock Nightfall

Sitting alone in a dark vacant room.
Shimmering and torchlight are never seen.
In front of my eyes is like lacquer produced in Jin.
Without hearing the bell
I spend the day in vain.
Only the sound of scurrying mice.
How do I have the mind
to think about paramita?

* * *

For those acquainted with Buddhist transmission, "Sitting alone in a dark vacant room" isn't the image of someone socially lonely and poor, seated in an unlit room. It includes that, but overall the figure is of one who has established independence from all phenomena, as we see in *Biyan lu*, Case 26:

A monk asked Baijang, "What is the most wonderful thing?"
Baijang replied, "To sit alone on the great sublime peak."

"Great sublime peak" means Mt. Dashyung, where Baijang resides, but it also refers to his own body and therefore to his whole world. Jaujou likewise is saying in this verse that he is living in the most wonderful time.

"In a dark vacant room" is an adverbial phrase to indicate place, but is actually used to describe the cause that enables Jaujou to establish himself and live in the most wonderful time. Attaining vacancy is our essential work ever since Sakyamuni Buddha taught us to do so. He gave a gatha when he entrusted Maha-kasyapa to transmit the Dharma:

The intrinsic Dharma of the Dharma is no Dharma.
The Dharma of no Dharma is also the Dharma.
Now when no Dharma is transmitted,
how can the Dharma of the Dharma ever be the Dharma?
(*Chuandeng lu*, vol. 1)

Bodhidharma faithfully brought this teaching to Emperor Wu:

> Emperor Wu of Liang asked Great Teacher Bodhidharma: "What is the first principle of the holy teachings?"
> Bodhidharma: "It is vacancy and no holiness."
> (Biyan lu, Case 1)

Bodhidharma expects us to be free of the authorities, functions, and bondages of both rupa and sunyata. But he isn't recommending that we deny any of them. In a practical sense, we mustn't be crushed by emperor, state, materials, or chronological time, and also we shouldn't cling to the personified Buddha, theology, or idea. Being free of both extremes and going on the Middle Way is here expressed by Jaujou as "Sitting alone in a dark vacant room."

"How do we practice the Middle Way?" is an often-asked question, though the very question we shouldn't ask others. Asking makes a decent person more decent, and shabby person more shabby.

> A monk asked Shyuefeng, "For a sravaka, it is said, seeing through one's nature is like seeing the moon in the night, whereas for a bodhisattva, seeing through one's nature is like seeing the sun in the daytime. How is it for Your Reverence?"
> Shyuefeng thrice struck the monk.
> The monk visited Yantou and asked the same question. Yantou also thrice struck him. (*Tetteki tosui* [Playing the iron flute upside down], Case 34)

Jaujou in his verse uses vision and hearing to express how he is attaining the Middle Way:

> Shimmering and torchlight are never seen.
> In front of my eyes is like lacquer produced in Jin.

"Shimmering" symbolizes klesa; "torchlight," Bodhi. Jaujou sees only blackness, "like lacquer produced in Jin." There are two kinds of not seeing: not seeing because of ignorance, and not seeing because of being in the midst of practicing.

Occasion 1:

Toutzy [Toutzy Detung, 819-914] one day pointed to a stone before the hermitage and said to Shyuefeng, "All Buddhas practicing in The Three Worlds are here, aren't they?"
Shyuefeng replied, "We must know those who aren't here."
Toutzy: "A pitch-dark lacquer pail."

Occasion 2:

Another day Toutzy was walking with Shyuefeng along the path Lungmian [path where a dragon sleeps] and he commented to Shyuefeng, "The path forks."
Shyuefeng asked, "Which is Lungmian?"
Toutzy pointed with his staff.
Shyuefeng said, "One leads east, the other leads west."
Toutzy said, "A pitch-dark lacquer pail."

Occasion 3:

Shyuefeng asked Toutzy, "Are there any that come here to study?"
Toutzy picked up a hoe and cast it forward.
Shyuefeng said, "In such case, here I will dig."
Toutzy said, "A pitch-dark lacquer pail."

Occasion 4:

Shyuefeng: "How do you think about one who accomplishes with a single blow of a sledge hammer?"
Toutzy: "Not wise."
Shyuefeng: "How about not accomplishing with a single blow?"
Toutzy: "A pitch-dark lacquer pail."

(*Wudeng hueiyuan*, vol. 3)

Shyuefeng in Occasion 1 doesn't see the truth of "All Buddhas in The Three Worlds are here." So he can have neither basic joy nor confidence in his life and makes a worldly problem, such as "are here" or "aren't here." He has yet to understand none of our profound problems can possibly be solved by any dualistic way of thinking. Toutzy says his ignorance is "A pitch-dark lacquer pail."

Shyuefeng in Occasion 2 still dwells in dualistic thought:

"One leads east, the other leads west." In Buddhism there's no such nonsense as the direction in which we precede will bring us a difference of truth or fault. We must study the Way wherever we are and not dream of anywhere else.

In Occasion 3, Shyuefeng seems to be asking Toutzy if he has any students. But we must understand Shyuefeng's "any that come" contains the sense of not only any students, or persons, but also any human thought and emotion coming to study. Toutzy was a good friend of Jaujou's. Both were poor in economy and number of students, but their standard of living up to being a Buddhist priest was the highest ever. Instead of voicing answer, Toutzy picked up a hoe and cast it forward. Doing so, he deepened Shyuefeng's "here" from its meaning "Toutzy's teaching" to its meaning "the presence of Shyuefeng here now." Shyuefeng understands his transition of meaning and says, "In such case, here I will dig." He is understanding the truth can be found only when he digs deep into where and what he is. Toutzy approves of his understanding and encourages: "A pitch-dark lacquer pail."

In Occasion 4, Shyuefeng revives his dualistic way of thinking. Especially for those to whom the great realization is yet to come, accomplishing is important, but by a single blow or not is irrelevant. This time Toutzy scolds, "A pitch-dark lacquer pail."

> Without hearing the bell
> I spend the day in vain.
> Only the sound of scurrying mice.

Coming to these lines, we are forced into the awareness that Jaujou's "Twelve Hours Verses" isn't a set of verses he created for his leisurely poetical amusement but is his standard he is recommending to his kasaya-donning monks for their practice. These lines here tell us how we should take the Four Sufferings, or Eight Sufferings, and how we should have the surplus to care for the life of others.

This "bell" is obviously the bell to announce regular ceremonial events such as chanting, meditating, lecturing, and working together. Even though the temple was poor, and had "less than twenty" students according to Dogen, Jaujou kept up the noble sangha life. Then why does he say "Without hearing the bell I spend the day in vain?" How can it be the standard recommended to kasaya-donning monks?

Yunmen is Shyuefeng's heir and a little later person than Jaujou, but as for the matter hidden in Jaujou's nightfall verse, it is the very subject Yunmen wished trainees to master:

> Yunmen said, "The world is so wide and free, why do you don the kasaya as soon as you hear the bell?"
> (*Yunmen lu*, vol. 1)

To be free from the torture of family and society, and from the four and eight basic human sufferings, we put ourselves under the teaching of Buddha and the patriarchs. Yet we must also obey the fussy and severe monastic rules and customs. Otherwise our chance to understand Bodhi and Nirvana will be drastically reduced, and social bondages and exploitations will await us without any reward of fundamental solutions to our basic sufferings.

Yunmen wishes us to be free of every suffering that comes in the form of color and sound. For the Buddhists' view, phenomena do not make us (us = Buddha nature). Rather, for the Buddhists' view, we make phenomena, and phenomena shouldn't be the cause of our suffering but should be the diversified function of Buddha nature. Jaujou's answer to Yunmen's question is amazing: "Without hearing the bell I spend the day in vain." This is the achievement of Jaujou. He sees, hears, smells, tastes, feels, and thinks, and he doesn't miss even the sound of scurrying mice, yet he doesn't hear any approach of the Four and Eight Sufferings.

> A monk asked, "What is Nirvana?
> Jaujou: "My ears are heavy."
> The monk asked again.
> Jaujou: "I'm not suffering deafness," and he composed a gatha:
>> Those who freely go on the Great Way
>> meet the gate of Nirvana.
>> Just by sitting, their sense is boundless,
>> and they are enabled to cherish an endless spring
>> year after year. (*Jaujou lu*, entry 518)

"Those who freely go on the Great Way" must be those

who courageously and righteously practice the conduct based on non-dualistic valuation. Not hearing, while hearing and practicing sitting meditation—this hearing and not hearing are the same act.

> Question: "Your student is dull and stupid and always keeps repeating up and down. How to get out of this?"
> Jaujou just kept sitting.
> The monk: "I am sincerely asking the advice of Your Reverence."
> Jaujou: "In which place do you keep repeating up and down?" (*Jaujou lu*, entry 188)

The "dull and stupid" student can obviously see Jaujou sitting. It is the figure of one who is "repeating up and down." But the monk can't see Jaujou who is simultaneously transcending "repeating up and down." So Jaujou asks, "In which place do you keep repeating up and down?" It is more like asking "In which of two places are you...?" The physical place is the same one place. The same one place can be the saha world, where we must endure all sorts of sufferings. Nevertheless, it is also Buddha's world. This different view depends on our faith in what Buddha and the patriarchs taught us, or seeing through Buddha nature in every phenomenon.

> Question: "What should I do when four mountains are pressing me?"
> Jaujou: "There is no path to approach the person who is called Jaujou." (*Jaujou lu*, entry 227)

"Four mountains" means the four basic sufferings. Jaujou says those sufferings have no path to approach him. If we are not awestruck by his achievement, have we ever any chance to experience such a feeling? He can say so because he has such faith or ability to see through nature, but we also must understand more simply that he becomes one with suffering as soon as it comes. With no distance between him and any suffering, there is no path.

In conclusion, Jaujou is fully practicing what he should do every day, hour after hour. The content of such a life is described as "Without hearing the bell I spend the day in vain." This is an example that no hearing can be the ultimate hearing.

> Only the sound of scurrying mice.

In either case, bell, or mice, Jaujou and his environment are fused into one. In the case of "bell," Jaujou's life (which is the direct effect of past karma) is highly focused, so in an active role he takes it. In the case of "mice," the environment surrounding him is formed by mutual relations and is called indirect effect, so in a passive role he takes it. The point is to make ourselves shed ourselves and make our environment shed our environment, regardless of which role we take, active or passive.

> How do I have the mind
> to think about paramita?

The content of the first line, "Sitting alone in a dark vacant room," and the content of the conclusion, "How do I have the mind to think about paramita?" are the same, as we should expect. Paramita is a Sanskrit word meaning "to reach the other shore, Nirvana, from this shore of suffering." In popular Buddhism it is believed that the great wisdom (*Mahaprajna*) is the important object necessary for us to practice in order to reach the other shore, as said in the *Maha-prajnaparamita-hrdaya-sutra*:

> When the Bodhisattva Avalokitesvara practiced the deep Prajna paramita, he perceived that the Five Skandhas are all empty and was freed from all sufferings.

The Five Skandhas are our mind and body. The sutra says it is necessary for us to perceive the truth that our mind and body are all empty in order for us to be free of all sufferings (= to reach the other shore, Nirvana). Then for the same subject what does Jaujou say?

> Question: "What is Maha prajna paramita?"
> Jaujou: "Maha prajna paramita." (*Jaujou lu*, entry 252)

Here Jaujou and "Maha prajna paramita" are one. Jaujou isn't simply Jaujou, and Maha prajna paramita isn't simply Maha prajna paramita. Jaujou is Jaujou as well as Jaujou is Maha prajna paramita, and Maha prajna paramita is Maha prajna paramita as well as Maha prajna paramita is Jaujou. When Jaujou and Maha prajna paramita are one, Jaujou is shedding both himself and Maha prajna paramita, and thus he is free of all sufferings. In true practical Buddhism, reaching the other shore means to make ourselves and our environment one. This is the sure definition of what religious training is for us.

Ten O'clock Settling

Who cherishes the moon before the gate?
Indoors my concern is how to sleep.
No upper or lower bedclothes, no covers.
Odd are Liou, the regulations monk,
and Jau, who keeps the Five Precepts.
With their mouth they preach the morals,
even though my bag has become empty.
Never do they understand whatever I ask.

* * *

The word "settling" serves two meanings, for "sleep" and the practice of dhyana.

Until Sixth Patriarch Hueineng (638-713), Buddhists believed that keeping the precepts (sila and vinaya) enables us to maintain dhyana, and dhyana enables us to attain prajna. It means they were believed each to be a relative virtue.

The Sixth Patriarch clarified that they are three aspects of the same one virtue: dhyana is the body (=torch) of prajna; prajna is the function (= light) of dhyana; and the nature of our mind, which is made with such dhyana and prajna, is our sila (=purity). By the word "settling," Jaujou means this one indivisible dhyana with three aspects.

(According to the gist of *Tanjing*, entry 5, these three indivisibles — dhyana, prajna, and sila — have three fundamental aspects: no form, no notion, and no dwelling. No form means detaching from form while involved with form; no notion means detaching from notion while having notion; and no dwelling means every notion keeps changing, notion after notion, never staying in any particular notion. This no dwelling is our primary nature. It is the reason we are not bound by anything, and it is called primary purity.)

Who cherishes the moon before the gate?

This first line doesn't mean that because the night grows late no one is outdoors to admire the moon. It is a positive statement in question form. The indefinable "who" is cherishing the moon. This "who" is a bodhisattva that is neither Buddha nature nor human being, but also a bodhisattva that is either Buddha nature or human being. The brightness of the moon such a bodhisattva sees isn't the sunlight reflected by our moon. It is the brightness beyond our dualistic brightness, that is, beyond the brightness perceived by our sense organs and conceptualized by our thinking facility. So in such context it can be said to be also darkness.

About this moon Jaujou was taught by Nanchyuan:

> Jaujou asked Nanchyuan, "Where will one who understands [the Way] go?"
> Nanchyuan: "One who understands will become a work cow at the layman's house over there."
> Jaujou: "Your Reverence, thank you for your guidance."
> Nanchyuan: "Last night at eleven the moon shined in the window." (*Jaujou lu*, entry 3)

The episode seems to tell us that those who understand wisdom should engage in compassionate conduct like a work cow, seeking no reward, like an inorganic planet or moon. If that were so, then gaining wisdom would become a process that precedes the practice of compassion, and it would be an atavism going back over the head of the Sixth Patriarch. Besides, without toxic endurance, no sensible human can engage in compassionate conduct, seeking no reward. Anyway, Buddhist compassion is functioning regardless of whether we are conscious or not.

The life of a work cow is not enjoyable even if the cow happens to be under the command of someone relatively kind. The farmer always holds his whip and maintains his work schedule. We have no record of Jaujou's becoming any sort of work force under a farmer.

What the episode is telling us is that understanding wisdom is an ongoing function, like the work of a work cow, and only when we are continuously studying are we transcending the conceptual restriction of wisdom—like the midnight moon beyond reach of forms or valuations such as illusion and awakening, compassion and wisdom. In this episode the moon is a symbol of total truth, a perfect blend of the human and human environment, both made out of Buddha nature, so naturally they blend.

> Jaujou asked Nanchyuan viewing the moon, "How long have you been so?"
> Nanchyuan: "From twenty years ago."
> (*Chanyuan mengchiou*, vol. 3)

From old times this episode has also been oddly interpreted as an illustration of Nanchyuan's great power to become one with the moon. Obviously nobody can become one with the moon. Yet if we insist on such an interpretation, we can't help but force ourselves to highly estimate Nanchyuan's ability to meanwhile forget himself and his environment by seeing the moon, like a dope. But that much is true even of people who never studied Buddhism.

Instead the episode is telling us of the ability to see Buddha nature intuitively in concrete form. Nanchyuan is intuitively seeing the moon (=Buddha nature) in the actual moon in the sky. "From twenty years ago" doesn't mean literally from twenty years ago. It means "I am accustomed to seeing Buddha nature in daily life from so long ago I can't actually recall from when."

Jaujou received from Nanchyuan the transmission of the function of wisdom. This function of wisdom is the central issue of Buddhism, and it is the free transport between rupa (phenomena) and sunyata (substance.) This wisdom was transmitted by the Sixth Patriarch to all followers whether they later belonged to the Nanyue-Matzu-Baijang lineage or to the Chingyuan-Shytou-Yaushan lineage.

> It gets polluted
> once it is expressed.
> It is bright at midnight,
> is invisible under the sun.
> It becomes the material, the world standard,
> functioning to give relief from suffering.
> (*Dungshan lu*, entry 117)

This is an extract from Dungshan's *Baujing sanmei ge*

(Verses for function of wisdom). Its content was transmitted to Dungshan from his teacher Yunyan through their intimate daily life. Dungshan gave it a literary form, and he gave it to one of his heirs, Tsaushan (Tsaushan Benji, 840-941). What it essentially describes is the same as the content of Dungshan's Five Classifications [of the relations between substance and phenomena] (ref. *Mind to Mind*, VI-52, pg. 727).

"It is bright at midnight" means substance is evident when we don't see any phenomena, and "is invisible under the sun" means substance will be hidden in phenomena. The purpose of bringing Dungshan's *Baujing sanmei ge* here is to clarify that "the moon" in Jaujou's verse carries the same meaning as "It is bright at midnight, is invisible under the sun." In short, Jaujou is attempting to describe the function of wisdom in his night verse Ten O'clock Settling. This moon Jaujou suggests is the moon to see Buddha nature in any phenomena. Jaujou isn't going to solve our problems directly with his hands and materials. He is enabling us to help ourselves.

> Indoors my concern is how to sleep.
> No upper or lower bedclothes, no covers.

Where Jaujou dwelled was Hebei, north of the Yellow River, where he hoped to have a warm hearth at night from November to February. It is hard to fall asleep when our feet don't get warm. Jaujou here is worrying not only about attire and bedcovers for a normal night but also about his funeral, wishing for dignified attire and a coffin cover. In the culture of the time, when manner and ceremony were reaching great height, Jaujou's life was so poor that religious observance was possible only as his wish. Well, at least he could die in the manner that Buddha died. It is recorded in *Chuandeng lu*, vol. 10:

> He died on the second of November, in the fourth year of Ganming, in the era of Tang, reclining on his right side.
> His age was one hundred and twenty.

His head was positioned north, his face west. North is where things are extinguished, west where they settle. This is a variation of the form of proper cross-legged sitting. His view about life-death is in the next two episodes. These questions were obviously asked near his life's end.

> There was a monk who asked, "Are the two phases life and death the same or different?"
> Jaujou made a gatha:
>> A trainee asks about life-death.
>> About that, how should I say?
>> It is the water of a pond between pairs of sala trees,
>> the bright moon shining in heaven and on earth.
>> He is wise with words
>> only to fool spirits.
>> Attempting to understand life-death
>> is like a lunatic's telling of his spring dream.
>> (*Jaujou lu*, entry 519)

Jaujou's view is in the second couplet. He describes overwhelming reality, which is beyond interpretation. Reality has its undeceivable cause and undeniable effect. Causation is another name for Buddha nature. Wherever there is causation or Buddha nature, there is peace, just as Buddha attained his Nirvana in a place with a pair of sala trees at each of its four corners. We are like the pond water between those sala trees. On such actual water the moon of Buddha nature shines.

> A monk asked: "It is said all Buddhas when they meet peril will hide in the flame. Your Reverence, where will you hide when you meet peril?
> Jaujou made a gatha:
>> He who talks as if he were Buddha meeting peril
>> is he who meets peril.
>> Just watch how I avoid peril:
>> Where does it follow after me?
>> Relative being or non-being is not preaching.
>> Coming and going are not coming and going.
>> What I just said is the way to avoid peril.
>> Face directly and see through.
>> (*Jaujou lu*, entry 520)

For Jaujou there is no such creature or dharma to be called "peril." For Buddhists since Sakyamuni Buddha after he attained the great realization, solving the Four and Eight Sufferings isn't the goal. By any means, we would like to be free of suffering, but it isn't the purpose of our life. Seeing through the nature of those sufferings is our goal. Veteran Buddhists like Jaujou see each one as Buddha nature. For Jaujou, seeing Buddha nature in each is the content of his life, and it was the most important concern for him. Having suffering or not was not his most important concern.

He concludes his gatha, "Face directly and see through." But however often, deeply, sharply he sees Buddha nature through daily phenomena, cold remains cold, pain as pain, hunger as hunger. So he says:

> Odd are Liou, the regulations monk,
> and Jau, who keeps the Five Precepts.
> With their mouth the preach the morals,
> even though my bag has become empty.
> Never do they understand whatever I ask.

The regulations monk and the acolyte who keeps the Five Precepts should behave and distinguish their belongings from those of another. But they too must be cold and, before thinking, using their master's winter wear and bedcovers as a matter of fact. It happens in poor and intimate circumstances. Jaujou finds his bag has become empty and asks those trainees whether they know the obvious trace of its contents. With serious looks they answer they don't know. They have become so intimate with his belongings that they no longer are aware of any distinction between themselves and their whereabouts.

Jaujou is enjoying these intimate trainees' attainment of understanding by not understanding instead of staying in the state of understanding. They are acting as lively Buddha nature. Jaujou isn't sparing his wisdom and compassion but giving it forth from his bag of Buddhist transmission, thus emptying his bag. Here in his temple is one of the highest accomplishments in one of the poorest lives. So this verse he calls "Settling."

Midnight

How does my mind cease even a moment?
Come to think of the monks in this world
dwelling in temples,
how many can be like me?
Earthen bed, unraveled bamboo mat,
a long time using an elm pillow without a cover.
For Buddha no benzoin in the incense burner.
Only the smell of cow dung.

* * *

Jaujou says even at midnight, when he should be settled, his mind doesn't cease even a moment. It means when we are settled in peace is when our mind ceaselessly functions with all sorts of sensing, feeling, thinking, wishing, caring, concerning. It also means ceaselessly functioning is the nature of our mind as well as the nature of all phenomena. The opening line "How does my mind cease even a moment?" carries the same meaning as what Sixth Patriarch Hueineng eagerly impresses upon us in the following episode:

A monk recited a gatha made by the Zen teacher Wolun:

> Wolun has the art
> to sever a hundred thoughts.
> No notion rises in any situation.
> Bodhi thus grows daily.

The Teacher [Dajian Hueineng, 638-713] commented: "This gatha shows an un-clarified mind. People if they follow this gatha will increase their restriction."

He then made his own gatha:

> Hueineng lost the art.
> Hundreds of thoughts cannot be severed.
> The mind rises as often as each situation turns.
> How can Bodhi be grown?

(*Lioutzu Tanjing*, chap. 7, ed. Tzungbau)

The Sixth Patriarch says our thoughts are not objects to be controlled and they naturally come and go according to the situation. Growth of Bodhi has nothing to do with our controlling our thoughts, but is rather the fundamental nature of our mind and environment, existing independent of any artificial effort or endurance. What is of great significance is for us to be awakened to the nature of this mind and environment. The importance of this awakening is emphasized by one of Hueineng's heirs, Shenhuei (Hetze Shenhuei, 670-762) inasmuch as he makes a slogan for his school: "Knowing this one letter is the gate to all wonders."

The Sixth Patriarch lectures about the incessant flow of our notions. This free flow of notion is the base of his entire teaching, as influenced by the Diamond Sutra:

> No form means detaching from form while involved in form. No notion means having no notion while having notion. No dwelling is human nature.
>
> When the flow of notion does not stop, notion ceaselessly functions from past to present and from present to future with no severance. If even one notion is severed, Dharma-kaya will be instantly separated from the physical body.
>
> No notion ever dwells in any phenomena at any time. Even if one notion dwells, the flow of notion will stagnate, and such a state is called restriction. When the flow of notion does not dwell in any phenomena, we have no restriction and this no dwelling is the primary state of our mind. (*Tanjing*, comp. Fahai, entry 5)

Seeing through the nature of notion which never dwells is so important to establish his teachings that he repeats toward the end of his relatively short, well-edited lecture:

> What is that which is called no notion? What it is, is not to attach to any phenomena amid every phenomenon and not to attach in any place amid everywhere.
>
> Keeping one's nature pure all the time, letting the six thieves go out from the six exits, not detaching from but also not attaching to the six dusts, and being free in coming and going is called Prajna Samadhi, and freely shedding [the phenomenal world] is called the practice of no notion.
>
> Do not try not to think anything, do not sever function of

notion. Severing notion is restriction and is an eccentric view. Those who are awakened by the teaching of no notion can utilize any teaching and can see Buddha's world. Those who are awakened by such fundamental teaching as no notion are accomplishing Buddha's state. (Ibid., entry 10)

It is thus apparent that Jaujou's opening line "How does my mind cease even a moment?" is reminding us of the Sixth Patriarch's teaching, and that Jaujou is describing how faithfully and thankfully he applies this teaching to his actual life.

Yet, there will be a shortage in our understanding of Jaujou if we take the rest of his lines as an example of his naturally flowing notion.

A shallow interpretation is 'Not many monks could endure so poor a temple life. My bed is built of mud and has no elaborate silk quilt. Its bamboo mat is unraveled, the pillow made of hard wood. But fortunately I am well and needn't good covering such as for an invalid. A costly import such as benzoin, representative of human concept, is only to be dreamed of as an offering to Buddha. Around here prevails the odor of burning cow dung. Isn't it a natural, practical, and earthy real life? It is the life of a bodhisattva, a work cow, promoted by Nanchyuan and Kueishan.'

One of Jaujou's episodes is helpful in leading us to the right understanding:

> Question: "How do you think of the person who does not forget that which is throughout the ancient time up to now?"
> Jaujou: "Do not restrict your mind. Always think of all Buddhas in the Ten Directions." *(Jaujou lu*, entry 353)

Jaujou reminds the monk not to be restricted by thought, even about the changeless truth throughout time. Yet, he advises the monk, "Always think of all Buddhas in the Ten Directions" because "to be unconscious" is not the Way (*Jaujou lu*, entry 1). Jaujou is denying discretionary thought and yet recommends to the monk that he have thought that exists beyond discretion. Thought that exists beyond discretion is more like intuition or thought undivided from our other life functions such as emotion, character, humanity, words, and behavior. In short, all Buddhas in the Ten Directions aren't separating any object from their character. It means the person and Buddha, the one who thinks and the one who is thought of, aren't divided, and this thought is called Right thought (*samyak-smarti*). Jaujou encourages us to engage in this Right thought.

Now we have to return to the Sixth Patriarch's teaching.

There we will frankly mumble "We understand our notion keeps moving, rising, falling, just as all phenomena do. However, there is sometimes a wretched stagnation when our notion doesn't flow smoothly, which the Patriarch refers to as "restriction." It is true each notion finishes sooner or later, but also a notion can appear repeatedly, sometimes with increased vigor and depth. A repeating notion can begin to control us as if it were a continuous notion, as if a genetically inherited character, as if a secondary instinct since our amoeba age.

To sum up, the repeated occurrences of notion consist of The Three Poisons, wrath, greed, and ignorance. We live in the environment consisting of these poisons, in the sense of both general humanity and human individuals throughout history up to now worldwide. We are victims as well as assaulters in this environment, and this environment is squirming both inside and outside our life. To live an all-rounded Buddhist life, it seems that our coming to be aware of the nature of our notion, which is not to dwell, is not good enough. Then what should we do about our tenaciously repeating occurrence of notion, especially when it's not welcomed?

To this question Jaujou replies, "Always think of all Buddhas in the Ten Directions," and his verse develops for this aim:

> Come to think of the monks in the world
> dwelling in temples,
> how many can be like me?

"Come to think," he says. Yes, we should think before repeated occurrences of notion set in, think before wrath, greed, and ignorance form a habit in us. We should repeatedly think those three poisons have no chance to enter us and won't want to stay long in our mind if they already happen to be active there. In this way they will leave by their own free wish. We should think at every opportunity, whenever we are aware of the movement of our notion. Think what? Right thought. What is that? It is obviously Buddha's thought. What is Buddha's thought? It is:

> Come to think of the monks in the world
> dwelling in temples,
> how many can be like me?

Jaujou isn't comparing himself with others. What he says is a variation of Sakyamuni Buddha's saying:

> In all the world of heaven and earth I alone am respectable. (*Biyan lu*, Case 31, or *Datang shiyu ji*, vol. 6)

This is the core of Buddha's thought. "I" is every being, addressed as first person singular. Buddha said also:

> When Venus appears, simultaneously I, the great earth, and all sentient beings are accomplishing the Way.
> (*Hotsu bodaishin* [To Raise Bodhi mind],
> vol. 63 of 75-vol. *Shobogenzo*)

"Great earth" is the general name for all insentient beings. I, the great earth, and all sentient beings are not divided, and so can accomplish the Way at the same time. It's the starting point of Buddha's teaching, and as Linji uttered when coming to an awakening, "Buddha's Dharma is consistent!" Buddha's teaching is the same wherever we dig in.

For instance, the First Primary Precept, Not killing, is only telling us that we shouldn't oppose Buddha's view and that all beings are Buddha without exception. I, the great earth, and all sentient beings are not divided. Naturally there is no life to be killed or to kill. Not understanding or not affirming this view means violating this precept. Dogen's annotation states:

> Not killing. *Kyoju kaimon*: Life cannot be killed,
> Buddha's seed keeps increasing. The life of Buddha's
> wisdom is to be continued, life is not to be killed.

So Jaujou must think before any repeated occurrences of his notion turn to wrath, greed, and ignorance. He thinks of each being as Buddha nature, accomplishing the Way, having the life not to be killed. In true Buddhism, each time of thinking the right thought is called To Raise Bodhi mind (To

Practice the Way, To Attain Bodhi, or To Attain Nirvana). And this is To have Right thought.

Jaujou is raising Bodhi mind anew whenever seeing his earthen bed, unraveled bamboo mat, and elm pillow, whenever noting the absence of benzoin scent and the faint presence of burning cow dung.

Even in his old age, he raises Bodhi mind when seeing his earthen bed. Lin Yutang's Chinese-English Dictionary gives the definition "Earthen bed in North China, covered with clay bricks and matting, used for sitting and sleeping, heated during winter from beneath."

His unraveled bamboo mat with its own unique history makes him more practice the Way. Elm is valued for its interlocking grain that doesn't split. For Jaujou it is the actual attaining of Bodhi.

> For Buddha no benzoin in the incense burner.
> Only the smell of cow dung.

The central image in Jaujou's temple was Avalokitesvara Bodhisattva. Avalokitesvara is no different from Buddha and the Tathagata, other names for the Whole World in the Ten Directions. Burning incense is to purify oneself and one's environment. There is no purer world than when one's life is the Whole World in the Ten Directions. So it is said "For Buddha no benzoin."

"Benzoin" and "cow dung" are put in contrast. However, they aren't clarifying only their difference but also their sameness. Benzoin is from an Indonesian tree, cow dung from hay through a cow's stomachs. But we aren't talking about material incense or about "For Buddha no benzoin" in the context of the preceding paragraph. This "For Buddha no benzoin" exists only when we raise Bodhi mind and when we wish to become an Avalokitesvara Bodhisattva. In that sense, this benzoin is greatly different from cow dung. This benzoin, which is the product of Buddhist right thought, can make such materials as cow dung into Buddha nature.

However, even this "no benzoin" and "cow dung" come from the same place, and if we observe them in short circuit, both come from Buddha nature. But the one who can bring

Buddha nature is the one who can burn no benzoin. Here is the key to living in perfect causation and it is also the key to transcending causation. The key to using this key depends on whether or not we raise Bodhi mind. Those who live for themselves know very well all about cow dung but cannot even dream of knowing about no burning of benzoin.

February, 2011

Notes

Chinese Romanization is based on Lin Yutang's *Chinese-English Dictionary of Modern Usage* (Hong Kong, 1972).

1. p. 123, In this Matzu essay, this episode "Nanyue's polishing a tile" up to this point is treated.

2. p. 152, Dahuei is the posthumous name of Nanyue Huairang (677-747), a disciple of the Sixth Patriarch, and later, when he became head priest of the temple Guanyin at Mt. Nanyue, he taught Matzu Dauyi (709-788).

3. p. 169, This "because there is no preference in the Dharma of no dwelling" is a complementary phrase found only in *Chuandeng lu*.

4. p. 290, Made a hermitage among the people,
   though no noise of horses and carts.
   How come to be so?
   The isolation of land accords
   with the distance of mind.
   I pick a stem of chrysanthemum
   beside an eastern hedge,
   and leisurely view the south mountains.
   The mountain air is beautiful at sunset.
   Birds fly back together.
   Here is the true meaning—
   I yearn to express it
   but have forgotten the words.
   (Tau Yuanming, 365-427)

Index

Ananda, 103-104;
  Mahakasyapa transmitted, 160-161, 206, 220, Sanavasin's kasaya, 260-262; 304
Asokavadana, 243
Avalokitesvara, keeping *dharani*, 21; the Treasured Orb, 21-22; awakening of, 27; bearer of Buddha's Heart Seal, 79, 118; for those who are to be helped, 171; practiced the deep Prajna paramita, 244, 278, 288, 329, 342
Avatamsaka Sutra (*Mahavaipulya buddhavatamsaka-sutra*), 14, 40, 52, vol. 8, *Bhadrapala Bodhisattva*, 60;143. See Huayan Sutra.
Baijang Huaihai (749-814), *Baijang lu*; "Mt. Himalaya is like The Great Nirvana," 84; "Lofty Dignified," 97; "Baijang and Wild Ducks," 99, 231-234; "The phrase of Baijang leaving the lecture hall," 154; "Studying from Matzu for the Second Time," 100-104; monastic rules 103, 240; "Baijang's Wild Fox," 223, 240; *Guang lu*, in *Sija wulu*, 224; "A day of no work is a day of no meals," 225; "To sit alone on the great suhlime peak," 233; "There is a tiger," 246-247
Biyan lu, Case 1; Bodhidharma's "Vacancy and No Holiness," 24, 77-78, 118, 171, 322; Case 2; Jaujou's Ultimate Way, 174, 316; Case 3; Matzu's "Sun-face Buddha, Moon-face Buddha," 116; Case 9: "Jaujou's Four Gates,"279-280; Case 11; Huangbo's "All of You are Draff-Eaters!", 225-6; Case 12; Dungshan's "Three Pounds of Hemp," 318; Case 18; Nat'l Teacher Nanyang's Seamless Pagoda, 75, 296; Case 19; Jyujy's Finger, 150; Case 24; Liou the Old Cow, 169; Case 26; To Sit alone on the great sublime peak, 233, 321; Case 38 Fengshuye's Iron Ox's Spirit; 157; Case 39; Yunmen's "Peony Garden," 20; Case 40; Nanchyuan's "As if in a Dream," Case 43; Dunghan's "Cold-and-Heat," 114; Case 46; Jingching's Sound of Raindrops, 67; Case 53; Baijang and Wild Ducks, 99, 100, 102, 231; Case 78: Sixteen Bodhisattvas in the Bath. 27; Case 88; Shyuansha's Man of Three Disabilities, 36; Case 96, Jaujou's Three Turning Words, 49; Case 100, Baliang's Sword That Can Cut a Blown Hair, 24
Bodhisattvas, 16, 19, 82, 84, 129, 138, 189, 209, 248, 249, 322,
Bodhi mind, 38, 48, 59, 60, 92, 127, 167, 187, 219, 236-7, 256, 280, 339-41
Bodhidharma, (?-528?) "Bodhidharma never came to this eastern land" 19, 20, 65; "Bring your mind," 27-28; "It is vacancy and no holiness," 77; "bearer of Buddha's

Heart Seal," 118; gatha on transmission, 208; gatha transmitting the Dharma, 217; "Make your mind like a fence or wall and enter the Way," 214
Brahma's Net Sutra, 41, 55, 144, 165, 259, 260
Buddha and the patriarchs, 29, 115, 129, 138, 152, 175, 176, 180, 200, 236-239, 241-243, 247, 267, 273, 293, 310, 314-5, 325-326
Buddha's Declaration, 14, 21, 25, 55, 62, 186, 202, 311
Buddha's Dharma, 11, 13, 14, 40, 44, 53, 54, 59, 63, 129, 131, 132, 144, 147, 153, 154, 157, 158, 164, 171, 188, 190, 193, 194, 195, 211, 212, 218, 219, 228, 241, 256, 260-261, 28-89, 290, 303, 310, 339,
Buddha's Way, 29, 46, 60, 125 132, 133, 142, 160, 212, 288
Causation, 223-228, 230-232, 235-246
Changching Hueileng (854-922), "What a great difference!" 42, 69; Today is a fine day to work outside," 69
Changsha Jingtsen (?-?), "The whole world in the ten directions," 17, 297, 198, 199, 200, 202
Changshuei Tzyshyuan (?-1038), "If all the worlds are primordially pure," 25, 203-205; "There is no different destination," 207
Chanyuan Mengchiou, 13, 55, 69, 108, 331
Chuandeng lu, 12, 14; vol. 3; 28, 208, 210, 257; vol. 5; 17, 19, 91, 124, 104, 105; vol. 6; 154; vol. 8; 158-159; vol. 7; 228, 286; vol. 9; 155, 156, 165, 246; vol. 10; 17, 197, 202, 332, vol. 14; 71, 148, 258, 287; vol. 17; 285; vol. 18; 16, 19, 25, 26, 35, 36, 62, 69, 119, 235, 306; vol. 19; 264; vol. 21; 80; vol. 24; 43; vol. 28; 282; added chapter on Bodhidharma, 215
Chaunshin Fayau (Essence of the Dharma of transmitting the Mind), 103, 105
Chinshan, 94
Christian faith, 60, 61
Chuanhua temple, 123
Compassion, klesa, and, 230; Middle Way, and, 169; sangha, and, 294; Great Endurance, The, and, 120; wisdom, and; 24, 91, 196, 155, 195, 201; Buddha, 33, 334; Buddha's Budy, 25; content of, 186; ocean of, 22; Avalokitesvara, of, 22, 78; no division, of, 189; Samatanhadra, "thinking the unthinkable," of, 125; phenomena, 70, 115; practice of, 129, 207, 210, 211; Sanavasin, and origin of, 259
Concentration (dhyana), importance of, 55; wisdom (prajna) and, 55, 89, 282
Confucius, "I carry One throughout," 55; "Not to be surely definite," 72; Four Do not's, 134; "I have no act I do not do together with you," 154; "Our teacher's way is to be sincere with himself and with others, 163,164, 211
Constitution of Japan, Article 9; 81, 82
Country of Chu, 195
Dachyuan (?-894), "The smoke rising under your feet," 113
Dahuei. See Nanyue Huairang

Daito (1282-1337), National Teacher, Admonition, 168
Dajeng, National Teacher, 194. See Nanyang Hueijung
Dajung, 95-97, 107
Daji (great quietude). See Matzu Dauyi
Daju Hueihai, 282
Dakuei Dayuan see Kueishan Lingyou
Damei Fachang (752-829), gatha, 150, 228; "the apricot has ripened," 171
Danyuan Yingjen (?-?), gatha, 75, 78; "It is located south of Shiang and north of Tan," 76, 295; "National Teacher Nanyang's Seamless Pagoda," 296
De, 267
dedicating, 54
Denko roku, 18, Buddha's Declaration, 83; vol. 1 [Transmission of the Light], 125; vol. 2, 177; 213, 214, 256, 259: See also Keizan Jhokin
demons' cave, 62- 64, 73, 76-79
Deshan Shyanjian (780-865), 15, 94, 111, 219
desires, 84, 205; klesa, 89, 262; happiness and, 92; shedding, 189, 211; "love and hate," 267
device, 25, 31, 34, 35, 120, 157, 158, 177, 187, 199, 264, 281, 282, 308, 309
Dharma Seal, 75, 156, 157. 214, 298
Dharma-kaya, activity of, 265, 298; appearance of, 115, 119; bright crystal orb, 68; environment, and, 202; eye to make pure, 21; figures of, 197; Huangbo as, 97; insentient beings, 194; intuition, and, 45; Nature nursed as, 193; nature of, 280; Nirmana-kaya, and 270; our

Buddha, 135, 190; our true life, 202; practice of, 91; presenting, 29, 192; pure, 202, 191, 192; substance of, 54; Body of Buddha, the, 45; Three Worlds, the; 45, 49; think the unthinkable, 133; Three Bodies of Buddha, 178; Tsuwei's teaching, 178; universal reason, 45, 49
Dharmapundarika-sutra. See Lotus Flower Sutra
dhyana. *See* Concentration
Diamond Eye, 21, 22
Diamond samadhi, (*vajra-dhyana*), 274
Diamond Sutra (*Vajracchedika-prajnaparamitra-sutra*), 16, 21, 41, 84-85, 95, 179, 216, 272, 298, 336
Danshia Tianran (739-824), 178
Dipankara-buddha, 189, 190
Ditsang. See Luohan Gueichen
Ditsang Temple, 39, 52, 43
Dunglin Changtzung (1025-1051), 191
Dungpo, see Su Dungpo
Dungshan Liangjie, (807-869) "What is your Name?" 67-68; "Together with Uncle Segmi at Mt. Lungshan," 108; "When Shyuefeng was sorting the rice, 111; "Fording the river," 112; "The smoke is rising under your feet," 113; "As soon as we go out of the gate, there are weeds," Five Classifications, 279; 114, 117,158-159, 178, 208, 218-221, 276, 280, 296-297, 304-306, 316, 335
Dungshan lu; entry 2; 304; entry 11; 303, entry 24, 108; entry 30; 243; entry 33; 218; entry 41, 68;

entry 46, 112; entry 49, 304; entry 50, 294; entry 64, 113; entry 73, 114; entry 75, 273; entry 101; 178, 313, entry 105, 110,111; entry 114; 277
Eight Right Ways, 112, 305
Eihei Dogen (1200-1253), 60, 118, 122, 130, 208, 222, 229-230, 336-8; *Bendo wa* [Essay on Studying the Way], 79, 95, 129, 132 148, 152, 153, 175; Dogen's poems, "Do no evil," 136; *Fukan zazen gi* [Recommendation for the protocol of sitting meditation], 123, 145, 160, 181, 183; *Gakudo yojinshu* [Cautionary Advice for Studying the Way], 60, 129, 144, 211, 261, 288; SHOBOGENZO (Treasure Repository Housing the Eye to See the Right Dharma): *Bodaisatta shishoho* [A Bodhisattva's Four Embracings], " Do all good," 137; *Butsudo* [Buddha's Way], 160; *Bussho* [Buddha Nature]; 86, 146, 173; *Dai-shugyo*, (Great training), 226; *Dharani*, 241; *Genjo koan* [koan manifested], 132; *Gyo butsuyigi* [Practicing Buddha's noble deeds], 115, 137; [Practising Buddha's behavior], 30; *Gyoji* [Keeping up the priestly acts], 117, 140; *Hotsu Bodaishon* [To Raise Bodhi Mind], 339; *Katto* [Ivy and Wisteria], 73, 218; *Kenbutsu* [To see/Become Buddha], 154, 236; *Kyoju kaimon* [Transmitted Essence]; 29, 35, 37, 42, 68, 72, 119-120, 129, 136, 137, 176, 208, 209, 210, 213, 227, 228, 240, 272, 286-287, 339; *Ikka no Meishu* [A Bright Crystal Orb] 11, 15, 63-64; *Jisho zanmai* [Samadhi in self-realization], 126; *Keisei sanshoku* (Sound of the brook, color of the mountain), 180, 237; *Makahannya haramitsu* [*Mahaprajnaparamita-sutra*], 134; *Shinjin inga* (Deep belief in Causation), 226; *Sanmai o Sanmai* [Samadhi among samadhis], 135, 154, 164, 175; *Sangai yuishin* [The Three Worlds are One Mind], 40, 46; *Senjo* [Purification], 152; *Sokushin zebutsu* [The Mind is Buddha], 116; Shoji [Life-Death], 70, 128; *Sokushin zebutsu* [The Mind is Buddha], 116; *Tenzo kyokun* [Kitchen discipline], 143,164, 216; *Yuibutsu yobustsu* [Buddha to Buddha],126; *Yuji* [A Certain (which is Existing) Time], 229
Ejo, Koun (1198-1280), 118, *Shobogenzo zuimonki* [Ejo's Record of the Master's Talks], 147, 226
Ekottaragama, vol 31-5; 92
Emperor Sutzung, 75
Emperor Wen, 11
Emperor Wu, 77, 78, 171, 262, 308, 322
endeavor 145, 147, 160, 177, 181, 182, 187, 214
endurance, see *ksanti-paramita*
evidence 143-145, 159, 181, 182
Fada, 85
faith, 59, 60, 295
Fashi Lingtzun, "What is the meaning of the Patriarch's

coming from the West?" 178-179
Fashin, 43
Fashing Temple, 88. See Hueineng
Fayan Wenyi, "Not knowing is the most intimate," 32, 36, 43; *Jinling Chingjing-yuan* Wenyi [Recorded Sayings of Fayan]. 43;"Everything is manifesting", 44; "Form rises from formless", 298
Fengshyue, "Fengshyue and the Patriarch's Dharma Seal," 156-158, 214, 296
Five Skandhas, 327
Four Earnest Observations (*smartyupasthana*), 76, 275
Four Obstacles, The, 13
Four Truths, 92
Foyin Liauyuan (1032-1098), "Where will you sit? 191
Fujou Daan (793-883), "I only tended a cow," 155
Freedom, 34, 35, 38, 52, 171, 172, 274
Gatha of Three spoonfuls, 133
Genshin (942-2027), Founder of Japanese Pure Land, 47
Gosho. See Kyogo
Guang lu. See Baijang Huaihai
Great Teacher Jenjiau, 29. See Shyuansha Shybei
Great Teacher Jenying, 39. See Luohan Gueichen
Great Teacher Tzungyi, 29. See Shyuefeng Yitsun
Hakuin Ekaku, 277
Hetze Shenheui (670-762), "Knowing this one letter is the gate to all wonders," 336, 346
Huangbo Shiyun, (?-856), 12, 98, 105-108, 112, 210, 246, 285, 286, "Rude monk," 95-96, "Lofty Dignified," 97; "Deafened for three days," 100, 102; "About studying from Matzu for the Second time," 103; "My teaching will prosper well in your generation," 104; "Huangbo studies from an old woman," 138-139; "no Zen teacher," 226; "The ancient person gave a wrong turning phrase," 244; "A tiger at Mt. Dashung," 246;
Huayan sect 203, 207
Huayan Sutra (*Mahavaipulya-buddhavatamsaka-sutra*), 203
Hueike Shenguang (487-593), "My mind is not yet settled," 26; "Your Reverence, I beg of you, please open the gate of sweet dew, Compassion, everywhere to help sentient beings," 210-216; "I have put your mind at peace," 211; "Your Reverence, just go straight on," 215; "Brightly, clearly, I always know." 215
Hueineng, Dajian (638-713), *Lioutzu Tanjing*, 89, 95, 102, 137, 185, 226, 260, 275, 298, 329, 335, 336, "Indeed there is no place to dwell," 15-16, 41, entry 16; 85 ; "For Buddha Nature there is no South or North," 86; "Not the wind, not the banner," 88; "How can Bodhi be grown?" 89
Hungjy Jengjyue (1091-1157), gathas for *Tsungrung lu*, 24, "A well-mannered old turtle," 56; "A colorful fish," 58, *Hungjy lu*, 126, Hungjy's gatha, 226, 310
Hungren, Huangmei Daman (601-674), 16, 85, 86, "A

person of Lingnan who
has no Buddha
Nature," 87, 88, 261
Indra, 188-190, 192, 241
Intuition, 339-340
Jataka, Abhiniskrama-sutra,
189
Jaujou lu, 188, 190, 313;
Biography, entry 5; 336;
entry 6;262; entry 1; 337;
entry 3; 330; entry 6; 265;
entry 76; 266; entry 77;
184; entry 93; 160; entry
99; 279; entry 132; 269;
entry 133; 270; entry 138;
310; entry 188; 326;
entry 209; 49, 256; entry
227; 328; entry 230; 161;
entry 252; 329; entry 291;
26; entry 353; 337; entry
356; 274; entry 363; 271;
entry 371; 26; entry 459;
309; entry 472; 279;
entry 518; 326; entry 519;
333; entry 520; 333;
Jaujou lu, Shingjuang,
169
Jaujou Tsungshen (778-899),
"From where should I
begin?" 26; "True Buddha
is in the depths of the
Hall," 49; 255; "Does a
dog have Buddha nature
or not?" 227, 269-270
Jauti Hueilang, 289
Jauwang Wangrung (873-
921), 265
Jengda ge, 79, 89, 180, 196
See Yungjia Shyuanjyue
Jinling Chingjing-yuan. See
Fayan Wenyi
Jingching Dafu (864-937),
"Jingching's Sound of
Raindrops," 67
Jingjau Weikuan (755-817),
"It is a nice mountain,"
286
Jungfeng Mingben (1263-
1323), 180
Jygung, 78, 118
karma, 13, 22, 23, 98, 129,
213, 227, 327, 369

kasaya, 55, 56, 110, 191, 251,
255, 256-261, 299, 325
Keizan Jhokin, (1268-1325),
17, 63
Kenzei ki [Kenzei's memo],
236
King Prasenajit, 243
klesa, 13, 16, 21, 34, 49, 89,
91, 92, 95, 110, 111, 112-
113,114, 165, 184-188,
190, 192-196, 201, 229,
255, 257, 273-275, 297,
322
ksanti-paramita (or, ksanti),
82, 83, 89,189
Kueishan Lingyou (771-853),
"A hundred years hence I
will go to a layman's
house at the foot of this
mountain and become a
work cow," 155;
"Kueishan lay down and
took his ease," 168; "Old
Cow, have you come?"
169; "Water levels
things," 179; "Express to
me one phrase for the
world before your parents
were born," 193;
"Kueishan expressed his
thanks," 231-232; "Fetch
me a chair,"317
Kumaralabdha (AD?-22), 226
Kumarajiva (350-409), "The
Cart pulled by the Great
White Cow," 146
Kyogo, *Shobogenzo*
Sho (Annotations to the
Zen precepts), [or *Gosho*]
166, 170, 176
Langshie Heuijyue (? -?),
"How do mortal
forms…repeatedly rise,
change and ruin?" 23, 25,
203, "There is no different
destination," 205
Lankavatara Sutra, 40,
leaving family 240,
251,262, 267, 269, 313
Li Fuguo, 297
life-death 70, 110, 128, 141,
314, 315, 333

Lingyun Shichin (?-?), 69, "Before the donkey affairs have left, the horse affairs have arrived," 164; gatha at sight of a flowering peach," 195-198, 200-201, 248
Linji Yishyuan (?-867), "Buddha's Dharma is consistent," 63; "Planting seedlings," 104; "Pecking at black beans," 105; "Visit to Reverend Ping," 106
Linji lu, 104, 106; lectures 13 and 17; 190; Dialogue, 40; section Lectures, 218
Liou Tiemo, "Old cow visits Kuieshan," 169
Lioutzu fabau tanjing. See Hueineng, Dajian
Lotus Flower Sutra, 30, 46, 52, 85, 113, 171, 210; (*Dharmapundarika-sutra*), *Tathagata-ayus-pramana* [Life Duration of the Tathagata] 28, 46, 53, 237, 239; *Upaya*, 29; *Aupamya* (Metaphor), 50; *Upayakausalya*, 217
Luohan Gueichen (867-928), "What do you call this?" 36, 39; "Not knowing is the most intimate [knowing]," 32, 43, 57; "Ditsang raised two fingers," 43; "everything is manifesting," 44; "Who does not understand?" 80
Lungshan, Tanjou (?-?), "I saw a pair of bulls made of mud enter the ocean as they fought and I have never seen them since."108-110; "a vegetable leaf in the deep mountain,"109; "the white cloud," 140; "I came from neither the heavenly world nor the human world," 158
Lutzu Bauyun (?-?), 182

Lunyu. See Confucius
Mahakarunacita-dharani, 21
Mahamangala-sutta, in Sutta-nipata in Sutta-pitaka, 92
Maha-prajnaparamita-hrdya-Sutra, 209, 329
Maha-prajnaparamita-sutra, 59, 209
Mahavaipulya-buddhavatamsaka-sutra, 14, 203, 281, 319. See Avatamsaka Sutra
Mahakasyapa, 15, 117, 118, 122, 160, 161, 196, 199, 248
Mahayana Buddhism 25, 258, 276
Maitreya Buddha, 228, 236, 246, 303, 304
Maitreya-vyakarana, 304
Manjusri "The Dharma of the Dharma king is like this," 24, 82, 125, 302
Matzu Dauyi (709-788), "Baijang and Wild Ducks," 99, 120; "Raising the whisk," 100-103, "Sunface Buddha, Moonface Buddha," 115, "Polishing a tile," 123, 128; "The Way is beyond color or form," 124; "No mind, no Buddha," 171; Daji, posthumous name, 287; native land, Shyfang, 116
Middle Way, 83, 169, 291, 312, 322
Mt. Baiyai, See Nanyang, Heuijung 90
Mt. Chingping, 178
Mt. Dashung. See Baijang Huaihai
Mt. Heng (in Hunan), *See* Nanyue Huairang, 287
Mt. Lu, 191
Mt. Lungshan, 108
Mt. Shigung (in Kimyou), 287
Mt. Shyuefeng, 29
Nagarjuna (c. 150-250 AD), 59, 172-173, 226. See

Mahaprajnaparamita-sastra
Nanchyuan Puyuan (748-834), "As if in a dream,," 43; "One who understands will become a work cow," 155, 261; "A reclining Tathagata," 168; When the Year of the Donkey comes," 182; "Buddha and patriarchs do not know being, whereas rat-catchers and bullocks know," 261; "Who will pay your sandal fee?" 285; "The ordinary mind is the Way," 294
Nanyang Hueijung (?-775), National Teacher, "A Seamless Pagoda," 75, 298; "Fence, tile and pebbles, all are the ancient Buddha," 90; "With no attachment to Buddha," 90-91, "Klesa is...shedding klesa," 297
Nanyue Huairang (677-747), "What comes thus?", 17; "Return to the native land and the Way is not practised," 117-122; "Nanyue's Polishing a tile," 123; "Is it right to whip the cart, or to whip the cow?" 144; "If you are studying sitting meditation," 164-5; "Buddha has no certain form," 169-175
Nirmana-kaya, 45, 46, 49, 97, 115, 133, 167, 178, 209, 265, 270, 279
no dwelling, 123, 173, 175, 330, 332, 336, 332
no form, 23, 225, 261, 331
no notion, 329, 335, 336
non pollution 19, 152
paying worship 86, 87, 94, 116, 117, 142, 143, 155, 158, 167, 177, 178, 210, 233, 240, 241, 242, 253, 306, 307, 308

pilgrimage, 15, 18, 28, 44, 65, 94, 113, 158, 225, 302, 311
Reverend Ping, 106
Prajna-paramita, 209, 276, 287
Prajnaparamita-hrdaya-sutra, 63, 199, 274
precepts, 41, 55, 165, 166, 176, 181, 207, 222, 241, 257, 258, 259, 260, 275, 287, 309, 329, 334
pure mind 16, 84, 85
The Purport of the Nirvana Sutra (*Mahaparinirvana-sutra*), 14, 89, 232, 310
Purnamaitrayaniputra, 22, 23, 203
Rahula 252, 306, 310, gatha, 311
Reverend Pindola 251
Right Effort (*samyag-vayayana*), 229
Right Thought (*samyak-smarti*) 285, 340-343
rupa, 134; *See* sunyata
Saicho (762-822), "Any person, any Being, illuminating a corner is a national treasure," 90
Sakyamuni Buddha (?- 485), "I and my companions," 18, 83; "I alone am respectable," 47, 139, 162, 186, 233, 339; "Make yourself like an island," 47, 206; "The Three Spheres," 50-51; "Mt. Himalaya is like the Great Nirvana, 84; "In seeking happiness, no one in the world has exceeded me," 92
samadhi, 124, 129, 135, 282
Samadhi of self-cherishing, 233, 234
Sambhoga-kaya 45, 49, 133, 167, 178, 247
Samyutta-nikaya, 307
Sanavasin (?-?), "Is your body going to leave family, or is your

mind...?" 125; "The Teacher...was born clothed," 257; "Ananda pulled the corner of Sanavasin's kasaya," 260
Sanbyaku soku, 28, 40, 179, 221, 267
Sanjushippon bodaibunpo [Thirty-seven divisions of higest wisdom], 135
Sariputra, 29, 50, 209
Sarvastivada-vinaya,311
self-proving, 249
Senne, *Okikigaki* [Memo of responses to Questions], 124, 170
Sengjau, *Jaulun*, 43
Sengtsan, Jianjy (?-606), 219,
Shaulin Temple, 27, 123, 149, 308
Shaushiou, 43
Shautang, 55-58
Shenshan, 218, 220. 221, 245
Shiangyan Jyshian (?-898), "Express to me in one phrase," 193; "Painted cakes cannot relieve hunger," 193; gatha to express Shiangyan's realization, 195
Shinshin Ming. 269, 270. See Sengtsan, Jiangy
Shobogenzo kyakutai ichijisan [Shobogenzo translated to Chinese with Annotations], 178
Shobogenzo. See Eihei Dogen
Shobogenzo sho (Annotations to the Zen Precepts), [(or Gosho). See Kyogo
Shobogenzo zuimonki. See Ejo, Koun.
Shuho Myocho. See National Teacher Daito.
Shyshuan Chingju (807-888), "As soon as we go out of the gate there are weeds," 114
Shyshuan Chuyuan, also known as Tsyming (987-1040), "What should I do when I meet you on a narrow path?"142
Shyuansha Shybei (835-908), 11, 12; "You are a tiger," 13; "This body is not real being," 15; "I dare not mislead others," 16; "The Whole World in the Ten Directions is a bright crystal orb," 62; "Bodhidharma never came," 17, 65, 119
Shyuansha Temple, 29
Shyu-Chuandeng lu, vol. 7, 142, 205
Shyuedou Jijian (1109-1192), 176-177
Shyuedou Jungshian (980-1052), 24, 27, 36-37, 39, 75, 95, 150, 203, 269, 277, 280
Shyuefeng Yitsun (822-908), "Every part of the great earth is the gate to attain freedom," 34; "A venomous turtle-nosed snake," 69; "Mt. Aushan attained the Way!" 94
sila, 55, 82, 181, 189, 329
Spiritual Recognition, 180
Sramana, 197
Su Dungpo (1036-1101), 27; *Liandeng hueiyau*, 12, 34; "Dungpo...handed over his belt with ornamenting gems, 191-192; *Pudeng lu*, "The sound of brook...the figure of the mountain," 192; 201
Surangama-sutra, 22, 220
Su Shy, see Su Dungpo
Sumedha, Prince, 189, 194
Shyshuan Chyuan (987-1040), 142
sunyata, activity of, 12; rupa and, 12, 17, 20, 44, 54, 63, 67, 84, 103, 110, 134, 141, 183, 186, 209, 221, 264, 270, 269, 278, 298; Buddha, 66; True Form, 83; recycling of, 85, 97, 99; thought and emotion,

87, 279, 78, 309; Buddha nature, 134; alternation, 145, 256, Sunyata King, 165, 166; not, 185; total worlds of, 210; right arm, 222; True human body and, 242, 247; wild fox, body of, 270; Ultimate Way, 271; transition, 279; nonexistence, 305, Dharma, 305; our innate nature, 309; practice, 312; freedom, 322, substance, 331
Sutralankara-sastra, 146
Tettsu Gikai (1219-1309), 63, 64
thought and emotion. See klesa
Three Bodies of Buddha, 45, 178
Three Inclusive Vows, 136, 227
Three Spheres, 50-52
Three Treasures, 53-54, 60, 96, 126, 127, 230, 241
Three Vehicles, 281
Three Wheels, 137, 176, 290
Three Worlds, 18, 29, 30, 34, 39, 40-42, 44-53, 59, 60, 113, 160, 180, 248, 325
Tiantung Rujing (1163-1228), 167, 176,"Actualize the place never polluted," 177, 178; 216, 244
time, 146, 211-212, 230-235, 239, 267, 276, 292, 296, 318, 322
Toutzy Detung (819-914), 15; "A pitch-dark lacquer pail," 325-326
training, 19, 20, 31, 45, 48, 63, 70, 71, 143, 144, 145, 151-153, 159, 160, 163, 182, 185-187
transcend, 133
transmigration, 22-23. 34
transmission, 20,32,98, 102, 122, 161, 208, 242, 262, 314, 321
Treasured Orb, 22
true Buddha, 49, 50, 256

True Existence, 235, 298
True Form, 28, 31-35, 54, 66, 120, 121, 141, 145, 146,, 148, 165, 180, 235
Truth, 196, 221, 291
Tsaushan Benji (840-941), *Tsaushan lu*, "Most precious is the skull of a dead cat," 79; "It is like the well seeing the well-pulley above," 265, 332
Tsungrung lu, 24, 26; Case 1, 83; Case 2; 149; Case 4; 188, 204; Case 7; 234; Case 8, 224; Case 18, 227; Case 23, 182; Case 81, 55; Case 100, 25, 203
Tsueiwei Wushyue (?-?), "This bamboo is quite tall, and that bamboo is quite short," 179
Tsyming, see Shyshuan Chuyuan
Tusita Heaven 253, 302, 303, 305
Tzengtzy, 163
Tzuing ji, See Hakuin Ekaku
Tzutang ji, 94, 139, 211, 224, 262, 283, 293, 310
Ultimate Way, 174, 270, 316, 317
Upagupta, 126
Vairocana Tathagata, 176, 178
Vajracchedika-prajnaparamita-sutra. See Diamond Sutra
Varanasi (Mrgadava), 307, 308
Vasubandhu, *Mahyana-samgraha-bhasya*, 82
vijjnapti-matrata [Universal Mind] 44
Vimalakirti, 23, 113
Vimalakirti-nirdesa-sutra, 23, 178, 298
vimukti or *vimoksa* see Freedom
vinaya, 43, 309, 329
wisdom (prajna). 23, 55, 58, 149, 181, 189, 202, 278, 282, 284, 329; content of;

209; continuous study, and, 331; function of, 331, 332; Prajna Samadhi, 336
Wumen Hueihai (1183-1260), 224
Wumen guan (Gateless barrier), 224
Wudeng hueiyan, 136, 225, 323
Yaksa's gatha, 90
Yangchi, 142, 143
Yangshan Hueiji (803-887), "With this deep mind," 104, "Yangshan stepped forward and paid worship," 155; "The time will come to understand," 299
Yanguan Chian (?-842), 94-95
Yanwang Likeyung (856-908), 264
Yantou, 15, 94, 112, 324
Yanyang, 275
Yaushan Weiyan (745-828), "Think the unthinkable," 71, 124, 148; "How can you suspect this old monk?" 153, 155, 221, 229, 234, 258; "The thousand sages do not know about that," 259
Yejou, 213, 227. *See* Hueike Shenguang
Yintzung, 88
Yuanwu Kechin (1063-1135), 21, 24, 58, 270
Yuanwu lu, 29
Yungjia Shyuanjyue (?-713), "By searching you cannot be found," 78-79; The lotus in the fire will never ruin," 89; 167. *See Jengda ge*, 79, 89, 167, 180, 196
Yunjyu Daying (835?-902), "My name is Daying, 67-68; "While fording the river," 112, 288; "What is it when you do not think either good or bad?" 295
Yunmen Wenyau (864-949),

"Peony Garden,"20-21, "[You are] A golden-haired lion," 18; 33-34; You aren't blind...deaf...dumb, 36; "All day long...he will not touch so much as a grain," 266, 326
Zen Teacher Dajy. 223, 230. *See* Baijang Huaihai
Zen Teacher Woshu, 88

www.ingramcontent.com/pod-product-compliance
Lightning Source LLC
Chambersburg PA
CBHW071651160426
43195CB00012B/1421